Contents

POETRY

LITERATURE

An Introduction to Fiction, Poetry, and Drama

Third Compact Edition

X. J. Kennedy

Dorothy M. Kennedy

Dana Gioia

Longman

New York   San Francisco   Boston
London   Toronto   Sydney   Tokyo   Singapore   Madrid
Mexico City   Munich   Paris   Cape Town   Hong Kong   Montreal

ACKNOWLEDGEMENTS

"Women at Fifty" by Andrea Hollander Budy from *House Without a Dreamer*. Copyright © 1993. Reprinted by permission of the author and Story Line Press. "Buck It" by Jerald Bullis. Reprinted by permission of the author. "Introduction to Poetry" from *The Apple That Astonished Paris*, poems by Billy Collins. Copyright © 1988 by Billy Collins. Reprinted by permission of The University of Arkansas Press. "Introduction to Poetry" from *Another Kind of Travel*, poems by Paul Lake. Copyright © 1988 by Paul Lake. Reprinted by permission of the author.

Vice President and Editor-in-Chief: Joseph Terry
Senior Supplements Editor: Donna Campion
Electronic Page Makeup: Dianne Hall

Instructor's Manual to accompany *Literature: An Introduction to Fiction, Poetry, and Drama*, Third Compact Edition.

ISBN: 0-321-11792-1

345678910—MV—05040302

DRAMA

WRITING

Preface

We've always found, before teaching a knotty piece of literature, no preparation is more helpful than to sit down and discuss it with a colleague or two. If this manual supplies you with such a colleague at inconvenient hours, such as 2:00 A.M., when there's no one in the faculty coffee room, it will be doing its job.

This manual tries to provide exactly that sort of collegial conversation—spirited but specific, informal but informed. We offer you a sheaf of diverse notes to supply—if you want them—classroom strategies, critical comments, biographical information, historical context, and a few homemade opinions. These last may be wrong, but we set them down to give you something clear-cut with which to agree or disagree. Candor, we think, helps to enliven any conversation.

The manual includes:

- Commentary on every story, poem, and play presented in the text, except for a few brief poems quoted in the text as illustrations;
- Additional classroom questions and discussion strategies;
- Thematic Indices at the beginning of the "Fiction" and "Poetry" sections.

To help you refer quickly to the parent book, page numbers are given at the top of each page in this manual. These correspond to pages in the book itself. There is also an alphabetical index of authors with titles at the back of this manual.

PLAN OF THE BOOK

There is a plan to *Literature,* but the book does not oblige you to follow it. Chapters may be taken up in any sequence; some instructors like to intersperse poetry and plays with stories. Some may wish to teach Chapter 22 on "Myth and Narrative" immediately before teaching *Oedipus the King.* Many find that "Imagery" is a useful chapter with which to begin teaching poetry. Instructors who prefer to organize the course by theme will want to consult the detailed thematic indices.

If, because you skip around in the book, students encounter a term unknown to them, let them look it up in the "Index of Terms" on the inside back cover. They will be directed to the page where it first occurs and where it will be defined and illustrated. Or, have them look it up in the "Glossary of Literary Terms" at the back of the book.

In the poetry chapters, the sections entitled "For Review and Further Study" do not review the whole book up to that moment; they review only the main points of the chapter. Most of these sections contain some poems that are a little more difficult than those in the body of that chapter.

CHANGES TO THIS EDITION

The third compact edition of *Literature* incorporates many changes. We have revised this edition with the simple aim of bringing in useful new features and selections without losing the best liked material. We have been guided in this effort by scores of instructors and students who use the book in their classrooms. Teaching is a kind of conversation—between instructor and student, between reader and text. Revising *Literature*, we try to help keep this conversation fresh by mixing the classic with the new, the familiar with the surprising.

New Casebooks on Major Authors

The most significant change in the current edition is the inclusion of six new casebooks on major authors. These special chapters present a variety of material—biographies, photographs, critical commentaries, statements by the authors, and a deep selection of the featured writer's work. Our aim has been to provide everything a student might need to begin an in-depth study of each author. Two major writers from each basic literary form have been featured. For fiction, the casebooks showcase Flannery O'Connor and Raymond Carver with five selections from each author (two stories and three critical statements), as well as a selection of responses from eight critics. For poetry, we present in-depth selections from Emily Dickinson and Langston Hughes with fourteen poems each— supplemented by others elsewhere in the volume—as well as ten critical articles, photographs, facsimiles, letters, and statements.

For drama we have gone even further by creating two extensive new chapters on Sophocles and Shakespeare. The critical casebook on Sophocles offers new commentary, photographs, and diagrams as well as a selection of critical articles. (But fear not—amid all the novel elements we have preserved the two popular Robert Fitzgerald and Dudley Fitts translation of *Oedipus the King*.) The casebook on Shakespeare includes *Othello*, as well as five critical excerpts on the author and his plays.

New Glossary of Literary Terms

We have also added a comprehensive "Glossary of Literary Terms" to the back of the book. This new feature includes every term heightened in boldface throughout the text as well as other important terms—over 350 entries in all—providing a clear and accurate definition usually with cross references to related terms.

New Stories, Poems, Plays, and Critical Prose

The FICTION section includes many new stories, bringing the total selection to 47—an all-time high. (There are also twenty-two pieces of critical prose—half of them new.) We have added ten new stories to broaden and update our coverage. Many of the new stories deepen our international and multicultural coverage like Chinua Achebe's "Dead Men's Path," Ha Jin's "Saboteur," and Octavio Paz's "My Life with the Wave."

In the POETRY section we proudly provide the most extensive selection of poems found in any comparable book in the field—a total of 355 poems in the new edition. We have added over 40 new poems to the book—to freshen the selections and update our coverage of contemporary work. There are too many new poems to list individually but instructors are advised not to miss Rhina Espaillat's marvelous "Bilingual / Bilingüe" reprinted here for the first time in any anthology. We predict this humane and illuminating poem will soon become a standard selection in textbooks.

The selection of poems by Emily Dickinson and Langston Hughes has also been greatly expanded for the "Casebooks" chapter on their works. Please note that the book contains 13 poems by Robert Frost, plus a passage of critical prose, so he, too, can be used as a research topic as easily as Dickinson or Hughes. Many other fine new poems have been added by writers including Louise Bogan, Bob Dylan, Adelle Foley, Thom Gunn, Sophie Hannah, Ha Jin, Marilyn Nelson, Yone Noguchi, Robert Pinsky, Kay Ryan, Benjamin Sáenz, Diane Thiel, C. K. Williams, and Chryss Yost.

The DRAMA section has been both revised and expanded. We have added two new plays. The two new contemporary works are Terrence McNally's moving play *Andre's Mother* and David Ives's hilarious *Sure Thing*. The chapter on classical Greek drama has been extensively revised and broadened. Both Sophocles and Shakespeare are also the subject of extensive new "Casebooks," which include 10 critical commentaries on the dramatists. Illustrations have been extensively integrated into the text to provide students with visual reference points to the texts.

Critical Approaches to Literature

"Critical Approaches to Literature" proved so popular in the last two editions that we have kept and slightly updated it in the new *Literature*. There are two selections for every major critical school—twenty selections in all. The critical excerpts have been carefully chosen both to illustrate the major theoretical approaches and to be accessible to beginning students. All the critical selections focus on literary works found in the present edition. Among the new critical excerpts are examinations of works by William Faulkner, Charlotte Perkins Gilman, and Andrew Marvell. Taken together with the many commentaries in the "Casebooks" and "Writer's Perspectives," *Literature* now includes a total of 91 critical excerpts. This expanded coverage gives *Literature* both more depth and flexibility for instructors who prefer to incorporate literary theory and criticism into their introductory courses.

Writing Material

The extensive writing material added in the previous edition has had numerous improvements and updates. All main chapters still include a "Writer's Perspective," a "Writing Critically" feature, and "Further Suggestions for Writing." The extremely popular "Writer's Perspective" provides an author's own comments on his or her work reprinted in the chapter. These 44 statements range across the literary spectrum from Ernest Hemingway discussing literary style and Gwendolyn Brooks explaining "We Real Cool," to Tennessee Williams describing an ideal production of *A Glass Menagerie* and Amy Tan recalling how she developed a narrative voice. Meanwhile the "Writing Critically" feature provides students with practical advice on planning and composing critical essays as well as offering specific assignments for possible term papers.

We have also reprinted the numerous student essays from the last edition— twelve complete papers to provide students with models for their own critical writing. (There is also a card report.) Six of the papers are found in final chapters on "Writing About Fiction," "Writing About Poetry," and "Writing About Drama" where they illustrate three different approaches to critical writing—explication, analysis, and comparison—as well as a drama review. Six papers (written by real students) will be found in earlier chapters. The papers provide close readings of the literary works that emphasize specific elements of their structure and meaning. The final chapters on critical writing have also been revised and updated. Students will find more complete guidelines and examples for preparing and formatting papers according to 1999 MLA standards.

STATISTICS ON POETRY

The third compact edition of *Literature* has been expanded to include 355 whole poems. In case you wish to teach a poet's work in greater depth than a single poem affords, these 19 poets are most heavily represented (listed by number of poems):

Emily Dickinson	19
Langston Hughes	15
Robert Frost	13
William Shakespeare	8
W. B. Yeats	8
Walt Whitman	6
W. C. Williams	6
William Wordsworth	6
William Blake	5
E. E. Cummings	5
Thomas Hardy	5
John Keats	5
Alfred, Lord Tennyson	5
W. H. Auden	4
John Donne	4

Also, there are three poems each by Elizabeth Bishop, Gwendolyn Brooks, Buson, H. D., George Herbert, Robert Herrick, Ben Jonson, Sylvia Plath, Alexander Pope, Adrienne Rich, Edwin Arlington Robinson, Theodore Roethke, and William Stafford. Many other poets are represented doubly.

TEXTS AND EDITORIAL POLICY

Spelling has been modernized and rendered American, unless to do so would change the sound of a word. However, the *y* has remained in Blake's strange "Tyger," and Whitman has been left with his *bloom'd* on the conviction that *bloomed* would no more resemble Whitman than a portrait of the poet in a starched collar. Untitled poems are identified by their first lines, except for those that have titles assigned by custom. The poems of Emily Dickinson are presented as edited by Thomas H. Johnson.

It would have been simpler to gloss no word a student could find in a desk dictionary, on the grounds that rummaging through dictionaries is good moral discipline; but it seemed best not to require the student to exchange text for dictionary as many as thirty times in reading a story, poem, or play. Glosses have been provided, therefore, for whatever seemed likely to get in the way of pleasure and understanding.

The spelling *rime* is used instead of *rhyme* on the theory that rime is easier to tell apart from *rhythm*.

ADDITIONAL TEACHING RESOURCE

Ask your Longman representative for our *Teaching Composition with Literature: 101 Writing Assignments from College Instructors*, a collection of proven writing exercises based on selections from the book contributed by dozens of teachers from across North America.

A NOTE ON LIVE READINGS

Many find that, for drumming up zeal for poetry, there is no substitute for a good live poetry reading by a poet whose work students have read before. Anyone who wants to order a live poet is advised to send for *A Directory of American Poets and Fiction Writers* from Poets and Writers, Inc., 72 Spring Street, New York, NY 10012. Not all poets give stirring performances, of course, so ask your colleagues on other campuses for suggestions, lest you get stuck with some mumbling prima donna.

If you want the poet to visit classes or confer with student writers, be sure to specify your expectations ahead of time. Some poets, especially media figures whose affairs are managed by agents, will charge for extra services; less-known visitors grateful for a reading are often pathetically happy to oblige (they may even walk your dog). All poets, if they are to do their best for you, need an occasional hour of solitude to recharge their batteries.

WITH A LITTLE HELP FROM OUR FRIENDS

If we have described this manual as a 24-hour teacher's lounge, we are pleased to report how many interesting colleagues have stopped in to chat. We receive a steady stream of letters on *Literature* from instructors throughout North America and abroad. Sometimes they disagree with our comments. More often they add new information or perspective. Frequently they pass on stories about what works or does not work in their classrooms. Much of this information is simply too good not to share. We have, therefore, supplemented our own comments with hundreds of comments from instructors (always properly credited to their authors).

For each new edition, we also solicit a few comments from contemporary authors whose work appears for the first time in *Literature*. These writers generously provide some extra perspective on their poems and stories found in the anthology. In addition to contributions carried over from the previous edition, you may be interested to read the brief commentaries specially written for us by Rhina Espaillat, Kay Ryan, Diane Thiel, and Chryss Yost.

THANKS

We decided to go through the entire Instructor's Manual for the new edition to revise, expand, and update the text. Michael Palma led the effort by going through the last edition and making innumerable additions, revisions, cuts, and suggestions. His contributions have been invaluable, and they guided us in numerous other changes.

Daniel Stone, Tami Haaland, Robert McPhillips, and Diane Thiel helped with some new entries. Meanwhile excellent advice came from: Cheryl Clements; Lee Gurga; Nan LaBoe; Richard Mezo; Jeff Newberry; Beverly Schneller; Janet Schwarzkopf; Theresa Welford; and William Zander.

Many instructors, most of whose names appear in this manual, generously wrote us with their suggestions and teaching experiences. Other instructors are noted in the introductory remarks to the textbook itself. We thank them all for their pragmatic and informed help. We are grateful to Donna Campion at the publisher and Dianne Hall for their formidable effort and good will in managing the design and production of the manual. Finally, we would like to thank Mary Gioia whose remarkable planning and editorial skills kept this manual in running order despite its erratic drivers.

On Teaching Literature

We'll close with a poem. It is by Billy Collins, from his collection *The Apple That Astonished Paris* (University of Arkansas Press, 1988), and it sets forth an experience that may be familiar to you.

INTRODUCTION TO POETRY

I ask them to take a poem
and hold it up to the light
like a color slide

or press an ear against its hive.

I say drop a mouse into a poem
and watch him probe his way out,
or walk inside the poem's room
and feel the walls for a light switch.

I want them to waterski
across the surface of a poem
waving at the author's name on the shore.

But all they want to do
is tie the poem to a chair with rope
and torture a confession out of it.

They begin beating it with a hose
to find out what it really means.

As you might expect, Billy Collins, who has recently been appointed U.S. Poet Laureate, is a professor of English himself—at Lehman College of the City University of New York.

May this manual help you find ways to persuade your students to set aside rope and hose, and instead turn on a few lights.

XJK, DMK, and DG

FICTION

Stories Arranged by Type and Element

If you prefer to teach a *different* story to illustrate an element of fiction—to discuss style, say, with the aid of "Cathedral" or "A Good Man Is Hard to Find" instead of the examples in the chapter on style—you will find the substitution easy to make. Many choices are at your disposal in Chapter 9, "Stories for Further Reading," and other stories in the book lend themselves to varied purposes. The following list has a few likely substitutions. If you teach other elements of fiction (e.g. humor, fantasy) or specific genres, you will find some nominations here.

FABLE, PARABLE, AND TALE

STORIES INCLUDED IN CHAPTER:
- Appointment in Samarra
- The North Wind and the Sun
- Godfather Death
- Independence

OTHER SUGGESTED STORIES:
- Before the Law
- My Life with the Wave
- The Parable of the Prodigal Son
- The Tell-Tale Heart

PLOT

STORY INCLUDED IN CHAPTER:
- A & P

OTHER SUGGESTED STORIES:
- Barn Burning
- The Lottery
- An Occurrence at Owl Creek Bridge
- A Rose for Emily
- Saboteur

POINT OF VIEW
First Person Narrator as Central Character:

STORIES INCLUDED IN CHAPTER:
- The Tell-Tale Heart
- Why I Live at the P.O.

OTHER SUGGESTED STORIES:
- A & P
- Araby (*mature narrator recalling boyhood view*)
- Cathedral
- Barbie-Q
- Gimpel the Fool (*innocent narrator*)
- Greasy Lake
- My Life with the Wave
- A Pair of Tickets
- The Yellow Wallpaper

First Person Narrator not the Protagonist:

STORIES INCLUDED IN CHAPTER:
- A Rose for Emily
- Sonny's Blue

ANOTHER SUGGESTED STORY:
- The Ones Who Walk Away from Omelas

POINT OF VIEW (Cont.)
Third person, all-knowing narrator:
SUGGESTED STORIES:

A Good Man Is Hard to Find
The Man to Send Rain Clouds
The Rocking-Horse Winner
The Storm
The Things They Carried
Where Are You Going, Where Have
You Been? (*paragraphs 1–13*)

Third Person, Limited Omniscience
(Narrator Seeing Into One Major Character):
SUGGESTED STORIES:

Barn Burning
The Gospel According to Mark
The Jilting of Granny Weatherall
Miss Brill
An Occurrence at Owl Creek Bridge
The Open Boat
Young Goodman Brown

Objective or "Fly-on-the-Wall" Point of View:
SUGGESTED STORIES:

A Clean, Well-Lighted Place
(*paragraphs 2–75*)
The Chrysanthemums

CHARACTER

STORIES INCLUDED IN CHAPTER:
Everyday Use
Gimpel the Fool
The Jilting of Granny Weatherall

OTHER SUGGESTED STORIES:
Barn Burning (*Sarty Snopes: a dynamic character, one who develops within the story*)
The Chrysanthemums
A Good Man Is Hard to Find
Miss Brill
Paul's Case
A Small, Good Thing
Sonny's Blues
The Things They Carried
Where Are You Going, Where Have
You Been?

SETTING

STORIES INCLUDED IN CHAPTER:
Greasy Lake
A Pair of Tickets

OTHER SUGGESTED STORIES:
A & P
Araby

SETTING (Cont.)

The Storm

The Chrysanthemums
A Clean, Well-Lighted Place
Gimpel the Fool
A Good Man Is Hard to Find
The Gospel According to Mark
Miss Brill
The Open Boat
Paul's Case
A Rose for Emily
Sweat
The Things They Carried
The Yellow Wallpaper
Young Goodman Brown

TONE AND STYLE

STORIES INCLUDED IN CHAPTER:
Barn Burning
A Clean, Well-Lighted Place

OTHER SUGGESTED STORIES:
Barbie-Q
Cathedral
Gimpel the Fool
Girl
Greasy Lake
The Jilting of Granny Weatherall
The Open Boat
A Rose for Emily
The Tell-Tale Heart
The Things They Carried
A Very Old Man with Enormous
    Wings
Where Are You Going, Where Have
    You Been?
Young Goodman Brown

IRONY

STORY INCLUDED IN CHAPTER:
Saboteur

OTHER SUGGESTED STORIES:
The Appointment in Samarra
Dead Men's Path
The Gospel According to Mark
Happy Endings
The Jilting of Granny Weatherall
The Lottery
An Occurrence at Owl Creek Bridge
The Open Boat (*irony of fate*)
The Rocking-Horse Winner
A Rose for Emily
The Storm
The Tell-Tale Heart

SYMBOL

OTHER ELEMENTS AND GENRES

HUMOR

A & P
Barbie-Q
Gimpel the Fool
Greasy Lake
Harrison Bergeron
Independence
Why I Live at the P.O.

MYTH, FOLKLORE, AND ARCHETYPE

The Appointment in Samarra
Gimpel the Fool
Godfather Death
The Lottery
My Life with the Wave
A Very Old Man with Enormous Wings
Where Are You Going, Where Have You Been?
Young Goodman Brown

SCIENCE FICTION

Harrison Bergeron
The Ones Who Walk Away from Omelas

FANTASY AND THE SUPERNATURAL

The Appointment in Samarra
Gimpel the Fool
Godfather Death

Stories Arranged by Subject and Theme

In case you prefer to teach fiction according to its subjects and general themes, we have provided a list of stories that may be taken up together. Some instructors who arrange a course thematically like to *begin* with Chapter 6, *Theme*, and its three stories.

ART, LANGUAGE, AND IMAGINATION
    Cathedral
    Everyday Use
    My Life with the Wave
    Sonny's Blues
    The Gospel According to Mark
    The Jilting of Granny Weatherall
    The Ones Who Walk Away from Omelas
    The Yellow Wallpaper

CHILDHOOD
    Araby
    Barbie-Q
    Girl
    The Rocking-Horse Winner

COMING OF AGE, INITIATION STORIES
    Araby
    Barn Burning
    Greasy Lake
    Paul's Case
    Where Are You Going, Where Have You Been?

DEATH
    The Appointment in Samarra
    Dead Men's Path
    Godfather Death
    A Good Man Is Hard to Find
    The Gospel According to Mark
    The Jilting of Granny Weatherall
    The Open Boat
    A Rose for Emily
    A Small, Good Thing
    Sweat

FRIENDSHIP AND CAMARADERIE
A & P
Araby
Barbie-Q
Cathedral
Greasy Lake
The Open Boat
The Things They Carried

GENERATION GAPS
A & P
Araby
Barbie-Q
Girl
Greasy Lake
Where Are You Going, Where Have You Been?

HOLDING A JOB, WORK
A & P
A Clean, Well-Lighted Place
Sweat

HUMANITY AGAINST THE ELEMENTS
The Open Boat

ILLUSION AND REALITY
Araby
The Chrysanthemums
Dead Men's Path
Gimpel the Fool
The Gospel According to Mark
Greasy Lake
An Occurrence at Owl Creek Bridge
Paul's Case
The Tell-Tale Heart
The Very Old Man with Enormous Wings
The Yellow Wallpaper
Young Goodman Brown

INDIVIDUAL VERSUS SOCIETY
A & P
Barn Burning
Dead Men's Path
Gimpel the Fool
Harrison Bergeron
Independence

The Lottery
The Ones Who Walk Away from Omelas
Paul's Case
A Rose for Emily
Saboteur
Young Goodman Brown

INGENIOUS DECEPTIONS
Good Country People
The Tell-Tale Heart
Young Goodman Brown

LONELINESS
The Chrysanthemums
A Clean, Well-Lighted Place
Miss Brill
Paul's Case

LOVE AND DESIRE
A & P
Araby
The Chrysanthemums
Gimpel the Fool
Happy Endings
The Jilting of Granny Weatherall
My Life with the Wave
The Storm

MACHISMO AND SEXISM
A & P
Greasy Lake
Sweat

MAGIC AND THE OCCULT
The Appointment in Samarra
Godfather Death
The Rocking-Horse Winner
Young Goodman Brown

MARRIAGES (THE GOOD, THE BAD, AND THE UGLY)
Cathedral
Gimpel the Fool
Happy Endings
The Storm
Sweat
The Yellow Wallpaper

MOTHER-CHILD RELATIONSHIPS
Everyday Use
Girl
Good Country People
The Jilting of Granny Weatherall
A Pair of Tickets
The Rocking-Horse Winner

MULTICULTURAL PERSPECTIVES
Dead Men's Path
Everyday Use
Gimpel the Fool
Independence
The Man to Send Rain Clouds
A Pair of Tickets
Sonny's Blues
Sweat

MURDER
A Good Man Is Hard to Find
The Gospel According to Mark
A Rose for Emily
The Tell-Tale Heart
Sweat

NATURE
The Man to Send Rain Clouds
The North Wind and the Sun
The Open Boat
The Storm

PRIDE BEFORE A FALL
Barn Burning
Dead Men's Path

RACE, CLASS, AND CULTURE
Barbie-Q
Barn Burning
Dead Men's Path
Everyday Use
Gimpel the Fool
Independence
The Man to Send Rain Clouds
A Pair of Tickets
Sonny's Blues
Sweat

Stories Students Like Most

At the end of the book is a short student questionnaire. This form solicits each student's opinion about his or her reactions to the book. The editors read and save each completed questionnaire they receive. These candid student responses often help improve the anthology from edition to edition.

These student responses are interesting in their own right, but they also add perspective on what really happens in the classroom. The stories students prefer often differ sharply from those that instructors rate most highly. Instructors can learn a great deal by remembering how younger readers find certain selections both exciting and illuminating that may seem overly familiar to seasoned teachers.

Here are some top stories from previous editions chosen by a large sample of students over the past four years.

FAVORITE STORIES *(Student Choices in Rank Order)*

1. William Faulkner, "A Rose for Emily"

2. Shirley Jackson, "The Lottery"

3. Edgar Allan Poe, "The Tell-Tale Heart"

4. T. Coraghessan Boyle, "Greasy Lake"

5. Charlotte Perkins Gilman, "The Yellow Wallpaper"

6. John Updike, "A & P"

7. Flannery O'Connor, "A Good Man Is Hard to Find"

1   Reading a Story

For a second illustration of a great detail in a story, a detail that sounds observed instead of invented (besides Defoe's "two shoes, not mates"), you might cite a classic hunk of hokum: H. Rider Haggard's novel of farfetched adventure, *She* (1887). Describing how the Amahagger tribesmen wildly dance by the light of unusual torches—embalmed corpses of the citizens of ancient Kor, left over in quantity—the narrator, Holly, remarks, "So soon as a mummy was consumed to the ankles, which happened in about twenty minutes, the feet were kicked away, and another put in its place." (Pass down another mummy, this one is guttering!) Notice the exact specification "in about twenty minutes" and the unforgettable discarding of the unburned feet, like a candle stub. Such detail, we think, bespeaks a tall-tale-teller of genius. (For this citation, we thank T. J. Binyon's review of *The Private Diaries of Sir Henry Rider Haggard* in *Times Literary Supplement*, 8 Aug. 1980.)

When you introduce students to the *tale* as a literary form, you might point out that even in this age of electronic entertainment, a few tales still circulate from mouth to ear. Ask them whether they have heard any good tales lately (other than dirty jokes). This tale reportedly has been circulated in Israel:

> Two Israeli agents, captured in an Arab country, are tied to stakes to be shot. While the firing squad stands in readiness, the Arab commander asks one of the captured men if he has any last request. For answer, the captive spits in the commander's face. From the other captive comes a wail: "For God's sake, Moishe, don't cause *trouble!*"

FABLE, PARABLE, AND TALE

W. Somerset Maugham
THE APPOINTMENT IN SAMARRA, page 4

Maugham's retelling of this fable has in common with the Grimm tale "Godfather Death" not only the appearance of Death as a character, but also the moral or lesson that Death cannot be defied. Maugham includes this fable in his play *Sheppey* (1933), but it is probably best known as the epigraph to John O'Hara's novel *The Appointment in Samarra* (New York: Random, 1934).

Students may be asked to recall other fables they know. To jog their memories, famous expressions we owe to Aesop ("sour grapes," "the lion's share," "dog in the manger," and others) may suggest the fables that gave them rise. At least, the fable of the hare and the tortoise should be familiar to any watcher of old Bugs Bunny cartoons.

Aesop
THE NORTH WIND AND THE SUN, page 5

Aesop's fables are still so familiar to many students that they may be tempted to treat them condescendingly as "kids' stuff." His fables are also so compact that they seem very slight. It may help students initially to point out that in classical times the notion of a special literature for children as opposed to other groups did not exist. Aesop told his stories to a mixed audience probably consisting mostly of adults. It might even be interesting to ask a fundamental question such as whether a story is necessarily different if it is directed toward adults or children.

Most fables involved animals endowed with human traits of character and consciousness. We have deliberately chosen a fable that endows astronomical bodies and natural physical forces with character traits—the sun and the wind—to demonstrate the range of imaginative possibilities open to the fabulist. Any student interested in pursuing the effect of such cosmic fables on contemporary literature might want to investigate two books by Italo Calvino—*Cosmicomics* (1965) and *t zero* (1967)—whose characters include planets, physical forces, and mathematical ideas.

Chuang Tzu
INDEPENDENCE, page 6

Chuang Tzu's parables are famous in Chinese culture, both as works of intrinsic literary merit and as pithy expressions of Taoist philosophy. Parables are important literary genres in traditional societies. They reflect a cultural aesthetic that appreciates the power of literary artistry while putting it to the use of illustrating moral and religious ideas. Clarity is a key virtue in a parable or moral fable. Its purpose is not merely to entertain but also to instruct.

Chuang Tzu's celebrated parable suggests the uneasy relationship between philosophy and power in ancient China. It was not necessarily a safe gesture to decline the public invitation of a king, and the refusal of employment could be construed as an insult or censure. Chuang understands that the only safe way to turn down a monarch is with wit and charm. He makes his moral point, but with self-deprecating humor.

In his indispensable book, *Essentials of Chinese Literary Art* (Belmont, CA: Duxbury, 1979, p. 46), James J. Y. Liu of Stanford University comments on the sly rhetoric of this parable:

Instead of solemnly declaring that worldly power and glory are all in vain, Chuang Tzu makes us see their absurdity by comparing them to a dead tortoise. At the same time, life unburdened with official duties is not idealized, but compared to the tortoise dragging its tail in the mud.

The *Tzu* following Chuang's name is an honorific meaning *master*. The philosopher's historical name was Chuang Chou. The Chinese surname is conventionally put first, so Chuang is the proper term to use for the author.

This parable was a favorite of the Argentinean writer Jorge Luis Borges, who was fascinated by the Chinese fabular tradition.

Jesus's "Parable of the Prodigal Son" (Luke 15: 11–32) is found in the chapter on "Theme." It may be interesting for students to compare the differing techniques of these two classic parables from different traditions.

Jakob and Wilhelm Grimm
GODFATHER DEATH, page 8

For all its brevity, "Godfather Death" illustrates typical elements of plot. That is the main reason for including it in this chapter (not to mention its intrinsic merits!). It differs from Updike's contemporary "A & P" in its starker characterizations, its summary method of telling, its terser descriptions of setting, and its element of magic and the supernatural. In its world, God, the Devil, and Death walk the highway. If students can be shown these differences, then probably they will be able to distinguish most tales from most short stories.

"Godfather Death" may be useful, too, in a class discussion of point of view. In the opening pages of Chapter 2, we discuss the ways in which this tale is stronger for having an omniscient narrator. If you go on to deal with symbolism, you may wish to come back to this tale for a few illustrations of wonderful, suggestive properties: the magical herb, Death's underground cave, and its "thousands upon thousands" of flickering candles.

This is a grim tale even for Grimm: a young man's attentions to a beautiful princess bring about his own destruction. In a fairy tale it is usually dangerous to defy some arbitrary law; and in doing so here the doctor breaks a binding contract. From the opening, we know the contract will be an evil one—by the father's initial foolishness in spurning God. Besides, the doctor is a thirteenth child—an unlucky one.

Possible visual aids are reproductions of the "Dance of Death" woodcuts by Hans Holbein the younger. Have any students seen Ingmar Bergman's film *The Seventh Seal,* and can they recall how Death was personified?

Anne Sexton has a sophisticated retelling of "Godfather Death," in which the doctor's guttering candle is "no bigger than an eyelash," in her *Transformations,* a collection of poems based on Grimm (Boston: Houghton, 1971). "Godfather Death" is seldom included in modern selections of fairy tales for children. Bruno Bettelheim has nothing specific to say about "Godfather Death" but has much of interest to say about fairy tales in his *The Uses of Enchantment* (New York: Knopf,

1976). Though Bettelheim's study is addressed primarily to adults "with children in their care," any college student fascinated by fairy tales would find it stimulating.

PLOT

THE SHORT STORY

John Updike
A & P, page 14

Within this story, Sammy rises to a kind of heroism. Despite the conventional attitudes he expresses in the first half of the story (his usual male reactions to girls in two-piece bathing suits, his put-down of *all* girls' minds: "a little buzz like a bee in a glass jar"), he comes to feel sympathy for the girls as human beings. He throws over his job to protest against their needless humiliation, and in so doing he asserts his criticism of supermarket society, a deadly world of "sheep" and "houseslaves" whom dynamite couldn't budge from their dull routines. What harm in a little innocent showing off—in, for once, a display of nonconformity?

Sammy isn't sophisticated. He comes from a family of proletarian beer drinkers and thinks martinis are garnished with mint. His language is sometimes pedestrian: "Really, I thought that was so cute." But he is capable of fresh and accurate observations—his description of the way Queenie walks on her bare feet, his comparison of the "clean bare plane" of her upper chest to "a dented sheet of metal tilted in the light." (Could Sammy be capable of so poetic an observation, or is this Updike's voice?)

Carefully plotted for all its seemingly casual telling, "A & P" illustrates typical elements. The *setting* is clear from Updike's opening paragraph ("I'm in the third checkout slot . . . with my hand on a box of HiHo crackers"). Relatively long for so brief a story, the *exposition* takes up most of the story's first half. Portraying Queenie and the other girls in loving detail, this exposition helps make Sammy's later gesture of heroism understandable. It establishes, also, that Sammy feels at odds with his job, and so foreshadows his heroism. He reacts against butcher McMahon's piggishness: "patting his mouth and looking after them sizing up their joints. *Dramatic conflict* arrives with the appearance of Lengel, the manager, and his confrontation with the girls. Lengel catches Sammy smiling—we can guess the clerk is in for trouble. Crisis and climax are practically one, but if you care to distinguish them, the *crisis* may be found in the paragraph "I thought and said 'No' but it wasn't about that I was thinking," in which Sammy hovers on the brink of his decision. The *climax* is his announcement "I quit"; the *conclusion* is his facing a bleaker future. The last sentence implies not only that Sammy will have trouble getting another job, but that if he continues to go through life as an uncompromising man of principle, then life from now on is going to be rough.

In "A & P" and the fairy tale "Godfather Death," the plots are oddly similar. In both, a young man smitten with a young woman's beauty, makes a sacrifice in order to defend her against his grim overlord. (It is far worse, of course, to have Death for an overlord than Lengel.) If this resemblance doesn't seem too abstract, it may be worth briefly pursuing. The stories, to be sure, are more different than similar, but one can show how Updike is relatively abundant in his descriptions of characters and setting and goes more deeply into the central character's motivation—as short-story authors usually do, unlike most writers of tales.

For a good explication of this story, see Janet Overmeyer, "Courtly Love in the A & P," in *Notes on Contemporary Literature* for May 1972 (West Georgia College, Carrollton, GA 30117).

Updike himself reads this story and five others on *Selected Stories*, a set of two audiotape cassettes (169 minutes) produced by Random House (ISBN 0-394-55040-4), and available in shops or from American Audio Prose Library, whose phone number is (800) 447-2275. This is a crisp, dry reading that brings out the humor of "A & P."

WRITER'S PERSPECTIVE

John Updike on Writing
WHY WRITE?, page 19

Although John Updike is probably the most prolific novelist-critic active in American letters, he has written surprisingly little about his own creative process. Perhaps he has been so busy examining the work of other writers that his critical attention has been mostly focused outward. A certain native reticence, however, must also surely be at play. His 1975 essay, "Why Write?" is, therefore, a key document in understanding his artistic perspective.

The passage excerpted is an elegant defense of imaginative writing as a special means of human communication not reducible to an abstract message. Art's indirection, silences, and complexity are essential to its essence. "Reticence is as important a tool for the writer as expression," Updike asserts. Genuine writing is "ideally as ambiguous and opaque as life itself."

2 Point of View

For other illustrations of the relatively scarce second-person point of view, see Richard Hugo's poetry collection, *31 Letters and 13 Dreams* (New York: Norton, 1977): "In Your Fugitive Dream," "In Your War Dream," "In Your Young Dream," and others. These also appear in Hugo's collected poems, *Making Certain It Goes On* (New York: Norton, 1984).

William Faulkner
A ROSE FOR EMILY, page 28

Over the past decade whenever we have polled college students about their favorite short stories, Faulkner's "A Rose for Emily" has usually ranked first. The story has immense appeal to students for its memorable title character, brooding atmosphere, and eerie surprise ending. It is also a story that immediately rewards rereading and study. After knowing the ending, one discovers details in virtually every paragraph that anticipate the conclusion—the poison, the smell, the vanished suitor, to mention only a few.

The style of "A Rose for Emily" is unusually conventional for Faulkner. There are no elaborate periodic sentences or stream-of-consciousness narration. The simple and direct style reflects the particular speaker Faulkner chose to tell the story. The unnamed narrator is a townsman of Jefferson, Mississippi, who has for some years watched Emily Grierson with considerable interest but also respectful distance. He openly describes his perspective as average; he always uses *we* in the story, never *I*. His tone and manner are informed but detached, and surprisingly cool given the horrific conclusion. He mixes his own observations with town gossip to provide a seeming reliable view of Jefferson's opinion of Miss Emily. (The story would be radically different if it were told from Emily Grierson's point of view.)

While the narrator notes and reports many things about Miss Emily's history and personality, he is not the man to analyze or ponder their significance. The careful reader, however, soon understands several important factors affecting her. Miss Emily's father has somehow kept her down—dominating her life and driving away suitors. She also has difficulty accepting loss or change. She will not, for example, initially admit that her father has died or let the doctors or minister dispose of the body. Miss Emily seems starved for affection and emotionally desperate enough to risk censure from the town when she takes Homer Barron as her lover. At the end the reader also sees her determination in killing Barron, though her motives are open to question. Did she want to exact revenge for his apparent refusal to marry her? Or did she want to keep him with her forever?

The genre of the story is Gothic—more precisely Southern Gothic—which may be another factor in its popularity. Gothic fiction tries to create terror and

suspense and is usually set in isolated old houses, castles, or monasteries, populated by mysterious individuals. Typical Gothic devices include locked rooms,
ancient servants, dusty chambers, and decayed mansions—all properties found
in "A Rose for Emily." Usually taking place in interior spaces of sinister buildings, Gothic fiction also thrives on cultivating an oppressively claustrophobic
atmosphere of disturbing mystery and implicit evil. This story provides a good
introduction to the genre for students, and compared to another Faulkner story
like "Barn Burning," it demonstrates how powerfully genre can shape an
author's work.

Students will want to make sure of exactly what happens in the story. From
the detail that the strand of hair is *iron-gray*, it appears that Emily lay beside
Homer's body recently, long after it was rotten; probably lay beside it many
times, for her pillow is clearly indented. Just as she had clung to her conviction
that her father and Colonel Sartoris were still alive, she had come to believe that
Homer Barron had faithfully married her, and she successfully ignored for forty
years all the testimony of her senses. The conclusion of the story is foreshadowed
by Emily's refusal to allow her father to be buried, by her purchase of rat poison,
by the disappearance of Homer Barron, and by the pervasive smell of decay. In
fact, these foreshadowings are so evident it is a wonder that, for those reading the
story for the first time, the ending is so surprising. Much of the surprise seems
due to the narrator's back-and-forth, unchronological method of telling the
events of the story. We aren't told in proper sequence that (1) Emily buys poison,
(2) Homer disappears, and (3) there is a mysterious odor—a chain of events
which might immediately rouse our suspicions. Instead, we hear about odor, poison, and disappearance, in that order. By this arrangement, any connection
between these events is made to seem a little less obvious.

Having satisfied their natural interest in the final horror of the story, students
can be led to discuss why "A Rose for Emily" isn't a mere thriller. Why (they may
be asked) is the story called "A Rose"? No actual rose appears in it. Perhaps Emily
herself is the white rose of Jefferson (like the heroine of *The White Rose of Memphis*,
a novel by Faulkner's grandfather). But the usual connotations of roses will apply.
A rose is a gift to a loved one, and the whole story is the narrator's tribute to Emily.

But, some may object, how can anyone wish to pay tribute to a decayed old
poisoner who sleeps with a corpse? The narrator patiently gives us reasons for his
sympathy. As a girl, Emily was beautiful, a "slender figure in white," fond of society. But her hopes were thwarted by her domineering father, whose horsewhip
discouraged suitors from her door. Her strength and pride vanquished all who
would invade her house: the new Board of Aldermen who tried to collect her
taxes, the Baptist minister sent to lecture her on her morals, the relatives from
Atlanta who eventually departed. "It is important," Ray B. West writes, "to realize that during the period of Emily's courtship the town became Emily's allies in
a contest between Emily and her Grierson cousins, 'because the two female
cousins were even more Grierson than Miss Emily had ever been'" ("Atmosphere
and Theme in Faulkner's 'A Rose for Emily,'" *Perspective* [Summer 1949]: 239–45).

Emily's refusal to recognize change is suggested in the symbol of her invisible watch (paragraph 7), with its hint that she lives according to a private, secret
time of her own. Her house seems an extension of her person in its "stubborn and

coquettish decay" (2). Now it stands amid gasoline pumps, refusing, like its owner, to be part of a new era. The story contains many such images of stasis: when Emily confronts the aldermen, she looks bloated, "like a body long submerged in motionless water"—a foreshadowing, perhaps, of the discovery of Homer's long-guarded dust.

Some have read the story as an allegory: Homer Barron is the crude, commercial North who invades, like a carpetbagger. Emily, with her faithful ex-slave, is the Old South, willing to be violated. In an interview with students at the University of Virginia, Faulkner played down such North-South symbolism. "I don't say that's not valid and not there," he said, "but . . . [I was] simply writing about people." (The whole interview in which Faulkner discusses this story, not very helpfully, is in *Faulkner in the University*, Frederick Gwynn and Joseph Blotner, eds., UP of Virginia, 1959.)

Still, it is clear that Emily, representing an antebellum first family, receives both Faulkner's admiration and his criticism for resisting change. "The theme of the story," according to C. W. M. Johnson, "can be stated: 'If one resists change, he must love and live with death,' and in this theme it is difficult not to see an implied criticism of the South" (*Explicator* VI [No. 7] May 1948: item 45). But Faulkner's criticism, Ray B. West, Jr., feels, is leveled at the North as well. West makes much of the passage in which Faulkner discerns two possible views of Time (55). If, for the South, Time is "a huge meadow which no winter ever quite touches," then for the North it is a mere "mathematical progression" and "a diminishing road." West would propose, for a statement of the story's theme: "One must neither resist nor wholly accept change, for to do either is to live as though one were never to die; that is, to live *with* Death without knowing it" (*Explicator* VII [No. 1] Oct. 1948: item 8).

Studying "A Rose for Emily" may help prepare students for Faulkner's "Barn Burning" (Chapter 5), whose central character, the son of a sharecropper, is Colonel Sartoris Snopes. "A Rose for Emily" clearly is in the tradition of the Gothic story, for it has a crumbling mansion, a mysterious servant, and a hideous secret. For comparison, one might have students read Poe's "The Tell-Tale Heart," if they don't know it already: another story of madness and murder, but told (unlike "A Rose") from the point of view of the mad killer.

For a valuable discussion of the story's point of view see John Daremo, "Insight into Horror: The Narrator in Faulkner's 'A Rose for Emily,'" in Sylvan Barnet, ed., *A Short Guide to Writing about Literature*, 5th ed. (Boston: Little, Brown, 1985). A more superficial view of the story is expressed in this limerick by a celebrated bard, Anonymous:

> Miss Emily, snobbish and cranky,
> Used to horse around town with a Yankee.
> When she'd wake up in bed,
> With the dust of the dead,
> She would sneeze in her delicate hanky.

Faulkner's story resembles a riddle, argues Charles Clay Doyle of the University of Georgia. The resemblance lies not so much in the story's structure or rhetoric "as in the tricky way it presents clues, clues that tell the truth but at the same time mislead or fail to enlighten. The pleasure of discovery experienced by readers of the story resembles the pleasure we take in learning the answer to a riddle: we are astonished that the solution, which now seems so obvious, so inevitable, could have eluded us." Furthermore, Doyle finds an allusion to a well-known riddle in Faulkner's final description of Emily's chamber: Homer's "two mute shoes and the discarded socks." The riddle is, "What has a tongue but can't speak?" (Answer: a shoe.) Taking the phrase *mute shoes* to echo the riddle, Doyle thinks the shoes a pair of silent witnesses who, in their way, resemble the narrator himself, who shows us the truth but does not state it outright ("Mute Witnesses: Faulkner's Use of a Popular Riddle," *Mississippi Folklore Register* 24 [1990]: 53–55).

Joanna Stephens Mink of Illinois State University, Normal, divided her class into several groups and conducted a mock murder trial of Emily Grierson, which ended, after spirited debate, with an acquittal of Miss Emily by reason of insanity. For Professor Mink's full account, see "We Brought Emily Grierson to Trial" in *Exercise Exchange*, Spring 1984: 17–19. Inspired by her example, Saul Cohen of County College of Morris in New Jersey tried a similar experiment. In this instance, enough suspicion was raised about the actions of Miss Emily's servant to create reasonable doubt, leading to a straight acquittal. Professor Cohen's account appears in *Exercise Exchange* for October 1990.

Edgar Allan Poe

THE TELL-TALE HEART, page 35

In *The Uses of Enchantment*, the celebrated study of the psychological dimension of fairy tales, Bruno Bettelheim maintains that people who read fairy tales to children should not talk to them about what the stories mean. Thus, it could be argued that a story such as Poe's "The Tell-Tale Heart" is not meant to be picked apart and subjected to analysis. XJK remembers that once, after a class had read a Poe tale, a wonderful controversy broke out when someone complained, "this story doesn't really say anything." Everyone tried to sum up the story's theme, he reports, but failed miserably, and at last decided that there is a place in literature for stories that don't say anything in particular, but supply their readers with memorable nightmares and dreams. Many a writer of horror stories might summarize his or her intentions in the famous words of Joe the fat boy in Charles Dickens's *The Pickwick Papers*—"I wants to make your flesh creep"—and leave it go at that.

On the other hand, "The Tell-Tale Heart" must have something more than a good scare going for it to have attracted the attention of so many critics over the years. Daniel Hoffman, for instance, in his highly personal and deeply stimulating *Poe Poe Poe Poe Poe Poe Poe* (1973), sees the old man as a father-figure, even a Father-Figure, and suggests that in striking at his eye "the young madman strikes, symbolically, at his sexual power." Hoffman also says that the narrator "is full of the praise of his own sagacity, a terrible parody of the true sagacity of a

Dupin or a Legrand. For what he takes to be ratiocination is in fact the irresistible operation of the principle of his own perversity, the urge to do secret deeds, have secret thoughts undetected by the otherwise ever-watchful eye of the old man."

This and other demonstrations of the narrator's imbalance come at the very beginning of the story, and provide the context in which we will evaluate everything else that he says and does. The first paragraph alone, brief as it is, should provide fertile ground for students sent to find evidence of his severe disturbance. From there, you can lead the class into a discussion of the subsequent manifestations of his madness—his perception of the old man's eye as a thing in itself, independent of its admittedly benevolent possessor; his extreme attention to details and matters that others could find insignificant is not irrelevant; his fixation on a single objective for an insanely long period of time; his need to flaunt his brilliance, even if only to himself, by inviting the police into the house; and so on.

Is it his own heart that the narrator hears at the end, as Hoffman and others have suggested, or is it the wholly imaginary manifestation of his own guilty conscience? No one can say for certain, and perhaps no one should. As suggested above, the claim that the story contains no larger meaning represents one extreme of possible responses, but it may be an equally extreme response in the opposite direction to impose a strict—and potentially reductive—interpretation upon every last detail. At least some of the story's considerable power lies in the fact that we can't explain everything away.

There is a substantial amount of support material on "The Tell-Tale Heart" in this anthology. An excerpt from Hoffman's analysis of the story appears in "Critical Approaches to Literature." There are also two student essays and a sample card report on this story included in the chapter "Writing About a Story." You may want to suggest that students review any or all of this material.

"The Tell-Tale Heart" was adapted for television in the PBS television series *The American Short Story*, and is available on videocassette. Additionally an A & E biography of Edgar Allan Poe is also available on videocassette. Both can be obtained from Teacher's Video Company at (800) 262-8837.

James Baldwin
SONNY'S BLUES, page 39

The narrative structure of "Sonny's Blues" is more complex and interesting than it may seem at first glance. The story reads so smoothly that it is easy to overlook the fact that it begins *in medias res*. "Sonny's Blues" opens with the title character's arrest for the sale and possession of heroin; it ends in a jazz club with the older brother's ultimate understanding and acceptance of Sonny. This linear narrative is interrupted, however, by a long flashback that describes the uneasy earlier relation between the brothers. Since their parents are dead when the story opens, we meet the father and mother only in the flashback. The mother is the central moral figure of the story. Her last conversation with the narrator ultimately becomes a crucial part of his impetus to reconcile with Sonny. (The other, more immediately compelling motivation is the death of the narrator's small daughter from polio:

"My trouble," the narrator confesses, "made his real.") When the narrator promises to take care of his kid brother, his mother warns him it will be hard. She has seen enough of the world's trouble to be fatalistic. "You may not be able to stop nothing from happening," she tells him, before adding, "But you got to let him know you's *there.*" In one sense, "Sonny's Blues" is essentially the story of the narrator's slow, difficult process of living up to the promise he gave his mother.

The basic conflict of the story, which is—it is essential to remember—*the older brother's story,* is the narrator's inability to understand and respect the life of the younger brother he so clearly loves. Baldwin carefully establishes the brothers as opposites. The narrator is a cautious, respectable family man. He teaches math and is proud of his professional standing. Living in a Harlem housing project, he consciously protects himself from the dangers that surround him. Notice how intensely he appears to dislike Sonny's friend, the drug addict, when he encounters him in the school courtyard at the beginning of the story. However, the narrator is also compassionate, and it is important to see, in the same episode, how quickly he recognizes and responds to the addict's battered humanity. That gesture prefigures his reconciliation with his brother. Sonny, by contrast, is a romantic artist who is not afraid of taking risks to pursue the things he desires. His passion for music makes him impatient with everything else. He drops out of school. In his brother's view he is "wild" but not "hard or evil or disrespectful."

The outer story of "Sonny's Blues" is the title character's rehabilitation from drug addiction, reconciliation with his estranged brother, and recognition as a jazz pianist. The inner story is the narrator's spiritual and emotional growth into a person who can understand his younger brother's unorthodox, but nonetheless valuable, life. There should be no doubt that Baldwin, the former boy preacher, saw the narrator's inner growth as in some sense religious. The final scene in the nightclub ends with a religious vision of the blues. Listening to the group leader, Creole, play, the narrator says:

> He hit something in all of them, he hit something in me, myself, and the music tightened and deepened, apprehension began to beat the air. Creole began to tell us what the blues were about. They were not about anything very new. He and his boys up there were keeping it new, at the risk of ruin, destruction, madness, and death, in order to find new ways to make us listen. For, while the tale of how we suffer, and how we are delighted, and how we may triumph is never new, it always must be heard. There isn't any other tale to tell, and it's the only light we've got in all this darkness.

That passage not only offers as good an explanation of the blues and jazz as one is likely to find anywhere; it speaks cogently on the purpose of all art. It is worth having students pause over it. The final scene of "Sonny's Blues" is set in a dark, smoky nightclub, and its lyric quality marks a noticeable shift in tone from the realistic narrative style that preceded it. As the closing episode gains force along with the music it describes, it becomes a kind of vision for the narrator. In intellectual terms (for, after all, the narrator is a reflective math teacher), the vision brings him to a deep understanding of the human importance of art and the terrible cost of its creation. In emotional terms, his comprehension of jazz is inseparable from his sudden and profound understanding of Sonny's identity and motivations as an artist.

Unless the reader can accept the narrator's capacity for this transforming insight, the story is flawed by the sudden change of tone. Several critics have expressed their problem with the conclusion. They feel that Baldwin's authorial voice has replaced the narrator's. As Joseph Featherstone said in an initial review of *Going to Meet the Man*, the volume in which "Sonny's Blues" first appeared:

> The terms seem wrong; clearly this is not the voice of Sonny or his brother, it is the intrusive voice of Baldwin the boy preacher who has turned his back on the store front tabernacles but cannot forget the sound of angels' wings beating around his head. (*New Republic*, Nov. 27, 1965)

> [reprinted in Kenneth Kinnamon's "Twentieth Century Views" collection, cited below]

On one level, Featherstone's criticism makes sense. The tone of the final scene is elevated and religious. It is quite unlike the narrator's opening voice. However, a reader, wrapped up in the power of the final scene, is entitled to respond that the entire story up until then exists to justify this passage. "Sonny's Blues" is not merely the story of the narrator's experiences; it is the tale of his inner transformation. The final scene is the demonstration of the older brother's spiritual growth which his earlier experiences of death and loss have motivated. In understanding and accepting Sonny, he has enlarged his soul enough to understand Sonny's music, too.

There is a large, interesting body of criticism on James Baldwin's work. Kenneth Kinnamon's "Twentieth Century Views" critical collection, *James Baldwin* (Englewood Cliffs, NJ: Prentice Hall, 1974) remains extremely useful. John M. Reilly's cogent sociological essay, "'Sonny's Blues': James Baldwin's Image of Black Community," will be interesting for students writing on the story. Sherley Anne Williams's "The Black Musician: The Black Hero as Light Bearer" examines the metaphoric role of the musician in Baldwin's work with special attention given to "Sonny's Blues." Bruce Bawer's insightful overview of Baldwin's fiction, "Race and Art: James Baldwin," in his critical collection, *The Aspect of Eternity* (St. Paul, MN: Graywolf, 1993) will be very useful for students planning a paper on the author. Bawer surveys Baldwin's career in a biographical context and candidly evaluates the strengths and weaknesses of the novels. Quincy Troupe's *James Baldwin: The Legacy* (New York: Simon and Schuster, 1989) contains memoirs, tributes, and appreciations by fellow writers, including Maya Angelou, William Styron, Toni Morrison, and Chinua Achebe. Carolyn Wedin Sylvander's *James Baldwin* (New York: Ungar, 1980) also provides a reliable survey of the author's work, though her discussion of "Sonny's Blues" is brief.

Before students plunge into the secondary material on Baldwin, however, they should be encouraged to read the author's own essays. Baldwin was one of the finest essayists of his time, and there is no better introduction to his work than the title piece of *Notes of a Native Son*, Baldwin's passionate memoir of his Harlem youth.

A lively interview with Baldwin in which the author comments on race relations in America and on the cultural role of black and white artists is available on audiotape cassette from the American Audio Prose Library, Inc., Box 842, Columbia, MO 65205; phone number for orders, (800) 447–2275.

Eudora Welty
WHY I LIVE AT THE P.O., PAGE 63

Critic Robert McPhillips offers the following note on reading and teaching "Why I Live at the P.O."

Joyce Carol Oates has written in "The Art of Eudora Welty" that it "is an outstanding characteristic of Miss Welty's genius that she can write a story that seems to me, in a way, about 'nothing'—Flaubert's ideal, a masterpiece of style—and make it mean very nearly everything." Readers confronting "Why I Live at the P.O." for the first time may indeed feel that it seems to *mean* nothing in terms of easily analyzable themes, but they are equally likely to recognize that they have *experienced* something at once raucously comic and profoundly human. For the story's triumph is its style and its style is the embodiment of the voice of Sister, its hilarious unreliable narrator.

"Why I Live at the P.O.," Welty's biographer tells us, derives from the author having seen an ironing board in a post office. This incongruous image—which appears unobtrusively at the story's end in paragraph 141—seemed to beg for an explanation, and Sister becomes the ideally distorted voice, a classic example of the Southern grotesque, to explain it. Her story describes her own curious juxtaposition of the domestic and the commercial resulting from her decision to move into the tiny post office of China Grove, Mississippi where she is the postmistress.

Sister is at once paranoid and intensely jealous of her sister, Stella-Rondo, whom she tells us is "exactly twelve months to the day younger than I am and for that reason . . . spoiled." The meticulously skewed logic apparent in this statement suggests the odd nature of the story that follows, Sister's tall tale explaining why she lives at the post office, or, as she notably phrases it, "the P.O.," for in Welty's narrative voice—dialect, cliches, non-sequiturs—and plot are virtually indistinguishable.

On one level, the plot of "Why I Live at the P.O.," as it is finally revealed by Sister, is relatively straightforward. It consists of encounters between the narrator and various members of her family on one memorable Fourth of July and the morning after, which prompt Sister's unusual move away from home. The five key characters in Sister's tale are her mother; Stella-Rondo and her "adopted" daughter, Shirley T.; her grandfather, Papa-Daddy; and Uncle Rondo. These encounters are set in motion by the jealousy reawakened in Sister by Stella-Rondo's return to her China Grove home with Shirley T. following her separation from her husband, Mr. Whitaker, the taker of "'Pose Yourself' photos" from Illinois. (Sister believes that Stella-Rondo stole Mr. Whitaker from her.) The encounters are related in dialogues which contain contradictory accounts of assertions made by the unreliable narrator, presenting multiple perspectives whose plots extend beyond the temporal frame of July 4th and 5th, and spatially beyond Sister's house to the Mississippi community represented by the China Grove post office and to Mr. Whitaker's Illinois.

With China Grove and Illinois serving as synecdoches for the South and the North respectively, Welty's story does seem ultimately to point to the universal "nearly everything" to which Oates refers, even if it doesn't resolve the conflicting claims of all of the plots, voices, and worlds which it calls forth. Welty, then, uses the convention of the tall tale spoken in comically naïve yet poetically rich dialect to create a subtly modernistic work that exposes the fault lines existing beneath the surface of a "traditional" Southern family. Not only, then, are voice and plot conflated in "Why I Live at the P.O.," theme is inherent in technique as well.

Students should be encouraged to read "Why I Live at the P.O." more than once—first for the unmediated pleasure related by its voice, and subsequently, to examine the complexities contained in its narrative technique. First, that is, for the sheer delight of the deceptive "nothing" of the story; then for the richness of the "very nearly everything" below the surface. Ideally, because this story, like a lyric poem, derives from an oral tradition, the first reading should really be a *listening*, for the human voice—and particularly Welty's—reveals a subliminal level of meaning that reading the story on the page can at best approximate. Further readings can begin by focusing on the comic aspects of Sister's language, and then move to comparisons of her versions of events with those of the family members against who she perceives herself as pitted and from whom she finds it necessary to escape.

Sister's function as an unreliable narrator is intimately connected to her role as a Southern grotesque whose verbal and psychological exaggerations both mirror and instigate her ultimate isolation from her family that eventually leaves her alone at the P.O. Sister's paranoia and jealousy lead her to question the veracity of her family members, particularly Stella-Rondo. They also lead her to engage in conversations with her family that lead to her final, comic alienation from them— usually because, as she perceives it, one family member falsely reports her comments to another.

The story's opening paragraphs frame Sister's narrative by emphasizing the differences between herself and Stella-Rondo. We learn that Stella-Rondo, who had "just separated from her husband and came back home again," married Mr. Whitaker after having broke up his alleged prior relationship with Sister "through a deliberate calculated falsehood." She now threatens Sister's relationship with her family with whom "she was getting along fine" in Stella-Rondo's absence. We also immediately witness Sister's amusingly irrational assertion that Stella-Rondo is "spoiled" *because* she's "exactly twelve months to the day younger than" Sister. We also hear a crucial detail about Stella-Rondo that so incites Sister's jealousy: "She always had anything in the world she wanted and then she'd throw it away," from "this gorgeous Add-a-Pearl necklace" to her husband.

If Stella-Rondo's "calculated falsehood"—telling Mr. Whitaker that Sister "was one sided. Bigger on one side than the other"—resulted in her marriage, escape to the North, and the apparent bearing of a daughter before her return to her family, the "lies" she tells when she does return lead to Sister's shorter flight to her isolation at the P.O. The first of these lies is to tell her mother that her daughter "Shirley-T.'s adopted, I can prove it." Whereas the mother is willing to believe Stella-Rondo ("She looks just like Shirley Temple to me"), Sister insists that "She looks just like a cross between Mr. Whitaker and Papa-Daddy." Sister claims to have told Stella-Rondo that Shirley T. "was the spit-image of Papa-Daddy if he'd cut his beard, which of course he'd never do in the world." Stella-Rondo, however, "turns Papa-Daddy against" Sister by reporting to him that "Sister says she fails to understand why you don't cut off your beard." Sister's suggestion that she is being maligned and misrepresented by Stella-Rondo may be called into question by the dissatisfaction she registers toward her grandfather and the job he used his influence to get as China Grove's postmistress: "'Oh, Papa-Daddy,' I says, 'I didn't say any of a thing. I never dreamed [your beard] was a bird's nest, I have always been grateful though this is the next smallest P.O. in the state of Mississippi, and I do not enjoy being referred to as a hussy by my own grandfather.'" Here, Sister narrates two versions of a conversation, and her protests do not prevent Papa-Daddy from believing Stella-Rondo's version—for Sister, evidence that Stella-Rondo "turns" everyone "against her"; for the reader, evidence both of her paranoia and her unreliability as a narrator.

This narrative strategy is repeated throughout the story. Sister's way of relating dialogue differs from how it is reported by and to other family members. The repetition of this disparity of points of view intensifies the story's humor through the sheer accumulation of detail with its attendant grotesque exaggeration of Sister's condition. It also subliminally registers the darker implications of Sister's isolation. Sister's implication to her mother that Shirley T.'s silence might be a sign of mental illness is comically overturned when the girl bursts into song and proves to be an adept tap dancer as well. This incident leads Sister to claim that Stella-Rondo has turned more family members against her:

> But Mama just turned on her heel and flew out, furious. She ran right upstairs and hugged the baby. She believed it was adopted. Stella-Rondo hadn't done a thing but turn her against me from upstairs while I stood there helpless over the hot stove. So that made Mama, Papa-Daddy and the baby all on Stella-Rondo's side.
> Next, Uncle Rondo.

Uncle Rondo, who had seemingly turned against Stella-Rondo at one time because "she did something horrible to him—broke a chain letter from Flanders Field," causing him to take back the radio he had given her and let Sister have it, is on an annual Fourth of July drunken binge during much of the story. He is wearing a kimono from Stella-Rondo's trousseau, leading to a conversation between the sisters. Stella-Rondo reportedly states that "Uncle Rondo looks like a fool in it, that's all." Sister defends him: "'Well, he looks as good as he can' I says. 'It's good as anyone in reason could.'" Yet this is a half-hearted defense at best, and when Stella-Rondo later tells Uncle Rondo that "Sister says, 'Uncle Rondo certainly does look like a fool in that kimono! '" we are again left to question which version of the conversation is the more reliable. Regardless, Uncle Rondo believes Stella-Rondo, leading him to ignite a package of firecrackers in Sister's bedroom early the next morning, the event that finally precipitates her packing of her things—many, like the "four-o'clocks" growing in the yard, of dubious ownership at best—and moving into the P.O. The possessions she brings with her—the radio, the ironing board, "my charm bracelet in [Stella-Rondo's] bureau drawer, under a picture of Nelson Eddy"—become the only tenuous markers of Sister's identity.

The story concludes with a resonant image of Sister, her fingers in her ears in order to prevent her hearing a hypothetical attempt by Stella-Rondo to explain the incidents of her life with Mr. Whitaker. Although she claims she'd "refuse to listen" to this narrative, we recognize it to be one of the absent perspectives in "Why I Live at the P.O." The reader would surely enjoy hearing the other side of this particular story, though certainly not at the expense of missing Sister's magnificently convoluted and sublimely dubious account of the events in China Grove.

WRITER'S PERSPECTIVE

James Baldwin on Writing

RACE AND THE AFRICAN-AMERICAN WRITER, page 73

Baldwin was an essayist of genius—forcefully intelligent, penetratingly insightful, and passionately consumed with pursuing his ideas to their inevitable conclusions. He wrote extremely well on most topics he addressed, but none so completely engaged his creative powers as himself. "One writes out of one thing only," he remarked, "one's own experience." Baldwin's talent for seeing both sides of an issue is never so apparent than in his autobiographical writing since he alternately views his own life as both representative and singular. One sees this open-minded ability—indeed what John Keats called "negative capability"—to embrace opposites in this excerpt from Baldwin's "Autobiographical Notes" in which the author examines the many imaginative sources of a writer.

3 Character

Katherine Anne Porter
The Jilting of Granny Weatherall, page 80

"I spend my life thinking about technique, method, style," Katherine Anne Porter told her friend and fellow novelist Glenway Wescott. "The only time I do not think about them at all is when I am writing." Marked by scrupulous and fastidious craft, by adherence to the highest standards of achievement, her fiction, including the novel *Ship of Fools*, fills less than a thousand pages. In her autobiographical statement for *Twentieth-Century Authors* (1942), Porter said, "As for aesthetic bias, my one aim is to tell a straight story and to give true testimony."

With its frequent excursions into the rambling consciousness of its dying protagonist, "The Jilting of Granny Weatherall" may not always be "a straight story" in terms of undemanding linear narrative, but it is certainly "straight" in the larger sense of fidelity to the realities of human nature and experience, the "true testimony" that the rest of her comment refers to. Its emotional power lies largely in its presentation of the complexities of emotion, in our understanding that no matter how much Granny Weatherall feels that her life has turned out better than it would have with George, and no matter how much the details of the story support her judgment, her jilting remains a raw, painful, irreducible fact that has, in its way, shaped the rest of her life. In paragraph 28, Granny thinks: "Don't let things get lost. It's bitter to lose things." Her own awareness of, and refusal to confront, the larger application of this insight is shown in her very next thought: "Now don't let me get to thinking, not when I am tired and taking a little nap before supper."

Suggested here are some possible answers to the questions at the end of "The Jilting of Granny Weatherall." Other answers, of equal merit, may occur to you and your students. Other questions may occur as well.

Questions

1. *In the very first paragraph, what does the writer tell us about Ellen (Granny Weatherall)?* That Ellen Weatherall is feisty, accustomed to having her way, and unwilling to be treated like the sick old woman she is, all comes through the story from the start.

2. *What does the name of Weatherall have to do with Granny's nature (or her life story)? What other traits or qualities do you find in her?* Granny has "weathered all"—unrequited love, marriage, the birth of five children, early widowhood, backbreaking labor, "milk-leg and double pneumonia," the loss of her favorite daughter, and the frustrations of old age. Her victories over adversity have made

her scornful of her daughter Cornelia, who seems to her weak and inadequate. Granny is tough and inclined to hold a grudge. She has never forgiven the man who jilted her. So overweening is her pride, in fact, that at the moment of her death, when she wants a sign and fails to perceive one, she decides she will "never forgive."

3. *"Her bones felt loose, and floated around in her skin, and Doctor Harry floated like a balloon" (paragraph 6). What do you understand from this statement? By what other remarks does the writer indicate Granny's condition? In paragraph 56, why does Father Connolly tickle Granny's feet? At what other moments in the story does she fail to understand what is happening, or confuse the present with the past?* Granny is very ill, her sense of reality distorted by lengthening periods of confusion. The story quite convincingly ushers Granny Weatherall by fits and starts into an altered state of consciousness preceding death. Granny's weakened grasp on reality is again apparent: when the doctor "appeared to float up to the ceiling and out" (paragraph 7); when "the pillow rose and floated under her" and she thought she heard leaves, or newspapers, rustling (8); when she pondered her impossible plans for "tomorrow" (17 and 26), in her belief that she could, if she wanted to, "pack up and move back to her own house" (24); in the distortions that creep into Granny's sense of the passage of time (28, 29, 36, 37, 42, 43, 50, 56, and 57); when she feels the pillow rising again (29); in Granny's sporadic inability to hear (31 and 32); in her belief that there are ants in the bed (40); in Granny's occasional inability to speak clearly enough to be understood (40 and 53); when Granny has hallucinations in which she confronts her daughter Hapsy (41, 50, and 60); in the doctor's "rosy nimbus" (51); in Granny's failure to comprehend that Father Connolly is not tickling her feet but administering the last rites of the Catholic Church (56). (In the anointing of the sick, formerly known as Extreme Unction, the priest makes a sign of the cross with oil upon the eyes, ears, nose, mouth, hands, and feet of the person in danger of death, while praying for his or her soul.)

4. *Exactly what happened to Ellen Weatherall sixty years earlier? What effects did this event have on her?* George, the man she was to marry, had failed to show up for the wedding. This blow to Ellen's pride had left permanent scars even though Ellen had subsequently lived a full and useful life. It is hard to say whether her exacting, imperious, unforgiving ways resulted from the jilting—or caused it!

5. *In paragraph 49, who do you guess to be the man who "cursed like a sailor's parrot"? In paragraph 56, who do you assume is the man driving the cart? Is the fact that these persons are not clearly labeled and identified a failure on the author's part?* The most likely guess about the man who "cursed like a sailor's parrot" is that he was John, the man Ellen eventually married. Presumably John had always loved her and was angry because she had been so deeply hurt. The identity of the man driving the cart is more nebulous. Was he George? John? A confused amalgam of the two? That the reader remains unsure is not a fault in the story. The dreamlike haze surrounding the man's identity beautifully reflects Granny's loosening hold on reality.

6. *What is "stream of consciousness"? Would you call "The Jilting of Granny Weatherall" a stream of consciousness story? Refer to the story in your reply.* The story's point of view is one of selective omniscience. The events are reported in the third person by a narrator who can see into Granny Weatherall's mind. When Granny is lucid, the story proceeds in tidy chronological order. In the story's most interesting passages—especially in paragraphs 17–18 and 24–31—Porter uses stream of consciousness with great skill to present the randomly mingled thoughts and impressions that move through Granny's dying mind. By fragmenting Granny's thoughts, by having her shuttle back and forth between reality and fantasy, by distorting her sense of the passage of time, the author manages to persuade us that the way Granny experiences dying must be nearly universal.

7. *Sum up the character of the daughter Cornelia.* Cornelia, evidently the oldest of Granny's children, is a dutiful daughter—a fact resented by her cantankerous mother (10). Granny feels demeaned by her knowledge that Cornelia often humors her to keep peace. And, like mothers everywhere, Granny regards her daughter as far less competent than herself. Cornelia is tenderer, less tough than Granny. She weeps beside the deathbed. The old woman fails to appreciate her daughter's care and compassion because she scorns her own need of them.

8. *Why doesn't Granny's last child, Hapsy, come to her mother's deathbed?* Hapsy, the youngest child and her mother's favorite, died young. Paragraph 41 suggests that she may have died giving birth to a son.

9. *Would you call the character of Doctor Harry "flat" or "round"? Why is his flatness or roundness appropriate to the story?* A "flat" character, the doctor is little more than a prop in this account of Granny's dying. There is no reason for him to be more than that, for it is Granny's life and death that we are meant to focus on.

10. *How is this the story of another "jilting"? What is similar between that fateful day of sixty years ago (described in paragraphs 29, 49, and 61) and the time when Granny is dying? This time, who is the "bridegroom" who is not in the house?* Before talking about the final paragraph, why not read aloud to your students the parable of the wise and foolish virgins (Matthew 25:1–13)?

Then shall the kingdom of heaven be likened unto ten virgins, which took their lamps, and went forth to meet the bridegroom.

2 And five of them were wise, and five were foolish.
3 They that were foolish took their lamps, and took no oil with them:
4 But the wise took oil in their vessels with their lamps.
5 While the bridegroom tarried, they all slumbered and slept.
6 And at midnight there was a cry made, Behold, the bridegroom cometh; go ye out to meet him.
7 Then all those virgins arose, and trimmed their lamps.

8   And the foolish said unto the wise, Give us of your oil, for our lamps are gone out.

9   But the wise answered, saying, Not so; lest there be not enough for us and you: but go ye rather to them that sell, and buy for yourselves.

10 And while they went to buy, the bridegroom came; and they that were ready went in with him to the marriage: and the door was shut.

11 Afterward came also the other virgins, saying, Lord, Lord, open to us.

12 But he answered and said, Verily I say unto you, I know you not.

13 Watch therefore; for ye know neither the day nor the hour wherein the Son of Man cometh.

Evidently, the bridegroom Granny awaits at the end of the story is Christ. When he does not appear, she feels jilted for a second time. Why doesn't he come? Why does Granny not receive the sign she asks for? Is it because her pride is so over-weening ("I'll never forgive it") as to keep her from salvation? Is it because of her refusal to stay prepared for death (18)? Or did she receive her sign (the last rites of the Church) and merely fail to perceive it? Students may object to the apparent grimness of the ending. Some of them are likely to insist that Granny gets worse than she deserves, that Porter has allowed her symbolism to run roughshod over her humanity. Divergent opinions may spark a lively discussion.

11. *"This is the story of an eighty-year-old woman lying in bed, getting groggy, and dying; I can't see why it should interest anybody."* How would you answer this critic? Such a critic will be hard to convince. But perhaps discussion can show that the story is remarkable for its condensation of a long life into a few pages. How does it feel to die? All of us find the question interesting, and Porter answers it. Although Edith Wharton has argued that it is not the nature of a short story to develop a character (in *The Writing of Fiction* [New York: Scribner's, 1925]), "The Jilting of Granny Weatherall" certainly makes character its central concern. We finish the story persuaded that we know Ellen Weatherall very well indeed—better than she knows herself.

Here is a bleak reading of the story for possible discussion: For sixty years Ellen Weatherall has suppressed the memory of George, the man she loved, who jilted her. She prays not to remember him, lest she follow him down into the pit of Hell (29). If she remembers him, she herself will be damned—yet she remembers him. She longs to see him again (42), imagines him standing by her deathbed (30). In the end she beholds the pit: a darkness that will swallow up light. For the sake of a man, she has lost her soul.

But is the story so grim an account of one woman's damnation? It seems hardly a mortal sin to remember a person and an event so crucial in one's life; damnation seems undeserved. We sense that the author actually admires Granny's defiance in blowing out the light at the end. To say the least, the story is splendidly ambiguous.

"The Jilting of Granny Weatherall" lent itself effectively to the PBS television film series *The American Short Story*, obtainable on videotape for classroom viewing from Teacher's Video Company at (800) 262-8837. Anyone interested in writing for television might care to see Corinne Jacker's excellent script, reprinted in

The American Short Story, Volume 2 (New York: Dell, 1980), together with a revealing interview with the scriptwriter on the problems of adapting "Granny"—such as a dearth of physical action in the present—and Carolyn G. Heilbrun's short critical essay on the Porter story.

Porter's familiarity with illness and the threat of death may have been drawn from memory. As Joan Givner recounts in her biography, *Katherine Anne Porter* (New York: Simon, 1982), Porter had to struggle for years against bronchial troubles and tuberculosis. Defiantly, she endured to age ninety.

Alice Walker
EVERYDAY USE, page 88

"Everyday Use" is a genuinely funny story ("Ream it out again," the mother says as she tries to learn her daughter's new name, and she keeps—possibly with tongue in cheek—slipping the new name in throughout the story) with serious undertones. Narrated by the mother, whose wry good sense contrasts vividly with her older daughter's pretensions, the story highlights not only a generation gap, but a contrast between two sharply different attitudes toward the idea of heritage.

Dee, having suddenly discovered that old quilts and dashers are potentially interesting decorations, accuses her mother and sister of not understanding their heritage because they fail to appreciate the artistic value of such objects. However, she herself is so divorced from her heritage that she does not know which member of the family made the dasher. It may be true, as Dee accuses, that Maggie and her mother don't "understand" their heritage—at least not in an intellectual way. The story suggests, however, that by using the quilt, and by having learned the traditional skills passed from generation to generation required to make one, Maggie, the homely, uneducated sister, knows more about her African-American heritage than does Dee (Wangero). Maggie and her mother *live* their cultural heritage; they are nourished by it through everyday use and versed in the craftsmanship needed to pass it on to future generations.

That the mother loves Dee is clear. Although she's aware of the unattractive elements in Dee's nature, her dream of Dee showing her appreciation for her mother on a television show reveals wistfulness: the older woman longs for Dee to return her love. Instead, Dee is scornful. "You ought to try to make something of yourself, too, Maggie," she says as she departs, as if she herself were a superior being, to be emulated. Dee, in spite of her education, has never learned to imagine how she appears to others.

"Everyday Use" is an accessible story for students that explores powerful issues. Although the setting is specifically African-American, the themes of family identity, intergenerational conflict, cultural heritage, and self-esteem are universal. The basic narrative situation—the educated daughter returning on a family visit to criticize her mother and stay-at-home sister—is also particularly relevant to many college students, and most students find it interesting to see this situation from the mother's perspective. Do your African-American students like this story, or are they offended by it? Do any of them feel that the story reinforces undesirable stereotypes? Do any of your black students side with Dee, who is trying so hard to leave poverty and ignorance behind? If the black students in your class are willing to be drawn out on this subject, the discussion might be lively and valuable.

Students wanting critical perspectives on Walker should consult *Alice Walker* (New York: Amistad, 1993), edited by Henry Louis Gates, Jr. and K. A. Appiah, which collects a representative cross-section of reviews, essays, and interviews with the author.

Issac Bashevis Singer
GIMPEL THE FOOL, page 95

Isaac Bashevis Singer's "Gimpel the Fool" cogently represents the author's distinctive contribution to the short story. It ingeniously and persuasively combines the traditions of the Jewish folk tale with the modern short story. Although his subject matter is supernatural and religious, Singer never lets his psychological portrayal of Gimpel become a traditional stereotype. Instead he takes the archetypal figure of the holy fool and deepens him into a credible individual. In this parable, the reader does not merely observe the protagonist's bitter lessons, but deeply feels the anguish that earns them.

Like Flannery O'Connor's "Revelation," Singer's story grows from a vision—Gimpel's dream of Elka, with her counsel, "Because I was false is everything false too?" (Several critics have pointed out similarities between Singer and Flannery O'Connor, two writers working with a conflict between new and traditional cultures. See Melvin J. Friedman, "Isaac Bashevis Singer: The Appeal of Numbers," in *Critical Views of Isaac Bashevis Singer*, edited by Irving Malin [New York: NYUP, 1969].) Singer was an avid reader of Spinoza, whose concept of the lesser or inferior reality of this world probably influenced the famous statement at the end of "Gimpel the Fool," "No doubt the world is entirely an imaginary world." But, in another sense,

> The world [Singer] recoils from is the world of the market place, of human passions, of vain ambitions, of misguided aspirations, and of all the human relationships which result from them. This is the world of Gimpel the Fool, where the simple and the sensitive are gulled, deprived, humiliated, and despised. It is the world in which the poverty of Frampol distorts the perspective of its people (J. A. Eisenberg, "Isaac Bashevis Singer: Passionate Primitive or Pious Puritan?" in Malin's collection).

Much of Singer's best fiction, including "Gimpel the Fool," takes place in the *shtetl* or Jewish village of Eastern Europe, a place of rutted streets and tumble-down houses—Singer doesn't romanticize it. He writes, according to Ben Siegel, "compassionate fables of Jews who cling tenaciously to their traditions but who otherwise interest no one but God, the devil, and themselves. And God's interest is never certain" ("Sacred and Profane: Isaac Bashevis Singer's Embattled Spirits," *Critique* 5 [Spring 1963]). Phantoms, demons, *dybbuks,* and the devil figure in Jewish folklore and popular stories; in Singer's fiction, a supernatural personage often embodies a character's passions or obsessions. And so in "Gimpel the Fool," when the Spirit of Evil speaks, he voices Gimpel's resentment against Frampol and his momentary distrust of humankind.

An incisive comment on Gimpel's wife Elka comes from Professor Stan Sulkes of Raymond Walters College.

> Do we agree that Gimpel's ability to love his wife emanates from his own goodness rather than hers? (An echo, perhaps, of the prophet Hosea's being commanded to marry a whore so he could appreciate God's love for the errant Israel.) On her deathbed she tells him the truth. (More of her selfishness, I think, since she is anxious over her impending fate rather than his feelings.)

Suggested writing assignment: "A Defense of Elka."

The character of the "simple creature of God," or holy simpleton, ridiculed in this world, rewarded only in afterlife, is a familiar figure in Jewish folk literature. Another famous story with such a character is I. L. Peretz's "Bontsha the Silent." Thus as a work of storytelling, "Gimpel the Fool" is both traditional and original, Sol Gittleman shows in *From Shtetl to Suburbia: The Family in Jewish Literary Imagination* (Boston: Beacon, 1978) 103–7.

Still, some readers have been bothered by Gimpel's passivity, among them Professor Sulkes. His letter deserves further quotation.

> I recall being dismayed when I first read this story. How could a post-holocaust Jewish writer, I wondered, defend the literary convention of the holy fool? Wouldn't someone as naive and accommodating as Gimpel find himself in the Nazi ovens? . . . How could I even be amused by him? Was Singer blinking away the holocaust?
>
> Rereading the story, I realized that it does belong in the context of that horror, though the horror is never mentioned. The holocaust lurks in the background of this tale. As a result I think that Singer is more distanced from Gimpel's simple goodness than he might be if he were a Christian author. He probably *admires* the gullible Gimpel of the first half of the story more than he *approves* of him.
>
> At the end, Gimpel embarks on a journey which reveals to him the evil of the world (events like the holocaust), but he does not allow it to destroy his sweetness and his faith. My class was particularly eager to discuss this point: how does one remain hopeful in light of the atrocities so prevalent in the world? I assume that Singer offers Gimpel's post-journey piety as one response [of] the post-holocaust Jew. But Gimpel's quietism disappoints me, so far removed as it is from the mainstreams of modern Jewry. . . .

Your class might care to discuss this serious objection.

Still another objection might be raised to Gimpel's conclusion, "No doubt the world is entirely an imaginary world." Is, then, the evil in the world only a dream? Isn't this assumption dangerous?

Sol Gittleman, cited above, reads the story to mean that Gimpel, whatever his philosophy, finds truth in his wanderings. Discovering that the world beyond Frampol is less malicious and cruel, Gimpel in the end reaffirms his belief in humanity. Would your students agree or disagree with this paraphrase?

Dr. Eleanor Carducci of Sussex County Community College (New Jersey) has shared with us an assignment that she finds works well for teaching Singer's story. She divided her class into two groups: one consisting of the townspeople and the other, of those sympathetic to Gimpel. The task of the former group was to demonstrate that Gimpel is a fool; the task of the latter, to defend him against the charge. Students were asked to indicate specific passages in the story as evidence. "The townspeople found their task easier, at first," Carducci reports. She continues:

> The others had to delve deeper, but found the search a challenge. After compiling sufficient evidence, the groups tried to convince each other. . . . Students were allowed to join the opposite group, if they were so convinced. It was interesting to note that many townspeople, after thinking more deeply, joined those who felt Gimpel was not a fool. At any rate, the discussion was quite lively and no one remained passive.

This translation of "Gimpel the Fool" offers the work of one Nobel Prize winner rendered into English by another. First published in *Partisan Review* for May 1953, Saul Bellow's translation was the first appearance in English of any Singer story.

In his speech on accepting the Nobel Prize, Singer said he regarded the award as a recognition of the Yiddish language. The language and its speakers—their conduct, their outlook on life—have been for him always identical.

> There is a quiet humor in Yiddish and a gratitude for every day of life, every crumb of success, each encounter of love. The Yiddish mentality is not haughty. It does not take victory for granted. It does not demand and command but it muddles through, sneaks by, smuggles itself amid the powers of destruction, knowing somewhere that God's plan for Creation is still at the very beginning (*Nobel Lecture* [New York: Farrar 1978] 8).

Comic actor Theodore Bikel reads "Gimpel the Fool" on an audiocassette (SWC 1200) available from American Audio Prose Library, Box 842, Columbia, MO 65205. For current price call (800) 447–2275.

QUESTIONS

1. *Is Gimpel a "fool" in the obvious sense—naïve, gullible, simple-minded, and truly blind to the reality before him?* Gimpel describes himself in paragraph 3 as "easy to fool," and he is certainly very far from being skeptical or suspicious-minded, but there are frequent places in the story where he makes clear that he sees through the deceptions that others are trying to practice on him. He does, however, show an extraordinary willingness to suspend judgment and to give others the benefit of the doubt, as well as an extraordinary openness to possibilities beyond the lim-

its of our understanding. In some sense Gimpel is a "holy fool," a traditional type of character often seen in Russian and Eastern European Jewish literature—a person who maintains a certain childlike innocence by refusing to learn the conventional hypocrisy of the adult world and who follows God's commandments simply and unquestioningly.

2. *If he knows better, why does he consistently act against his own interests?* This question can provoke a larger discussion about self-interest and human motivation in general. It might be claimed that all actions are motivated by self-interest—that most of us, for example, derive more satisfaction from behaving honorably and responsibly than we would from stolen goods or adulterous liaisons—and that one cultivates virtue, therefore, not through self-denial but through the refinement and elevation of one's desires. From this point of view, the question might be better restated as: What are the things that matter most to Gimpel, for which he is willing to be such a "fool"? More than anything else, of course, Gimpel is motivated by love, especially for the children. Most people can relate to a willingness to do anything, even to commit treason and mass betrayal, in the name of love when love means a romantic attachment that essentially seeks its own satisfaction, as witness the success of the film version of *The English Patient*. Instead of mocking, should we not be even more admiring of a love that seeks not its own stimulation and fulfillment, but rather the well-being of others, especially young and innocent others? Gimpel is motivated also by the love of God, and the desire to be what, in his judgment, God expects of him.

3. *Is Gimpel's conclusion, "No doubt the world is entirely an imaginary world," a dangerous assumption?* Perhaps it is, if we cite only the first half of the sentence. But the rest of the statement—"but it is only once removed from the true world"—is crucial to a proper understanding of Gimpel's, and presumably Singer's, view: this world is all we have to go by in trying to comprehend the true world, and while here we should strive to live as if we were in that finer place so that we will be worthy of it in time. Students who object to the unreality, i.e. absurdity, of such an attitude might be asked about relevant parallels in their own experience. How often do we seek to put a hopeful interpretation on some tragic occurrence or at the very least console ourselves with the inscrutability of "God's will"?

WRITER'S PERSPECTIVE

Isaac Bashevis Singer on Writing
THE CHARACTER OF GIMPEL, page 106

Few writers ever explain the particular quality of their characters as clearly and succinctly as Singer elucidates Gimpel in this 1968 *Paris Review* interview. In a few sentences he places his creation in relation to Jewish social history and literature.

His comments will not only help contemporary students, who have been raised on action heroes, understand the cultural context of Singer's tale, but the passage may even provide the basis for an interesting classroom discussion. Singer's modest notion of heroism can be provocatively compared to the standards of male heroism portrayed—explicitly or implicitly—in several other stories such as Kurt Vonnegut's "Harrison Bergeron," John Updike's "A & P," or Stephen Crane's "The Open Boat."

4 *Setting*

Kate Chopin
THE STORM, page 114

Kate Chopin wrote "The Storm" at a single sitting in July 1898. Its four adult characters had previously appeared in "At the 'Cadian Ball," written in 1892 and published in *Bayou Folk* (1894), Chopin's first collection of short fiction. The earlier story recounts the relationship of Calixta and Alcée and the circumstances that led to their marriages.

The setting of "The Storm" provides its most powerful unifying element. The raging storm initiates the plot—trapping Bobinôt and Bibi at Friedheimer's store and providing Alcée with an excuse to seek shelter at the home of his former lover, Calixta. Setting and plot reinforce each other. The storm not only affects the situation of each character; it also reflects the tempestuous inner states of Alcée and Calixta, who find themselves unexpectedly alone. Their passionate adultery is supremely satisfying—the classic Chopin touch that so outraged her contemporaries. No wonder she never published the story in her lifetime. The frank depiction of sexual passion in "The Storm" (especially in terms of the woman's desire and enjoyment), the complete lack of remorse or guilt on the part of the adulterous lovers, and Chopin's apparent acceptance of the situation, put it well beyond the limits of what was acceptable a century ago.

Present-day students will not be shocked or outraged by the story the way that Chopin's contemporaries would have been, but they may still vigorously debate both the behavior of the lovers and Chopin's own intentions particularly in terms of the story's very last sentence. Is that last sentence ironic? If so, at whose or what expense—the lovers themselves, the betrayed spouses, the institution of marriage?

Any discussion of the setting should not overlook the story's cultural milieu—the French Catholic bayou country of Louisiana. This region was not Chopin's native territory. She was born an Irish-American in St. Louis and came to New Orleans at nineteen. She sees the milieu, therefore, with the relative objectivity of an outsider who is nonetheless rooted by family and children. Part of the special charm of her fiction is its careful depiction of this exotic local culture so different from the rest of the South.

QUESTIONS

1. *What causes Calixta's infidelity?* Her husband loves her, in his way. He buys a can of shrimp because he knows she likes it. He stands in awe of her scrupulous housekeeping, but he seems to know nothing of her sensuality. We're told that

after he buys the shrimp, he sits "stolidly." It is this stolidness, perhaps, that has prevented his ever having plumbed his wife's passionate nature.

2. *Doesn't Calixta love her husband?* She does, apparently: she worries about him and her son when the storm comes up. She seems genuinely glad to be reunited with them when they come home. But passions, Chopin seems to say, cannot be denied. Their force is equal to that of a storm, and the marriage bed is not the likeliest place for release of that force. The author indeed hints that marriage and sexual pleasure are incompatible in Parts IV and V of the story, where Alcée urges his absent wife to stay away another month and where we learn that for Clarisse, "their intimate conjugal life was something which she was more than willing to forgo for a while."

T. Coraghessan Boyle
GREASY LAKE, page 119

It is rebellious adolescence in general that Boyle describes in his opening paragraph; but he's also talking about the late 1960s, when adolescents were in plentiful supply, "bad" behavior was much admired, and "courtesy and winning ways went out of style." In 1967 when the American attack on Khe Sanh (mentioned in paragraph 7) took place, Boyle himself was nineteen years old. We can only guess that's about the year in which "Greasy Lake" is set. Not only the epigraph but also the title of the story come from that bard of a slightly later era, Bruce Springsteen, whose first album appeared in 1973.

Are Digby and Jeff really "bad"? Well, no, and neither is the narrator. They're just engaging in the kind of behavior they think is expected of them (1, 3, 4). When, on the night of the story, their rebellion backfires, throwing them into a grimmer world than they had bargained for, they feel revulsion. As is clear at the end, they have had enough of being "bad." Like the boy in James Joyce's "Araby," they have grown up painfully. (For other stories of a young man's initiation into maturity, see "A & P," "Araby," and "Barn Burning.")

That the narrator of "Greasy Lake" grows and changes during his adventures is apparent from the two views of "nature" he voices, one in paragraph 2 and one in paragraph 32. Early in the story, "nature" was wanting "to snuff the rich scent of possibility on the breeze, watch a girl take off her clothes and plunge into the festering murk, drink beer, smoke pot, howl at the stars, savor the incongruous full-throated roar of rock and roll against the primeval susurrus of frogs and crickets." By the end of the story, these swinish pleasures have lost their appeal. When, at dawn, the narrator experiences the beauties of the natural world as if for the first time, he has an epiphany: "This was nature."

Students can have fun demonstrating how Greasy Lake is the perfect setting for Boyle's story. Like the moral view of the narrator (at first), it is "fetid and murky, the mud banks glittering with broken glass and strewn with beer cans and the charred remains of bonfires. There was a single ravaged island a hundred yards from shore, so stripped of vegetation it looked as if the air force had strafed it" (2). The lake is full of "primordial ooze" and "the bad breath of decay" (31). It also hides a waterlogged corpse. Once known for its clear water, the unlucky lake has fallen as far from its ideal state as the people who now frequent its shores have fallen from theirs. (If you teach the chapter on symbol, hark back to Greasy Lake once more.)

Still, in its way, Greasy Lake is a force for change. Caught trying to rape the girl in the blue car, the narrator and his friends run off into the woods, into the water. Waiting in the filthy lake, the narrator is grateful to be alive and feels horror at the death of the "bad older character" whose body he meets in the slime. His growth has begun. When at the end of the story, two more girls pull into the parking lot, the subdued narrator and his friends are harmless. Cold sober, bone tired, they know they have had a lucky escape from consequences that might have been terrible. Also, the narrator knows, as the girls do not, that Al is dead, his body rotting in the lake. He won't "turn up"—except perhaps in the most grisly way. It is this knowledge and the narrator's new reverence for life that make him think he is going to cry.

Students might enjoy spelling out the change in the narrator's outlook. By what hints does Boyle show us that some time has elapsed since the events of the fateful night? Surely the story displays little admiration for the narrator's early behavior, which he now regards with sarcasm, as when he says, "Digby wore a gold star in his right ear and allowed his father to pay his tuition at Cornell" (3), or when he speaks of "new heights of adventure and daring" (6). Other ironic remarks abound, showing his altered view. The maturity the narrator acquired that night seems to have been permanent.

Critics have cited Boyle as a writer socially and politically disengaged; but satire, he points out, can be corrective. "It can hold up certain attitudes as being fraudulent, and in doing that suggest that the opposite might be an appropriate way to behave. And I hope that if my work is socially redemptive, it is in that way" (interview with David Stanton in *Poets & Writers*, January/February 1990). Surely "Greasy Lake," a story some readers find shocking, is socially redemptive.

In a letter to the editor of the *New York Times Book Review* (February 27, 2000), Boyle took issue with a critic who had thought "Greasy Lake" to be about characters in a popular song:

> The story itself was inspired by Bruce Springsteen's song "Spirit in the Night" and employs an epigraph from that song, but it is not . . . "about its characters." As anyone who has read the story will know, the characters and situations are wholly invented. I see "Greasy Lake" as a kind of riff on the song, a free take on its glorious spirit.

Candace Andrews of San Joaquin Delta College argues that, while on the surface "Greasy Lake" seems merely to recount the misadventures of a nineteen-year-old delinquent, a careful reading will show that much of the story retells the narrator's experience in Vietnam—"It is a tale of a young man who has been to war and back." For a writing assignment, she had her students list every reference or allusion to war, and told them, "Then bring your 'research' together into some kind of coherent statement which supports the idea that the narrator is a Vietnam veteran." We do not believe, ourselves, that Boyle's several references to war necessarily require the narrator to be an ex-GI. He would have followed the war news and come to feel that the war was senseless violence—like the action out at Greasy Lake on a Saturday night. When he tells us (in paragraph 40) that he and Digby looked at the girl "like war veterans," we take that to be a metaphor: he too feels a sort of battle fatigue. However, you may care to check out Ms. Andrews's provocative theory for yourself. What do your students think of it?

Amy Tan
A PAIR OF TICKETS, page 127

"A Pair of Tickets" is a story of self-discovery—born in pain but eventually resolved in joy. Pain unites characters from different countries and decades. The narrator's still-fresh sorrow at her mother's death, the mother's abiding despair at losing her twin daughters on the war-torn road to Chungking, and the daughters' ache at losing their mother not once, but twice (first as babies in 1944 and then again as adults after they learn their mother is dead) are all caused by the same tragic historical circumstance and its far-reaching consequences. Joy, however, eventually links June with her two half sisters. Acknowledging what they have lost, they find that much remains.

QUESTIONS

1. *How is the external setting of "A Pair of Tickets" essential to what happens internally to the narrator in the course of this story?* "A Pair of Tickets" is a story that grows naturally out of its setting. June's journey to China is one of both external and internal discovery. Finding China, she also finds part of herself. Tan announces the theme at the end of the first paragraph: "I am becoming Chinese." China becomes a spiritual mirror for the narrator, just as her glimpse of her half-sisters' faces provides a living mirror of her own and her late mother's face. One might say that "A Pair of Tickets" is the story of Americanized June May Woo (born, as her passport says, in California in 1951) becoming Jing-mei Woo by discovering her ethnic and cultural roots in her ancestral homeland.

2. *How does the narrator's view of her father change by seeing him in a different setting?* Although June's mother haunts the story, her father is also a quiet, important presence. As the title says, this story is about a *pair* of tickets. June's seventy-two-year-old father, Canning Woo, accompanies her on the trip to China. He is returning after four decades. He is June's physical as well as psychological link with the homeland, as well as her living link with the family history that she (like most children) only half knows. His revelations teach her about both her mother and herself. Seeing him in China, June gets a glimpse of his past, what he was like as a young man before she was born. "He's a young boy," she

observes on the train to Shenzen, "so innocent and happy I want to button his sweater and pat his head."

3. *In what ways does the narrator feel at home in China? In what ways does she feel foreign?* June is Chinese-American, which means that she experiences the two cultures from both the inside and the outside. Just as going to China helps her understand how she is Chinese, it also reminds her how much she has been shaped by America. She understands Mandarin Chinese but cannot speak it well. She does not know the Cantonese of her relatives or her father's Mandarin dialect. Although she is purely Chinese in ancestry, not only her clothes betray her American upbringing—she is also too tall. "I stand five-foot-six," June observes, "and my head pokes above the crowd so that I am eye level only with other tourists." And yet she physically resembles her half-sisters, realizing at the end of the story: "And now I also see what part of me is Chinese. It is so obvious. It is my family. It is in our blood."

4. *What do the narrator and her half sisters have in common? How does this factor relate to the theme of the story?* She and her half sisters share a biological and spiritual link to their common mother, and through her they share a bond to one another. "Together we look like our mother," June observes. "Her same eyes, her same mouth." Their fates are interrelated, as reflected by their names. In China, June asks her father the meaning of her Chinese name, Jing-mei, and he interprets her name to signify the younger sister who is the essence of the other lost daughters. As she discovers on meeting them, she does share their essence—they are all daughters of the same mother.

5. *In what ways is the story interesting because it explores specifically Chinese-American experiences? In what other ways is the story grounded in universal family issues?* Although "A Pair of Tickets" is saturated in Chinese history and culture, and its plot reflects a situation unlikely to be repeated in other contexts, it also explores nearly universal themes of self-discovery, cultural awareness, and family history. One might say that Tan's broader theme is dual identity—an especially relevant theme for many Americans who come from immigrant families. Tan explores this quintessentially American experience with humor, compassion, and imagination.

Amy Tan reads an abridged version of her novel *The Joy Luck Club* on audiocassette tape available from the American Audio Prose Library, Inc., Box 842, Columbia, MO 65205; phone number for orders (800) 447-2275. ("A Pair of Tickets" is the last chapter in this book.) Wayne Wang's 1993 film version of *The Joy Luck Club* will probably disappoint most of Tan's readers as much as it did movie critics. The subject matter is so interesting that it carries the film along, but Wang sentimentalizes and sensationalizes the story into a sort of Asian-American soap opera. The final episode (drawn from "A Pair of Tickets") is condensed and simplified. The *pair* of tickets is, alas, reduced to a single passage: June flies to China alone, and poor Canning Woo gets left in the States. The film may nonetheless be useful to students who need help in visualizing the American and Chinese milieus of the story. Under pressure, one might assign a particularly movie-struck student the task of comparing and contrasting the movie's version of "A Pair of Tickets" to the original story.

WRITER'S PERSPECTIVE

Amy Tan on Writing

SETTING THE VOICE, page 142

Tan's 1989 essay on the relation between finding her authorial voice and remembering her mother's "broken" English provides a fascinating glimpse into the relationship between life and art. It also highlights the issue of audience. An artist's strategy of literary creation necessarily includes the image of his or her ideal reader. The act of imaginative identification has often been problematic for minority or immigrant writers. Should they address their own communities or try to reach a mainstream that may be ignorant of their particular experiences? Such writers must often imagine an audience that does not yet exist and hope their work summons it into being. Tan's immensely popular books have done just that by creating a huge diverse audience of readers. This passage describes how Tan gradually developed the distinctive style for the stories that made up *The Joy Luck Club*.

5 Tone and Style

Ernest Hemingway
A CLEAN, WELL-LIGHTED PLACE, page 149

This celebrated story is a study in contrasts: between youth and age, belief and doubt, light and darkness. To the younger waiter, the café is only a job; to the older waiter, it is a charitable institution for which he feels personal responsibility. Of course, he himself has need of it: it is his refuge from the night, from solitude, from a sense that the universe is empty and meaningless, expressed in his revised versions of the Hail Mary and the Lord's Prayer. The older waiter feels kinship for the old man, not only because the waiter, too, is alone and growing old, but because both men are apparently atheists. Willing to commit suicide, the old man (unlike his pious daughter) evidently doesn't think he has any immortal soul to fear for. Robert Penn Warren is surely right in calling Hemingway, at least in this story, a religious writer. "The despair beyond plenty of money, the despair that makes a sleeplessness beyond insomnia, is the despair felt by a man who hungers for the sense of order and assurance that men seem to find in religious faith, but who cannot find grounds for his faith" ("Ernest Hemingway," in Warren's *Selected Essays* [New York: Random, 1951] 80–118). What values are left to a man without faith? A love of cleanliness and good light, of companionship, of stoic endurance, and above all, of dignity. (Another attempt to state the theme of the story is at the beginning of Chapter 7.)

At the heart of the story is the symbol of the café, an island of light and order surrounded by night and nothingness. Contrasting images of light and darkness begin in the opening paragraph: the old man, not entirely committed either to death or to life, likes to sit in the shadow of the leaves. Every detail in the story seems meaningful: even, perhaps, as L. Rust Hills points out, "the glint of light on the soldier's collar . . . an attribute of sexual potency" (*Writing in General and the Short Story in Particular* [Boston: Houghton, 1977] 85).

The story has been much admired for Hemingway's handling of point of view. The narrator is a nonparticipant who writes in the third person. He is all-knowing at the beginning of the story: in the opening paragraph we are told how the old man feels, then what the waiters know about him. From then on, until the waiters say "Good night," the narrator remains almost perfectly objective, merely reporting visible details and dialogue. (He editorializes for a moment, though, in observing that the younger waiter employs the syntax of "stupid people.") After the waiters part company, for the rest of the story the narrator limits himself to the thoughts and perceptions of the older waiter, who, we now see, is the central character.

It is clear all along, as we overhear the conversation of the two waiters, that Hemingway sides with the elder's view of the old man. The older waiter reveals himself as wiser and more compassionate. We resent the younger man's abuse of the old man, who cannot hear his "stupid" syntax, his equation of money with happiness. But the older waiter and Hemingway do not see things identically—a point briefly discussed in the text in a comment on the story's irony.

A small problem in reading the story is to keep the speakers straight. Evidently it is the younger waiter who has heard of the old man's suicide attempt and who answers the questions at the beginning of the story.

Jan Hodge of Morningside College has written to contest our interpretation. He offers an interesting revisionist reading of the text:

> I was a bit taken aback by your note [on paragraphs 20 and 21] that "The younger waiter says both these lines. A device of Hemingway's style is sometimes to have a character pause, then speak again—as often happens in actual speech." This may be the case, though I don't know of any instances offhand in his writing where there is not some kind of indication when this is what is happening, or where context wouldn't make it clear that the same speaker speaks successive lines, each enclosed in quotation marks.
>
> As I read the story, the young waiter speaks the first of the lines in question here, and the older waiter the second. This would be consistent not only with their respective characters, but with conventionally alternating lines of dialogue in the rest of that section *if* . . . and herein lies the critical problem, paragraphs 39–42 read in your text:
>
> "You can't tell. He might be better off with a wife."   *[clearly the older waiter]*
> "His niece looks after him."
> "I know. You said she cut him down."—
> "I wouldn't want to be that old. An old man is a nasty thing."
> *[clearly the young waiter]*
>
> But the words "You said she cut him down" must be spoken by the young waiter, because the older waiter has told him that earlier. The passage makes perfect sense if the lines are adjusted this way:
>
> "You can't tell. He might be better off with a wife."   *[older]*
> "His niece looks after him. You said she cut him down."   *[young]*
> "I know."   *[older]*
> "I wouldn't want to be that old . . ."   *[young]*
>
> I haven't checked the critical record recently, but many years ago a student doing a research paper on this story ran across an article on the passage which argued (as I recall, though I can't swear to it) that the compositor had slipped, and that the manuscript has the dialog as in the second version above. Voila! All difficulties vanish.

Hemingway's device of assigning two successive speeches to the same character without identifying him (paragraphs 20–21 and probably 32–33) has given rise to much confusion among readers—also to twenty or more scholarly articles on the correct reading of the story. David Kerner's "The Foundation of the True Text of 'A Clean, Well-Lighted Place'" settles the question. Demonstrating that the device appears many times in Hemingway's novels and stories, Kerner suggests—with evidence—that Hemingway may have learned it from Turgenev or Joyce (*Fitzgerald/Hemingway Annual* [1979]: 279–300). Later, Kerner examined manuscripts of books Hemingway saw through press and found thirty-eight clear instances of the device ("The Manuscripts Establishing Hemingway's Anti-Metronomic Dialogue," *American Literature* 54 [1982]: 385–96).

How original Hemingway's style once seemed may be less apparent today, after generations of imitators. Ford Madox Ford described the famed style: "Hemingway's words strike you, each one, as if they were pebbles fetched fresh from a brook" (introduction to *A Farewell to Arms* [New York: Modern Library, 1932]). Students may be asked to indicate some of the more prominent pebbles: the repetitions of such words as *night, light, clean, late, shadow, leaves,* and (most obviously) *nada*. The repetitions place emphasis. Students may be asked, too, to demonstrate whether Hemingway's prose seems closer to formal writing or to speech. It might help to have them notice the preponderance of one-syllable words in the opening paragraph of the story and to compare Hemingway's first paragraph with that of Faulkner's "Barn Burning." Faulkner's second sentence is a 117-worder, clearly more recondite in its diction (*dynamic, hermetic*). Most of Hemingway's story is told in dialogue, and usually we notice that a character *said* (unlike Faulkner's characters, who often *whisper* or *cry* their lines).

Frank O'Connor comments adversely on the Hemingway style:

> As practiced by Hemingway, this literary method, compounded of simplification and repetition, is the opposite of what we learned in our schooldays. We were taught to consider it a fault to repeat a noun and shown how to avoid it by the use of pronouns and synonyms. This led to another fault that Fowler christened "elegant variation." The fault of Hemingway's method might be called "elegant repetition" (*The Lonely Voice* [Cleveland: World, 1963]).

This criticism may be well worth quoting to the class. From "A Clean, Well-Lighted Place," can students see what O'Connor is talking about? Do they agree with him?

In a preface written in 1959 for a selection of his stories that did not materialize as a book, Hemingway congratulated himself for his skill at leaving things out. In his story "The Killer," he had left out Chicago; in "Big Two-Hearted River," the war. "Another time I was leaving out good was in 'A Clean, Well-Lighted Place.' There I really had luck. I left out everything. That is about as far as you can go, so I stood on that one and haven't been drawn to that since" ("The Art of the Short Story," *Paris Review* 79 [1981]: 100).

Hemingway himself had reason to empathize with the older waiter. "He was plagued all his adult life by insomnia and in sleep by nightmares," notes biographer Carlos Baker (*Ernest Hemingway: A Life Story* [New York: Scribner's, 1969] viii–ix).

Among its other practical uses, literature provides great names for businesses. Taking a leaf from Hemingway, three California bookshops (in Cupertino, Larkspur, and San Francisco) bear the name "A Clean Well-Lighted Place." Their give-away bookmark states: "We are of those who like to stay late at a bookstore. . . . Each night we are reluctant to close because there may be someone who needs to relax in A Clean Well-Lighted Place"—or perhaps, someone who needs to seek relief from insomnia?

William Faulkner
BARN BURNING, page 153

"Barn Burning" makes an interesting contrast to "A Rose for Emily." Whereas the earlier story (first collected in 1931) is written in a realist mode with Gothic elements, "Barn Burning" (1939) shows Faulkner in his Modernist mode—not opaque but richly textured and subtly nuanced. There are many ways to contrast the two stories, but one interesting way for students is to discuss how the different narrative points of view help shape radically different styles and effects.

The unnamed narrator of "A Rose for Emily" speaks in a public voice; he intends to represent the town's collective and considered view on Miss Emily Grierson. His style is lucid, measured, informed, and detached. "Barn Burning," however, is narrated from an objective third person point of view that enters the main character Sarty's mind. The objective external view is, therefore, constantly mixed with the confusion and emotions of a boy undergoing terrible stress. The narrator is not constrained to describe things only in the boy's limited vocabulary but can examine and represent his innermost thoughts and feelings. The narrator also helps the reader understand the boy's situation better than the character himself does.

The protagonist of "Barn Burning" is a poor ten-year-old boy with the unusual and very Faulknerian name of Colonel Sartoris Snopes (called Sarty by his family). His father, Abner Snopes, is a primitive and vengeful man who divides the world into two opposing camps—blood kin ("us") and enemies ("they"). He is the poor, ignorant, and vicious patriarch of an impoverished family. (Significantly, Faulkner gives Ab several features that link him on an associative level with the devil, as Edmond Volpe demonstrates in his discussion of "Barn Burning" in the section on "Critical Approaches to Literature.") The main psychological story of "Barn Burning" is Sarty's growing awareness of his father's depravity and the boy's internal struggle between blood loyalty to his father and a vague but noble ideal of honor suggested by the aristocratic Major de Spain. The boy loves his father but he also understands his immoral destructiveness. Sarty sees himself as an individual different from his father and kinfolk. By the end of the story he has achieved a difficult and tortured moral independence from his father.

From the opening paragraph, we can tell that the tone of the story will be excited and impassioned—at least in the moments when we see through Sarty's eyes. Even his view of canned goods in the general store (where court is being held) is tinged with intense emotion. Fear, despair, and grief sweep over Sarty because his father is on trial as an accused barn burner.

The boy's wonder and dismay are conveyed in a suitably passionate style. Whenever Sarty is most excited, Faulkner's sentences grow longer and more complex and seem to run on like a torrent. The second sentence of the story is a good illustration, as is the sentence in which Sarty jumps out of the way of Major de Spain's galloping horse and hears the barn going up in flames (at the climax of the story, the long sentence in paragraph 107). A familiar student objection is that Faulkner embodies the boy's feelings in words far beyond a ten-year-old's vocabulary—especially one who can't even read, as we learn about Sarty in the opening paragraph. You might anticipate this objection by making clear that a story about a small boy, even when the story is presented largely in terms of his own perceptions, need not be narrated by the boy himself; nor does the author need to confine himself within the limit of the boy's ability to comprehend and to express what he observes and feels (refer to the discussion of the quotation from *As I Lay Dying* at the beginning of the chapter). "Barn Burning" is told by an omniscient narrator who, much of the time, gives us the viewpoint of the main character.

Now and again, the narrator intrudes his own insights and larger knowledge. At times Faulkner rapidly shifts his perspective from outside Sarty's mind to inside it. Two such shifts take place in a sentence in paragraph 7 ("For a moment . . ."), in which, first, we get the boy's thoughts and then an exterior look at his crouched figure ("small for his age . . . with straight, uncombed, brown hair and eyes gray and wild as storm scud"), followed by a return to the boy's perceptions. In the paragraph telling how Ab Snopes's "wolflike independence" impressed strangers (25), Faulkner makes a judgment far beyond the boy's capacity. In paragraph 26, the narrator again separates his view from the boy's to tell us what Sarty would have thought if he were older—"But he did not think this now." The narrator is again clearly in evidence in the story's last two paragraphs.

Lionel Trilling wrote a good defense of the style in this story: the complexity of Faulkner's rhetoric reflects the muddlement and incompleteness of the boy's perceptions and the boy's emotional stress in moving toward a decision to break away from father and family (*The Experience of Literature* [New York: Holt, 1967] 745–48). He is perplexed and innocent, and we realize that somehow he loves his terrible father. In the next-to-last paragraph, Sarty's impressions of his father's war service are set beside the grim truth—which only the father (and the narrator) could know. Wayne C. Booth comments on this passage: "We can say with some confidence that the poignancy of the boy's lonely last-ditch defense of his father is greatly increased by letting us know that even that defense is unjustified" (*The Rhetoric of Fiction* [Chicago: U of Chicago P, 1961] 308).

If you teach "Barn Burning" together with "A Rose for Emily" (Chapter 2) to demonstrate that point of view, remember that "Barn Burning" is the more difficult story. You may want to take up "A Rose for Emily" first and to spend a little while getting students into the universe of Faulkner. Any brief discussion of the Civil War and its effects will help prepare them for "Barn Burning." Though her perch in society is loftier, Miss Emily, like Ab Snopes, is fiercely proud and capable of violent revenge, and she too holds herself above the law. As with Miss Emily, Snopes is characterized in part through symbolic use of details. The neat, "shrewd" fire (paragraph 26) reflects his cautious nature; his weapon of revenge, fire, is to be "regarded with respect and used with discretion." The rug that he soils and then ruins is emblematic of the social hierarchy that he defies and that he refuses to make amends to. His deliberately dirtied boots communicate his contempt for his employer as well as his own dirtiness of spirit. Clearly, Faulkner's impressions of both Snopes and Miss Emily are as complex as his feelings about the South itself.

"A Rose for Emily" also introduces the legend of Colonel Sartoris, war hero, mayor, and first citizen, whose fame and influence linger. Coming to "Barn Burning," students may then appreciate the boy hero's given name. Addressing the boy (in 10), the Justice foreshadows the story's conclusion: "I reckon anybody named for Colonel Sartoris in this country can't help but tell the truth, can he?" Truthfully, Sarty warns Major de Spain that his father is going to burn the major's barn; in so defying Ab, Colonel Sartoris Snopes rises to his namesake's nobility. (But, according to Frederick R. Karl, the line from Sartoris to Snopes is not one of simple degeneration. Karl points out that Colonel Sartoris "uses his power for white supremacy, harasses and even murders carpetbaggers, and makes certain that Negroes lose the vote. He . . . is a power-hungry, politically obsessed individual whose will is law. He establishes a dynasty, and its elements, while high and grand, are little different from the dynasties at the middle level established by Will Varner and at the lower levels by the Snopeses" [*William Faulkner: American Writer*, New York: Weidenfeld, 1989].)

Question 1 directs the student to paragraph 107, a crucial passage that repays close attention. From the roar Sarty hears, and from the detail that the night sky is "stained abruptly," it is clear that Ab Snopes and Sarty's older brother succeed in setting fire to de Spain's barn. We had long assumed that, although a total of three shots ring out, the barn burners get away, for they turn up in a later volume of Faulkner. But Joseph L. Swonk of Rappahannock Community College, North Campus, persuades us that the outcome is grimmer. Sarty cries "Pap! Pap!"—then trips over "something," looks back, and sobs "Father! Father!" "I contend," says Professor Swonk, "that he tripped over the bodies of his father and brother, that he was looking backward at the bodies, and that his shift from 'Pap' to 'Father' was eulogistic. Furthermore, he continues in this manner: '*Father. My Father* . . . He was brave! . . . He was! He was in the war!'" Now referring to his father in the past tense, Sarty is delivering a final tribute over Ab's corpse.

"Barn Burning," to place the story in the chronicles of Yoknapatawpha County, is a prelude to the Snopes family history later expanded in Faulkner's trilogy *The Hamlet* (1940), *The Town* (1957), and *The Mansion* (1959); in fact, a heavily revised version of "Barn Burning" forms the first chapter of *The Hamlet*. At the conclusion of "Barn Burning," Sarty Snopes turns his back on his father and his clan; so, in the trilogy, the primary figure is Flem, Sarty's brother, who remained. Meeting Flem Snopes, whose father Ab is still well known as a barn burner, Jody Varner in *The Hamlet* says dryly, "I hear your father has had a little trouble once or twice with landlords."

"Barn Burning" was adapted for television in the PBS television series *The American Short Story*, and stars Tommy Lee Jones. It is available on videocassette from Teacher's Video Company at (800) 262-8837. A paperback, *The American Short Story, Volume 2* (New York: Dell, 1980), includes short scenes from Horton Foote's television script based on Faulkner's story.

For a stimulating attack on Faulkner's style, see Sean O'Faolain, *The Vanishing Hero* (Boston: Little, Brown, 1957) 101–3, 111–12, 133. Charging that Faulkner can't write plain English because "his psyche is completely out of his control," O'Faolain cites lines of Faulkner that he thinks rely on pure sound instead of sense ("the gasoline-roar of apotheosis"); and complains that Faulkner needlessly uses "second-thought words" ("He did not know why he had been compelled, or anyway needed, to claim it"; "This, anyway, will, shall, must be invulnerable"). In O'Faolain's view, when Faulkner begins a sentence, "I mean," it is a tipoff that he doesn't know what he means and won't know until he says it. O'Faolain's objections might make for a provocative class discussion.

IRONY

Ha Jin

SABOTEUR, PAGE 168

This bitter political story depicts how an unjust system gradually corrupts its innocent victims—or to quote W. H. Auden, "Those to whom evil is done / Do evil in return." The protagonist, Mr. Chiu, is a gentle man of strong personal integrity but seemingly no passionate political views. His malicious arrest, which is a vicious joke by two railroad policemen, puts him in a difficult and painful ethical dilemma. If he lies about his innocence and signs a phony confession—thereby denying the gross misjustice done to him—the police will let him go. If he refuses to lie, he will continue to be punished. Mr. Chiu initially refrains from endorsing the official lie at considerable personal cost. Only when he has been weakened by a relapse of hepatitis and dismayed by the public torture and humiliation of his lawyer, does Mr. Chiu reluctantly agree to sign the false confession. His rage at the injustice he has suffered and his impotence in preventing it lead him to seek revenge the only way he can—a murderous plan that is not only disproportionate, but also one that eventually punishes the guilty and innocent alike.

Jin's story contains irony upon bitter irony. Chiu's honeymoon ends in jail. The police are the perpetrators of injustice. The innocent Mr. Chiu must pretend to be guilty to be set free. A man with no crimes must sign a confession. The ultimate irony is that by falsely claiming to be a saboteur, Mr. Chiu secretly becomes one. It is a sign of Jin's talent that these ironies emerge naturally—and usually surprisingly—from the narrative.

Jin's story reminds us of how pervasively irony is used in political fiction, especially works written in Communist societies. As the work of such disparate writers as Milan Kundera (Czech), Mikhail Bulgakov (Russian), Solwomir Mrozek (Polish), and Ha Jin demonstrate, a sense of irony helps in presenting the painful distance between the noble aims of the revolutionary worker societies and the often brutal realities. "In China," Jin has commented, "I still have the feeling that evil very often prevails and the good suffer." Jin's story also reminds us that irony is not necessarily a comic device, but can be a very dark, indeed tragic instrument. There is nothing funny about Mr. Chiu's humiliations, punishments, or murderous revenge.

WRITER'S PERSPECTIVE

Ernest Hemingway on Writing
THE DIRECT STYLE, page 176

Hemingway was internationally famous during his lifetime, and he gave many interviews. He talked expansively about travel, sports, food, politics, and personalities, but he usually became evasive when asked about his own work. He was almost entirely silent on his immensely influential style. This passage from Edward Stafford's "An Afternoon with Hemingway," therefore, is especially valuable to students of the writer's work. Connoisseurs of literary journalism may enjoy Stafford's old style of interviewing, which has now been almost entirely replaced by the *Paris Review* question-and-answer format. The 1964 publication date may seem confusing since Hemingway died in 1961. The interview was conducted in the late fifties, but Stafford did not publish it until after the novelist's death.

Hemingway's remarks are particularly interesting because he relates his style to his creative process. Hemingway wrote and revised his work in three stages—pencil, typescript, and proof. At each stage he consciously worked on conveying the "feeling or emotion" he wanted in each scene. Note, too, how Hemingway mentions that a writer needs to present the different sides of a story without judging. (His view here recalls John Keats's theory of "negative capability" as the mark of a particular kind of literary artist.)

6 Theme

Instructors who wish to teach all the stories in the book according to themes (not just the stories in this chapter) will find suggestions in this manual in "Stories Arranged by Subject and Theme."

Stephen Crane
THE OPEN BOAT, page 181

It may interest students to know that "The Open Boat" is based on Crane's own experience of shipwreck, but they may need some discussion to realize that factuality does not necessarily make a story excellent. Newspaper accounts may be faithful to the fact, but few are memorable; on the other hand, fine stories often are spun out of imagined experience—as was Crane's novel *The Red Badge of Courage,* a convincing evocation of the Civil War by a writer who was born six years after it ended.

For what reasons is "The Open Boat" a superb story? Its characters are sharply drawn and believable; captain, cook, oiler, and correspondent are fully realized portraits, etched with great economy. Crane deeply probes the mind of his primary character, the correspondent, from the point of view of limited omniscience. The author knows all, but confines his report to what he sees through the correspondent's eyes.

The story seems written with intense energy; students will find many phrases and figures of speech to admire. In a vigorous simile, Crane conveys the motion of the boat and a sense of its precarious balance: "By the very last star of truth, it is easier to steal eggs from under a hen than it was to change seats in the dinghy" (paragraph 31). In the same passage, a man changing places in the boat picks himself up and moves his body as carefully as if he were a delicate piece of china. One way to get students to sense the degree of life in a writer's style is to have them pick out verbs. In the opening sentence of Part II (21): "As the boat *bounced* from the top of each wave the wind *tore* through the hair of the hatless men, and as the craft *plopped* her stern down again the spray *slashed* past them." Building suspense, Crane brings the men again and again within sight of land and then drives them back to sea. He aligns enemies against them: sharks, the ocean current, the weight of water that sloshes into the boat and threatens to swamp it. The climax of the story—the moment of greatest tension, when the outcome is to be decided—comes in paragraph 204, when the captain decides to make a run through the surf and go for shore.

The situation of having one's nose dragged away before he can "nibble the sacred cheese of life" (70, 143) is a clear instance of irony of fate, or cosmic irony. (These slightly ponderous terms are defined as briefly as possible in the Glossary of Literary Terms.) Crane, who sees Fate as an "old ninnywoman" (70), knows that the rain falls alike on the just and the unjust. There is no one right way to state the theme of this rich story, but here are some attempts by students, each with some truth in it:

The universe seems blind to human struggles.

Fate is indifferent, and doesn't always reward the brave.

It's an absurd world; only people are reasonable.

This theme (however it is stated) may be seen also in the symbol of the giant tower (204) and Crane's remarks on what it suggests: "The serenity of nature amid the struggles of the individual," a presence not cruel or beneficent or treacherous or wise. Students who like to hunt for symbols sometimes want to see the boat as the universe, in which man is a passenger. A case can be made for reading the story in this way. But everything in the story (ocean, waves, shark, beach, lighthouse), however full of suggestions, is first and foremost a thing concrete and tangible.

Although the secondary theme of comradeship is overtly expressed only in paragraph 43 ("the subtle brotherhood of men that was here established"), it informs the entire story. Until they quit the boat, the men are willing to spell one another at the oars; and even in the water, the captain still thinks of the correspondent's safety. The word "heroism" remains unspoken, but it is clearly understood: in "The Open Boat," a hero seems to be one who faithfully does what needs to be done. All four men thus qualify for the name.

Remembering the scrap of verse by Victorian bard Caroline Norton (179), the correspondent finds himself drawn into sympathy with any sufferer who, like himself, has to die in a remote place. The sentimental lines give rise to a feeling that, under the circumstances, seems heartfelt and real. In their time, the stormy life and dashing Byronic ballads of Caroline Norton (1808–1877), granddaughter of Richard Brinsley Sheridan, attracted wide notice. Joyce mentions another poem of hers in "Araby," paragraph 23.

For its view of people as pawns of nature, Crane's story has been classified as an example of American naturalism. Clearly, "The Open Boat" also has elements in common with more recent fiction and drama of the absurd: its notion of Fate as a ninny, its account of Sisyphean struggles in the face of an indifferent universe. For critical comment on these aspects of the story, see Richard P. Adams, "Naturalistic Fiction: 'The Open Boat,'" *Tulane Studies in English* 4 (1954): 137–47; and Peter Buitenhuis, "The Essentials of Life: 'The Open Boat' as Existentialist Fiction," *Modern Fiction Studies* 5 (1959): 243–50.

The late William Maxwell, novelist and for many years a *New Yorker* fiction editor, was once asked in an interview, "As an editor, in deciding whether or not to read a story how much weight do you place on the first sentence?" "A great deal," Maxwell replied. "And if there is nothing promising by the end of the first page there isn't likely to be in what follows. . . . When you get to the last sentence of a [story], you often find that it was implicit in the first sentence, only you didn't know what it was." Asked for his favorite opening lines in fiction, Maxwell's first thought was of "None of them knew the color of the sky," from "The Open Boat" ("The Art of Fiction," *Paris Review* 82 [December 1982]). Students may be asked what this first line reveals. (That the sea compels the survivors' whole attention.) How does the final sentence in the story hark back to the first?

Luke 15: 11–32.
THE PARABLE OF THE PRODIGAL SON, page 200

The original setting of this famous parable may help clarify its principal theme. Jesus has been preaching in the towns and villages along the road to Jerusalem. He has attracted great crowds, including many disreputable people whom Jewish religious leaders would traditionally have avoided or spurned. The Pharisees (strict practitioners of Jewish dogma) and the Scribes (doctors of religious law) expressed shock that Jesus would be willing to receive and even dine with sinners (not to mention tax collectors). In Luke 15, Jesus answers their criticism with three parables: the lost sheep, the lost coin, and the prodigal son. These parables implicitly preach compassion and concern for sinners. The righteous, Jesus implies, don't reject sinners; they seek to bring them back to virtue.

Most parables from the Gospels have a slightly abstract quality. Short, simple, and allegorical, they illustrate their morals through exemplary but deliberately generalized characters and action. The characters in "The Parable of the Prodigal Son," however, feel like individual human beings. We experience their motivations, emotions, and thoughts. The parable reads like a short story. The philosopher George Santayana called it "a little masterpiece."

The human theme of the parable might be summarized as "genuine virtue includes the power to forgive" or "true goodness requires love and compassion, not just outward virtue." The elder son has led an outwardly virtuous life, but when his erring brother returns home, he cannot put aside his jealousy to greet him. He resents his father's joy as well as his brother's behavior. His external righteousness has not nourished his heart: he feels neither joy nor compassion. The father, however, rejoices in the younger son's safe return. Santayana thought that the parable also had a psychological theme: "There is more joy in finding what was lost than there would be in merely keeping it."

We tend to remember this parable as the story of the younger son. (Its traditional title, "The Parable of the Prodigal Son," surely contributes to this overly narrow focus.) However, the parable is more richly complex; it is, as the opening line tells us, the story of two brothers: "A certain man had two sons." In his excellent commentary on the Gospel, *Saint Luke* (London: Penguin, 1963), G. B. Caird points out that the loving and generous father has actually lost both sons, "one in a foreign country, the other behind a barricade of self-righteousness. The elder contrived, without leaving home, to be as far away from his father as ever his brother was in a heathen pigsty. Both brothers are selfish, though in totally different ways." (p. 182) The theme of the parable would be less dramatically presented if we did not see (and probably feel some sympathy with) the older brother's uncharitable reaction to the prodigal's return.

The father refuses to be drawn into an argument with his older son. When the son complains to him, he answers with, to quote G. B. Caird again, "the gentlest of rebukes": "Son, thou art ever with me, and all that I have is thine. It was meet that we should make merry, and be glad: for this thy brother was dead, and is alive again; and was lost, and is found."

It may be worthwhile to point out a few memorable details along the way. Ask for someone to define the word *prodigal*. You will be surprised how few students know what it means. (On second thought, maybe you won't be surprised.) You may want to point out that tending pigs—unclean animals, according to Jewish belief—was a horribly degrading job for the younger son. You may also wish to store up the prodigal's phrase, "I will arise and go to my father" in your memory for the next time you teach William Butler Yeats's "The Lake Isle of Innisfree." Yeats's poem begins, "I will arise and go now, and go to Innisfree," and the poet intends a biblical echo to let us know that his return to this spot is no mere weekend holiday. Finally, you might want to point out how the image of killing "the fatted calf" has become a traditional symbol for extravagant and joyful feasting. (Students in the Boston area may recognize it as the name of a local restaurant.)

A good writing exercise is to ask students to retell the parable from the older brother's perspective. Can they present his version of the story without losing the original theme? (For a comic retelling of the parable from just this slant, see Garrison Keillor's satiric skit, *The Prodigal Son*.)

Another version of the prodigal son's story occurs in Rainer Maria Rilke's novel, *The Notebooks of Malte Laurids Brigge* (1910). Rilke's powerful retelling of the parable appears as the last few pages of the book, and it can be easily understood by someone who has not read the rest of the novel. (In the German-speaking world, his parable is frequently anthologized separately.) In Rilke's version, the younger brother is "a man who didn't want to be loved," a person who could not bear the weight and responsibility of another's affection. A savvy student could write an excellent term paper on comparing Rilke's parable to the Gospel original.

Kurt Vonnegut, Jr.
HARRISON BERGERON, page 201

"Harrison Bergeron" is a story that tends to divide teachers. Many instructors like Vonnegut's science fiction satire immensely, but a vocal minority of college instructors consider "Harrison Bergeron" too boisterously direct. Students, however, usually find the story powerful and provocative. They consistently rate it among their favorite works. (Science fiction remains one of the few literary genres truly popular among students.) Whenever we have dropped the story from *Literature*, letters pour in asking for its reappearance.

We suspect that the gap between some instructors and students reflects differences between high literary culture and popular literary culture. Vonnegut's gutsy satire is no deathless masterpiece. Its humor is elementary, and its characters are flat. Vonnegut's style has neither the evocative conciseness of a Hemingway nor the lyrical resonance of a Porter.

But to catalogue what Vonnegut is *not* misses what he *is*—a contemporary satirist who uses science fiction conventions to frame his iconoclastic ideas. Vonnegut's roots are in science fiction. Viewed from the vantage of that genre, the particular qualities of "Harrison Bergeron" become more obvious. One particularly interesting classroom use for the story is to use it as a platform for examining the idea of genre. Have students compare it to a classic, realist story like "Araby" or "Paul's Case" and enumerate the differences in style, structure, setting, and characterization.

Science fiction short stories are more concerned with exploring ideas than with careful portrayal of psychological and social reality. The classic sci-fi short story makes a few changes in technology and then speculates on their social, political, psychological, or moral implications. The purpose is not to predict the future, but to explore the possible consequences of present trends abetted by future technology. In "Harrison Bergeron" Vonnegut explores the idea of a futuristic society which has developed the technology to enforce an extreme version of social equality at all costs. Vonnegut's story belongs to a long tradition of anti-utopian satire usually called dystopian fiction. (Modern dystopian fiction developed out of Menippean satire, which emphasizes ideas and employs loose form, a tradition that includes Jonathan Swift's *Gulliver's Travels*, or Francois Rabelais's *Gargantua and Pantegruel*.) Among the best known dystopian literary works are George Orwell's *1984*, Aldous Huxley's *Brave New World*, Eugene Zamyatin's *We*, and Anthony Burgess's *A Clockwork Orange*, but there are countless other anti-utopian novels, stories, films, and television shows. Describing all sorts of possible nightmare futures proved one of the late twentieth century's favorite pastimes.

The theme of "Harrison Bergeron" strikes most students with great force, and they can usually summarize it one way or another. "Down with mediocrity and conformity" is one common answer, or "Individual excellence involves risk." A more elegant and comprehensive statement of the story's themes might be, "By attempting to enforce equality too vigorously, society risks penalizing excellence." Vonnegut's story also objectifies the well-known American distrust of intellectuality, and it exaggerates this prejudice to an insane degree. Some students may read the story remembering how in high school or junior high they were ridiculed by classmates for showing interest in ideas or learning. Vonnegut imagines a society so dedicated to a perverse concept of equality that it condemns absolutely all excellence, including good looks, physical grace, and imagination. The story is probably best seen as a fable. It certainly has a moral: don't be afraid to excel. As in most fables, rounded characterization is unnecessary to its purpose.

Until Vonnegut began to reach a wide general audience in the 1960s, his following was mainly limited to science fiction fans—but he has insisted that his work is not confined to science fiction. In an essay, "Science Fiction" for the *New York Times Book Review* (September 5, 1965), he said that until he read the reviews of his first novel, *Player Piano* (New York: Delacorte, 1952), he had not thought of himself as a science fiction writer; "I supposed that I was writing a novel about life, about things I could not avoid seeing and hearing in Schenectady, a very real town, awkwardly set in the gruesome now. I have been a sore-headed occupant of a file drawer labeled 'science fiction' ever since, and I would like out."

There is little criticism on Vonnegut's short stories. What exists can mostly be found in Gale Research's *Short Story Criticism*, vol. 8 (Detroit: Gale, 1991). There are many excellent books and articles on Vonnegut's novels. *The Vonnegut Statement*, edited by Jerome Klinkowitz and John Somer (New York: Delacorte, 1973), is a lively anthology of criticism of Vonnegut's work by various hands. Vonnegut's most interesting commentator, however, may be the author himself. There is a thick book of interviews, *Conversations with Kurt Vonnegut*, edited by William Rodney Allen (Jackson: UP of Mississippi, 1988) that contains a great deal of interesting biographical and literary material. Additionally, *Harrison Bergeron* was filmed in 1995. Directed by Bruce Pittman, the film is available on videotape. Finally, a 56 minute audio cassette interview of Vonnegut by Heywood Hale Broun is available from the American Audio Prose Library at (800) 447-2275.

WRITER'S PERSPECTIVE

Kurt Vonnegut, Jr. on Writing

THE THEMES OF SCIENCE FICTION, page 207

Kurt Vonnegut has spent much of his career telling the literary world that he is not a science fiction writer. He realizes that a genre label keeps a writer from serious critical attention. (Both he and Ursula Le Guin have suffered from such critical stereotyping.) And yet Vonnegut's literary roots are indisputably in science fiction, and his best novels—most notably *Cat's Cradle* (1963) and *Slaughterhouse Five* (1969)—grow out of the genre's enlivening traditions without being limited by its narrower conventions. In Vonnegut's voluminous published interviews, these two passages best represent his interest in using the possibilities of science fiction to describe the technologically dependent modern world. He also discusses the ghettoization of science fiction writers by the literary establishment.

7 Symbol

John Steinbeck
THE CHRYSANTHEMUMS, page 212

John Steinbeck was a writer whose best work came relatively early in his career. His later work—much of it ambitiously allegorical fiction or literary journalism—has tended to obscure his genuine achievement. In the second half of the 1930s, however, Steinbeck published in quick succession his greatest works of fiction: *In Dubious Battle* (1936), *Of Mice and Men* (1937), *The Long Valley* (1938), a collection of stories that includes "The Chrysanthemums," and his masterpiece, *The Grapes of Wrath* (1939). With great feeling for his characters and often intense emotional impact, he shows us the lives of hard-working people whose desire for fulfillment are balked by custom and circumstance, by powerful economic forces that thrive upon their exploitation, and, at times, by their inability to comprehend their own longings.

Elisa is a complex study in frustration. She is a strong, intense woman with far more energy than she can put to use: we learn at the outset that "even her work with the scissors was over-eager, over-powerful" and that her house is "a hard-swept looking little house, with hard-polished windows." Trapped under a "grey-flannel fog" that encloses the valley like a lid on a pot, she works behind a symbolic barrier: a wire fence "that protected her flower garden from cattle and dogs and chickens" and that also protects her from the wider world. Custom denies her and her restless energy the adequate outlets that men enjoy. She cannot buy and sell cattle as Henry does. She cannot drift about the countryside mending utensils as the traveling repairman does, though his unfettered lifestyle powerfully appeals to her. "That sounds like a nice kind of a way to live," she declares on meeting him. "I wish women could do such things," she tells him later, and adds, "I can sharpen scissors, too. . . . I could show you what a woman might do." But she will never be given such an opportunity.

Besides her frustration at the passive role thrust upon her, Elisa is thwarted because her considerable gifts for nurturing—her "planting hands"—have little value in the wider world. The remarkable chrysanthemums are richly symbolic of her feminine talents. Yet the practical and shortsighted Henry, because the flowers are not a cash crop, says, "I wish you'd work out in the orchard and raise some apples that big." The traveling repairman feigns an interest in the chrysanthemum shoots for his own gain and then throws them on the road and saves the pot. In the sight of the flower pot's contents discarded in the road, Elisa sees the end of her brief interlude of hopes and dreams.

Mordecai Marcus, in his critical commentary, sees Elisa's flowers as substitutes for the children she (now thirty-five) was apparently unable to have ("The Lost Dream of Sex and Childbirth in 'The Chrysanthemums,'" *Modern Fiction*

Studies 11 [1965]: 54–58). The suggestion is not unlikely; according to Elizabeth E. McMahan, however, "it does not necessarily have anything to do with a longing for children" ("'The Chrysanthemums': A Study of a Woman's Sexuality," *Modern Fiction Studies* 14 [1968]: 453–58).

Given to speaking in impassioned poetry ("Every pointed star gets driven into your body"), Elisa is further thwarted by having to live a life devoid of romance. Although kind and considerate, Henry is dull. When he tries to turn a compliment, the best he can do is, "Why—why Elisa. You look so nice!" When pressed for details, he says: "You look strong enough to break a calf over your knee, happy enough to eat it like a watermelon."

Though crafty and unkempt, the repairman has a touch of the poet. He can describe a chrysanthemum as "a quick puff of colored smoke." Elisa's short-lived belief that he values her flowers (and by extension, recognizes her womanliness) releases in her a long-pent eroticism for which the repairman is ill prepared. He changes the subject.

Elizabeth McMahan finds a "purification ritual" in the scene that follows. Elisa "felt shame after her display of passion before the stranger. Now she cleanses herself before returning to her husband, the man to whom she should lawfully reach out in desire," punishing herself with the abrasive pumice until her skin is "scratched and red."

Elisa's battle with her stifled sexuality is conveyed in detail ("her hand went out toward his legs in the greasy black trousers. . . . She crouched low like a fawning dog"). William R. Osborne demonstrates that Steinbeck, in revising the story, heightened Elisa's earthiness and the sexual overtones of her encounter with the repairman (*Modern Fiction Studies* 12 [1966]: 479–84). The revised version as it appeared in *The Long Valley* (New York: Viking, 1938) is the text used in this book.

In the end, Elisa tries to satisfy her spiritual and erotic cravings by asking Henry if they might order wine with their dinner. "It will be enough if we can have wine. It will be plenty." It isn't enough, of course, and she cries "weakly— like an old woman"—she who had briefly thought herself strong. Her new interest in prize fights, in the spectacle of blood-letting she had formerly rejected, manifests Elisa's momentary wish for revenge on men: her desire to repay them for her injured femininity. At least, this is the interpretation of Marcus and of McMahan. Alternatively, one may see in this curiosity about the violence of the boxing ring a woman's envy of the opportunities given to men to work off their aggressions and frustrations in socially acceptable ways.

If your students are familiar with *Of Mice and Men*, you may encourage them to make connections between Elisa's situation and those of the many stunted characters—whether physically, mentally, or emotionally—in that classic novella. A particularly apt comparison, of course, is with Curley's wife, who speaks movingly of the loneliness and confinement of her life and complains, "Seems like they ain't none of them cares how I gotta live." One may also discuss Elisa in terms of George, the protagonist of *Of Mice and Men*, who also—albeit on a much more profound level—responds to the ruin of his dreams by resigning himself to being swallowed up in the emptiness and meanness of spirit all around him.

The story and the novella also bear comparison on a technical level, in that both are attempts by Steinbeck to confine himself to the objective point of view, presenting his characters, as far as possible, from the outside only, and allowing us to deduce what is taking place within them. Steinbeck acknowledged that *Of Mice and Men* was a formal experiment, an attempt to write a work that was simultaneously narrative fiction and playable drama. (Not surprisingly, the work has been successfully adapted as a play, film, TV drama, and opera.) "The Chrysanthemums" also illustrates the objective point of view, or "the fly on the wall" method. After some opening authorial remarks about the land, Steinbeck confines himself to reporting external details. Although the reader comes to share Elisa's feelings, we do not enter her mind; we observe her face and her reactions ("Elisa's eyes grew alert and eager"). This cinematic method of storytelling seems a hardship for the author only in paragraph 109, when to communicate Elisa's sadness he has to have her whisper aloud.

Like his early model, D. H. Lawrence, Steinbeck is fond of portraying people swept up by dark forces of the unconscious. (A curious book for additional reading: Steinbeck's early novel *To a God Unknown* [New York: Viking, 1933] which shows the influence of both Lawrence and Robinson Jeffers.) "The Chrysanthemums" invites comparison with Lawrence's "The Blind Man," which also conveys a woman's struggle for intellectual survival while living with a mindless husband on a farm. Henry Allen is no match, though, for Lawrence's impressive Maurice. If the two stories are set side by side for evaluation, Lawrence's may well seem (in our opinion) the deeper and more vivid. Though finely perceptive, "The Chrysanthemums" has something methodical about it, as if the young Steinbeck were deliberately trying to contrive a short-story masterpiece. But this is to dissent from the judgments of Mordecai Marcus, who thinks it indeed "one of the world's great short stories," and of André Gide, who in his *Journals* finds it in a league with the best of Chekhov (Vol. IV [New York: Knopf, 1951] 79).

Shirley Jackson
THE LOTTERY, page 221

Shirley Jackson's famous story shocks us. By transferring a primitive ritual to a modern American small town and by making clear in passing that the same ritual is being carried out in surrounding towns, the author manages to create in us a growing sense of horror over what is happening. Very early—in paragraphs 2 and 3—she mentions the stones that have been gathered in preparation for the day's events. Not until much later in the story does the importance of the stones begin to dawn.

Students might be asked to sum up the rules of Jackson's lottery, which are simple and straightforward. The male head of each household—or, if he is absent, another representative of the family—draws a slip of paper out of a big black box. One householder pulls out a piece of paper that has a black circle crudely penciled on it. Each member of his family is then obliged to participate in a second drawing. This time the unlucky recipient of the black circle is stoned to death by the other townspeople, including the members of his or her own family. Whatever justification might ever have existed for the ritual has long since been forgotten. The people simply accept the proceedings as an annual civic duty, the up-to-date version of an ancient fertility ritual ("Lottery in June, corn be heavy soon").

What is spine-chilling in Jackson's story is the matter-of-factness with which the ritual is carried out. Each June the townspeople assemble to murder one of their neighbors. The discrepancy between ordinary, civilized, modern behavior and the calm acceptance of something as primitive as human sacrifice gives "The Lottery" a terrible power. Among the story's many ironies, some of the most notable are:

1. *The point of view.* An objective narrator tells the story, remaining outside the characters' minds, yet the narrator's detachment contrasts with the attitude of the author, who presumably, like the reader, is horrified. That the day's happenings can be recounted so objectively lends them both credence and force.

2. *The setting.* The beauty of the June day is out of keeping with the fact that what takes place on the town green is a ritual murder.

3. *The misplaced chivalry.* Though women can be stoned to death in these yearly proceedings, they are whenever possible protected from having to take part in the general drawing (paragraph 13).

4. *The characters.* The townspeople are perfectly ordinary types, "surveying their own children, speaking of planting and rain, tractors and taxes" (3). Mr. Summers is in charge because he "had time and energy to devote to civic activities" (4). Old Man Warner is a stickler for tradition. Neighbors chat amiably. Children play. All are grateful that the proceedings will be over in time for them to enjoy their noon meal.

As a matter of course, even the small son of the victim is given some stones to throw at his mother. That is perhaps the most horrifying detail of all.

The story's very outrageousness raises questions about unexamined assumptions in modern society. Do civilized Americans accept and act upon other vestiges of primitive ritual as arbitrary as the one Jackson imagines? Are we shackled by traditions as bizarre and pointless as the lottery in Jackson's story? What determines the line between behavior that is routine and that which is unthinkable? How civilized in fact are we?

In *Private Demons: The Life of Shirley Jackson* (New York: Putnam's, 1988), Judy Oppenheimer gives a good account of the story's genesis. Jackson wrote "The Lottery" in 1948 while pregnant with her third child. She had been reading a book on ancient customs of human sacrifice and had found herself wondering how such a rite might operate in the village of North Bennington, Vermont, where she lived.

Peter Hawkes of East Stroudsburg University finds an obstacle to teaching "The Lottery" in that many students think its central premise totally unrealistic and absurd. How, they assume, can this story have anything to do with me? Hawkes dramatizes the plausibility of the townspeople's unswerving obedience to authority. With a straight face, he announces that the Dean has just decreed that every English teacher give at least one F per class to reduce grade inflation, passes around a wooden box, and tells students to draw for the fatal grade! "While I pass the box around the room, I watch carefully for, and indirectly encourage, the student who will refuse to take a slip of paper. When this happens, I ask the class what should be done. Invariably, someone in the class will say that the person who refused to draw deserves the F. Hearing this, the student almost always draws." See Mr. Hawkes's account in "The Two Lotteries: Teaching Shirley Jackson's 'The Lottery,'" *Exercise Exchange* for Fall 1987. We would expect a class to greet this trick with much skepticism! But what if you were to try it on them *before* assigning the story?

Jackson once remarked that in writing "The Lottery" she had hoped "to shock the story's readers with a graphic demonstration of the pointless violence and general inhumanity in their own lives" (quoted by Lenemaja Friedman, *Shirley Jackson* [New York: Twayne, 1975]). For class discussion: What is the point of Jackson's comment? Is it true? In our own society, what violent behavior is sanctioned? How are we comparable to Jackson's villagers? Don't we too casually accept the unthinkable?

"The Lottery" invites comparison with Hawthorne's "Young Goodman Brown": in each, an entire community is seen to take part in a horrifying rite.

Yet another interpretation is possible. Jackson ran into parental opposition when she announced her intention of marrying fellow Syracuse University student Stanley Edgar Hyman, and some of her housemates warned her of the perils of living with a Jew. Shocked by these early run-ins with anti-Semitism, Jackson once told a friend (according to Judy Oppenheimer) that "The Lottery" was a story about the Holocaust.

There are dangers, of course, in reading more meaning into the story than it will sustain. Jackson herself, in *Come Along with Me* (New York: Viking, 1968), insists that we accept the story at face value. After its debut in the *New Yorker* in 1948, Jackson was surprised by the great amount of mail she received about the story. Some letter writers demanded to know what "The Lottery" meant, others supplied interpretations that they wished confirmed, others angrily abused the author for writing such a story. She even had letters from people asking where these lotteries were held, that they might go and watch the drawings.

Octavio Paz
MY LIFE WITH THE WAVE, page 229

Octavio Paz's fascinating "My Life with the Wave" triumphantly defies easy classification. Depending upon the angle from which it is viewed, the piece can be seen as a Modernist parable, an erotic allegory, a Surrealist prose poem, or a Magical Realist short story. Each approach offers some insight—and may spur some interesting class discussion—but ultimately the story must be accepted on its own terms—alluring, troubling, and elusive.

The exposition is notably short and matter-of-fact. By the end of the first paragraph the wave has left the sea to follow her lover into town, and she has refused to leave him. Paz clearly has no interest in verisimilitude. He has unapologetically established the impossible premise—no scientific, supernatural, or mythic explanation is offered—and he now explores the consequences. Once the considerable difficulty of transporting the wave into the city is solved—which costs the narrator a year in prison—the pair begin a passionate love affair. At first their lovemaking is a sunlit sea of pleasure.

Slowly the relationship darkens. At the center of the problem is the unalterable differences between the two lovers who remain unknowable to one another. The narrator studies the wave earnestly. "But never did I reach the center of her being," he confesses. The wave exists beyond humanity. She, too, now finds her human lover unsatisfying. They alternate between love and anger. After the wave nearly drowns the narrator (for throwing away her fish towards which he feels jealous), he starts "to fear and hate her." He begins to visit an old girlfriend and plot an escape.

The ending of the story becomes a terrifying parable of sexual revulsion and cold-hearted revenge. The couple grows increasingly estranged. In winter he abandons her for a month and returns to find her frozen. There is no touch of compassion in the narrator. "I was unmoved by her weary beauty," he comments. Rather than warm her or return her to the sea, he sells her to a waiter who chops her into little pieces of ice to use in the restaurant.

What is one to make of Paz's compelling tale? It depends entirely on how one approaches the work. On a realistic level—if we accept its fantastic central premise—the story depicts a passionate but failed love affair that eventually becomes murderous. But few readers will entirely resist the urge to interpret the text symbolically. The key is probably to accept each meaning the story suggests without insisting on any one reading, though the temptation to read it as a dark allegory of male and female sexuality may be strong in many. Although cast as prose fiction, "My Life with the Wave" unfolds and resolves very much like a poem, and this compressed and evocative tale deserves to be read with the same care one would lavish on poetry.

The poet Diane Thiel, who teaches at the University of Miami, offers the following provocative reading of Paz's story, which she sees as an allegory of the creative process. This interpretation both illuminates and justifies the story's disturbing conclusion.

Paz's "My Life with the Wave" has a many-layered nature which eludes immediate definition. Is it a love relationship the wave describes, or is it an aspect of himself? Is it memory? Or is it the muse, inspiration—which follows him from the sea, causes his imprisonment, and then is waiting for him on his return home, ready to toss him in many directions?

The wave is vested with human qualities (a voice, a body, feelings, and moods), and the speaker has a relationship with her which is both physical and emotional. The personification of the wave, along with bizarre physical details of her elemental nature (such as the speaker's hiding her in the water tank on the train, her "falling in a fine rain" into the engine to travel to his home) give the piece a surreal or magically real quality. A superficial reading might lead to the conclusion that the wave is merely a representation of a love relationship. The sensuous nature of the wave and the erotic and tempestuous relationship of the speaker with her support this impression. A closer reading, however, reveals some inconsistencies. The wave presents some non-human qualities. Her tempests, like those of the sea, are tied to the weather. She lacks the human center of mortality, and the vulnerability which comes from it.

The origin of this piece—its inclusion in *Aguila o Sol* (*Eagle or Sun*), a collection of prose poems which deals with the creative process—offers a useful clue to the deeper, possible meanings of the wave. The pieces in *Aguila o Sol* describe the artistic process as a physical, erotic encounter, sometimes violent. Paz's choice of a wave to depict the experience is an evocative one. As a writer, he struggles with the volatile demands of the Muse. It is a relationship which strikes a familiar chord with all writers. The wave will follow you home. You have no choice in the matter. It will come in search of you. You will do anything for this wave. Going to prison will not keep you from writing. But it is a tempestuous relationship—tortuous at times, because you may not know what the Muse requires.

The double metaphor—the creative process as a wave, and the wave as a person—is effective because it can describe the relationship with the Muse simultaneously on intellectual, emotional, and visceral levels. The erotic connotations are particularly effective because they heighten the intensity of the piece. Paz chooses a feminine noun (*la ola*) for his character, which requires the feminine pronoun in Spanish. The effect in the original language is somewhat subtler than the use of "she" in English. The translation strongly encourages one to initially read the piece as a description of a love relationship.

"My Life with the Wave" embodies many qualities of the prose poem (though this form itself, as a fusion of genres, often eludes definition). Paz's piece feels drawn by the drift of the unconscious, while simultaneously steeped in wry humor and the details of the everyday world—elements which are central to prose poetry. The piece develops around the image of the wave—from the gentle caress to a howling storm which calls up the monsters of the depths. These primordial images occur in stark contrast to the world of trains, police, apartments and ice buckets.

The final image of the wave, broken up to fill ice buckets, may be chilling, but it is also a clue to her identity. The ideas generated by the creative process become tortuous at times. One may have to leave the project for a while, in order to allow the inspiration to solidify into words. For the writer, inspiration can be a monster with which one must battle, until it is broken up into pieces—words, poems, stories. The fact that the speaker "sells" the wave further suggests her nature as Muse. Is the waiter the editor, who uses small shards of the product of inspiration to enrich the lives of readers, like chilled wine? It is an unfortunate fate—the wave of inspiration reduced to restaurant ice. One cannot truly capture the wave, Paz seems to suggest, only serve it in the tiniest of pieces.

Ursula K. Le Guin
THE ONES WHO WALK AWAY FROM OMELAS, page 234

Ursula Le Guin's "The Ones Who Walk Away from Omelas" may be the most unusual story in the book in its relation to the conventions of storytelling. It does not describe the actions of a particular character or small group of characters. It has no plot or protagonist in the usual sense. A skeptical critic of old-fashioned taste might even claim that it is not truly a short story—a fiction, yes, but not a story. Le Guin's central character is an imaginary society. Her plot is a survey of the civilization that leads up to a single shocking revelation. Yet this unusual work has been recognized as a small classic from the beginning. It won a Hugo (science fiction's most prestigious award) after its first magazine appearance, and it has been frequently anthologized in both science fiction and mainstream anthologies.

"The Ones Who Walk Away from Omelas" seems only slightly less unusual when seen in the context of science fiction. The story belongs to a standard genre of science fiction that presents an imaginary civilization in order to criticize some aspect of our own culture, and yet even when viewed against such science fiction conventions, Le Guin's story is an unusually plotless, subtly ironic, and intellectually complex piece. This story's genre is often called utopian fantasy (after Thomas More's 1516 *Utopia*), though some readers might claim that she actually describes a dystopia, a conspicuously flawed society. (Some famous dystopian fictions would include George Orwell's *1984*, Aldous Huxley's *Brave New World*, and Anthony Burgess's *A Clockwork Orange*.) Actually, Le Guin's story borrows elements from both the utopian and dystopian traditions. Le Guin's narrator fervently believes that Omelas is a perfect society; the narrator intends the story to be a utopian vision. The reader, however, sees the horrifying moral compromise at the center of the society, and, as the story's title suggests, the author also sees Omelas as a covert dystopia.

Le Guin's story is overtly disturbing—and all the more so because the narrator blithely accepts the undeserved suffering that shocks the reader. Her penetrating parable raises the same ethical issue as Dostoyevsky's famous tale of "The Grand Inquisitor" from *The Brothers Karamazov:* would it be morally acceptable to purchase universal happiness at the cost of injustice to one innocent child? Le Guin appears to say that no society should rest on such injustice. Surely, it is not coincidental that by the time the narrator tells this story, the happy civilization of Omelas has apparently ceased to exist. In this detail, Le Guin suggests perhaps that Omelas has rotted from within and that any civic or cultural achievements purchased at such a price will not endure.

Although Le Guin admits she knew *The Brothers Karamazov*, she claims in a note on this story in her collection, *The Wind's Twelve Quarters* (New York: Harper, 1975), that she got the idea for the story from William James's essay, "The Moral Philosopher and the Moral Life." Le Guin's note is excerpted in the "Writer's Perspective" that follows the story.

There are two dominant symbols in "The Ones Who Walk Away from Omelas" that deserve discussion. The first is the city of Omelas itself, "bright-towered by the sea." What does Omelas symbolize? At the very least, it suggests the dream of human happiness. ("They were not simple folk, you see," the narrator tells us, "though they were happy.") The citizens of Omelas are "Joyous!" as well as "mature, intelligent, passionate adults whose lives are not wretched." To the narrator at least, Omelas represents a happiness no longer possible in a cheerless time. In a moral sense, however, Omelas symbolizes the hidden compromises that prosperous societies must make. "It is the existence of the child, and their knowledge of its existence," the narrator claims, "that makes possible the nobility of their architecture, the poignancy of their music, the profundity of their science."

The unforgettable symbol of Le Guin's story, however, is the filthy, feeble-minded child locked in the dark cellar. The symbolic significance of this pathetic figure and its grim setting ramifies in many directions. The child is imprisoned in the basement of "one of the beautiful public buildings of Omelas." It is the hidden injustice on which the city is built. The child symbolizes all the evil that citizens in a society must learn to accept without question in order to enjoy their own position. "They all know that it is there, all the people of Omelas," the narrator assures us. The child does not suffer because the good citizens of Omelas are ignorant: it suffers because the citizens are willing to trade its "abominable misery" for their peace, pleasure, and prosperity. Although the child is universally known, it is also kept out of sight. In psychological terms, the child symbolizes the horrible knowledge the conscious mind wishes to repress in order to maintain its happiness.

Students planning to write on Le Guin's story might compare it to Dostoyevsky's powerful "The Grand Inquisitor" (*The Brothers Karamazov*, Volume I, Book 5, Chapter 5). How does Le Guin's parable differ from Dostoyevsky's? How does her work resemble his? Le Guin's other fiction will also provide fruitful areas for research. Her finest work is her novels, especially *The Left Hand of Darkness* (1969), *The Lathe of Heaven* (1971), and *The Dispossessed* (1974). (Her "Earthsea" trilogy of novels for young adults is also superb.) *The Dispossessed* would be a particularly interesting book to compare and contrast to "The Ones Who Walk Away from Omelas," since the novel presents two radically different societies, each with conspicuous strengths and weaknesses that puzzle the narrator, who wrestles with the ethical issue of which to consider superior.

WRITER'S PERSPECTIVE

Ursula K. Le Guin on Writing
NOTE ON "THE ONES WHO WALK AWAY FROM OMELAS," page 240

Ursula Le Guin's passage provides the intellectual background of her disturbing parable. The quotation from William James is not only interesting for the specific insight it offers on the origins of Le Guin's work, but it also suggests a general lesson on how new literary works emerge from older ones. Since many students believe that writers simply snatch absolutely original and unprecedented ideas out of the air in the creative process, this lesson is important to point out. In literature, new texts always grow out of other texts—sometimes in emulation, expansion, or qualification, sometimes in rejection, ridicule, or rebellion. A strong artist nonetheless stamps his or her personality on the new work and thereby makes it in some sense unique. Le Guin's story is particularly instructive. She clearly draws her parable from an identifiable source, and yet who would mistake "The Ones Who Walk Away from Omelas" for the work of William James? Le Guin has transformed his idea into something distinctly her own.

8 Two Critical Casebooks: Flannery O'Connor and Raymond Carver

FLANNERY O'CONNOR

Flannery O'Connor is generally acknowledged as one of the greatest American fiction writers of the last century—a reputation that rests mostly on her emotionally powerful, incisively drawn, and exuberantly original short stories. Although her prose style is lucid and accessible, her fiction is by no means easy going. The stories violate the usual standards of good taste—presenting violence, racism, madness, deceit, despair, and sexual perversity—and challenge the reader's worldview. She is at once the darkest satirist and brightest religious visionary in modern American fiction. Students may find her initially troubling, perhaps even infuriating, but few contemporary writers so deeply reward study and discussion.

If you think Flannery O'Connor's Southern world is likely to strike your students as remote and unfamiliar, you might begin by telling the class a little about it. Should your library own a copy of Barbara McKenzie's book of photographs, *Flannery O'Connor's Georgia* (Athens: U of Georgia P, 1980), by all means bring it in and show it around. McKenzie recalls John Wesley's remark in "A Good Man Is Hard to Find," "Let's drive through Georgia fast so we won't have to look at it much," and supplies a series of pictures of some "oppressive" landscapes. Besides, there is a stone marker announcing Toomsboro, a town whose name foreshadows the ending of "A Good Man Is Hard to Find," and a glimpse of a pig parlor of which Mrs. Turpin of "Revelation" might have been proud.

An essay worth quoting aloud is Alice Walker's sympathetic tribute, "Beyond the Peacock: The Reconstruction of Flannery O'Connor," *In Search of Our Mothers' Gardens* (New York: Harcourt, 1983). "She was for me," declares Walker, "the first great modern writer from the South," and she praises O'Connor for not trying to enter the minds of her black characters, not insisting on knowing everything, on being God. "After her great stories of sin, damnation, prophecy, and revelation, the stories one reads casually in the average magazine seem to be about love and roast beef."

O'Connor's *Collected Works* has been accorded the honor of appearing in the Library of America series. This volume, along with three works of O'Connor criticism, was reviewed by Frederick Crews in the April 26, 1990, issue of the *New York Review of Books*. Crews has interesting things to say about O'Connor's debt not only to New Criticism, but also to Edgar Allan Poe and Nathanael West. He offers insight as well into what he calls her "stern fanaticism" and her "twisted feelings about segregation."

GOOD COUNTRY PEOPLE, page 247

Critic Robert McPhillips has provided this commentary on O'Connor's "Good Country People."

Flannery O'Connor is a writer of paradox—a religious writer in a secular world, a Catholic novelist in the Protestant South. O'Connor saw herself writing in the tradition of the Southern grotesque, a tradition she insightfully connects to that of the American romance, as defined by Nathaniel Hawthorne, as opposed to tradition of the novel. The former can be loosely identified as allegorical, the latter realistic. O'Connor specifically uses the allegory of the romance tradition, casting her stories with grotesque characters (who for O'Connor—one of the paradoxes of her vision—are entirely real) to point toward a deeper level of truth which for her potentially resides in human salvation through Christ's grace. In "Good Country People," O'Connor presents an allegory of modern man's simultaneous yearning for salvation and his isolation from a state of grace.

"Good Country People" has four main characters that function in various ways as doubles of each other: Joy/Hulga; her mother, Mrs. Hopewell; their tenant farmer, Mrs. Freeman; and the Bible salesman, Manley Pointer. (Needless to say, much can be made of the allegorical significance of these names.) Mrs. Hopewell is a divorced woman managing her own farm who depends on tenant workers to keep it running smoothly. For this help, she depends on Mrs. Freeman, her husband, and her two daughters, Glynese and Carramae, "good country people," as Mrs. Hopewell platitudinously refers to them. Joy is her rather joyless thirty-two-year-old daughter with a Ph.D. in philosophy who has a chronic heart condition and lost her leg in a hunting accident at age ten. While away at college, Joy legally changed her name to Hulga, in a perverse effort to represent the hulking ugliness of her physical self. Joy/Hulga is the story's central grotesque, marked as such both by her unusual intellect, embodied by her Ph.D., and her physical deformity, symbolized by her artificial leg. Manley Pointer is the seemingly naive and devoutly Christian Bible salesman who arrives at the Hopewell farm and instigates the story's action.

The story is framed by the dialogue of one of the story's set of doubles, the two mothers whose discussions of farm business combined with gossip enclose the central, complex drama of seduction and betrayal played out between the pair of younger people. On the surface of these doublings, Mrs. Hopewell and Joy/Hulga would seem to represent sophistication, Mrs. Freeman and Manley Pointer simplicity, naivete, and innocence. Both of these dichotomies, however, are ironically overturned in the story. But they point to another level of doubling as well, between mother and daughter and mother and (symbolic) son, as Frederick Asals points out in *Flannery O'Connor: The Imagination of Extremity* (Athens, GA: U of Georgia P, 1982). On this level, the "good country people" are shown to be far shrewder than the Hopewells.

The plot of "Good Country People" derives from the material the Catholic O'Connor found in the Protestant Bible Belt of her South. One day, a young man, seemingly a devout Christian, arrives at the Hopewell farm selling Bibles. He points out to the would-be devout Mrs. Hopewell that she has "no family Bible in your parlor," a situation he would hope to change. (One of the points that

O'Connor makes in "The Catholic Novelist in the Protestant South" is that Catholics differ from Protestants in that they "are not accustomed to seeing religion Biblically"—i.e., they do not derive their sense of religion through reading the Bible but through the Church's teachings about it. By pointing out the absence of a family Bible—there is one hidden somewhere in the attic—O'Connor is perhaps allegorically aligning Mrs. Hopewell and Joy/Hulga with Catholics.)

Though Mrs. Hopewell has no intention of buying a Bible from this young man, he moves her when he reveals that he has a heart condition like her daughter's and impulsively invites him to stay to dinner. At the table, Joy/Hulga, a self-proclaimed nihilistic atheist, conceives of a plan to seduce the seemingly innocent young Bible salesman. She arranges to meet him the next day for a picnic to initiate her plan. Joy/Hulga neglects to bring food to their outing, but Manley Pointer does bring along his suitcase of Bibles. When the couple climbs into a hayloft where, from Hulga's perspective, her seduction may proceed, the Bible salesman reveals one of his Bibles to be hollow, containing a flask of whiskey, a box of condoms, and a deck of pornographic cards. Having convinced Hulga to teach him how to remove her prosthetic leg (which she "took care of as someone else would his soul"), Manley reveals himself to be something quite different from the "perfect Christian" that Hulga continues to protest he *must* be. Instead, he demonstrates himself to be the true nihilist who doesn't "believe in that crap!" and who has "been believing in nothing ever since I was born!" Indeed, he eventually reveals himself, as he abandons Hulga in the barn, her prosthesis in his suitcase, to be a sexual deviate with a perverse fetish for handicapped women (he has a glass eye among his stash). "Pointer ain't really my name," he adds as a final refutation to Hulga's naive trust.

The story ends with Mrs. Hopewell and Mrs. Freeman again in conversation, who see the Bible salesman in the distance. Mrs. Hopewell ironically assumes that "that nice dull young man that tried to sell me a Bible yesterday . . . must have been selling them to Negroes back in there." Mrs. Freeman, similar to Pointer in her lurid obsession with "secret infections, hidden deformities, assaults upon children," reveals her own superior intelligence when she observes to her interlocutor: "Some can't be that simple, . . . I know I never could."

"Good Country People" presents a complex web of the ironies that structure modern life. The title itself is ironic, of course. Neither Mrs. Freeman nor Manley Pointer are "good country people"—naive, exemplary Christians. The real naive is Mrs. Hopewell, whose chatty jargon represents her inability to correctly see the world. More crucially, so too is the facade of Joy/Hulga's atheism, her lack of "illusions," her ability "to see *through* to nothing." When the hypocritical Bible salesman asked her, in response to her revealing her atheism to him, "Then you ain't saved?" she replies that "In my economy . . . I'm saved and you are damned." Yet, during her comically deluded attempt to seduce Manley, Joy/Hulga also reveals another level of romantic illusion that she thought herself to have transcended:

> She decided that for the first time in her life she was face to face with real innocence. This boy, with an instinct that came from beyond wisdom, had

touched the truth about her. When after a minute, she said in a hoarse high voice, "All right," it was like surrendering to him completely. It was like losing her own life and finding it again, miraculously, in his.

In the surface narrative Hulga's surrender is sexual and emotional, but O'Connor's allegory points the reader to another level of religious meaning. Underneath her cynical atheism and nihilism, Joy/Hulga betrays a nostalgia for salvation, which neither the philosophical or scientific intellect, nor sexual or romantic love could provide: not her renaming of herself; not her Ph.D.; not her "surrendering" of herself to a false image of Christ. If, as a writer, Flannery O'Connor saw herself as limited in her material to the "real" world as she perceived it in the time and place in which she lived; as a *Catholic* writer, she felt the freedom, through the use of allegory (the defining genre of the Catholic Middle Ages) to see—in a way inaccessible to her characters—*through* the things of the world, which her God created, and perceive the possibility for redemption that only the openness to divine grace can provide.

A GOOD MAN IS HARD TO FIND, page 262

Without some attention to its Christian (specifically Catholic) assumptions, this story won't make much sense to students, who might mistake it for a tale of meaningless violence. Their seeing what O'Connor is driving at depends on their reading with great care the conversation about Jesus between the Misfit and the grandmother, and the account of the old woman's epiphany and death (paragraph 137).

Who is the central character? Clearly, the grandmother. This is her story from beginning to end, the story of her long overdue moral and spiritual growth. She causes things to happen; the Misfit merely reacts to her. She persuades the family to depart from the main road to see the old plantation. She causes the accident by letting the cat out of the basket. She dooms the family when she recognizes the Misfit. Her final gesture incites the Misfit to murder her.

O'Connor loves to pick unlikely, ordinary people and show how, by the sudden and unexpected operation of God's grace, they are granted the possibility of sanctity. In "A Good Man Is Hard to Find" the nitwit grandmother dies loving (and presumably forgiving) the Misfit. In the course of "A Good Man Is Hard to Find," the grandmother grows and changes. At first, she seems a small-minded biddy, selfish or at least self-centered, capable of stupid remarks like "Oh look at the cute little pickaninny!" (18) and "People are certainly not nice like they used to be" (36), capable of blaming Europe for "the way things were now" (45), of regretting that she hadn't married Mr. Teagarden "because he was a gentleman and had bought Coca-Cola stock when it first came out" (27).

In the end, when we are told that "her head cleared for an instant," the grandmother becomes newly perceptive. She reveals—and offers to the Misfit—her vast, compassionate heart. We have no reason to doubt the Misfit's shrewd remark, "She would have been a good woman . . . if it had been somebody there to shoot her every minute of her life." In slaying her, the Misfit has done her a tremendous favor: he has made a martyr of her. For one moment just before she dies, the old lady doubts Jesus, or at least feels forsaken: "Maybe he didn't raise the dead" (134). It is an understandable reaction, after the colossal shock she has undergone: she knows that her family has been massacred. But this moment of confusion passes. In O'Connor's Catholic worldview, the grandmother is headed straight to heaven for her final Christ-like act of love the moment before she dies. She realizes that there is a chance that the Misfit will repent, and she reaches out to him lovingly, as though he were a child. By this time, she already knows that the Misfit's gang has murdered her son and daughter-in-law and all the children. The Misfit may be a ruthless murderer, but that doesn't prevent her from loving him and hoping for his redemption. Symbolically, in death the old woman's body lies with legs in the form of a cross, a look of childlike sweetness on her face. The Misfit, naturally, is glum, having just declined a chance for his own salvation.

The scene at Red Sammy's Barbecue is no mere filler. It tightens the suspense and enforces the hint that the much talked-about Misfit is bound to show his face. In his highway signs, Red Sammy boasts of his uniqueness: NONE LIKE FAMOUS RED SAMMY'S. He considers himself a hard-to-find good man. In calling him a good man (36), the grandmother first introduces the theme. The barbecue proprietor agrees with her, even declares, thinking of how many bad characters are on the loose these days, "A good man is hard to find" (44). In the end, the title leaves us thinking: yes, a good man (a saint) certainly is hard to find. We find, at the end, a serenely good woman whose salvation has been achieved only through traumatic suffering and the amazing arrival of grace.

An insightful and outspoken student might wonder about the appropriateness of imposing Catholic terms of redemption on all these Southern Protestants. (That the eight-year-old is named John Wesley suggests that the family is at least nominally Methodist.) The story may draw other objections as well. O'Connor's use of familiar racist epithets will outrage some African-American students unless they see that O'Connor is only reporting faithfully how the characters think and talk, not condoning it or thinking that way herself.

For O'Connor's own reading of this famous story, see her critical comments following the stories in this chapter. Her interpretation will certainly startle many students reading the story for the first time. If you choose to consider O'Connor's comments in class, it may be worth asking how authoritative a writer's interpretation of her own work is. Are there limitations or inherent biases in a writer's self-assessments? According to the intentional fallacy, we cannot uncritically accept an author's statement of intended meaning, since the author is unable to see his or her own work objectively. An author necessarily sees the finished work through the veil of the original intent, with the possibility of projecting onto the text meanings that were intended but that have not been realized and therefore are not communicated to any other reader through the text itself. Still, knowing an author's conscious intentions may help point a reader in the right direction—at least in general terms.

In an incisive essay on Flannery O'Connor, Clara Claiborne Park points out that while O'Connor may have objected to readers' attempts to reduce her stories to literal meanings or themes, she herself tended to do so in her own commentaries on the stories. Despite their excellence, the stories, when so reduced, may be faulted as oversimplified fables of Christian salvation through suffering. "A Good Man Is Hard to Find" seems vulnerable to this charge. Park observes: "As incursions of grace through arson and through murder and through sudden stroke become familiar to the point of predictability, all moral ambiguity evaporates, leaving the stories that puzzled us all too clear" (*Rejoining the Common Reader*, Chicago: Northwestern UP, 1991). A question for class discussion is: can O'Connor be defended against this charge? (Perhaps she intends no ambiguity.) Evidence of the story's depth and complexity can be found in a volume containing critical essays by various hands, *A Good Man Is Hard to Find*, edited by Frederick Asals (in a series, "Women Writers: Texts and Contexts," New Brunswick: Rutgers UP, 1993).

FLANNERY O'CONNOR ON FLANNERY O'CONNOR

THE ELEMENT OF SUSPENSE IN "A GOOD MAN IS HARD TO FIND," page 274

O'Connor's comments came from a reading she gave in 1963 (the remarks were reprinted in her posthumous critical collection, *Mystery and Manners* [New York: Farrar, 1969] 107–14).

Southern students, she had learned, tended to recognize the grandmother as exactly like one of their own relatives, "and they knew, from personal experience, that the old lady lacked comprehension, but that she had a good heart." When her head clears for an instant, the grandmother:

> realizes, even in her limited way, that she is responsible for the man before her and joined to him by ties of kinship which have their roots deep in the mystery she has merely been prattling about so far. At this point, she does the right thing, she makes the right gesture. I find that students are often puzzled by what she says and does here, but I think myself that if I took out this gesture and what she says with it, I would have no story.

It is important to note O'Connor's warning against equating the Misfit with the devil. Instead, in her view, this murderous criminal is a potential saint gone terribly wrong. She even claims that the grandmother's gesture, "like the mustard seed, will grow to be a great crow-filled tree in the Misfit's heart" and redeem him. Can we accept O'Connor's statement that "in this story you should be on the lookout for such things as the action of grace in the grandmother's soul, and not for the dead bodies"?

Frederick Asals points out in a fruitful critical reading that it remains hard to ignore all those dead bodies. In Asals's view no other O'Connor story sets up such extreme tension between matters sacred and profane, between comedy and violence. See *Flannery O'Connor: The Imagination of Extremity* (Athens: U of Georgia P, 1982), 142–54.

ON HER CATHOLIC FAITH, page 277

O'Connor's brief statement on her faith is extraordinarily revealing. To say that her self-description avoids conventional Catholic pieties is an understatement. The Church itself, she maintains, is part of the burden a Catholic bears only because one believes in the divinity of Christ. The key statement is her explanation why her violent and grim stories are never bitter: "You have to cherish the world at the same time you struggle to endure it."

THE SERIOUS WRITER AND THE TIRED READER, page 277

O'Connor's remarks about "the serious writer" and "the tired reader" constitute a brilliant defense of real literary artistry in an age that mostly demands light entertainment. Now decades later—in the literary era of Oprah Winfrey—O'Connor's tough-minded and commonsensical stance seems more relevant than ever. She insists that storytellers aim for their art to be a "redemptive act." Art seeks to transform its audience not merely to entertain it. Such art, O'Connor states, does not come without cost. The cost to the writer is the requirement "to operate at the maximum of his intelligence and his talents." The cost to the tired reader is to wake up and pay attention. There was nothing middlebrow about O'Connor's aesthetic. She aimed high and expected her readers to do the same.

QUESTIONS

1. What is Flannery O'Connor's opinion of book clubs? Explain her remark on this subject in the second paragraph.

2. Does O'Connor condemn people who want fiction to leave them "lifted up"? What is her attitude toward them?

3. By what means can writers write the great novels of the future?

CRITICS ON FLANNERY O'CONNOR, pages 278–287

We have presented a selection of critical perspectives on O'Connor to supplement the three statements she made on her own work. (She was a formidably lucid explicator of her own methods.) The four articles excerpted on her work by literary critics provide different perspectives. **Robert Brinkmeyer Jr.** offers a reader-response analysis of O'Connor's complex relation to her readers. **J. O. Tate** provides a historical analysis of the factual sources of O'Connor's memorable character, the Misfit, in "A Good Man Is Hard to Find." (We even reproduce the original newspaper article O'Connor saw in 1952 that inspired the story.) **Mary Jane Schenck** deconstructs the same story. Finally, **Kathleen Feeley** provides a formalist analysis of irony and paradoxical perversity in "Good Country People."

RAYMOND CARVER

In searching for a second fiction writer to represent in depth, we chose Raymond Carver, whose stark and reticent stories provide a strong contrast to those of Flannery O'Connor. The contemporary settings of his stories should provide no obstacle to students, who can focus on understanding his quietly complex characters and direct but resonant narratives.

Shortly after Carver's death, Jay McInerney, who had been his student in fiction writing at Syracuse University in the early 1980s, published a warmly affectionate memoir, "Raymond Carver: A Still, Small Voice," in the *New York Times Book Review* (August 6, 1989). McInerney recalls Carver as a man given to quiet understatement, so shy and soft-spoken that an interviewer once had to put the tape recorder in the author's lap and still found his responses almost inaudible. His harshest criticism to a writing student was, "I think it's good you got that story behind you." That mild rebuke reveals the humanity found everywhere in Carver's work. Often sad and even tragic, he remains the gentlest and most generous of contemporary writers.

CATHEDRAL, page 289

In the relatively brief time since its first appearance in the *Atlantic Monthly* in 1981, Raymond Carver's "Cathedral" has become an acknowledged classic of American fiction. Widely anthologized, frequently analyzed, and almost universally admired, the short story perfectly blends the compressed and understated qualities of Minimalism with the lyrical emotionalism of realists like Sherwood Anderson. It also portrays in a credible way a positive transformation of character. Initially a man of petty prejudice and small worldview, the narrator grows in humanity and understanding as the story develops. Few contemporary stories have such a cogently uplifting effect.

According to Raymond Carver, "None of my stories really happened, of course. But there's always something, some element, something someone said to me or that I witnessed, that may be the starting place." In her introduction to *Carver Country*, Carver's widow, the poet Tess Gallagher, makes clear that a great many of the details of "Cathedral" were rooted in an actual experience. In his essay "The Origin of 'Cathedral,'" editor Tom Jenks relates how Carver and Gallagher made similar statements to him about the story's basis in reality. Carver was uneasy when a blind man Gallagher knew came for a visit and became jealous of the man's relationship with her. As interesting as these facts may be, in the end, of course, they matter less than their reworking into an independent artistic pattern, an entertaining narrative that also communicates movingly about attitudes and relationships.

On the surface, "Cathedral" is a simple story told flatly by a narrator of limited awareness, both of himself and of others. His misgivings about the visit, rooted in his lack of experience with the blind, are clearly spelled out in paragraphs 1, 5, 9, and 17; the fact that his perceptions are veiled by unexamined assumptions is shown further in paragraphs 31 and 44. His blundering attempts at small talk lead to increased discomfort (25), and it seems to be a combination of thoughtlessness and the wish to cover over the awkward situation that impels him finally to turn on the television set.

Throughout, his wife demonstrates a much more relaxed attitude, seeing Robert not as an abstraction or the representative of an alien group, but as an individual, a valued friend and former colleague—so much so, in fact, that in some ways she seems to have an easier and more intimate rapport with him than she does with her own husband. The narrator initially reacts with jealousy and resentment at his seeming exclusion from this closeness; but as the story proceeds, he slowly achieves an emotional breakthrough.

Students have phrased the story's theme in different ways: "Barriers tend to break down when people try to communicate with one another," or "Even those not physically blind sometimes need to be taught to see," or "Stereotypes render sighted people blind to the common humanity we all share." Obviously, the story itself is much more effective and affecting than any possible statements of its theme.

For a writing topic, a student might be asked to read D. H. Lawrence's "The Blind Man" (in *Complete Short Stories,* Volume II [Penguin Books]) and compare the characters of the blind man and the sighted man with the similar pair in "Cathedral."

Tami Haaland of Montana State University has provided a critical analysis of "Cathedral" for inclusion in this manual:

> The unnamed narrator of "Cathedral" is a man confined—intellectually and emotionally. He thinks he knows things, but he is intentionally labeling and limiting. His first words, "the blind man," show this tendency, and his subsequent comments indicate his desire not to move beyond his most superficial impressions or his tendency to stereotype ("I wasn't enthusiastic about his visit. He was no one I knew. And his being blind bothered me").

"Cathedral" presents a succession of psychological and spiritual openings brought about because the narrator is repeatedly thrown out of his comfort zone. He can either accept new information (understanding that blind men have beards, for instance) or find a way to block the information. The culmination comes in the final scene, where he "didn't feel like [he] was inside anything." Perhaps Carver recalled the story of Tiresias and Oedipus: the blind man observes more than the seeing man, and when the seeing man becomes symbolically blind at the end of the story, his world opens up.

The narrator in "Cathedral" is intent on stopping up his senses. He doesn't want to know any more than he has to, so it seems appropriate that he watches television, drinks, eats, and smokes pot through much of the story. The blind man, Robert, joins him, but for the narrator this binge seems to be a daily pattern. The emphasis on drinking, eating, and smoking early in the story (drinking is one of their "pastimes") alleviates some of the tension between husband and wife as well as the narrator's discomfort in having "the blind man" in his home. During the meal, the narrator begins to refer to Robert by his name instead of "the blind man." This marks the beginning of a change in the narrator.

Initially, the narrator seems surprised that other people have experiences and perceptions that are different from his. He even remarks on word choice that he finds unusual: "my wife's word, inseparable." It is also "beyond [his] understanding" that Robert was never able to see his wife and that the wife could never be seen by her husband. This remark implicitly invites comparison to the narrator and his wife. How much does he really see of her? Does he understand her at all? Does he try? Only a few lines later he sees her pull into the driveway with Robert: "She was still wearing a smile. Just amazing." Apparently he sees something in her that he didn't expect. When she looks at him a moment later, he says, "I had the feeling she didn't like what she saw."

It would be interesting to trace imagery and language associated with sight through this story. The wife is uptight too, like her husband, but her primary concern is that her husband will misbehave. This fear becomes evident very early after the three of them are together in the living room. The narrator asks which side of the train Robert sat on, and she reacts by saying, "What a question." Robert shows himself to be more open than either husband or wife.

In the last scene, Robert takes on a kind of fatherly role, encouraging the narrator to explain and eventually draw the cathedral. A key statement here comes after the narrator attempts to describe and explain: "I guess I don't believe in it. In anything. Sometimes it's hard." This admission seems to be the psychological or spiritual reason for the narrator's limitations. He has no faith, not even in himself. A few lines later he says, "But I can't tell you what a cathedral looks like. It just isn't in me to do it. I can't do anymore than I've done." He then confesses that, "My legs felt like they didn't have any strength in them." He is exhausted, empty, and his preconceptions no longer seem to be in the way. He also believes that he is incapable of continuing the conversation on cathedrals.

Apparently Robert sees his potential and encourages the narrator to start drawing. It's as if he is coaxing a child through a difficult project. The cathedral could be seen as a symbol of faith both in its function as a place of worship and also in the way that it was built by successive generations, many of whom would never see the finished structure. The narrator doesn't see his finished structure either, though he knows that it as well as his sense of not being contained was "really something." It is as if the narrator has developed a new sensibility, an emotional and intellectual openness that he didn't have before.

In my experience, students often don't get the ending. They react much like the wife who steps into the scene and finds it bizarre that these two men sit side by side, their hands linked, drawing a cathedral on a paper bag.

A SMALL, GOOD THING, page 299

Though people sometimes act badly, most people are basically good. This simple assumption seems to inform "A Small, Good Thing," in which Carver shows how people can suffer from isolation. When on rare occasions they reach out to one another, sharing their concerns and perceptions, their lives are enriched. Carver hints at much the same thing in "Cathedral."

Carver tells his story in the third person; because the point of view alternates between the mother's and the father's, readers cannot help sharing in the parents' suffering. The flat, numb tone seems to intensify the reader's sense of Howard and Ann's pain. The hospital setting further dramatizes the family's ordeal by cutting them off, as hospitals do, from the rest of the world. When they leave that world, they are subjected to the cruelty of the baker's anonymous phone calls. Thus, except for the mother's brief exchange in the hospital with a family similarly afflicted, the Weisses are completely isolated in their pain. The doctors are false prophets, holding out hope when there is no hope at all.

When Ann finally figures out, in paragraph 160, that it is the baker who has been harassing them with the terrifying phone calls, she and Howard set out to vent their anger upon him. Ironically, in the warmth and fragrance that surround them in the baker's shop, they find solace. The baker is not a menacing madman but a fellow sufferer, alone in the world. Their isolation ends as the baker's does, through the comforting discovery of their common humanity, symbolized by the cinnamon buns, the "small, good thing" the baker offers them along with his explanation for the way he has behaved.

What have students experienced that confirms Carver's observations about people—how they react to suffering and loss, how they seek mutual comfort? Such a class discussion of this story might become too painfully personal, but perhaps the topic might be approached like this: "Has anything like this ever happened to anyone you know?"

Tami Haaland of Montana State University at Billings has observed that:

> Carver uses a great deal of situational irony here, deliberately contradicting the reader's expectation. Scotty is injured on his birthday. The narrator refers to him as "the birthday boy" just before he steps off the curb and is seriously injured. But even as we think he might be dying, he gets up and walks home. When we're beginning to expect that he might be okay, he becomes unconscious and limp. The doctor's repeated assurances that Scotty is fine turn out to be completely inaccurate. When Scotty does emerge from his coma, it is only to scream and die.
>
> Ann recognizes the irony in her own responses after Scotty dies. "She . . . thought how unfair it was that the only words that came out were the sort of words used on TV shows where people were stunned by violent or sudden deaths. She wanted her words to be her own."

RAYMOND CARVER ON RAYMOND CARVER

COMMONPLACE BUT PRECISE LANGUAGE, page 317

This excerpt from Carver's "On Writing" is both an explicit announcement of his literary aims and an implicit defense for his minimalist aesthetic, which at the time of writing was being hotly debated by critics. Carver insists that the imaginative endeavor "to write about commonplace things and objects using commonplace but precise language" is not a retreat from fiction's greater ambitions since the author still tries to evoke "immense, even startling power." Notice the names that Carver invokes—Vladimir Nabokov, Isaac Babel, Guy de Maupassant, Henry James, and Evan Connell (the last is the author of two classic contemporary American novels, *Mrs. Bridge* and *Mr. Bridge*). Carver places his own imaginative enterprise in the great tradition of Realist fiction (all his names but Nabokov are major Realists). Finally, Carver asserts that the sort of writing he practices is hard to do well—a statement subsequently proved by his many less talented and scrupulous imitators.

QUESTIONS

1. What does Raymond Carver's statement tell us about the qualities he prizes in literature? About his personal writing habits?

2. Consider "Cathedral." How does it show that this writer practices what he advocates?

MY BIASES IN FICTION, page 318

These two paragraphs provide perhaps the clearest statement Carver made about his aesthetic for fiction. "I lean toward realistic 'lifelike' characters—that is to say, people—in realistically detailed situations," he asserts, admitting that his methods are "traditional" and even "old-fashioned." He also stresses his own need for exact and concrete language versus "the abstract or arbitrary or slippery word."

HONESTY IN WRITING, page 319

Some of Carver's most interesting remarks on the craft of fiction are found in interviews. In this excerpt Carver discusses the need for honesty in writing and looks at "A Small, Good Thing" in this regard. Note how Carver insists that a writer must have a genuine emotional connection to his fictional subject. Otherwise "the reader feels my non-involvement on the very first page of the story."

CRITICS ON RAYMOND CARVER, pages 319–323

The critical excerpts on Carver's work also offer a variety of perspectives. The first two excerpts by **Tess Gallagher** (Carver's widow) and **Tom Jenks** (his editor) discuss the autobiographical sources of "Cathedral." The blind man in the story was based on an actual person, Jerry Carriveau (whose photo appears in the book next to Gallagher's memoir). As Jenks reveals, even the TV show on cathedrals was real. Students who read these two short memoirs will gain insight into the odd ways that life transmutes into art. **Paul Skenazy's** discussion on Carver's minimalism takes a broad cultural perspective viewing the author in the context of literary and social trends. Finally, **Arthur Saltzman** examines the social identity of Carver's characters—the beleaguered product of "proletarian America."

OTHER RESOURCES

Carver talks with frankness and humor about his work in an interview available on a fifty-one minute audiotape cassette from the American Audio Prose Library (AAPL). Among other things, he says he chose to write short stories because he found he lacked time to write novels when, at age nineteen, he found himself a father. You may order by phone: (800) 447-2275. AAPL's whole catalog is worth a look.

9 Stories for Further Reading

Chinua Achebe

DEAD MEN'S PATH, page 325

Chinua Achebe is the senior eminence of English-language African fiction. His first novel, *Things Fall Apart* (1958), almost immediately achieved classic status, and his subsequent books have only reinforced his reputation. Achebe's literary sensibility is rooted in British Realist fiction, and he stands unapologetically in the tradition of George Eliot, Joseph Conrad, E. M. Forster, and even—despite the evident differences of themes and settings—Jane Austen. Part of the pleasure of reading Achebe surely comes from his penetrating social intelligence and capacity for realistic psychological portrayal. He is also masterfully concise. (His short novels brilliantly depict broad canvases just as this very short story tells a great deal about Nigerian society.) Achebe's great innovation is to bring these Austen-like qualities to the complex and turbulent world of post-colonial West Africa. His forms feel familiar but his content is strikingly new and historically significant. Achebe directly addresses social and political issues in his work, but he never puts his fiction in the service of a particular ideology.

"Dead Men's Path" enacts in miniature one of the central themes of Achebe's novels—the clash between modern European ideas and traditional African values, progressive international standards and deeply rooted local custom. The story's protagonist, Michael Obi, is a well-educated forward-thinking idealist with a passion for "modern methods." Quite intelligent and undoubtedly dedicated to education, Obi is more comfortable in abstract thought than in facing the complexities of real life. He doesn't notice unspoken feelings; for example, his wife's considerable disappointment upon learning that the other teachers are all unmarried. His view of the world is rational and therefore incapable of fully understanding the parts of life ruled by emotion, intuition, or custom. Obi looks down on the older headmasters of the Mission schools. Note how Achebe subtly undercuts Obi in the opening paragraphs. Only twenty-six, the newly appointed headmaster appears much older with his "stoop-shouldered" posture and "frail" build.

Achebe's story was first published in 1953 just as the newly independent nations of Africa were making their first strides towards modernization. Michael Obi represents the new African, the progressive who hopes to rebuild his society. The tragic histories of most post-Colonial African nations in the latter half of the twentieth century reveals how prescient Achebe's diagnosis of modernization was. No standardized international idea of progress could be imposed on traditional African societies without terrible cost and probably failure.

Names are often significant in Achebe's fiction. Michael Obi's name demonstrates his divided heritage. Michael is a Christian baptismal name of European heritage. (Remember Obi works for "Mission" schools—as did Achebe's father, who was a devout Christian.) Obi, by contrast, is an African name. His name itself embodies the cultural conflict he is about to enter.

Having introduced his protagonist and set up the narrative premise, Achebe focuses his story on a single incident—Obi's attempt to close the footpath that the locals believe is used by dead and unborn souls to enter the village. Obi uses rational, progressive arguments in discussing the matter with the village priest (who ironically seems both more rational and open-minded than the ideological headmaster). "What you say may be true," admits the priest, adding "but we follow the practices of our fathers." The results of Obi's idealistic obstinacy ultimately prove disastrous for both the school and his own career.

An interview with Chinua Achebe covering a variety of topics, including Achebe's view on what is uniquely African about his role as artist in the community, is available on audiocassette tape from American Audio Prose Library at (800) 447-2275.

Margaret Atwood
HAPPY ENDINGS, page 328

Margaret Atwood's "Happy Endings" is a representative as well as an unusually engaging example of post-modern metafiction. Like much metafiction, it makes no attempt to make the reader believe in the verisimilitude of the narrative but instead overtly and exuberantly explores the nature of narrative structure. The author sets up the simple situation in one short line, "John and Mary meet." Then she asks the obvious narrative question, "What happens next?"

The bulk of the story consists of six mutually exclusive or minimally overlapping "endings" to the story. Despite the story's title, most of the endings are *not* "happy." Only the first alternative is unconditionally blissful. The second involves suicide, the third includes a triple murder, the fourth presents a tidal wave that kills thousands, the fifth depicts mortal illness. By now even the dimmest reader will begin to suspect that the piece's title was ironic.

Atwood is making several points through her multiple endings. First is that there is something unconvincing and inauthentic about most narrative endings. Second, all human endings are ultimately the same—we all die. Mortality is the central fact of human existence. Finally, Atwood suggests that "Beginnings are always more fun," possibilities are more pleasant than actualities. A sure sign of Atwood's literary talent is her ability to communicate these often disturbing, slightly abstract themes in such an accessibly comic way. Her humor may be dark, but it is genuine. Grim as the narrative often progresses in parts, "Happy Endings" nonetheless has fun with the conventions of storytelling in a way most readers can appreciate.

Ambrose Bierce

AN OCCURRENCE AT OWL CREEK BRIDGE, page 332

"Bitter Bierce" was what his contemporaries called him, and as both man and writer he earned the title. In life, he seems to have quarreled with and become estranged from everyone he ever met, including his wife and sons. In literature, he is still best known for *The Devil's Dictionary*, among whose acid definitions are: "History: an account mostly false, of events unimportant, which are brought about by rulers mostly knaves, and soldiers mostly fools" and "Marriage: the state or condition of a community consisting of a master, a mistress, and two slaves, making, in all, two."

But "An Occurrence at Owl Creek Bridge" remains Bierce's most popular piece of writing. One reason for its enduring popularity is, of course, the surprise ending. Yet this story affects the reader on a deeper level than those of some of Bierce's clever contemporaries, such as Frank L. Stockton's "The Lady or the Tiger?" One reason for the story's greater expressive power is certainly Bierce's superior artistry. And another must surely be his evocation of life through the heightened senses of a man about to die, in all of its splendor and its "blessings." Here as elsewhere in his work, life turns out to be a cruel cheat in the end, but here much more than elsewhere, he makes clear, in vivid and sensuous detail, why we cling to it so desperately.

QUESTIONS FOR DISCUSSION

1. *What has brought Peyton Farquhar to the brink of hanging?* Incited by the Federal Scout, he has apparently tried to burn down Owl Creek Bridge, which is in the hands of the Union Army.

2. *One student, after reading Bierce's story, objected to it on the grounds that the actions of the Federal Scout (paragraphs 9–17) are not believable. "Since when do military men dress up like the enemy and incite civilians to sabotage?" was her question. How would you answer it?* One possible answer might be that Farquhar, "a slave owner and like other slave owners a politician," has managed in his own way to engineer damage to the enemy and so has become a marked man. A believer in "at least a part of the frankly villainous dictum that all is fair in love and war" (8), Farquhar is lured into a fatal trap by someone in the enemy camp who assents to the same view.

3. *Are you surprised by the story's conclusion? Can you find hints along the way that Farquhar's escape is an illusion? At what point in the story does the illusion begin?* Bierce lays in enough hints to make most readers accept the surprise ending, though they may want to reread the story just to make sure. In paragraph 5, though Farquhar makes a conscious effort to think about his wife and children, he has already begun to experience an alteration in his sense of time. Recall the old general belief that at the moment of death we see our whole lives pass by again in a flash. As soon as an escape plot forms in Farquhar's mind

(6), the sergeant moves off the plank and the noose tightens around the doomed man's neck. Since we know from the ending that the rope does not break, what happens to Farquhar after the flashback (8–17)—except for the physical sensations of hanging—has to be a fast-moving hallucination in the mind of a dying man.

Bierce has planted clues that this is so. With "superhuman" effort Farquhar manages to free his bound hands. His senses are "preternaturally keen and alert" (20). His ability to dodge all the bullets fired at him seems miraculous. The forest through which he walks is unfamiliar and menacing; the stars above him are "grouped in strange constellations"; he hears "whispers in an unknown tongue" (34). Soon "he could no longer feel the roadway beneath his feet" (35). His wife greets him with "a smile of ineffable joy" (36)—then he is dead.

4. *From what point of view is "An Occurrence at Owl Creek Bridge" told?* In the third person by a nonparticipating narrator able to see into Farquhar's mind.

5. *At several places in the story Bierce calls attention to Farquhar's heightened sensibility. How would you explain those almost mystical responses to ordinary stimuli?* They are the out-of-body sensations of a dying man. Much has been written about such experiences in the popular press. For some interesting, serious comments on the subject see Elisabeth Kübler-Ross, *On Death and Dying* (New York: Macmillan, 1969). Dr. Ross quotes the testimony of persons who, after being declared clinically dead, were resuscitated. Some reported finding themselves floating in space, gazing down upon their own bodies.

6. *Where in Bierce's story do you find examples of irony?* There is irony in the contrast between the understated title and the extravagant style of the narrator. Ironic, too, is the mention of Farquhar's belief that "all's fair in love and war"—a belief shared by the Federal Scout who lures Farquhar to his capture and death. Verbal irony occurs in "Death is a dignitary who when he comes announced is to be received with formal manifestations of respect, even by those most familiar with him" (paragraph 2), and "The liberal military code makes provision for hanging many kinds of persons, and gentlemen are not excluded" (3). Students may find other examples as well.

7. *Do you think the story would have been better had Bierce told it in chronological order? Why or why not?* In defense of the way the story is told, we'd argue mainly that Bierce's use of flashback heightens the suspense created by the opening scene on the bridge.

A topic for writing: Compare this story with Borges's "The Gospel According to Mark." Both stories deal with men on the brink of death and their inner experiences.

A half hour video adaptation of "An Occurrence at Owl Creek Bridge," made in 1962, is available on video cassette from Teacher's Video Company at (800) 262-8837.

Jorge Luis Borges
THE GOSPEL ACCORDING TO MARK, page 339

Jorge Luis Borges, who considered himself primarily a poet, is almost certainly the most influential short story writer of the last half century. His mix of fantasy and realism was the catalyst to the Latin American literary "boom" of magical realism. His use of nonfiction forms—like the essay, book review, or scholarly article—as vehicles for the short story not only inspired experimental writers of metafiction; it also helped challenge, among literary theorists, the traditional distinctions between fiction and factual writing. Writers as diverse as John Barth, Italo Calvino, Gabriel García Márquez, John Updike, Thomas Disch, Donald Barthelme, J. G. Ballard, Michel Foucault, and Angela Carter all reflect Borges's influence.

Many Borges stories—including "The Gospel According to Mark"—operate simultaneously on two levels. The surface of the story usually offers a conventional narrative, often with a surprise ending. Borges's masters in fiction were traditional storytellers like Robert Louis Stevenson, Rudyard Kipling, and G. K. Chesterton. (He was also particularly fond of mystery and supernatural tales.) Borges frequently employed old-fashioned narrative devices borrowed from their work, but he was equally fascinated by the literature of mysticism and the occult, not only the Christian and Jewish traditions but also the Islamic and Chinese. From these mystics and metaphysicians, he developed an obsession for speculating on secret patterns in reality. For Borges, the search for hidden significance was not a literary game; it was an essential undertaking, part of humanity's attempt to uncover God's plan, and the temporal world's means of understanding eternity. Not surprisingly, one of Borges's favorite modern writers was Kafka.

Borges's fascination with hidden significance leads to a consciously constructed second level of meaning in many of his stories in which surface details can be discovered to have secret implications. The amazing thing about Borges's stories is the sheer density of meaning the careful reader will find embedded in the text. One need not catch or understand all these hidden clues to appreciate his stories, but discovering them does enrich one's experience. They are not trivial details, but the individual threads to a complex pattern of expression.

"The Gospel According to Mark" is an example of how tightly interwoven Borges's symbolic subtext can be. In this story, his main technique is irony, the traditional way of saying one thing while meaning another. Virtually everything that happens in the story has an ironic significance. The questions addressed below elucidate some, but by no means all, of the ironic underpinnings of this haunting story.

QUESTIONS FOR DISCUSSION

1. *What is about to happen to Baltasar Espinosa at the end of this story?* If students don't understand Borges's surprise ending—the point, that is, where the overt and ironic narratives meet—they will not be able to figure anything else out. Most students will catch the ending at once—Baltasar Espinosa is about to be crucified

by the Gutre family. However, it may be worth asking this basic question to make sure no one misses it.

2. *How old is Espinosa? What is ironic about his age?* Espinosa is thirty-three, the age at which Jesus is traditionally thought to have been crucified.

3. *What is the background of the Gutre family? How did they come to own an English Bible? Why is it ironic that they own this book?* Like America, Argentina is a country populated largely by immigrants. (Borges himself was a mixture of English, Italian, Jewish, Uruguayan, and Argentinean stock.) The Gutre family are the descendants of Scottish immigrants, but they have lived on the Argentinean pampas so long that they have forgotten not only their English but even their ancestry. Their name is a corruption of the name *Guthrie*. Significantly, Borges links their Scottish ancestry to Calvinism, with its belief in absolute predestination. (In retrospect, Espinosa's sacrificial death seems fated.) The irony of their owning an English Bible is multiple: they cannot read; they know no English; they are seemingly ignorant of Christianity; they have forgotten their Scottish roots. However, there is, of course, a deeper irony. Although they have forgotten everything else, the Gutres have unconsciously maintained a Calvinistic sensibility that leads them to interpret the Gospel with absolute literalism.

4. *The narrator claims that the protagonist, Espinosa, has only two noteworthy qualities: an almost unlimited kindness and a capacity for public speaking. How do these qualities become important in the story?* Espinosa's two qualities seal his fate. His gift for public speaking makes his renditions of the Gospel particularly effective to the illiterate Gutre family. He even rises to his feet when reading the parables. His unlimited kindness makes Espinosa a perfect Christ figure—the gentle man who sacrifices himself to redeem others. (One can find significance to virtually all of Espinosa's other attributes, as listed in the first paragraph.)

5. *When Espinosa begins reading the Gospel of Saint Mark to the Gutres, what changes in their behavior does he notice?* Once Espinosa begins reading the Gospel, he suddenly makes an intense connection with the Gutre family. Until then conversation had proved difficult. They treat him with ever-greater respect and follow his orders. He catches them talking about him respectfully, but he does not understand the significance of their change in behavior until too late.

6. *What other action does Espinosa perform that earns the Gutres' gratitude?* Espinosa helps treat the Gutre girl's injured pet lamb. (Borges's choice of that symbolic animal is surely not coincidental.) The family seem to consider his intercession miraculous, although Espinosa does not understand their reaction. There is a consistently ironic gap between what he notices in their behavior and what their actions really signify. It is a good exercise to have students list as many ironic episodes or situations as possible.

7. *Reread the last paragraph. Why is it ironic that the Gutres ask Espinosa's blessing and the daughter weeps?* The irony is that the three people asking his bless-

ing are about to murder him. The weeping girl is both one of his assassins and a Mary (or, perhaps more appropriately, a Mary Magdalene) figure crying at the crucifixion.

8. *Why do the Gutres kill Espinosa? What do they hope to gain?* The Gutres kill Espinosa to achieve salvation. The father questions Espinosa quite explicitly on that point the morning before his execution. For obvious reasons, old Gutre is particularly anxious to know if the soldiers who executed Christ were also saved.

9. *Is the significance of Espinosa's death entirely ironic? Or does he resemble Christ in any important respect?* The central question in interpreting Borges's story is whether it merely depicts a grotesquely ironic misunderstanding or rather suggests a deeper religious vision. Whatever one's conclusions, it is certain that Borges had a lifelong fascination with the idea of Christ and redemption. Some of his best stories, like "Three Versions of Judas" and "The Circular Ruins," explicitly concern the Incarnation. Borges never used the Christian mythos carelessly. A narrowly ironic reading of "The Gospel According to Mark" is easy to make. It is an ironic horror story in which the protagonist unwittingly creates the conditions for his own ritual murder. Read this way, the story is quite satisfactory—like a superior episode of "The Twilight Zone." The story, however, also allows a deeper, though still ironic religious reading. Here, too, Espinosa is an unwitting Christ-figure, but one understands him not to represent real Christianity, but a shallow parody of it. He is a Christ without divinity, a figure whose teaching lacks moral weight and whose death will save no one. When quizzed by the Gutre father about particular points in the Gospel, Espinosa asserts things he does not believe in order to save face. His theology is "rather dim," and so he answers other questions without examining their logical or theological consistency. In his bewildered way, Espinosa enjoys the authority of his divine position, but he neither understands nor deserves it. He is a well-meaning sham, quite unable to comprehend that the Gutres (whom he unmaliciously, but also un-Christianly, considers beneath him) might take matters of salvation seriously. He is a dilettante unsuitably cast in the role of a deity. Although he seems to accept his death meekly (we do not know for sure what follows his realization), he has only the outward features of a redeemer. His dabbling in the divine has not only destroyed him, but morally corrupted his followers. Espinosa may be a Christ-figure, but he is no Christ.

Students wishing to do a paper on Borges might profitably compare "The Gospel According to Mark" with Borges's ingenious tale, "Three Versions of Judas." For more sophisticated students, a comparison between "The Gospel According to Mark" and Flannery O'Connor's "A Good Man Is Hard to Find" could be an absorbing project. Both stories end in senseless murders, and both depict complex and heretical reaction to the Gospels. A 75 minute video interview with Borges, *Profile of a Writer*, is available on video cassette from Teacher's Video Company at (800) 262-8837.

Willa Cather
PAUL'S CASE, page 343

"Paul's Case" may put you in mind of several other intractable "cases" in modern American fiction, for example, the title character of Nathanael West's *Miss Lonelyhearts* or Tommy Wilhelm in Saul Bellow's *Seize the Day*. Both protagonists move us by their zeal to live meaningfully in a world of callousness and easy accommodations, and both appall us with their idiotic choices and almost willed self-destructiveness. If you have ever tried teaching either of these short novels, you will have realized the difficulty of leading students to understand the complexities of the characters and the themes, especially when most of their questions begin with "Why doesn't he just . . . ?"

Such youthful frustration is surely appropriate. There would be something freakish about young people embracing middle-aged defeat and disillusion. But with an adolescent protagonist such as Paul, a teacher might assume a greater degree of understanding and sympathy in students' responses, and perhaps be surprised at their rejection or even hostility toward Paul. Perhaps it isn't too surprising: imagine for a moment how students would react to him if he were one of their classmates. And remember that it is much easier to sympathize with Paul as a fictional character than it would be to deal with him as one of your own students.

Even within the context of the fiction, it is a tribute to the depth of Cather's art and insight that she has not made it overly easy for us. What Paul aspires to be, is, from any mature perspective, hollow and superficial. What he rejects, however unglamorous it may be, is not on its face hateful. The reactions of his teachers and even his father to Paul's behavior are not harsh or punitive; just about everyone, including his fellow ushers as they sit on him until he has calmed down, seems to want to help. And he is, after all, a thief and an unrepentant one at that—a fact that will no doubt be seized upon by students seeking justification for their dislike of him.

QUESTIONS FOR DISCUSSION

1. *What is it about Paul that so disturbs his teachers? Recall any of his traits that they find irritating, any actions that trouble them. Do they irritate or trouble you?* The boy's dandyism, his defiance, and his unconcealed contempt disturb his teachers beyond all reason. They also disturb many readers, who find a discrepancy between their own negative feelings about Paul and the fondness Cather seems to feel toward him. The school principal and Paul's art teacher are able to muster sympathy for the boy (paragraphs 7–8), but they don't claim to understand him.

2. *What do the arts—music, painting, theater—mean to Paul? How does he react when exposed to them? Is he himself an artist?* Oddly, when he hears a concert, it's "not that symphonies, as such, [mean] anything in particular to Paul" (11). The romance and beauty in the air excite him to hysteria. He reacts in the same way to fine food and wine, good clothes, a lavishly decorated room. For all his sensitivity, he is not an artist, and he doesn't respond to art as an artist would. It's the

idea of art and beauty, the pleasure they afford his senses, that evoke a response in him. In *Willa: The Life of Willa Cather*, Phyllis C. Robinson points out that Paul "may have had the sensitivity of an artist but, unlike his creator, he was without discipline, without direction and, saddest and most hopeless of all, he was without talent." In that fact lies his private tragedy.

3. *In what different places do we follow Paul throughout the story? How do these settings (and the boy's reactions to them) help us understand him, his attitudes, his personality?* Cather shows us Paul in school, at home, in the art gallery, in the theater, and, finally, in the big city. Everywhere, he functions apart from the ordinary beings who surround him. Isolated and unhappy, Paul regards his aesthetic longings as evidence of his superiority to other human beings. Absence of hope and cool disdain for the ordinary ways of attaining wealth and finery and an invitation to New York drive him to one grand, suicidal fling in the beautiful, glamorous world where he imagines he belongs.

4. *Does Cather's brief introduction into the story of the wild Yale freshman from San Francisco (in paragraph 54) serve any purpose? Why do you suppose he and Paul have such a "singularly cool" parting? What is Cather's point?* In New York Paul expects to find wealthy persons of taste and temperament similar to his own. He finds instead the disappointing Yale student who, far from sharing Paul's reverence for beauty, seems to the boy hopelessly crass. Ironically, though he seems to have grown up with all the advantages Paul has lacked, this worldly student disappoints Paul as much as do his family and friends at home. Who could measure up to Paul's impossible standards? For the rest of his stay, Paul is content to observe his fellow guests from afar.

5. *Is Paul a static character or a dynamic one? If you find him changing and developing in the course of the story, can you indicate what changes him?* The only change in Paul's character during the story seems to be the fairly minor one mentioned in paragraphs 42–43. Once settled in at the Waldorf, he realizes he is no longer "dreading something." Is this change enough to justify our calling him a dynamic character? The change seems to signal in Paul a deepening involvement in an unreal world rather than any growth. We think he's a static character. His perceptions and values, and the actions that follow from them, remain unchanged.

6. *Comment on some of the concrete details Cather dwells on. What, for instance, do you make of the portraits of Washington and John Calvin and the motto placed over Paul's bed (paragraph 18)? Of the carnation Paul buries in the snow (paragraph 64)?* Paul's sensibilities recoil from all that is ugly, even ordinary. His room, featuring pictures of those austere and well-disciplined heroes George Washington and John Calvin, is hateful to him. Working-class Cordelia Street, where he lives, induces in him "a shuddering repulsion for the flavorless, colorless mass of every-day existence; a morbid desire for cool things and soft lights and fresh flowers" (19). By paragraph 64, after Paul has run away from New York, he realizes that fresh flowers do not stay fresh forever. He sees the parallel between "their brave mockery" and his own "revolt against the homilies by which the world is run" and

characterizes both as "a losing game in the end." He dies like the flowers, his "one splendid breath" spent.

7. *What implications, if any, does the title "Paul's Case" have for this story? Is Paul mentally ill, or does Cather place the roots of his malaise elsewhere?* Robinson has this to say about Cather's view of Paul:

> As if to underscore her own intuition in regard to the story, Willa gave it the subtitle "A Study in Temperament," and to the modern reader the pathological attributes of Paul's malaise are more persuasive than the romantic aspects. Willa told George Seibel that she drew on two boys who had been in her classes for the character of Paul, but to others she confessed how much of her own hunger and frustration were embodied in the unhappy boy's flight from the drab reality of his daily life and in his instinctive reaching out for beauty.

In other words, we today tend to think Paul seriously disturbed, but apparently Cather didn't see him that way. In conflict with school, neighbors, and family, Paul seems to her an admirable victim. Cather often sticks up for the lonely, sensitive individual pitted against a philistine provincial society—as in her famous story "The Sculptor's Funeral."

"Paul's Case" was featured in the PBS television film series *The American Short Story*. It is available on video cassette from Teacher's Video Company at (800) 262-8837. Short scenes from the script of Ron Cowen's adaptation are included in *The American Short Story, Volume 2* (New York: Dell, 1980), and invite comparison with the original.

A detailed plan for teaching "Paul's Case" is offered by Bruce E. Miller in *Teaching the Art of Literature* (Urbana, IL: NCTE, 1980). To get students involved in the story before they read it outside of class, Miller suggests reading passages from the early part of the story (before Paul flees to New York) and summarizing what happens, and then asking students how they'd imagine Cather would continue the story. He advises the instructor to show the class a few photographs of adolescent boys and to ask how closely the pictures reflect students' mental images of Paul. The point is to spark a discussion of Paul's complex character. Is he a cheat? A victim? A hero? Various opinions are likely to emerge, and students may come to see "that the different views of Paul are not necessarily incompatible with each other, and that Cather has accomplished the difficult feat of delineating a complex character who, though flawed, engages the reader's sympathy."

Sandra Cisneros
BARBIE-Q, page 358

Sandra Cisneros began as a poet, and there are moments when "Barbie-Q" seems as much a prose poem as a short story. The narrative is slight, though in a few pages Cisneros finds time for a clever plot twist. What makes "Barbie-Q" interesting is its language and its psychology—which are cunningly interwoven. In this story, Cisneros explores the language of advertising and marketing. She understands how advertising exploits and excites the desires and fantasies of its target consumers. Barbie and her friends become projections of the narrator's appetite for romance and glamour. Observe how exquisitely the narrator remembers every detail of dress and appearance of each doll. In the flea market, she does not merely see boxes of Barbie clothes; she observes two small fantasy worlds:

> One with the "Career Gal" ensemble, snappy black-and-white business suit, three-quarter-length sleeve jacket with kick-pleat skirt, red sleeveless shell, gloves, pumps, and matching hat included. The other, "Sweet Dreams," dreamy pink-and-white plaid nightgown and matching robe, lace-trimmed slippers, hairbrush and hand mirror included. How much? Please, please, please, please, please, please, please, until they say okay.

The hyperbolic language of toy marketing reflects the psychology of the narrator and her friend. On the edge of adolescence, they explore the traumas of love and experience through play. Notice how their games always end with the two Barbies fighting over a nonexistent Ken. The girls may be young, but they already understand that romance can be divisive to friendship. It might be worthwhile to ask students how old the narrator and her friend are. There is no right answer, of course, but the question will focus them on the psychological and behavioral changes behind the story.

There is also a social dimension to the story. The narrator and her friend are not well-to-do. They cannot afford a Ken doll. They must wait until Christmas to get a new Barbie outfit. They shop at a decidedly downscale Chicago flea market ("tool bits, and platform shoes with the heels all squashed"). Cisneros does not bemoan their pecuniary plight; she simply states it as the condition of their daily lives. Without compromising her stinging social subtext, Cisneros makes "Barbie-Q" a happy story. The girls get their fantasy outfits at fire-sale prices.

Cisneros is not alone in finding Barbie interesting. The vast popular appeal of the character Barbie—700 million units sold worldwide—has enabled Barbara Bell of San Anselmo, California, to publish a *Barbie Channeling Newsletter*. So serious are some of her readers that Ms. Bell is able to charge them a fee for "channeling the spirit of Barbie" and answering their questions such as: "Dear Barbie, should I get involved with this man?" and "Should I quit my job?" (So Steve Rubinstein reports in a *San Francisco Chronicle* feature article reprinted in other newspapers in April 1993.)

Thirty serious writers, not all of whom take Barbie seriously, appear in *Mondo Barbie*, edited by Lucinda Ebersole and Richard Peabody (New York: St. Martin's Press, 1993), an anthology of stories and poems, all Barbie-inspired. "As icons go," notes Robert Plunket, "Barbie is right up there with Elvis" (review of *Mondo Barbie* in the *New York Times Book Review*, April 18, 1993). Plunket goes on to observe that Barbie "is a totemic object through which a certain kind of feminine knowledge is passed along from older girls to younger girls." A question for class discussion is: Good grief, why?

Sandra Cisneros reads from her books, *The House on Mango Street* and *Woman Hollering Creek*, on audiocassette tape available from the American Audio Prose Library, Inc., Box 842, Columbia, MO 65205; phone number for orders (800) 447-2275. (The story "Barbie-Q" is not recorded.)

Gabriel García Márquez
A VERY OLD MAN WITH ENORMOUS WINGS, page 360

"Magic Realism" (*el realismo magical*) was a term first coined in 1949 by the Cuban novelist Alejo Carpentier to describe the matter-of-fact combination of the fantastic and everyday in Latin American fiction. About the same time it was also used by European critics to describe a similar trend in postwar German fiction exemplified by novels like Gunter Grass's *The Tin Drum* (1959). (German art critic Franz Roh had employed the same term in 1925, but he applied it only to painting.) Magic Realism has now become the standard name for a major trend in contemporary fiction that stretches from Latin American works like Gabriel García Márquez's *One Hundred Years of Solitude* (1967) to *norteamericana* novels like Mark Helprin's *Winter's Tale* (1983) and Asian works like Salman Rushdie's *Midnight Children* (1981). In all cases the term refers to the tendency among contemporary fiction writers to mix the magical and mundane in an overall context of realistic narration.

If the term "Magic Realism" is relatively new, what it describes has been around since the early development of the novel and short story as modern literary forms. One already sees the key elements of Magic Realism in *Gulliver's Travels* (1726), which factually narrates the fabulous adventures of an English surgeon. Likewise Nikolai Gogol's short story, "The Nose" (1842), in which a minor Czarist bureaucrat's nose takes off to pursue its own career in St. Petersburg, fulfills virtually every requirement of this purportedly contemporary style. One finds similar precedents in Dickens, Balzac, Dostoyevsky, Maupassant, Kafka, Bulgakov, Calvino, Cheever, Singer, and others. Seen from an historical perspective, therefore, Magic Realism is a vital contemporary manifestation of a venerable fictive impulse.

The possibilities of storytelling will always hover between the opposing poles of verisimilitude and myth, factuality and fabulation, realism and romance. If mid-century critics (like F. R. Leavis, V. S. Pritchett, F. W. Dupee, Irving Howe, and Lionel Trilling) almost exclusively favored the realist mode, their emphasis reflected their generation's understandable fascination with the immediate past. They still lived in the shadow of what Leavis called the "Great Tradition" of the psychological and social novel. This tradition encompassed (to expand Leavis's Anglophilic list a bit) Jane Austen, George Eliot, Henry James, Edith Wharton, Joseph Conrad, Virginia Woolf, D. H. Lawrence, Willa Cather, Ernest Hemingway, and early James Joyce. As the realistic novel confidently continued in the first decades of the century, it was all too easy to imagine that this particular line of development had decisively superseded the older pre-novelistic modes of storytelling. These London, Oxford, and New York critics would hardly have imagined that a radically different kind of fiction was being developed beyond their ken in places like Argentina, Colombia, and Peru. By the time García Márquez and his fellow members of *"el boom"* (the boom) in Latin-American fiction came to maturity, the reemergence of the fantastic heritage in fiction seemed nearly as revolutionary as the region's politics.

All of the main features of Latin American Magic Realism can be found in García Márquez's story, "A Very Old Man with Enormous Wings," which appeared in his 1972 volume *The Incredible and Sad Tale of Innocent Eréndira and Her Heartless Grandmother.* (The English translation also appeared in 1972 as part of *Leaf Storm and Other Stories.* Since *Leaf Storm* was originally published in Spanish in 1955, the translation volume has led some American editors and critics to misdate "A Very Old Man with Enormous Wings," which is not an early work but written soon after García Márquez's *magnum opus, One Hundred Years of Solitude.*)

As a young law student, García Márquez read Kafka's *The Metamorphosis.* It proved a decisive encounter, and the influence is not hard to observe in the early stories, which so often present bizarre incidents unfolding in ordinary circumstances. If Kafka reinvented the fable by placing it in the modern quotidian world, García Márquez reset it in the unfamiliar landscape of the Third World. If Kafka made spiritual issues more mysterious by surrounding them with bureaucratic procedure, his Colombian follower changed our perception of Latin America by insisting that in this New World visionary romanticism was merely reportage. García Márquez also had another crucial mentor closer at hand—the Argentinean master, Jorge Luis Borges. Only thirty years García Márquez's senior, Borges had quietly redrawn the imaginative boundaries of Latin American fiction. Almost single-handedly he had also rehabilitated the fantastic tale for serious fiction. Removing religion and the supernatural from any fixed ideology, he employed the mythology of Christianity, Judaism, Islam, and Confucianism as metaphysical figures. Paradoxically he expressed his sophisticated fictions in popular rather than experimental forms—the fable, the detective story, the supernatural tale, the gaucho legend. He was the first great post-modernist storyteller, and he found an eager apprentice in García Márquez, who developed these innovative notions in different and usually more expansive forms.

The plot of García Márquez's story is easily summarized. At the end of a three-day rainstorm Pelayo discovers an old man with enormous wings lying face down in the mud of his courtyard. He immediately returns with his wife Elisenda to examine the bald, nearly toothless man who seems barely alive. They try to converse, but no one understands anything the winged ancient says. After consulting with a neighbor who identifies the man as an angel, Pelayo drags the filthy, passive creature into a chicken coop. Soon people visit—first to mock and tease the winged captive, then to seek miracles. The local priest tries to determine if the mysterious prisoner is truly an angel or merely some diabolic trick. He notices the old man's stench and his parasite-infested wings, but writes to the bishop and eventually Rome for a verdict. (Rome seeks additional information but never makes a decision—a very Kafkaesque situation.)

Soon Pelayo and his wife begin charging admission to see their angel. The crowds grow until they draw other carnival attractions. One visiting sideshow features a young woman who was transformed into a tarantula the size of a ram with the head of a maiden. Since the spider woman eagerly talks to customers—unlike the silent, nearly immobile angel—she begins to draw the audience away. By now, however, Pelayo and his wife have earned enough to build a fine two-story mansion. Several years pass. Their child, who was a newborn at the story's opening, is now old enough start school. The feeble angel drags himself around their property greatly to Elisenda's annoyance. He also loses his last bedraggled feathers. That winter the old man almost dies of fever, but by spring his feathers begin to grow back. One day, as Elisenda watches from the kitchen, the old man clumsily takes flight and flaps away across the sea.

The plot of García Márquez's story—the magical elements aside—is positively drab. The ending so conspicuously lacks any overt narrative ingenuity as to seem anticlimactic. The flatness of the plot gives the story an odd quality—as impersonal as a newspaper article, and as episodic as a legend. This feeling of detachment is heightened by the tale's omniscient narrator who reports the odd events with deadpan objectivity. The story's particular power comes from its extraordinary details, which are seldom drab and often dazzling. A motley procession of people and things (ranging from an ordinary parish priest to an enchanted tarantula woman) parade by in such profusion that the reader never knows what to expect next—the mysterious, the mundane, or the magic? That distracting but disorienting effect is crucial to the experience of Magic Realism and to a certain extent, it is the element that most clearly differentiates it from its predecessors. Gogol, Kafka, and Singer may have created similar modes of fiction, but they never lavished so many fabulous details with such profligate nonchalance.

"A Very Old Man with Enormous Wings" seemingly invites all sorts of symbolic and even allegorical readings, but García Márquez constantly undercuts or frustrates any easy interpretation. If this bedraggled, sickly creature truly represents the descent of the miraculous into the everyday world, he does not fit the preconceptions of anyone in this world—priest, petitioner, or even paying sideshow customer. This putative angel not only remains uninspiring and unknowable, but slightly repulsive. No one in the story ever successfully communicates with him. If he speaks the language of the divine, we cannot understand a word of it. He arrives, stays, and leaves without explanation or apparent purposes. If the story is to be read symbolically, all one can ultimately say is that the winged old man embodies both the impenetrable mysteries of this world and the next one. Whatever he truly is—mortal or supernatural—he exists beyond our comprehension. We can project our own assumptions on the blank screen of his history, but his essence remains forever invisible. When he flies away, we know nothing important about him with more certainty than when he arrived.

"A Very Old Man with Enormous Wings" can be profitably compared and contrasted to Isaac Bashevis Singer's "Gimpel the Fool." Both stories mix the supernatural and the ordinary, though Singer accepts the tradition of fable's responsibility to draw moral conclusions from the story—an impulse García Márquez steadfastly declines.

Charlotte Perkins Gilman
THE YELLOW WALLPAPER, page 365

"The Yellow Wallpaper" is now such a famous short story that it is interesting to recall how recently it was rescued from oblivion. The facts behind the original creation of the tale and its modern rediscovery are worth recounting. Gilman completed the story in 1890 after the breakup of her first marriage. Based on her own experience with depression and the debilitating effects of her medical treatment of the condition, "The Yellow Wallpaper" was written, she later claimed, to "save people from being driven crazy." Gilman sent the story to William Dean Howells, then the most influential critic in American fiction. Admiring it, he sent the story to Horace Scudder, the editor of the *Atlantic Monthly*, who turned it down on the basis of its stark and unsettling contents. As Howells later commented, it was "too terribly good to be printed" there. The story was eventually published in *New England Magazine* in 1892, where it stirred up a minor controversy. Howells later reprinted it in his 1920 anthology, *The Great American Short Stories*. For the next fifty years the story remained out of print. In 1973, the Feminist Press reissued it as a separate pamphlet with an admiring afterword. Six years later, Sandra Gilbert and Susan Gubar discussed it in their pioneering feminist study, *The Madwoman in the Attic* (1979). Soon thereafter, "The Yellow Wallpaper" became one of the most widely discussed texts in feminist criticism of American literature.

"The Yellow Wallpaper" lends itself to many different readings, but most obviously it invites—some critics might say *demands*—a feminist approach. Gilbert and Gubar explore the rich subtext of the story. The narrator is not only physically imprisoned in her comfortable, airy room; she is spiritually and intellectually confined in a patronizing male world that reduces her to childish dependency. Whatever critical approach one adopts, the important thing is not to simplify Gilman's complex and richly ambiguous narrative.

The first issue for students to deal with is the narrative situation. "The Yellow Wallpaper" is told by a woman undergoing a nervous breakdown. She suffers visions and is plagued by obsessions. Forbidden to write by her concerned but patronizing husband, she secretly jots down her thoughts and experiences. Her prose is conspicuously anxious and disconnected. Not only is the narrator unreliable, her reports are complicated further by the untrustworthy behavior of her husband and his sister, who take care of her. With good but misguided intentions, they talk down to her, and much of what they say appears to be deliberately misleading. A chief irony of the story is that the further the narrator sinks into madness the more clearly she understands the hypocrisy and paternalism of her keepers. Nothing anyone says in the story can be accepted uncritically.

A good way to acclimatize students to the uncertainty of the narrative situation is to ask them to recount everything they know about the room the narrator shares with her husband in the rented mansion. (The husband, however, has also selected the room because it has another bedroom nearby that he can move into if need be.) The narrator initially describes it as follows:

It is a big, airy room, the whole floor nearly, with windows that look all ways, and air and sunshine galore. It was a nursery first and then playroom and gymnasium, I should judge; for the windows are barred for little children, and there are rings and things in the walls.

No one in the story ever questions that the room was once a nursery, but as later details pile up (the stripped wallpaper, the bolted-down bed, the stairway gate), the alert reader wonders if it was not really once a genteel cell for an affluent lunatic. Like many other things in the story, a pleasant surface covers an authoritarian reality. Students should be encouraged to examine every aspect of this story with equal care and skepticism.

Another question to ask students is, who is the woman the narrator sees in the wallpaper? If this were a supernatural tale, the reader might eventually assume that it was a ghost or demon who inhabited the yellow wallpaper, and there are overtones of the macabre in Gilman's story. However, Gilman—like Poe before her—uses the outward narrative forms of Gothic and supernatural fiction to explore uncomfortable psychological territory. The woman imprisoned in the wallpaper is the narrator's double, probably the parts of her being confined and repressed by her suffocating life. Only as the narrator sinks into madness do her own inhibitions drop sufficiently that she can liberate these forbidden or unacknowledged aspects of her psyche.

In "The Yellow Wallpaper," Gilman uses the traditional figure of the *Doppelgänger* (a German term that, translated literally, means "double-goer"), in an original, feminist way. In Romantic literature the double usually represented an evil self that had broken free of the dominant, moral, conscious self. The evil double often battles the "real" self for control of the person's life. In Gilman's story, the repressed self that is finally liberated also wants to take over the narrator's life, but the double is neither obviously evil nor morally dangerous. Once free, the double seems to merge into the narrator. "I wonder if they all come out of the wallpaper as I did?" she suddenly comments. Although the narrator's outer life is crumbling, she is achieving a new authenticity in her inner life. Robert Louis Stevenson's classic *Doppelgänger* story, *The Strange Case of Dr. Jekyll and Mr. Hyde*, was published with immense acclaim in 1886—only four years before Gilman wrote "The Yellow Wallpaper." One wonders if Gilman knew it. She seems to take Stevenson's conventional moral themes and revise them radically from a feminist perspective.

Finally, students may want to explore the complex central image of Gilman's story, the yellow wallpaper. The "repellent, almost revolting," "smouldering unclean" yellow wallpaper resists neat allegorical interpretation; it is a troubling, changing symbol of the forces that haunt, imprison, and torment the narrator. At first its "bloated curves and flourishes" seem to have no shape, but gradually the obsessively observant narrator starts to comprehend its shape. In a probing essay, "Feminist Criticism, 'The Yellow Wallpaper,' and the Politics of Color in America" (*Feminist Studies* 15:3 [Fall 1989]), Susan S. Lanser compares the narrator's analysis of the wallpaper to deciphering the text of her own imprisoned female identity:

The narrator is faced with an unreadable text, a text for which none of her interpretative strategies is adequate. . . . But from all this indecipherability,

101

from this immensely complicated text, the narrator—by night, no less—finally discerns a single image, a woman behind bars, which she then expands to represent the whole.

Students wishing to write on Gilman may want to read her feminist utopian novel, *Herland* (1915), which describes a trio of American men visiting an all-female country. Gilman was, first and foremost, a writer on social issues. Even her champions concede that none of her other short stories is up to the level of "The Yellow Wallpaper." *Herland*, a novel of ideas, shows Gilman at her best—it is a radical, progressive questioning of the traditional assumptions of her age. They may also wish to consult Carol Farley Kessler's long, interesting essay on Gilman's life and work in *Modern American Women Writers* (New York: Scribners, 1991).

Instructors interested in providing biographical and historical context to classroom discussion of "The Yellow Wallpaper" may want to read Gilman's public statement about her short story, which appeared in the October 1913 issue of *The Forerunner*.

Why I Wrote "The Yellow Wallpaper"

Many and many a reader has asked that. When the story first came out, in the *New England Magazine* about 1891, a Boston physician made protest in *The Transcript*. Such a story ought not to be written, he said; it was enough to drive anyone mad to read it.

Another physician, in Kansas I think, wrote to say that it was the best description of incipient insanity he had ever seen, and—begging my pardon—had I been there?

Now the story of the story is this: For many years I suffered from a severe and continuous nervous breakdown tending to melancholia—and beyond. During about the third year of this trouble I went, in devout faith and some faint stir of hope, to a noted specialist in nervous diseases, the best known in the country. This wise man put me to bed and applied the rest cure, to which a still-good physique responded so promptly that he concluded there was nothing much the matter with me, and sent me home with solemn advice to "live as domestic a life as far as possible," to "have but two hours' intellectual life a day," and "never to touch pen, brush, or pencil again" as long as I lived. This was in 1887.

I went home and obeyed those directions for some three months, and came so near the boderline of utter mental ruin that I could see over.

Then, using the remnants of intelligence that remained, and helped by a wise friend, I cast the noted specialist's advice to the winds and went to work again—work, the normal life of every human being; work, in which is joy and growth and service, without which one is a pauper and a parasite—ultimately recovering some measure of power.

Being naturally moved to rejoicing by this narrow escape, I wrote "The Yellow Wallpaper," with its embellishments and additions, to carry out the ideal (I never had hallucinations or objections to my mural decorations) and sent a copy to the physician who so nearly drove me mad. He never acknowledged it.

The little book is valued by alienists and as a good specimen of one kind of literature. It has, to my knowledge, saved one woman from a similar fate— so terrifying her family that they let her out into normal activity and she recovered.

But the best result is this. Many years later I was told that the great specialist had admitted to friends of his that he had altered his treatment of neurasthenia since reading "The Yellow Wallpaper."

It was not intended to drive people crazy, but to save people from being driven crazy, and it worked.

There are two stories in this book that could provide students with particularly interesting topics to compare and contrast with "The Yellow Wallpaper." Poe's "The Tell-Tale Heart" uses Gothic conventions and an unreliable narrator to depict the consequences of a mental breakdown. (One might also consider Poe's "The Fall of the House of Usher" with its meticulously described house, neurasthenic protagonist, and *Doppelgänger* motif.) William Faulkner's "A Rose for Emily" provides interesting parallels to Gilman's story. Faulkner's mad Emily Grierson is also trapped in an old house by different sorts of male presences.

"The Yellow Wallpaper"/Charlotte Perkins Gilman, a volume devoted to "The Yellow Wallpaper," edited by Thomas L. Erskine and Connie L. Richards, appeared in 1993 from "Women Writers: Text and Context," a series of casebooks about short fiction from Rutgers University Press. It includes historical documents and critical commentaries on the story by various critics including Elizabeth Ammons, Sandra M. Gilbert and Susan Gubar, Susan S. Lanser, and others with an introduction by the editors. Additionally, Professor Denise Knight edits the *Charlotte Perkins Gilman Newsletter* out of SUNY College at Cortland, Cortland, New York 13045. The newsletter is also available online (http://orchard.cortland.edu), as are numerous Gilman web sites and resources. Check a search engine for the most recent addresses. Also of interest, University of South Carolina in Columbia hosted the third International Gilman Conference in April of 2001.

Nathaniel Hawthorne
YOUNG GOODMAN BROWN, page 378

"Young Goodman Brown" is Hawthorne's most frequently reprinted story and probably the most often misunderstood. Some initial discussion of the story's debt to American history may be helpful—most students can use a brief refresher on the Salem witchcraft trials, in which neighbor suspected neighbor and children recklessly accused innocent old women. The hand of the devil was always nearby, and it was the duty of all to watch for it. From Cotton Mather's *Wonders of the Invisible World* (1693), Hawthorne drew details of his imagined midnight Sabbath. In revealing to Brown the secret wickedness of all the people he knew and trusted, the story seems to illustrate the Puritan doctrine of innate depravity. Humankind was born tarred with the brush of original sin and could not lose the smudge by any simple ritual of baptism. Only the elect—communicants, those who had experienced some spiritual illumination which they had declared in public—could be assured of salvation. Brown's unhappy death at the end of the story seems conventional: Puritans held that how one died indicated his chances in the hereafter. A radiantly serene and happy death was an omen that the victim was Heaven-bound, while a dour death boded ill.

The devil's looking like a blood relative may reflect another Puritan assumption. Taken literally, perhaps the resemblance between the devil and Brown's grandfather suggests that evil runs in Brown's family, or in the Puritan line as the devil asserts (18–19). Or that wickedness lurks within each human heart (as well as good) and that each can recognize it in himself, as if he had looked into a mirror. Of course, donning the family face may be one more trick of the devil: an attempt to ingratiate himself with Brown by appearing as a close relative. Hawthorne's great-grandfather, the witch trial judge, would have agreed that the devil often appears in disguise. The Salem trials admitted "spectral evidence"—testimony that the devil had been seen in the form of some innocent person. Spectral evidence was part of the case against Goody Cloyse, Goody Cory, and Martha Carrier—all named in Hawthorne's story, all of whom Judge John Hathorne condemned to death. For more on Puritan doctrines (and how they eroded with time), see Herbert W. Schneider's classic study *The Puritan Mind* (U of Michigan P, 1958). Of Hawthorne's tales and *The Scarlet Letter*, Schneider observes:

> "[Hawthorne] did not need to believe in Puritanism, for he understood it. . . . He recovered what the Puritans professed but seldom practiced—the spirit of piety, humility, and tragedy in the face of the inscrutable ways of God" (262–63).

We realize that this story is often interpreted as highly ambiguous, highly ambivalent in its attitude toward Puritanism and the notion of innate depravity. But we read it as another of those stories in which the Romantic Hawthorne sets out to criticize extreme Puritanism and to chide the folly of looking for evil where there isn't any. In this regard, the story seems much like "Ethan Brand," in which the protagonist sets out to find the unpardonable sin, only to receive God's pardon anyway; and like "The Minister's Black Veil," in which Mr. Hooper makes himself miserable by seeing the world through a dark screen. (The latter is, admittedly, a more ambivalent tale: Hawthorne also finds something to be said in favor of that black veil and its wearer's gloomy view.) Brown's outlook has been tainted by dark illusion, conjured up, it would seem, by the devil's wiles.

Some students will take the devil's words for gospel, agree that "Evil is the nature of mankind," and assume that Brown learns the truth about all those hypocritical sinners in the village, including that two-faced Faith. One likely point of departure is the puns on *Faith* in Brown's speeches:

"I'll cling to her skirts and follow her to heaven" (paragraph 5).

"Faith kept me back awhile" (12).

"Is there any reason why I should quit my dear Faith . . . ?" (39)

"With Heaven above, and Faith below, I will yet stand firm against the devil" (46).

"My Faith is gone!" (50)

What Faith does Hawthorne mean? Surely not Puritanism—in this story, hardly a desirable bedfellow. More likely Brown's Faith is simple faith in the benevolence of God and the essential goodness of humankind. Brown's loss of this natural faith leads him into the principal error of the Salem witch-hangers: suspecting the innocent of being in league with the devil. At first, Brown assumes that his Faith is a pretty little pink-ribboned thing he can depart from and return to whenever he feels like it. Brown believes he is strong enough to pass a night in the evil woods and then return to the bosom of his faithful spouse unchanged. Of course this conviction is blind pride, and it works Brown's ruin.

Why does Brown go out to the woods? Apparently he has promised the devil he will go meet him, but go no farther. By meeting the devil he has "kept covenant" (15). The initial situation—that Brown has a promise to keep out in the woods—is vague, perhaps deliberately like the beginning of a dream.

And was it all a dream? Hawthorne hints that the devil's revelations to Brown and the midnight Sabbath are all one grand illusion. When Brown staggers against the supposedly flaming rock, it proves cold and damp, and a twig that had been on fire suddenly drips cold dew. (We are indebted here to F. O. Matthiessen's discussion in *American Renaissance* [Oxford: Oxford UP, 1941] 284.) If we read him right, Hawthorne favors the interpretation that Brown dreamed everything ("Be that as it may . . ."). Leave it to the devil to concoct a truly immense deception.

Still, some ambiguity remains. As Hawthorne declared in a letter to a friend in 1854, "I am not quite sure that I entirely comprehend my own meaning in some of these blasted allegories." If what Brown saw at the witches' Sabbath really did take place, then his gloom and misery at the end of the story seem understandable. Some have read the story to mean that Brown has grown up to have a true sense of sin, and therefore ends a good Puritan; he has purged himself of his boyish good cheer. But we find the morose Brown deluded, not admirable, and suspect that Hawthorne does too.

Students may not have met the term *allegory* in this book unless you have assigned the chapter "Symbolism," but some will know it already. Not only

Faith can be seen as a figure of allegory, but Young Goodman Brown himself—the Puritan Everyman, subject to the temptation to find evil everywhere. For a class that has already begun symbol-hunting, "Young Goodman Brown" is a fair field. Among the more richly suggestive items are the devil's snaky staff or walking-stick (13), with its suggestions of the Eden snake and the serpentine rods of the Egyptian magicians (Exodus 7:8–12). When the devil laughs, it squirms happily (22). It works like seven-league boots, and its holder enjoys rapid transportation. The devil gives it to Goody Cloyse and then plucks Brown a fresh stick from a maple (38–41); when Brown grasps it in despair (51), it speeds him on to the unholy communion. Other symbolic items (and actions) include the forest—entering it is to be led into temptation, and Brown keeps going deeper and deeper; the withering of the maple branch at the devil's touch (38); and the proffered baptism in blood or fire at the evil meeting (67).

But the richest symbol of all is Faith's lost pink ribbon that flutters to the ground, prompting Brown to conclude that Faith too is a witch and let fall her ribbon while riding on a broomstick to the midnight Sabbath. (Many students, unless you help them, will miss this suggestion.) Sure enough, when Brown arrives, Faith is there too. The ribbon, earlier suggesting youthful beauty and innocence, becomes an ironic sign of monstrous evil and duplicity. This terrible realization causes Brown to decide to follow the devil after all—even though, presumably, the fluttering ribbon was another diabolical trick. When Brown meets the real Faith once more, she is still all beribboned, as if she hasn't lost anything.

How to state the theme? Surely not "Evil is the nature of mankind" or "Even the most respected citizens are secretly guilty." That is what the devil would have us believe. A more defensible summing-up might be "Keep your faith in God and humankind" or "He who finds evil where no evil exists makes himself an outcast from humanity."

Compare this story with Shirley Jackson's "The Lottery." There, too, a whole town takes part in a blood-curdling rite—but public, not clandestine.

Zora Neale Hurston
SWEAT, page 388

Hurston's stark tale of a bitter marriage turned murderous first appeared in the one and only issue of the Harlem arts journal, *Fire!!* in November 1926. *Fire!!*, which carried the subtitle, "A Quarterly Devoted to the Younger Negro Artists," presented some of the leading talents of the new generation, including Langston Hughes, Countee Cullen, and Arna Bontemps. "Sweat," with its use of authentic black dialect and folkways, its forthright presentation of harsh subject matter, and (to quote Alice Walker) its "sense of black people as complete, complex, *undiminished* human beings," makes it a representative work of the Harlem Renaissance.

QUESTIONS FOR DISCUSSION

1. *What importance does the setting of "Sweat" have to its action?* The story takes place mostly in a house on the outskirts of a small Florida town (which critics identify with Hurston's hometown of Eatonville). The isolation of Delia's home is essential to the plot. Its distance from town means that she has no protection there from Sykes's violence, just as its isolation ultimately gives Sykes no escape from his slow, painful death by snakebite. The setting is also important to the story's motivation. Delia has bought the house with her own hard work. Sykes wants to kill her for the house so that he can bring another woman home to it. The house also becomes a symbol to the otherwise disappointed Delia of what she has managed to accomplish in her hard, painful life. ("It was lovely to her, lovely.")

2. *What has Delia and Sykes's marriage been like?* Delia married out of love. Sykes, she believes, brought only lust to the union ("a longing after the flesh"). Two months after the wedding, he gave her the first of many brutal beatings. In town, he is notorious for beating her and she for surviving his savage assaults. Sykes has frequently disappeared to squander his irregular earnings while Delia has worked as a laundress to pay their bills. Delia's hard work wounds Sykes's masculine pride: it reminds him that he cannot support her. Sykes is now adulterously involved with Bertha. Delia is not surprised to discover that he is trying to kill her.

3. *What is the significance of the story's title?* Hurston's title describes Delia's existence. Trapped in a brutal, loveless marriage and getting no help from Sykes in supporting the two of them, Delia has almost nothing in her life except work. Defending herself against Sykes's threats, she summarizes her life as "Sweat, sweat, sweat! Work and sweat, cry and sweat, pray and sweat!" The title also suggests why Delia is deaf to Sykes's pleas at the end of the story: love and compassion have been sweated out of her.

4. *Is Delia right to let Sykes die at the end of the story?* This may be an uncomfortable question for students, but the point of Hurston's story is to make us consider uncomfortable issues. It may be important to remind students that Delia is not responsible for Sykes being bitten by the snake; he has fallen into his own trap. If she is guilty of anything, it is only of not trying to help her husband—a sin of omission rather than commission. There is little question that a jury would acquit her of any charge. If ever a woman could claim extenuating circumstances, it is Delia. The more interesting question is whether Delia is morally culpable. In this regard, Hurston seems to suggest that Sykes has made Delia a person callous enough to watch coldly her own husband die. The ending has led one critic, Robert Bone, in his *Down-Home: Origins of the Afro-American Short Story* (New York: Columbia UP, 1988) to call "Sweat" a self-indulgent "revenge fantasy." But most critics have agreed with Lillie P. Howard, who viewed "Sweat" as a complex moral investigation of a good woman in an extreme situation:

Delia could have warned him, saved him, but she understandably does not. She has been hardened by his constant abuse and has built up a "spiritual earthworks" against him. Poetic justice has been rendered. (*Zora Neale Hurston:* New York, Twayne, 1980. 65)

What do your students think?

5. *How does the language of "Sweat" contribute to the story's effect?* There are two different levels of language employed in the story. Hurston presents the narration in sharp and evocative standard English, whereas the dialogue is written in the rural black dialect of her native Central Florida. Their constant alternation heightens the story's considerable nervous energy and suspense. The dialect also adds realism to the story: it evokes real people and a real region. Students sometimes experience some initial difficulty in reading dialogue in dialect because it looks different from conventional English. It is important to get them to hear it. You might ask the class why Hurston chose to write the dialogue in dialect. Would the story be different if the dialogue were written in standard American English?

A volume of critical essays dealing with "Sweat," edited by Cheryl Wall, is available from Rutgers UP (in its series dealing with short fiction, "Women Writers: Texts and Contexts"). Students planning to write on Hurston will find it helpful to read Laura M. Zaidman's comprehensive article on the author in *Dictionary of Literary Biography 86: American Short-Story Writers, 1910–1945,* edited by Bobby Ellen Kimbel (Detroit: Gale, 1989), which provides an insightful and highly readable introduction to her life and work.

Beverly Bailey of Seminole Community College in Sanford, Florida has informed us that Hurston's hometown of Eatonville hosts an annual festival in her honor. In addition to music, crafts, food, and entertainment, there are also scholarly presentations. For information on the Zora Neale Hurston Festival write to: Hurston Festival, P.E.C., PO Box 2586, 227 E. Kennedy Blvd., Eatonville, FL 32851. Prof. Bailey also recommends Steven Glassman and Kathryn Lee Seidel's *Zora in Florida* (Orlando: U of Central Florida, 1991), which Bailey calls "a fine study of the place that nurtured and inspired Hurston's work, the frontier wilderness of central Florida and the all-black town of Eatonville."

James Joyce
ARABY, page 398

Set in the city Joyce called "dear old dirty Dublin," "Araby" reveals a neighborhood so dreary that it seems no wonder a sensitive boy would try to romance his way out of it. In paragraphs 1–3, details stack up tellingly, painting a scene of frustration and decay. We see the dead-end street with an abandoned house at its "blind end"; the boy's house where the priest had died, its room full of "musty air" and "old, useless papers"; dying bushes, a rusty bicycle pump; a street of shadows and dark, dripping gardens lit by somber violet light. Still, the description is not unrelievedly sad. Playing in the cold, the boys feel their bodies glow. From "dark, odorous stables" comes the "music" of jingling harnesses. And for the boy, Mangan's sister lends the street enchantment.

Most students won't need help to see that "Araby" is told by its main character. They may need class discussion, though, to realize that the narrator is a man who looks back on his boyhood memories. One indication of the narrator's maturity is his style. In the first paragraph, he remarks, in unboyish language, that the houses, "conscious of decent lives within them, gazed at one another with brown imperturbable faces." Besides, this mature storyteller is about to step back and criticize his younger self: "her name was like a summons to all my foolish blood" (paragraph 4).

Mangan's sister, whose name is never told, seems an ordinary young woman who summons her kid brother to tea. She is a vague figure: the boy glimpses her from afar, sometimes while peering at her from shadow. John J. Brugaletta and Mary H. Hayden suggest that the conversation in which the boy promises to bring her a gift takes place only in his mind. Mangan's sister, they argue, may never have set foot in the room where the priest died (6), into which the boy retreats to have his visionary experience. In this musty shrine, his senses swoon. He clasps his hands in an attitude of prayer, murmurs an incantation over and over (*O love! O love!*), and conjures her face before him—"At last she spoke to me." Even the spikes he sees her clasping are unreal, for they couldn't be there in the dead priest's drawing room. In the end, at the bazaar, the image of Mangan's sister fades before the physical presence of the banal, flirtatious English salesgirl who says, "O, I never said such a thing." Neither did Mangan's sister say a word to the narrator that bound him to his imagined promise ("The Motivation for Anguish in Joyce's 'Araby,'" *Studies in Short Fiction* [Winter 1978]: 11–17).

The boy's daydreams of Mangan's sister are difficult to take seriously. Amid barrels of pigs' cheeks, he carries her image in his mind as a priest carries a chalice. He regards her with "confused adoration" and feels himself a harp on which she plays (5). From early in the story, the boy has projected a dazzling veil of romance over the commonplace. At the end, he realizes with shock that illusion has had him in thrall. Araby, the enchanted fair, turns out to be merely a drab charity bazaar where gimcracks are peddled, men count money, and a scatterbrained salesclerk makes small talk till the lights go out. The boy's intense anguish seems justified.

Nearly everything Joyce wrote has a thread of allegory, and "Araby" may be no exception. Making much of the identity of Mangan's sister, William York Tindall remarks: "Since [James Clarence] Mangan, one of Joyce's favorite poets, dedicated 'Dark Rosaleen,' his most famous poem, to his country, it seems likely that Mangan's sister is Ireland herself, beckoning and inviting." Tindall thinks the boy's frustrated quest is for Ireland's Church, toward which Joyce, too, felt bitter disillusionment. Rather than pursue Dark Rosaleen, the mature Joyce (and his protagonist Stephen Dedalus) chose exile. "Araby" makes a good introduction to *Portrait of the Artist as a Young Man*. (Tindall discusses the story in *A Reader's Guide to James Joyce* [New York: Noonday, 1959] 20.)

Araby, the bazaar with the "magical name," is paramount. Besides, the apple tree in the unkempt garden (2) hints of the tree in some lost Eden. Dublin, clearly, is a fallen world. Other items also suggest sterility and decay: the "blind" or dead-end street and its "uninhabited house ... detached from its neighbors" (1). the dead priest's rusty bicycle pump (2). Counting coins on a tray like that used to serve communion, the men in paragraph 25 perform a little act with symbolic overtones. The darkening hall has seemed to the boy "a church after a service," and the two money changers are not driven out of the temple—they drive out the boy.

Elizabeth A. Flynn compares reactions to this story by twenty-six male and twenty-six female college students in "Gender and Reading," *College English* 45 (Mar. 1983): 236–53. Some men felt uncomfortable with the boy's solipsistic infatuation. Recalling similar experiences of their own, they had trouble attaining distance. Several men, Flynn reports, were harsh in their judgment on Mangan's sister. They saw the girl as manipulating the boy for her own ends: "just using him," "playing him along." Most of the women students made better sense of the story. They didn't condemn Mangan's sister, and they understood the ending. They recognized that as the lights of the bazaar go out, the boy passes a painful judgment on himself: he has been a vain fool. Some women saw him gaining from his experience. Freed from his delusion, he can now reenter reality. If your men students have trouble understanding the story, you might have them take a good look at the last line.

On the popular poem "The Arab's Farewell to His Steed," which the uncle remembers, Matthew A. Fike of the University of Michigan writes, citing an insight by Stanley Friedman: "Joyce's reference to this poem, a work notable for its sentimentality, directs attention to the main significance of 'Araby': the assault on sentimentality and illusion" (Friedman, *The Explicator* 24:5 [Jan. 1966], item 43). There seems more than a little resemblance between the boy's worship of Mangan's sister for "the white curve of her neck" and the Arab's devotion to his horse, with its "glossy neck." Ironically, the Arab's glamorized view of his steed contrasts with the awareness that Joyce's narrator achieves, or as Mr. Fike puts it, "The nomad never parts with his horse, but the boy abandons his illusion." (Thanks to Mr. Fike for prompting XJK to greater precision in his footnote on "The Arab's Farewell.")

Franz Kafka
BEFORE THE LAW, page 403

Kafka's endlessly fascinating parable, which occupies a pivotal position in his novel *The Trial* (1925), was first published independently in 1915, and later collected in his book of tales *A Country Doctor* (1919). The parable, therefore, was originally meant to stand alone.

"Before the Law" represents the quintessence of Kafkaesque narrative art. It opens itself naturally to many possible interpretations, all of them feasible but none exclusively correct. It is possible, for instance, to analyze the parable from a political, ethical, psychological, religious, or existential perspective. Each approach meaningfully fits the circumstances of the story. For classroom discussions, it often works nicely to develop one or more of these interpretations in an almost allegorical way from beginning to end. (What does "the Law" mean, for example, in religious terms? From that perspective, who is "the doorkeeper"? and so forth.) After one interpretation is completed, start another. The ultimate aim of the exercise is to demonstrate how easily these multiple readings work in Kafka's fiction in a way that is intriguing rather than frustrating. One note of warning: if you chose to try a religious reading of the parable, you may have to offer multiple versions of the approach. The "Law" for a Muslim, Jew, and Christian are slightly different propositions, and that fact may subtly change other elements in interpreting the story.

Here are a few facts that you may want to work into your classroom discussion. Kafka studied law, but he never practiced it. Although he wrote privately, Kafka made his career as a bureaucrat in the state accident insurance company. Kafka was a Jew living in the predominantly Catholic Austro-Hungarian Empire. Do any of these biographical facts affect our reading of the tale?

Jamaica Kincaid
GIRL, page 405

"Girl" is the first story in Jamaica Kincaid's first book *At the Bottom of the River*. As such, it might be seen—like Hemingway's "Indian Camp" in *In Our Time*—as a kind of keynote to the body of her work. It is also worth noting that the first half of the volume's dual dedications reads: "For my mother, Annie, with love."

The form of "Girl" is worth considering in class because its compact length makes it easy for students to see the parts and the whole simultaneously. The form of "Girl" can be reasonably viewed in at least two ways. It can be cogently argued that "Girl" is a character sketch rather than a short story. Kincaid does not—at least overtly—describe a significant action with its motivations and consequences. Instead she presents a memorable character (and deftly implies another) through a speech. If "Girl" is viewed as a character sketch, therefore, it must be considered a sketch of *two* people—mother and daughter. The story reminds us that a person need not be presented at length to be credibly characterized. The daughter has only two short and perhaps silent (but italicized) comments. Yet we see her life vividly rendered throughout her mother's torrent of advice.

Considered as a sketch in this fashion, "Girl" could conceivably be analyzed as one would analyze a poem, emphasizing such things as tone, voice, rhythm, and selection and placement of detail as vehicles and even components of meaning. From the most trivial of matters to the most significant, the recurring theme of the mother's advice is that there is one right way to do everything, and that way must be followed in order to avoid all of life's many dangers. (Again, one may draw a comparison with Hemingway.)

If "Girl" is viewed as a short story, however, then the mother's speech is itself the central action. Her motivations are almost self-evident—love, worry, and a conviction that traditional ways are best. Her speech to the girl even hints at the central conflicts in their relationship—the mother's desire for her daughter to be a lady and the girl's feeling of being unjustly criticized (not to mention being overwhelmed by so many orders all at once).

Without much difficulty, students (who may have heard from their own parents long lists of advice more or less similar in tone) will identify the speaker in "Girl" as a mother and the listener as her daughter. The mother's diatribe is interrupted only twice when the daughter protests. (The italics leave it ambiguous whether the daughter responds aloud or merely mentally.) From the language, such as the names of foods (*dasheen, doukona*) and the details of daily life, we soon see that the setting is another country—the author's native Antigua, we might guess. The mother's words seem an accumulation of instructions repeated over many years. Her intent is to teach her daughter to measure up, to grow into a lady and not a "slut." Any deviation from her rules, the mother worries, may be a fatal step toward sluthood. Clearly, she sees a woman's role in life as traditionally restricted and restricting. But the mother is not merely delivering negative, binding orders; she tries to impart a whole body of traditional wisdom about the right way to do things. She offers her daughter the secrets of catching fish, avoiding bad luck, curing a cold (or a pregnancy), bullying a man, lovemaking, and making ends meet.

Some students, especially female students, will no doubt roll their eyes in recognition at the portrait of the mother and identify with the daughter, although they will grudgingly acknowledge that the mother is motivated by love and concern for her daughter's well-being. They may identify more directly with the mother—and find a greater depth and resonance in the text—if they perceive her to be also motivated, no doubt unconsciously, by self-concern as well: by the need to justify the choices and especially the sacrifices that she has made in her own life, and by the need to validate her own insights through their adoption by someone else.

Poet Cindy Milwe, who teaches at Santa Monica High School in Santa Monica, California, has contributed this note on teaching "Girl":

"Girl" never fails to engage teenagers and, despite its brevity, has proven useful in many classroom contexts. I have even used it with ninth graders as an introduction to *Romeo and Juliet*, with tenth graders as way into *A Doll's House*, and with seniors in a creative writing class to help them understand the notion of voice (focusing on the imperative nature of the piece and its almost relentless repetition).

Regardless of grade level, I have students read the story the night before and ask two good readers to be prepared the following day to read aloud (one as the mother and one as the daughter). During the in-class reading, I ask students to focus on the voices of these two characters and then I ask the following discussion questions:

1. What do we know about the mother and daughter? What don't we know? What can we infer? (For critical reading purposes and to facilitate a richer discussion, I will often have students jot down what they consider to be important lines from the text and then have them explain, in writing, what they are able to infer from those lines.)

2. What kinds of things is the mother trying to teach her daughter? Which commands and instructions seem particularly useful or problematic? Why?

3. Do you think she's a good mother based on the advice and warnings she offers? Why or why not?

4. Why is this story called "Girl" when the girl only "speaks" two sentences? What might Kincaid be suggesting about being a girl in general or about being a girl in this situation?

After talking about the story at length, I open up the discussion by asking students to share the various things they've learned about being a "boy" or a "girl" and from whom they've learned them. In a creative writing class, I ask students to make two columns on a piece of notebook paper and list the various "commands"—using the imperative—and the various "instructions" (using the repeated phrase "This is how to . . .") that they've heard from people in their own lives. They will then use these lists as preliminary notes to craft their own story with two voices, using "Girl" as a model.

An audiocassette tape of Kincaid reading "Girl" (in addition to other fiction pieces) and an interview about her experiences as a writer is available from American Audio Prose Library at (800) 447-2275 or <www.americanaudioprose.com>.

D. H. Lawrence
THE ROCKING-HORSE WINNER, page 406

Students have no difficulty with the conventions of Realism, as it is the dominant narrative mode of the fiction and the films with which they are most likely to be familiar. Likewise, the popularity of J. R. R. Tolkien, J. K. Rowling, super-hero comics, and the *Star Wars* movies, indicates that students are equally at home with the mode of Romance, especially fantasy. But they may find themselves uncomfortable with mixing the two modes as in "The Rocking-Horse Winner," a fantastic story that takes great pains to create a generally realistic atmosphere and to have its characters respond to external stimuli in the ways that "normal" people would. They may be resistant to details such as the picking of winning horses through a frenzied and debilitating ride on a rocking-horse, especially when such things are central to the unfolding of the narrative. Thus, it might be advisable at the outset of the presentation of "The Rocking-Horse Winner" to frame the discussion in terms of the conventions of Magic Realism. (See the discussion of García Márquez's "A Very Old Man with Enormous Wings" in this manual, for an extended treatment of the subject.) Past a certain point, however, explanation is useless: one either accepts the conventions or does not.

"The Rocking-Horse Winner" has occasioned some superb criticism. Any student wishing to write on the story should read the excerpt from Daniel P. Watkins's penetrating economic analysis of the tale found in this anthology in "Critical Approaches to Literature." Poet W. D. Snodgrass has also written a brilliant essay on the subject, "A Rocking-Horse: The Symbol, the Pattern, the Way to

Live," which examines the psychological and symbolic underpinning of "the perfect story by the least meticulous of serious writers." Originally published in the *Hudson Review* (Summer, 1958), Snodgrass's essay has been widely reprinted and still represents one of the foundational articles in Lawrence studies.

QUESTIONS FOR DISCUSSION

1. *The family members in Lawrence's story harbor a number of secrets. What are they?* The mother's secret is that "at the center of her heart was a hard little place that could not feel love, no, not for anybody" (paragraph 1). Paul's secret is that, by furiously riding his wooden rocking-horse, he is often able to predict which horses will win races. Bassett's secret, and Uncle Oscar's, is that they profit from Paul's predictions, even while the boy is on his deathbed. Their winnings are kept secret. Paul gives his mother 5,000 pounds, but does it anonymously. The house itself whispers a secret, "There must be more money" (5, 6, 181). The three children hear the whisper, but no one talks about it.

2. *What motivates each main character? What sets Paul's quest apart from that of the others?* It is the desire for more money that motivates them all. Perhaps the most blatant evidence of the family's obsession with riches appears in Uncle Oscar's attempt to console his sister after her son's death: "My God, Hester, you're eighty-odd thousand to the good and a poor devil of a son to the bad" (244)—as if he were enumerating her assets and liabilities on an imaginary balance sheet.

Paul's frenzied pursuit of money differs from the greed of the others in that he wants wealth not for himself but for his mother. Clearly he hopes that, by being "luckier" than his father, he will win his mother's love and attention.

3. *Some details in Lawrence's story are implausible. What are they?* Those students who can appreciate Lawrence's particular blend of reality and fantasy will like "The Rocking-Horse Winner." A house that whispers is unusual, but even a hardheaded realist can probably accept it at least as a metaphor. That a boy can learn to predict the winner in a horse race by riding his rocking horse is perhaps harder to believe.

4. *At what places in his story does Lawrence make use of irony?* Paul, intent upon stopping the whispers in the house, anonymously gives his mother 5,000 pounds as a birthday present. Ironically, his gift has the opposite effect. The whispers grow louder. Given his mother's insatiable greed for money, this result comes as less of a surprise to the reader than to Paul.

There is irony in the story's title. Paul, the rocking-horse winner, loses his life.

Ironic, too, are Paul's final words: "I *am* lucky" (241). In his mother's definition of luck, in paragraph 18 ("It's what causes you to have money"), Paul *is* lucky, of course—or was.

5. *In what sense may Paul's periodic rides on the rocking horse be regarded as symbolic acts?* The single-minded frenzy with which Paul rides his rocking horse par-

allels the intensity of the money-lust that dominates Paul's family. There is no joy in his riding, as there is no joy in his house.

6. *What is the theme of "The Rocking-Horse Winner"?* The love of money is destructive of all other love, and even of life itself.

Katherine Mansfield
Miss Brill, page 418

Like many practitioners of the modern short story, Katherine Mansfield frequently uses small details and seemingly trivial incidents to suggest a sense of a character's entire life. We might borrow James Joyce's term "epiphany," applied to the way in which a small gesture may lead to a revelation of or insight into character, in discussing Mansfield's "little sketch." (In fact, in the situation of its protagonist and her sense of herself, "Miss Brill" calls to mind "Clay" and "A Painful Case," two of the stories in Joyce's masterful collection, *Dubliners*.) In the second half of the story, Miss Brill herself undergoes two such revelations, with far different reactions and consequences. Her own sense of oneness with her fellow concert-goers, in which her assumptions about their pettiness and absurdity is replaced by a larger human sympathy, is quickly undercut by her awareness of her own pettiness and absurdity in the eyes of others.

The narrative point of view in "Miss Brill" is interesting—third-person, selective omniscience. The narrator is detached from the characters but can also see events through the eyes of the protagonist. This narrative strategy allows the reader to experience the action inwardly with the emotional intensity of Miss Brill, but it does not limit itself to only the exact words and ideas that the protagonist would use (as a first-person narrative would). At times Mansfield's narrative style could be called stream of consciousness since it often portrays the title character's interior monologue and the momentary play of thoughts and images on her mind. But the author alternates these stream of consciousness techniques with more Flaubertian selective omniscience. A close examination of Mansfield's opening paragraph will reveal how both methods co-exist in the story. In classroom discussion you might explore whether students identify more strongly with "the hero and heroine" whose cruel comments Miss Brill overhears, or do they identify with the title character? This line of questioning could be used to explore how the reader's sense of identification colors his or her sense of a fiction work.

Questions for Discussion

1. *What is the point of view in "Miss Brill"? Why is the story the better for this method of telling?* "Miss Brill" is written with selective omniscience: from the third-person viewpoint of a nonparticipant, but one who sees events through the eyes of the story's protagonist. In paragraph 5, Miss Brill notices that there is "something funny" about her fellow park sitters: "They were odd, silent, nearly all old, and

from the way they stared they looked as though they'd just come from dark little rooms or even—even cupboards!" (That she might look the same to them never enters her head—until she is forced to see herself as others see her.) Because we as readers experience the day's happenings from the perspective of Miss Brill, we come to understand and to sympathize with the sweet old dear, even go along with her sudden view of herself as an actress in a play performed every Sunday. To an intense degree we share her dismay and hurt when she overhears herself called a "stupid old thing" and her furpiece ridiculed as "exactly like a fried whiting."

2. *Where and in what season does Mansfield's story take place? How do we know? Would the effect be the same if the story were set, say, in a remote Alaskan village in the summertime?* In the opening paragraph Mansfield makes clear that Miss Brill is in the *Jardins Publiques* and, therefore, somewhere in France: in a small town, it seems, since the Sunday band concert is a big feature of local life. In paragraph 6 we learn that the sea is visible from the park. We also know that the season is autumn. Miss Brill has taken her fur out of its box for the first time in a long while. The trees are covered with "yellow leaves down drooping" (6). A chill in the air foreshadows the chill of Miss Brill's dashed spirits at the end of the story.

3. *What details provide revealing insights into Miss Brill's character and lifestyle?* Miss Brill lives frugally, alone in a small room, eking out a meager living by teaching English and reading the newspaper aloud to an invalid gentleman four afternoons a week. She seems happy with her lot even though her daily activities are drab by most standards and her pleasures are small ones. Her well-worn fur delights her, and an almond in the Sunday honey-cake is cause for rejoicing.

4. *What draws Miss Brill to the park every Sunday? What is the nature of the startling revelation that delights her on the day this story takes place?* Because she lives on the fringes of life in her small French town, Miss Brill regards her solitary Sundays in the park as the highlight of her week. Here, watching the people who come and go and eavesdropping on their conversations, she feels a connection with her fellow human beings. The smallest details about them excite her interest. She comes to feel herself one of them, an actor in life's drama. So caught up does she become in the sudden revelation that all the world's a stage and that she, like everyone else, has a part to play, that she has a mystical experience. In her mind, she merges with the other players, and "it seemed to Miss Brill that in another moment all of them, all the whole company, would begin singing" (10).

5. *Comment on the last line. What possible explanations might there be for Miss Brill's thinking that she "heard something crying?"* Miss Brill, who loves her fur as if it were a living pet or companion, is probably capable of thinking it was that "little rogue" she heard crying over the cruelty of the young couple in the park. It's possible, too, for the reader to believe that Miss Brill actually does hear a sound and that the "something crying" is herself. Perhaps she has, as Eudora Welty surmises in "The Reading and Writing of Short Stories," suffered a defeat that "one feels sure . . . is forever" (*Atlantic Monthly*, Feb.–Mar. 1949).

Joyce Carol Oates

WHERE ARE YOU GOING, WHERE HAVE YOU BEEN?
page 422

Like many another celebrated work of fiction, Oates's story was inspired by an account of an actual event. As she has pointed out, the germ of the story was an article entitled "The Pied Piper of Tucson," which appeared in Life magazine in 1966. The article concerned a man in his twenties, dressing and acting like a teenager, who seduced (and sometimes murdered) young girls. Interesting as this fact may be, one should avoid overemphasizing it in presenting the story. For one thing, Oates used the article only as a starting point, and in fact she claims that she never finished reading it, so as to leave room for her imagination to do its work. For another, literature seeks not merely to record fact but to transform it, by incorporating it into a larger, meaningful whole. Serious fiction—especially fiction like that of Oates, which is often drawn from violent and sensational occurrences—is at pains to dispute the journalistic cliché by probing the recesses of human nature to show that there is no such thing as "a senseless act."

QUESTIONS FOR DISCUSSION

1. *Describe Connie as you see her in the first few paragraphs of the story. In what ways is she appealing? In what respects is she imperceptive and immature?* Connie, Oates implies, is still growing and doesn't know whether to act "childlike" or "languid." Still discovering her identity, she behaves one way at home and another way elsewhere. Her mind is "filled with trashy daydreams," and the first caresses of love seem to her just "the way it was in movies and promised in songs."

2. *Describe the character of Arnold Friend. In what ways is he sinister? What do you make of his strangely detailed knowledge of Connie and her family, of his apparent ability to see what is happening at the barbecue, miles away? Is he a supernatural character?* Perhaps Arnold's knowledge was obtained merely by pumping Connie's friends for information and by keeping close watch on her house, and perhaps his reported vision of the barbecue is merely feigned for Connie's benefit. Much about him seems fakery: his masklike face and "stage voice," his gilded jalopy, his artificially padded boots, his affecting the speech, dress, and music of the youth culture (although he is over thirty). Still, there are hints that he is a devil or a warlock. Perhaps Ellie Oscar, the "forty-year-old baby," is his imp or familiar; perhaps his bendable boot conceals a cloven hoof. He works a kind of magic: on first spying Connie he draws a sign in the air that marks her for his own. He threatens to possess her very soul: he will enter her "where it's all secret" and then, after the sex act, she will give in to him (paragraph 104). A charismatic like Charles Manson, he seeks young girls to dominate. According to Oates, the character of Arnold Friend was inspired by the author's reading a newspaper story about a traveling murderer in the Southwest.

3. *Why doesn't Connie succeed in breaking loose from Arnold Friend's spell?* She seems in a trance, like a dazed and terrified bird facing a snake. Everything appears unreal or "only half real" (94). Like a practitioner of brainwashing, Arnold Friend denies reality: "This place you are now—inside your daddy's house—is nothing but a cardboard box I can knock down any time" (152). Arnold suggests that Connie's beating heart isn't real ("Feel that? That feels solid too but we know better") and soon she thinks her body "wasn't really hers either" (155). Perhaps, some male student will suggest, Connie really wants to give in to Arnold Friend—after all, she loves to flirt with danger and when Friend first looked at her in the parking lot, she looked back. But Connie's terror seems amply justified; Friend after all has threatened to kill her family unless she submits to him.

4. *What seems ironic in the names of the leading characters?* Friend is no friend; a better name for him would be Fiend. Ellie Oscar, like his first name, seems asexual. His last name suggests a trophy from the Motion Picture Academy—fitting for a media-slave who keeps his ear glued to his transistor radio. His androgynous name perhaps recalls that of another assassin, Lee Oswald. Connie is a connee—one who is conned.

5. *What is the point of view of this story? How is it appropriate?* Limited omniscience, with the author seeing into only one character's mind. Besides, the author perceives more than Connie does and observes Arnold Friend and Ellie more shrewdly than Connie could observe them.

6. *Explain the title. Where is Connie going, where has she been?* She has been living in a world of daydreams, and now, at the end, she is going out into a sunlit field to be raped. In the beginning of the story, we are shown that Connie lives mainly in the present; in the opening paragraph she sees "a shadowy vision of herself as she was right at the moment." She doesn't seem bothered by the ultimate questions asked in the title of the story. Arnold Friend answers the questions in paragraph 152: "The place where you came from ain't there any more, and where you had in mind to go is cancelled out." She has been nowhere, she is going nowhere—for in his view, there is no reality.

7. *What significance, if any, do you find in this story's being dedicated to Bob Dylan?* No doubt some of Dylan's music flows through Connie's mind, and some of Friend's repartee seems a weak-minded imitation of Dylanese: surreal and disconnected, as in his tirade to Ellie (133): "Don't hem in on me . . ." Arnold Friend bears a faint resemblance to Dylan: he has "a familiar face, somehow," with hawklike nose and hair "crazy as a wig," and he talks with a lilting voice "as if he were reciting the words to a song." His approach is "slightly mocking, kidding, but serious and a little melancholy" and he taps his fists together "in homage to the perpetual music behind him" (77). Joyce Carol Oates has remarked that Dylan's song "It's All Over Now, Baby Blue" (1965) was an influence on her story. Dylan's lyric addresses a young girl, Baby Blue ("My sweet little blue-eyed girl," Arnold calls Connie), who must make a hasty departure from home across an unreal, shifting landscape. A vagabond raps at her door, and she is told, "Something calls for you

/ Forget the dead you've left." Oates's title recalls a line from another Dylan song, "Mr. Tambourine Man": "And there is no place I'm goin' to."

In teaching this story to her students at the University of Georgia, Professor Anne Williams had "a couple of minor epiphanies." She has written to share them with us:

> "Ellie" may be a diminutive of "Beelzebub," lord of the flies. The story is certainly full of references to flies. I also noticed a series of comic allusions to various fairy tales, all of which, according to Bettelheim, concern the difficulties of coming to terms with adult sexuality:
>
> "Snow White" (in reference to the mother's jealousy over Connie's looks, so much like her own faded beauty [1–2]);
>
> "Cinderella" (the pumpkin on Arnold's car [36]);
>
> "Little Red Riding Hood" (here, there seems a fundamental structural parallel—and Arnold is described: "the nose long and hawk-like, sniffing as if she were a treat he was going to gobble up" [46]).

In spite of *hawk-like*, we agree the description makes Arnold sound distinctly like a wolf. Professor Williams refers, of course, to Bruno Bettelheim's *The Uses of Enchantment* (New York: Knopf, 1976). Perhaps Oates's story might be taken up together with the Grimm tale "Godfather Death."

Joyce Carol Oates reads an excerpt from this story on an audiocassette available from American Audio Prose Library, Box 842, Columbia MO 65205. For current price, call (800) 447-2275.

A film has been based on Oates's story: *Smooth Talk* (1987), directed by Joyce Chopra, with screenplay by Tom Cole. In an interview, Oates remarked that although she had nothing to do with making the movie, she respects the "quite remarkable" results. "The story itself is a Hawthornian parable of a kind, 'realistic' in its surface texture but otherwise allegorical" (interview with Barbara C. Millard, *Four Quartets*, Fall 1988). Is it, then, an account of a confrontation with the Devil, comparable with "Young Goodman Brown"?

Tim O'Brien
THE THINGS THEY CARRIED, page 435

In 1987 O'Brien published a wonderfully odd and powerful short story in *Esquire* titled "How to Tell a True War Story." (It was reprinted in his 1990 collection *The Things They Carried*.) In "How to Tell a True War Story," O'Brien mixes the techniques of memoir, literary criticism, and fiction to discuss how one conveys the grotesque atmosphere of the Vietnam War. Early in the story O'Brien's narrator observes:

> A true war story is never moral. It does not instruct, nor encourage virtue, nor suggest models of proper human behavior, nor restrain men from doing the things they have always done. If a story seems moral, do not believe it . . . You

can tell a true war story by its absolute and uncompromising allegiance to obscenity and evil.

That artistic credo illuminates but does not entirely describe "The Things They Carried." This story includes the obscene, the immoral, and the improper, but it uses those darker elements to portray a certain harsh and uncomfortable sort of virtue. By incorporating the evil and the obscene, "The Things They Carried" transcends the rules of the genre that O'Brien proclaims—admittedly through the voice of a fictionalized narrator—in "How to Tell a True War Story."

O'Brien's style in "The Things They Carried" (and in several other works) is both distinctive and unusual. He builds the story out of a series of fragmentary portraits, and he shifts aggressively from one character to another. He relishes bold shifts in tone or setting. His diction is omnivorous—from the soothingly domestic to the gritty and bellicose. He often provides elaborate catalogues as if the reality of the Vietnam War could only be described by listing all the disparate persons, places, and things it brought together. On some level the entire story is a list—the things the platoon carry into combat. The bold juxtaposition of scenes and the evocative catalogues give O'Brien's story a strongly poetic quality, and his expressive effects are as often lyric as narrative.

The reader soon recognizes that "the things" these young men carry into battles are as often mental as material. Along with weapons, food, supplies, and personal effects, they also carry hope, fear, love, hate, and belief. Kiowa, for example, carries both his Christianity and his distrust of white men. These internal possessions are reflected by two physical objects—an illustrated New Testament given to him by his Sunday-school-teaching father, and his grandfather's hunting hatchet. Each of his fellow soldiers carries a similarly complex load of objects and obsessions.

The ending of "The Things They Carried" is especially suggestive. After Lavender's death, First Lieutenant Jimmy Cross burns his most precious possession—the letters and photographs from Marthe, a college girl back home. Destroying these physical objects represents an emotional change inside Cross. Burning letters he knows by heart and cherishes as his most intimate connection with the innocent world of home, Cross deliberately razes part of himself, a source of his own humanity. He seemingly destroys this part not out of anger but from both duty and resolve. He must become a stronger if narrower person to protect his men. He must distance himself from his own civilian identity to become a better combat officer. The incident is simultaneously grim, tender, and honest. Now Cross carries something else into combat—perhaps the heaviest burden of all—Lavender's death and the fate of his men.

O'Brien's story teaches itself in a classroom. One sure-fire approach is to ask students to list all the members of the platoon with their combat specialties and then add the most important things (internal and external) each carries into combat. Then ask what these things suggest about the person in question. A good writing assignment is to ask students what three things they would carry into combat and why. (Conscientious objectors can choose what they would carry into the Peace Corps.)

120

Leslie Marmon Silko

THE MAN TO SEND RAIN CLOUDS, page 448

"The Man to Send Rain Clouds" was—amazingly—Leslie Marmon Silko's first published story. Appearing in 1969 when the author was still in college, it shows her sensibility already fully formed. ("The Man to Send Rain Clouds" was later incorporated in Silko's *Storyteller* [1981], a miscellany of stories, memoirs, anecdotes, poems, and photographs that portray her native Laguna Pueblo in New Mexico.)

The compression of Silko's story is particularly noteworthy. In a few pages she sketches the complex cultural heritage of the Laguna Pueblo, which combines both tribal and Catholic elements. To the Laguna Indians, their tribal and Catholic rituals are not mutually exclusive. Over the centuries they have incorporated Christian elements into their native rites. To the local priest, however, their combination of "pagan" and Christian beliefs seems at first sacrilegious. (Indeed, a priest's involvement in their burial custom would be forbidden by strict Catholic protocol.)

The story centers on Leon's attempt to bury his grandfather in such a way as to guarantee that the rains will come for the pueblo. In order to perform the necessary ritual, Leon must obtain holy water from the parish priest. Father Paul does not want to cooperate because the dead man did not receive last rites and will not even have an orthodox Christian burial. This initial conflict could easily have been developed stiffly and abstractly. The characters, especially in so short a work, might have remained stereotypes. Silko's achievement in "The Man to Send Rain Clouds" is to create a small cast of credible people who reveal their inner character as the action unfolds. She never reduces her characters to ideological counters but develops them as feeling, thinking, and often surprising human beings. Silko does not lecture; she shows.

The gift of storytelling has been central to Silko's artistic mission. It also appears to be part of her heritage. In an interview with German journalist Thomas Irmer, Silko claimed storytelling is an essential part of pueblo tribal culture:

> The education of the children is done within the community, this is in the old times before the coming of the Europeans. Each adult works with every child, children belong to everybody and the way to teaching is to tell stories. All information, scientific, technological, historical, religious, is put into narrative form. It is easier to remember that way. So when I began writing when I was at the University of New Mexico, the professor would say now you write your poetry or write a story, write what you know, they always tell us. All I knew was my growing up at Laguna, recallings of some other stories that I had been told as a child (Thomas Irmer, "An Interview with Leslie Marmon Silko"). <http://www.altx.com/interviews>

Commenting on this story, novelist Louis Owen also admires its evocative compression and humanity:

There is a wonderful beauty about the story, as clean and sparse as the New Mexican landscape where it's set. Like Hemingway at his best, Silko leaves almost everything out . . . She presents a Pueblo world with simple and profound clarity—no sentimental posturing, no romantic lens filter, no explanation. She expects us to enter the terrain of the Pueblo worlds the same way the priest in the story does, through accommodation made with understanding and above all, respect (Ron Hansen and Jim Shepard, eds. *You've Got to Read This* [New York: Harper, 1994]).

Anyone particularly interested in this story will want to read *Storyteller*. For a fascinating portrait of Silko's early development, look at *The Delicacy and Strength of Lace* (St. Paul: Graywolf, 1985) which reprints her correspondence with poet James Wright during the last eighteen months of his life.

A 1991 audio cassette tape of Silko reading from *The Almanac of the Dead*, her epic novel, and talking about a return to tribal values in the Americas is available from New Letters on the Air at (816) 235-1159.

POETRY

Poems Arranged by Subject and Theme

This list sorts out and classifies most of the poems in the entire textbook. Besides subjects or themes, it includes some genres (i.e., elegies, poems of spring and other seasons).

How to Use This Information. Browse through this list and you will find many poems worth teaching side by side. This list will be particularly helpful to the instructor who wishes to organize a whole poetry course differently from the way the book is structured: to teach poetry not by the elements of poems, but by themes. But, however you prefer to organize your course, you will find this list a ready source of possible writing assignments.

For Writing Topics. You might have students read three or four poems in a group (say, those in the category "Apocalypse," or a few of your choice from "Coming of Age"), then ask them to reply, in a page or two, to the question, "What do these poems have in common?" Or, "How do these poets differ in their expressions of a similar theme?"

What follows is thorough, but not exhaustive. We have left out some categories that sounded unpromising. Would you have cared that the book has four locomotive poems (by Dickinson, Stillman, Whitman, and William Carlos Williams), three (by Yeats, Hollander, and Anonymous) about swans, and two (by Cunningham and Tichborne) about persons literally or figuratively decapitated? Not all these themes and subjects are central to their poems, but all will be fairly evident.

ANGELS, DEVILS, GHOSTS, WITCHES AND ASSORTED MONSTERS

Anonymous	The Cruel Mother
Atwood	Siren Song
Bogan	Medusa
Poe	Annabel Lee
Robinson	Luke Havergal
Simic	Fork
Yeats	The Second Coming

ANIMALS (BEAST AND BIRD)

Blake	The Tyger
Frost	Design
Hollander	Swan and Shadow
Hopkins	The Windhover
T. Hughes	Hawk Roosting
Jeffers	The Beaks of Eagles
Layton	The Bull Calf
Lowell	Skunk Hour
Tennyson	The Eagle
Whitman	A Noiseless Patient Spider

APOCALYPSE

Dylan	The Times They Are a-Changing'
Frost	Fire and Ice
Hughes	Harlem [Dream Deferred]
Hughes	End
Yeats	The Second Coming

ART

Auden	Musée des Beaux Arts
Blake	The Tyger
Cherry	Advice to a Friend Who Paints
Keats	Ode on a Grecian Urn
Pastan	Ethics
Stevens	Anecdote of the Jar

ASIAN EXPERIENCE / ASIAN POETRY

Basho	Heat-lightning streak
Basho	In the old stone pool
Buson	On the one-ton temple bell
Buson	The piercing chill I feel
Issa	Cricket
Issa	Only one guy and
Jin	Missed Time
Lim	To Li Po
Shu-ning Liu	My Father's Martial Art
Moritake	The falling flower
Satyamurti	I Shall Paint My Nails Red
Song	Stamp Collecting

BELONGING TO A MINORITY (see also BLACK EXPERIENCE, INDIAN LIFE)

Alarcón	The X in My Name
Cofer	*Quinceañera*
Espaillat	Bilingual / Bilingüe
Hughes	Harlem [Dream Deferred]
Hughes	Theme for English B
Lim	To Li Po
Shu-ning Liu	My Father's Martial Art
Olds	The One Girl at the Boys' Party
Rose	For the White Poets Who Would be Indian

BLACK EXPERIENCE (see also BELONGING TO A MINORITY)

Brooks	The Bean Eaters
Brooks	We Real Cool
Cullen	For a Lady I Know
Dove	Daystar
Hayden	Those Winter Sundays
Hayden	The Whipping

Hughes	Dream Deferred [Harlem]
Hughes	A Negro Speaks of Rivers
Hughes	I, Too
Hughes	Song for a Dark Girl
Hughes	Subway Rush Hour
Hughes	Theme for English B
Nelson	A Strange Beautiful Woman
Randall	Ballad of Birmingham
Smith	Jailhouse Blues
Stillman	In Memoriam John Coltrane
Walcott	The Virgins

CARPE DIEM

Herrick	To the Virgins, to Make Much of Time
Housman	Loveliest of trees, the cherry now
Marvell	To His Coy Mistress
Waller	Go, Lovely Rose
Yost	Lai with Sounds of Skin

CHILDHOOD (see also FATHERS AND CHILDREN, MOTHERS AND CHILDREN)

Bishop	Sestina
Cleghorn	The Golf Links
Cummings	in Just–
Espaillat	Bilingual / Bilingüe
Frost	Birches
Grosholz	Listening
Hayden	The Whipping
Justice	On the Death of Friends in Childhood
Lawrence	Piano
Olds	The One Girl at the Boys' Party
Roethke	My Papa's Waltz
Thiel	*Memento Mori* in Middle School
Thomas	Fern Hill

CITY LIFE

Blake	London
Brooks	We Real Cool
Eliot	The *Boston Evening Transcript*
Eliot	The Love Song of J. Alfred Prufrock
Eliot	The winter evening settles down
Ginsberg	A Supermarket in California
Hardy	The Ruined Maid
Hughes	Lenox Avenue: Midnight
Hughes	Ballad of the Landlord
Miles	Reason
Simic	Butcher Shop
Wilbur	Love Calls Us to the Things of this World

COMING OF AGE

Cofer	*Quinceañera*
Espaillat	Bilingual / Bilingüe
Housman	When I was one-and-twenty

DEATH (see also ELEGIES)

Ashbery	At North Farm
Auden	Funeral Blues
Brooks	The Mother
Cornford	The Watch
Dickinson	Because I could not stop for Death
Dickinson	I heard a Fly buzz – when I died
Donne	Death be not proud
Frost	Birches
Frost	"Out, Out—"
Gunn	The Man with Night Sweats
Housman	To an Athlete Dying Young
Hudgins	Elegy for My Father, Who Is Not Dead
Jonson	On My First Son
Justice	On the Death of Friends in Childhood
Keats	This living hand, now warm and capable
Keats	When I have fears that I may cease to be
Kooser	Carrie
Lennon/McCartney	Eleanor Rigby
Merwin	For the Anniversary of my Death
Owen	Anthem for Doomed Youth
Pastan	Ethics
Pinsky	ABC
Plath	Lady Lazarus
Poe	Annabel Lee
Robinson	Luke Havergal
Roethke	Elegy for Jane
Rossetti	Uphill
Stevens	The Emperor of Ice-Cream
Stillman	In Memoriam John Coltrane
Tennyson	Break, Break, Break
Tennyson	Tears, Idle Tears
Tichborne	Elegy
Wordsworth	A Slumber Did My Spirit Seal

ELEGIES (see also DEATH)

Housman	To an Athlete Dying Young
Hudgins	Elegy for My Father, Who Is Not Dead
Jonson	On My First Son
Justice	On the Death of Friends in Childhood
Merwin	Elegy (quoted in Scholes, How do we make a poem?)
Poe	Annabel Lee

Roethke	Elegy for Jane
Stillman	In Memoriam John Coltrane
Tichborne	Elegy

FAITH, DOUBT, AND RELIGIOUS VISION

Arnold	Dover Beach
Bible	The Parable of the Good Seed
Brutschy	Born Again
Dickinson	Because I could not stop for Death
Dickinson	Some keep the Sabbath . . .
Donne	Batter my heart, three-personed God . . .
Donne	Death be not proud
Hardy	The Oxen
Herbert	Easter Wings
Herbert	Love
Herbert	Redemption
Hopkins	God's Grandeur
Hopkins	Pied Beauty
Hopkins	The Windhover
Hudgins	Elegy for My Father, Who Is Not Dead
Menashe	The Shrine Whose Shape I Am
Milton	When I consider how my light is spent
Rossetti	Uphill
Sáenz	To the Desert
Wilbur	Love Calls Us to the Things of This World
Wordsworth	The World Is Too Much with Us
Yeats	The Second Coming

FAME

Dickinson	Victory comes late
Dickinson	I'm Nobody! Who are you?
Guiterman	The Vanity of Earthly Greatness
Keats	When I have tears that I may cease to be
Shelley	Ozymandias

FAMILIES / PARENTS AND CHILDREN

Alvarez	The women on my mother's side . . .
Anonymous	Edward
Anonymous	The Cruel Mother
Brooks	The Mother
Dove	Daystar
Espaillat	Bilingual / Bilingüe
Foley	Haiku ("Learning to Shave")
Grosholz	Listening
Gwynn	Scenes from the Playroom
Hayden	Those Winter Sundays
Heaney	Digging

Hudgins	Elegy for My Father, Who Is Not Dead
Kees	For My Daughter
Lawrence	Piano
Liu	My Father's Martial Art
Olds	Rites of Passage
Plath	Daddy
Roethke	My Papa's Waltz
Wilbur	The Writer
J. Wright	Autumn Begins in Martins Ferry, Ohio

FARM AND COUNTRY
Frost	Birches
Frost	"Out, Out—"
Frost	Stopping by Woods on a Snowy Evening
Hardy	The Ruined Maid
Layton	The Bull Calf
Toomer	Reapers

FATE
| Hardy | The Convergence of the Twain |
| Slavitt | Titanic |

FATHERS AND CHILDREN
Foley	Haiku ("Learning to Shave")
Hayden	Those Winter Sundays
Heaney	Digging
Hudgins	Elegy for My Father, Who Is Not Dead
Jonson	On My First Son
Kees	For My Daughter
Shu-ning Liu	My Father's Martial Art
Plath	Daddy
Roethke	My Papa's Waltz
Thomas	Do not go gentle into that good night
Wilbur	The Writer

FRIENDSHIP
| Whitman | I Saw in Louisiana a Live-Oak Growing |

GLORY BE TO GOD/RELIGIOUS EXPERIENCE
Donne	Batter my heart, three-personed God
Herbert	Easter Wings
Herbert	Love
Herbert	Redemption
Hopkins	God's Grandeur
Hopkins	Pied Beauty
Hopkins	The Windhover
Sáenz	To the Desert

GRIEF (see also ELEGIES)

Dickinson	Success is counted sweetest
Dickinson	After great pain, a formal Feeling comes
Dickinson	The Bustle in a House
Hughes	Island
Jonson	Slow, slow, fresh fount, keep time with my salt tears
Niedecker	Sorrow Moves in Wide Waves
Poe	Annabel Lee
Tennyson	Break, Break, Break

HAPPINESS

Anonymous	Carnation Milk
Cummings	somewhere i have never travelled
Dickinson	I taste a liquor never brewed
Howes	Looking Up at Leaves
Kenyon	The Suitor
Yeats	The Lake Isle of Innisfree

HATRED AND INVECTIVE

Anonymous	Edward
Atwood	You fit into me
R. Browning	Soliloquy of the Spanish Cloister
Frost	Fire and Ice
H. D.	Helen
S. Smith	This Englishwoman
Steele	Epitaph
Stephens	A Glass of Beer

HEROES

Anonymous	Sir Patrick Spence
Carroll	Jabberwocky
Cummings	Buffalo Bill 's
Tennyson	Ulysses

INDIAN LIFE

Anonymous	Last Words of the Prophet (Navajo Mountain Chant)
Erdrich	Indian Boarding School: The Runaways
Momaday	Simile
Revard	Birch Canoe

INNOCENCE AND EXPERIENCE

Hopkins	Spring and Fall
Kees	For My Daughter
Pastan	Ethics

LANGUAGE (see also WRITING)

Alvarez	The women on my mother's side were known

| Carroll | Jabberwocky |
| Espaillat | Bilingual / Bilingüe |

LEAVE-TAKING

Hughes	Homecoming
Larkin	Poetry of Departures
Levertov	Leaving Forever
Lovelace	To Lucasta

LONELINESS AND ALIENATION

Anonymous	Western Wind
Bogan	Medusa
Collins	Embrace
Dickinson	After great pain, a formal feeling comes
Dickinson	I felt a Funeral, in my Brain
Dickinson	I'm Nobody! Who are you?
Dickinson	Success is counted sweetest
Dickinson	The Soul selects her own Society
Eliot	The Love Song of J. Alfred Prufrock
Eliot	The winter evening settles down
Frost	Acquainted with the Night
Frost	Desert Places
Ginsberg	A Supermarket in California
Hughes	Homecoming
Hughes	Island
Jonson	Slow, slow, fresh fount, keep time with my salt tears
Lennon/McCartney	Eleanor Rigby
Lowell	Skunk Hour
Millay	What lips my lips have kissed . . .
Nelson	A Strange Beautiful Woman
Niedecker	Sorrow Moves in Wide Waves
Robinson	Luke Havergal

LOVE AND DESIRE

Addonizio	First Poem for You
Anonymous	Bonny Barbara Allen
Anonymous	Western Wind
Arnold	Dover Beach
Bloch	Tired Sex
Bridges	Triolet
Burns	Oh, my love is like a red, red rose
Cope	Lonely Hearts
Cummings	somewhere i have never travelled . . .
Dickinson	The Soul selects her own Society
Dickinson	Wild Nights - Wild Nights!
Donne	The Flea
Frost	The Silken Tent

MOTHERS AND CHILDREN

Alvarez	The women on my mother's side were known
Anonymous	The Cruel Mother
Anonymous	Edward
Bradstreet	The Author to Her Book
Dove	Daystar
Grosholz	Listening
Gwynn	Scenes from the Playroom
Lawrence	Piano
Niedecker	Sorrow Moves in Wide Waves
Olds	Rites of Passage
Olds	The One Girl at the Boys' Party
Plath	Metaphors
Randall	Ballad of Birmingham

MUSIC

Herrick	Upon Julia's Voice
Hughes	Song for a Dark Girl
Hughes	The Weary Blues
Stillman	In Memoriam John Coltrane

MYTH AND LEGEND (other than poems in Chapter on "Myth and Narrative"; see also SCRIPTURE AND APOCRYPHA)

Atwood	Siren Song
Tennyson	Ulysses
Thiel	*Memento Mori* in Middle School
Yeats	Leda and the Swan
Yeats	Sailing to Byzantium
Yeats	Who Goes with Fergus?

NATURE (See also ANIMALS, THE SEASONS)

Bishop	The Fish
Blake	To see a world in a grain of sand
Blake	The Tyger
Dickinson	A Route of Evanescence
Dickinson	The Lightning is a yellow Fork
Frost	Desert Places
Gioia	California Hills in August
Hollander	Swan and Shadow
Hopkins	Pied Beauty
Hopkins	Spring and Fall
Hopkins	The Windhover
Housman	Loveliest of trees, the cherry now
Howes	Looking Up at Leaves
T. Hughes	Hawk Roosting
Jeffers	The Beaks of Eagles
Layton	The Bull Calf

Roethke	Root Cellar
Ryan	Blandeur
G. Snyder	Mid-August at Sourdough Mountain Lookout
Stafford	Traveling Through the Dark
Stephens	The Wind
Stevens	Anecdote of the Jar
Stevens	Thirteen Ways of Looking at a Blackbird
Teasdale	The Flight
Tennyson	Flower in the Crannied Wall
Tennyson	The Eagle
Williams	Spring and All
Wordsworth	I Wandered Lonely as a Cloud
Yeats	Lake Isle of Innisfree

OLD AGE (AND AGING)
Brooks	The Bean Eaters
Niedecker	Sorrow Moves in Wide Waves
Shakespeare	That time of year thou mayst in me behold
Tennyson	Ulysses
W. C. Williams	To Waken an Old Lady
Yeats	Sailing to Byzantium
Yeats	When You Are Old

POVERTY
Alarcón	The X in My Name
Brooks	The Bean Eaters
Cleghorn	The Golf Links
Niedecker	Popcorn-can Cover

PRAISE AND EXULTATION
Blake	To see a world in a grain of sand
Burns	Oh, my love is like a red, red rose
Hopkins	God's Grandeur
Hopkins	Pied Beauty
Howes	Looking Up at Leaves
Shakespeare	Shall I compare thee to a summer's day?
Tennyson	The splendor falls on castle walls
Wilbur	Love Calls Us to the Things of This World
Wordsworth	My heart leaps up when I behold

PROTEST POEMS
Alarcón	The X in My Name
Blake	London
Cleghorn	The Golf Links
Cullen	For a Lady I Know
Dylan	The Times They Are a-Changing'
Hughes	Dream Deferred

Hughes	I, Too
McKay	America
Owen	Dulce et Decorum Est
Randall	Ballad of Birmingham
Rich	Aunt Jennifer's Tigers
Wordsworth	The World Is Too Much with Us

SCIENCE AND TECHNOLOGY
Eberhart	The Fury of Aerial Bombardment
Frost	Design
Reed	Naming of Parts

SCRIPTURE AND APOCRYPHA
Bible	Parable of the Good Seed

THE SEASONS
Spring
Frost	Nothing Gold Can Stay
Housman	Loveliest of trees, the cherry now
W. C. Williams	Spring and All

Summer
Gioia	California Hills in August
Howes	Looking Up at Leaves
G. Snyder	Mid-August at Sourdough Mountain Lookout
Toomer	Reapers

Autumn
Hopkins	Spring and Fall
Longfellow	Aftermath
Robinson	Luke Havergal
Stephens	The Wind
J. Wright	Autumn Begins in Martins Ferry, Ohio

Winter
Bly	Driving to Town Late to Mail a Letter
Frost	Stopping by Woods on a Snowy Evening
Hayden	Those Winter Sundays
Niedecker	Popcorn-can cover
Shakespeare	When icicles hang by the wall

SPORTS
Housman	To an Athlete Dying Young
Shu-ning Liu	My Father's Martial Art
Updike	Ex-Basketball Player
Whitman	The Runner
J. Wright	Autumn Begins in Martins Ferry, Ohio

TIME, THE PASSAGE OF (see also *CARPE DIEM*, OLD AGE)

Auden	As I Walked Out One Evening
Cummings	anyone lived in a pretty how town
Eliot	The Love Song of J. Alfred Prufrock
Housman	Loveliest of trees, the cherry now
Jeffers	To the Stone-cutters
Pastan	Ethics
Shakespeare	Not marble nor the gilded monuments
Shakespeare	That time of year thou mayst in me behold
Shelley	Ozymandias
Wordsworth	Mutability
Yeats	Sailing to Byzantium

VIOLENCE

Eberhart	The Fury of Aerial Bombardment
Hayden	The Whipping
Hughes	Song for a Dark Girl
Levine	Animals Are Passing from Our Lives
Owen	Dulce et Decorum Est
Randall	Ballad of Birmingham

WAR

Arnold	Dover Beach
Eberhart	The Fury of Aerial Bombardment
Jarrell	The Death of the Ball Turret Gunner
Kees	For My Daughter
Komunyakaa	Facing It
Lovelace	To Lucasta
Owen	Anthem for Doomed Youth
Owen	Dulce et Decorum Est
Reed	Naming of Parts
Whitman	Beat! Beat! Drums!
Whitman	Cavalry Crossing a Ford

A WOMAN'S IDENTITY (see also MOTHERS AND CHILDREN)

Alvarez	The women on my mother's side were known
Brooks	The Mother
Clifton	Homage to my hips
Cofer	*Quinceañera*
Dove	Daystar
Nelson	A Strange Beautiful Woman
Olds	The One Girl at the Boys' Party
Plath	Daddy
Rich	Aunt Jennifer's Tigers
Rich	Women
Sexton	Cinderella

Poems for Further Reading, Arranged by Elements

Many instructors tell us that they use the poems in Chapter 27, "Poems for Further Reading," as an extra reservoir or second fuel tank of illustrations. Others, to be sure, think the book already offers too many examples. If that is your feeling, don't bother with this section.

If, however, you would like a few more poems (or some different poems) to illustrate matters taken up in the body of the book, then the following list can help you put your finger on them. It classifies only poems in the "Poems for Further Reading" section, and it works through the book chapter by chapter.

For Writing Topics. After your students have studied a chapter of the book, you can direct them to certain poems in the "Poems for Further Reading." Assign a poem or two and a short paper that springs from their reading. (An essay of two or three paragraphs might be enough: at this stage, overlong papers on topics such as figures of speech, rime and meter, stanza form, etc., might be debilitating.) Topics will occur: The Character of the Soliloquist in Browning's "Spanish Cloister" (after studying *The Person in the Poem*); The Attitude of the Daughter in Plath's "Daddy" *(Tone)*, and more.

For suggesting that this manual could use such a classification of the "Poems for Further Reading," thanks to Professor Harvey Birenbaum of San Jose State University.

11 Listening to a Voice

TONE

Some poems in which the poet's attitude is especially clear:

Jonson	On My First Son
Owen	Anthem for Doomed Youth
Plath	Daddy

Some poems that express, as Auden says, "a clear expression of mixed feelings":

Eliot	The Love Song of J. Alfred Prufrock
Larkin	Poetry of Departures
Lowell	Skunk Hour
Nelson	A Strange Beautiful Woman

THE PERSON IN THE POEM

Some poems in which the identity of the speaker is interestingly different from the poet's "I":

R. Browning	Soliloquy of the Spanish Cloister
Gunn	The Man with Night Sweats

| Levine | Animals Are Passing from Our Lives |
| Pound | The River Merchant's Wife: a Letter |

IRONY

(other kinds besides ironic point of view, as in the poems just listed):

| Hardy | The Convergence of the Twain (irony of Fate) |
| Reed | Naming of Parts (a discrepancy between the study of a gun and the study of nature, between the voice of the instructor and the view of the soldier; verbal irony in the pun "easing the spring") |

12 Words

LITERAL MEANING: WHAT A POEM SAYS FIRST

Poems that can be taken at face value, without looking for symbols, endless suggestions, huge significance (not that they won't repay thought and close reading):

Gioia	California Hills in August
Larkin	Poetry of Departures
Slavitt	Titanic
Updike	Ex-Basketball Player

THE VALUE OF A DICTIONARY

Poems containing two or more brief allusions:

| Eliot | The Love Song of J. Alfred Prufrock |

Poems with central allusions:

Auden	Musée des Beaux Arts
Keats	On First Looking into Chapman's Homer (the celebrated blooper in the allusion to Cortez)
Milton	When I consider how my light is spent
Tennyson	Ulysses

WORD CHOICE AND WORD ORDER

Poems in dialect:

| Anonymous | Edward |

Poems whose diction and syntax depart from those of speech:

Blake	The Tyger
Coleridge	Kubla Khan
Cummings	somewhere i have never travelled
Hardy	The Convergence of the Twain
Hopkins	Spring and Fall
Hopkins	The Windhover
Keats	On First Looking into Chapman's Homer (inverted syntax: "Much have I . . . ," "Yet did I never breathe," "Then felt I," etc.)

| Moore | Poetry |
| Thomas | Fern Hill |

Poems containing technical words:

| Reed | Naming of Parts |

Poems in colloquial diction:

Frost	Birches
Frost	Stopping by Woods on a Snowy Evening
Levine	Animals Are Passing from Our Lives
Olds	The One Girl at the Boys' Party
Updike	Ex-Basketball Player

Poems containing an interesting mix of formal and colloquial diction:

Ginsberg	A Supermarket in California
Larkin	Poetry of Departures
Simpson	American Poetry

13 Saying and Suggesting

Some poems especially full of words rich in connotations:

Coleridge	Kubla Khan
Cummings	somewhere i have never travelled
Eliot	The Love Song of J. Alfred Prufrock
Thomas	Fern Hill

14 Imagery

Erdrich	Indian Boarding School: The Runaways
Gioia	California Hills in August
Thomas	Fern Hill
W. C. Williams	Spring and All
W. C. Williams	To Waken an Old Lady

15 Figures of Speech

METAPHOR AND SIMILE

Poems with central metaphors:

Hopkins	The Windhover
Song	Stamp Collecting
Whitman	I Saw in Louisiana a Live-Oak Growing
W. C. Williams	To Waken an Old Lady
Wroth	In this strange labyrinth

Other poems with prominent metaphors:

Shakespeare	That time of year thou mayst in me behold
Simic	Butcher Shop
Wilbur	The Writer

Poem with a prominent simile:

| Keats | On First Looking at Chapman's Homer |

OTHER FIGURES

Frost	Birches (understatement)
Levine	Animals Are Passing from Our Lives (personification)
Marvell	To His Coy Mistress (hyperbole)
Plath	Daddy (hyperbole)
Reed	Naming of Parts (pun)
Waller	Go, Lovely Rose (apostrophe, personification)
W. C. Williams	Spring and All (personification)

16 Song

SINGING AND SAYING

Some poems originally sung (see also BALLADS):

Anonymous	Western Wind

BALLADS

Anonymous	Edward

A balladlike poem:

Auden	As I Walked Out One Evening

17 Sound

ALLITERATION AND ASSONANCE

Blake	The Tyger
Coleridge	Kubla Khan
Hopkins	Spring and Fall
Hopkins	The Windhover
Thomas	Fern Hill
Waller	Go, Lovely Rose

RIME

Poems whose rimes may well repay study:

Eliot	The Love Song of J. Alfred Prufrock
Lowell	Skunk Hour
Owen	Anthem For Doomed Youth
Plath	Daddy

18 Rhythm

STRESSES AND PAUSES

In any good metrical poem, rhythms matter, of course, and can't be disentangled from meanings. Here are some poems in open or syllabic forms in which rhythms play strong parts:

Reed	Naming of Parts
Thomas	Fern Hill

METER

Wyatt   They flee from me that sometime did me sekë

19 Closed Form

FORMAL PATTERNS, SONNETS, EPIGRAMS, OTHER FORMS

Poems in blank verse:
Frost   Birches
Tennyson   Ulysses
Updike   Ex-Basketball Player

Poems in closed (heroic) couplets:
Jonson   On My First Son

Poems in tercets:
Hardy   The Convergence of the Twain

Poems in tightly structured riming stanzas:
Donne   The Flea
Frost   Stopping by Woods on a Snowy Evening
Gunn   The Man with Night Sweats
Herbert   Love

Poems in syllabic stanzas:
Moore   Poetry
Noguchi   Hokku
Thomas   Fern Hill

Sonnets:
E. B. Browning   How Do I Love Thee?
Hopkins   The Windhover
Keats   On First Looking into Chapman's Homer
Keats   When I have fears that I may cease to be
MacLeish   The End of the World
Milton   When I consider how my light is spent
Owen   Anthem for Doomed Youth
Shakespeare   This time of year thou mayst in me behold
Shakespeare   When, in disgrace with Fortune and men's eyes
Wroth   In this strange labyrinth

Villanelles:
Bishop   One Art

20 Open Form

A few classics of open form poetry:
Cummings   somewhere i have never travelled
Ginsberg   A Supermarket in California
Pound   The River Merchant's Wife: a Letter
Roethke   Elegy for Jane

Whitman	I Saw in Louisiana a Live-Oak Growing
W. C. Williams	Spring and All
W. C. Williams	To Waken an Old Lady

21 Symbol

Ashbery	At North Farm
Eliot	The Love Song of J. Alfred Prufrock
Lowell	Skunk Hour

22 Myth and Narrative

| Atwood | Siren Song |

23 Poetry and Personal Identity

Brooks	The Mother
Browning	How Do I Love Thee?
Gioia	California Hills in August (regional identity)
Gunn	The Man with Night Sweats (gay identity)
Hayden	Those Winter Sundays (being a son)
Heaney	Digging
Jonson	On My First Son
Larkin	Poetry of Departures
Liu	My Father's Martial Art
Lowell	Skunk Hour
Milton	When I consider how my light was spent (Milton on his disability)
Nelson	A Strange Beautiful Woman
Owen	Anthem for Doomed Youth (war poem written by a soldier)
Plath	Daddy
Thomas	Fern Hill

24 Recognizing Excellence

| Hardy | The Convergence of the Twain (a poem surely bad in parts—e.g., stanza 5—but good in its entirety!) |

RECOGNIZING EXCELLENCE
[Your choice]

Poems Students Like Most

At the end of the book is a short student questionnaire. This form solicits each student's opinion about his or her reactions to the book. The editors read and save each completed questionnaire they receive. These candid student responses often help improve the anthology from edition to edition.

One of the most interesting insights afforded by these questionnaires is a good sense of the poems students like most. (Their favorites often differ from the poems instructors rate most highly, though there is also much overlap.) Significantly, both students and instructors lean heavily toward twentieth century poems and poets. Instructors might enjoy learning the poems and poets most frequently chosen by students. Some choices may surprise you.

Students often identify their favorite poets rather than a specific poem. The five poets most frequently named by students (in order) are:

FAVORITE POETS

1. William Carlos Williams

2. Robert Frost

3. E. E. Cummings

4. Emily Dickinson

5. Langston Hughes

The individual poems most frequently praised by students are listed below. Some are familiar favorites; others are pleasant surprises. There may be some poems high on this list that some instructors do not teach. It might be worthwhile to consider adding them to your reading list.

FAVORITE POEMS (Student Choices in Rank Order)

1. Robert Frost, "Fire and Ice"

2. Stevie Smith, "Not Waving but Drowning"

3. Margaret Atwood, "You fit into me"

4. Robert Frost, "Out, Out—"

5. Elizabeth Bishop, "The Fish"

6. Robert Browning, "My Last Duchess"

7. Robert Frost, "The Road Not Taken"

8. Sylvia Plath, "Metaphors"

9. James Stephens, "A Glass of Beer"

10. W. H. Auden, "The Unknown Citizen"

11. William Blake, "The Tyger"

12. E. E. Cummings, "anyone lived in a pretty how town"

13. Emily Dickinson, "Because I could not stop for Death"

14. Stephen Crane, "The Heart"

15. A. E. Housman, "To an Athlete Dying Young"

16. Robert Frost, "The Secret Sits"

17. Theodore Roethke, "My Papa's Waltz"

18. Lewis Carroll, "Jabberwocky"

19. William Shakespeare, "Shall I compare thee to a summer's day?"

This list of student favorites is not statistically reliable, and it changes slightly with each new batch of responses, but the results are nonetheless interesting to ponder. A purist might blanch at the particular Whitman poem chosen from the many in the book, but if the list indicates anything, it is that the students responding have pretty good taste in poetry. No matter how discouraging some days in the classroom may occasionally feel, you can take heart that you are making a strong impression on many students.

10 Reading a Poem

William Butler Yeats, THE LAKE ISLE OF INNISFREE, page 457

As a young man in London in 1887–91, Yeats found himself hating the city and yearning for the west of Ireland. He recalled: "I was going along the Strand, and passing a shop window where there was a little ball kept dancing by a jet of water, I remembered waters about Sligo and was moved to a sudden emotion that shaped itself into 'The Lake Isle of Innisfree'" (*Memoirs* [New York: Macmillan, 1972] 31). In London (he recalled in his *Autobiography*), he sometimes imagined himself "living in imitation of Thoreau on Innisfree, a little island in Lough Gill." The nine bean rows of the poem were evidently inspired by Thoreau's bean patch.

Yeats's lines provide rich rows of sound for the student to hoe: assonance (from *I . . . arise* in the first through the o-sounds in the closing stanza), onomatopoeia *(lapping)*, initial alliteration, internal alliteration *(arise, Innisfree; hear, heart's core)*. Sound images of bees, cricket, linnet, and lake water are predominant. Whatever noises come from roadway or pavement, however, are left unspecified.

Perhaps, in London, Yeats thought himself one of Ireland's prodigal sons. At least, A. Norman Jeffares has noticed in the first line an echo from the parable of the prodigal son (Luke 15:18): "I will arise and go to my father" (*A Commentary on the Collected Poems of W. B. Yeats* [Stanford: Stanford UP, 1968] 35).

In later years, according to John Unterecker, Yeats was shocked that "The Lake Isle" had become his most popular poem. He had taken a dislike to its "Biblical opening lines." But audiences always demanded it of him, and his sonorous reading of the poem is available on a recording (Spoken Arts, 753).

LYRIC POETRY

D. H. Lawrence, PIANO, page 460

About the first question: it's really a quick writing assignment. Ten minutes of class time might be enough to let students write their paraphrases. To be sure, you could let them wing it and paraphrase the poem out loud, but the results may not be so thoughtful or accurate. A few of the students might then be asked to read their efforts aloud, for others to agree or disagree with.

Reader response theory, if crudely applied, might claim that every paraphrase is valid. But we think it greatly helps a class discussion to assume that it is possible to find an interpretation of a poem that all or most will agree comes closest to it.

"Piano" isn't a flawless poem. Lawrence was seldom at ease in rime, and the strained juxtaposition of *clamor* and *glamor* indicates his discomfort. Still, *glamor* is an accurate word in its context: the mature man knows that the child's eyes endowed the past with an illusory beauty. The quality of Lawrence's poem may be seen in the specificity of its detail: "the boom of the tingling strings," "the small, poised feet." Lawrence enters into the child's perspective, while able to criticize it from outside. The speaker is resisting his urge to cry, as the connotations of his words indicate (the song is *insidious*, it *betrays).* But at last he is unable to hold back his tears and, sensibly, yields to them.

How does Lawrence's poem escape bathos? Robert Pinsky has offered an explanation in "Poetry and Pleasure," in *Threepenny Review* (Fall 1983). The subject of "Piano," Pinsky finds, is a stock source for poems, "as mothers-in-law or airplanes with ethnically various passengers are stock sources for jokes." Yet the poem strikes us with "something fresh, not stock." Its language is vivid, unconventional; its words *insidious* and *betrays* add a "steely spring"; it sets up an energetic tension between present and past.

Adrienne Rich, AUNT JENNIFER'S TIGERS, page 461

Rich's own comments on "Aunt Jennifer's Tigers" (found in this chapter's "Writer's Perspective") provide an interesting view of the poem. Rich explains how an artist can put many things into a poem which he or she is not fully conscious of until much later. Today Rich is universally recognized as the chief poet of American feminism, but that was neither her public image nor private identity in 1951. Yet Rich's feminist perspective had already begun to emerge intuitively in her early poems like "Aunt Jennifer's Tigers."

It is apparent in the poem that the poet perceived something wrong with the passive role assigned to women. The pride, confidence, and fearlessness ("masculine" virtues, whatever the sex of the tigers) of Aunt Jennifer's imaginary creations contrast sharply with Aunt Jennifer herself—a frail lady with fluttering fingers, *terrified hands.* Worth comment is the poet's use of the word *ringed*—suggesting "encircled"—to refer both to the wedding ring that "sits heavily upon Aunt Jennifer's hand" and to "ordeals she was mastered by," specifically marriage and being expected to conform. Although she goes down in defeat, her tigers triumph.

Some possible questions for discussion include:

1. In literal terms what are Aunt Jennifer's tigers? What sort of "panels" does she appear to be making?

2. The speaker depicts Aunt Jennifer mainly through her hands. What specific details characterize these hands?

3. Why are Aunt Jennifer's hands "terrified"?

4. What attributes characterize the tigers?

5. What does Aunt Jennifer express in the panel she weaves that she does not so easily express in her daily life?

Compare Aunt Jennifer with the dead woman who once embroidered fantails in Wallace Stevens's "The Emperor of Ice-Cream." For another contrast between a dull world of reality and the colorful life of the imagination, see Stevens's "Disillusionment of Ten O'Clock" in which:

> Only, here and there, an old sailor,
> Drunk and asleep in his boots,
> Catches tigers
> In red weather.

For an interesting classroom discussion, ask students why this poem is lyric rather than narrative. There is certainly a story implied in the images that describe Aunt Jennifer and her surroundings, and Rich surely intends us to ponder the significance of these images. The poem remains essentially lyric, however, in its brevity, musicality, and evocative emotionality. A lyric poem characteristically focuses on a particular instant in time and explores—usually in subjective and imagistic terms—the emotional, intellectual, and imaginative implications of that instant. (A narrative poem, by contrast, must move from one significant point in time to another.) A good lyric poem, however, will often contain secondary narrative elements just as a strong narrative poem will incorporate lyric effects to heighten its impact.

Mary Slowik discusses "Aunt Jennifer's Tigers" and other early poems of Rich in "The Friction of the Mind," *Massachusetts Review* (Spring 1984): 142–60.

NARRATIVE POETRY

Anonymous, SIR PATRICK SPENCE, page 462

On the questions in the book: We really don't think the king's motive cán be known for sure from this bare portrait of him; we ask this question mainly to prompt students to pay attention to what they find on the page and be wary of deep extrapolations. As far as we see him in the poem, the king sits around drinking wine, leading a life of ease, and (with a deliberate official gesture) sends his best sea-captain and a loyal contingent of naval officers to their doom. Although the poet takes a sour view of the comfortable life at court, he feels for the Scots nobles, and we too are moved by his spare sketch of the bereaved ladies, futilely waiting for their men, who will never return. The great stanza about the new and old moons, apparently an ill omen, serves further to heighten the tension of the story and foreshadow its conclusion.

Here are two more questions:

1. Comment on Sir Patrick's character. What do you make of his abrupt transition from laughter to tears (lines 13–16)? (He is not only brave and loyal to obey the king's order; he is a passionate man with quick, open, unconcealed feelings.)

2. In what lines do you notice a wry comment on the soft life that the nobles led at court? What does this attitude suggest about this anonymous poet? (lines

29–30: The nobles are loath to get their fine shoes wet. Probably the poet wasn't a noble, but a sarcastic commoner.)

In the famous image of the slim new moon, W. D. Snodgrass finds visual reminders of the king's golden crown and of the gold combs in the ladies' hair. For him, withering scorn for the Scottish lords afraid to dampen their fancy French pumps comes naturally to the singer, who probably went barefoot for much of his life. And he concludes: "This ballad, at least partly because of its scorn for the ignorant court, seems superbly successful in recognizing a more genuine nobility. Not that I need agree with its values: personally, I'd prefer (though not expect to find) a captain with more loyalty to his men than to king and office. Yet while the song lasts, I partake of the Scottish singer's world, and am broadened by entrance to another's experience, another's values." See "Shapes Merging and Emerging," *Shenandoah* (Winter 1991): 58–83.

Robert Frost, "OUT, OUT—," page 464

Like Sir Patrick Spence, the boy's initial reaction to his terrible realization is to laugh—then, almost at once, dismay sets in. And like the folk ballad, "Out, Out—" tells a story of sudden, meaningless death, and does so with spare economy.

Perhaps the "they"—the doctor and the hospital staff—who turn to their own affairs are not merciless. The "watcher at his pulse" grows frightened when the pulse fails; no one wants to believe the boy will die. Radcliffe Squires finds no one to blame for the "faceless accident." In his view, "Simultaneously, one sees the human watchers touched by normal griefs and fears. And yet life must turn to a more important task finally, that of continuing. . . . Only the grand composer could hold together in one poem the two severe and mutually accusing ideas that one must be moved to pity and compassion and that one must coldly and sternly pursue the duty of endurance and survival" (*The Major Themes of Robert Frost* [U of Michigan P, 1963] 46). Frost's poem offers no comfort, but seems a realistic view of what happens in an emergency ward. Any student interested in a career in medicine might be asked for a response to this poem.

Frost's allusion to *Macbeth* is part of the meaning of the poem, and the students may be asked to think about it. Perhaps Frost suggests that the snarling buzz-saw full of sound and fury, reaching out its friendly handshake, just doesn't make sense. This, as Stanley Burnshaw has noticed, is one among several of Frost's poems that seem to question the existence of a benevolent order in the universe. Others include "A Servant to Servants," "The Housekeeper," "Home Burial," and (we would add) "Design" (*Robert Frost Himself* [New York: Braziller, 1986] 298).

Frost based his poem on an actual incident: an accident that had happened in 1910 to a sixteen-year-old boy he knew in Bethlehem, New Hampshire; five years went by before the poem took form (in 1915–16). See Lawrance Thompson, *Robert Frost: The Early Years* (New York: Holt, 1966) 566–567.

In the article just cited in the previous entry, W. D. Snodgrass contrasts "Sir Patrick Spence" with "Out, Out—." The first poem is about a man who looks unflinchingly at the world's horror ("the buzz-saw of the world"); the second, about a boy who tries to avoid beholding it.

Of Frost's poem, he remarks: "The one thing you must never do while working with machinery is to lift your eyes. The boy does just that—not to count ranges, but perhaps to count time 'saved from work' by his sister's call. A horrifying salvation is granted him: not just a half hour, but a lifetime, saved from work." Why the vision of five mountain ranges on the horizon (lines 4–6)? "To lift one's view from saw to horizon, reveals a terrifying similarity. We are given one glimpse, ironically lovely, of the edged and jagged teeth of a world only too ready to take us for its 'Supper.'" If the poem had a superscription, it ought to come from the old hymn: "Work, for the night is coming when man (or boy) works no more."

Jean Tobin, who teaches at the University of Wisconsin Center in Sheboygan County, reports the powerful effect Frost's poem usually has on students.

> Your discussions of narrative, lyric, and dramatic poetry works well for the kinds of students I have. I read Frost's "Out, Out—" and was pleased by absolute silence at the end followed by one student's under-the-breath "Damn." As the discussion roared along, even that first hour, one student remarked how strange it was that the boy's first reaction was to laugh. "Oh, no," said a girl, holding up a hand and keeping it raised until we all saw it had no fingers, "that's exactly what you do." After that I didn't have to convince anybody about the relevance of poetry to daily life.

DRAMATIC POETRY

Robert Browning, MY LAST DUCHESS, page 465

We have brought this famous dramatic monologue back into the book because of instructor demand; we received more requests to reinstate the poem than any other new selection. Students generally find it fascinating, and instructors consider it an invaluable means of teaching the idea of a persona poem.

Some teachers may want to assign this poem in conjunction with Browning's "Soliloquy of the Spanish Cloister," which is in the "Poems for Further Reading" chapter. These two dramatic poems, both uttered by speakers we find unsympathetic, may be taken together as memorable works of character-drawing. In each poem, Browning places us in the midst of a society remote from our own in time, and thoroughly undemocratic. Of the two, only "My Last Duchess" is a typical dramatic monologue. "Soliloquy," as its title indicates, addresses no listener.

"My Last Duchess" may be familiar to students from high school literature courses; and if a show of hands indicates that they have met it before, we would spend less time with it. Whether or not it is familiar, it makes a useful companion to "Soliloquy." Students may be asked to define their feelings toward the Duke, to point to lines in the poem that helped define those feelings. Browning stresses the Duke's arrogance ("I choose / Never to stoop"; "I gave commands; / Then all smiles stopped together") and engages our sympathies for the poor Duchess in lines 21–31, despite the Duke's contempt for her facility to be gladdened. We know one instructor who in teaching this classic takes the tack, "Shouldn't we feel sorry for the Duke, with all his marital troubles?" (Students of both sexes are usually provoked to rise and trounce him.) Another question: to what extent is the Duke's attitude toward women presumably typical of his society? That the Count, the visitor's master, would offer a daughter to a man who had just disposed of his wife, suggests that the Duke is not alone in regarding women as chattel. Still, even for a Renaissance duke he seems cold-hearted: wives and works of art seem identified as objects to collect.

What were the Duke's commands that stopped the Duchess's smiles? "That she should be put to death, or he might have had her shut up in a convent," Browning once explained. But lines 2 ("Looking as if she were alive") and 46–47 ("There she stands / As if alive") seem to hint that she was executed. Hypocrisy is still another aspect of the Duke's character: compare his protest that he lacks skill in speech (lines 35–36) with his artful flattery of the Count (49–53).

Instructors should note that this book includes Robert Langbaum's insightful commentary on "My Last Duchess" in the "Critical Approaches to Literature" chapter.

WRITING CRITICALLY

William Stafford, ASK ME, page 469
William Stafford, A PARAPHRASE OF "ASK ME," page 469

The author himself so skillfully paraphrases this poem in the prose excerpt that follows it, that an editor offers further analysis at his own risk. A few comments, however, may provide a departure point for classroom discussions. Notice how the speaker asks several questions in the poem that are never specifically answered. *What* mistakes has the speaker made? *What* difference has love or hate made in his life? *Is* what he has done his life? The speaker answers the questions only with the final enigmatic and imagistic line. Stafford clearly trusts the reader's intuition to understand the ending.

Stafford's paraphrase is a bit freer and more interpretive than we might want from a student, but he proceeds through the poem line by line, image by image. Notice how Stafford spends more time on the final image than on earlier ones. He knows it requires more commentary—and a small imaginative leap—to explain. Stafford's deft paraphrase of "Ask Me" should demonstrate to students that close reading and critical discussion are not antithetical to the spirit of poetry.

11 *Listening to a Voice*

Theodore Roethke, MY PAPA'S WALTZ, *page 472*

Theodore Roethke's poem is one of the most widely taught selections in the book, and it usually proves a provocative topic for classroom discussion. We have revised the critical discussion of the poem in the new edition to reflect the broad range of opinion on this powerful poem. We have also included a new student essay focused directly on the main issues that usually emerge from classroom discussions.

Many instructors have shared their reactions with us:
Steven Hind of Hutchinson Community College disagreed with a previous edition's comments on this poem—"It seems to me that the poem is richer than Professor Kennedy's discussion would allow"—and finds its view of Papa ambivalent. "Kennedy hears a 'playfulness' in the slant rhyme *dizzy* and *easy*. Would it be possible to hear that as a slight dissonance? The only other double rhyme in the poem is *knuckle* and *buckle,* which has a hard edge to it, to my ear, [Mother] doesn't seem to be having such a good time. The involuntary response suggests that this isn't a novel experience. She will be the one who picks up the pans, one supposes. *Scraped* is a harsh verb. The ear is a sensitive organ. Certainly the boy loves his father and relishes the recollection of the dear brute's drunken revelry that included him, but these verbs present an unavoidable tension, it seems to me. The father may, as Professor Kennedy says, be 'happily using his son's head for a drum,' but that doesn't mean the drum is entirely comfortable with the impact."

Professor Hind adds a sobering anecdote:

> Last year in composition class I taught the recovering alcoholic son of an alcoholic father. He wrote papers about the loving and terrible bond he felt with his father, and some of his experiences reminded me of this poem. I saw Rick in the hall two weeks ago and asked how his summer had gone. "It would have been better if I hadn't learned that my father has been molesting his daughter the past four years and I didn't know about it," he said. They are in therapy. "My mother's countenance / Could not unfrown itself."

Ann Barnard of Blackburn College, in a provocative article, also thinks the poem's dark side worth emphasis. She and a colleague had expressed chagrin that half their students had read "My Papa's Waltz" as a poem about child abuse, reducing it to a social tract. But their mutual rediscovery of the poem "included the idea of covert *emotional* abuse." Papa, whose waltz gives the child both pleasure and pain, is a figure of ambivalence. See "'My Papa's Waltz' as a Problem in Pedagogy," *Teaching English in the Two-Year College* 18 (Feb. 1991): 43–47.

Fred Roux of Shippensburg University of Pennsylvania reports that his students' interpretations of "My Papa's Waltz" have differed according to sex. Young men almost unanimously respond to the poem as a happy childhood memory of a loving father's exuberant horseplay. A few young women react negatively. For them, "I hung on like death" and "You beat time on my head," as well as "battered" and "scraped," suggest that the speaker's recollection is unhappy. They also assume that a man with whiskey on his breath must be drunk. None has perceived an ironic parallel between their responses and that of the speaker's frowning mother. "From this," adds Professor Roux, "it would appear that student response to 'My Papa's Waltz' is, to a degree, the result of a difference in socializing experiences during early childhood." Haven't any young women had boisterous fathers? We'd like to hear other classroom experiences.

As Alan Seager discerns in his biography of Roethke, *The Glass House* (New York: McGraw, 1968) 23, the mature Roethke seems to have felt a certain guilty resentment against his father, a sense of how (as an awkward, chubby, bookish, and sensitive child) the young poet had failed to make the old man proud of him.

"My Papa's Waltz" may have had its genesis in a wish-fulfilling dream. After his father's death Roethke wrote a memoir (calling himself "John"): "Sometimes he dreamed about Papa. Once it seemed Papa came in and danced around with him. John put his feet on top of Papa's and they'd waltz. Hei-dee-dei-dei. Rump-tee-tump. Only babies expected dreams to come true" (qtd. in Seager, 24).

Countee Cullen, FOR A LADY I KNOW, page 473

From Cullen's first book, *Color* (1925), this is one of a series of twenty-nine epitaphs. Compare it with another brief poem that makes a biting social comment: Sarah N. Cleghorn's "The Golf Links." Cleghorn's poem seems angrier; the tone of Cullen's poem seems to be wry amusement at stupidity.

Cullen's early biography is sparsely documented. Raised by his grandmother until he was eleven, he was then adopted by the Reverend Frederick A. Cullen, pastor of a Methodist church in Harlem, who gave the future poet not only a name but a new life of books and conversation. Famed as the leading poet of the Harlem Renaissance, Cullen suffered a decline in reputation when militant black critics of the 1960s reevaluated his work and found it wanting in anger and social consciousness. But his wit can bite, as it does in "For a Lady I Know"; and Houston A. Baker has rightly called much of his work an "ironical protest . . . against economic oppression" in his short study of Cullen, *A Many-Colored Coat of Dreams* (Detroit: Broadside, 1974).

Anne Bradstreet, THE AUTHOR TO HER BOOK, page 473

The "rags" (line 5) worn by this bastard brat of a book may have been the first edition's abundance of typographical errors. Although Bradstreet patiently revised her work, she did not live to see her "brat" appear in better dress. This poem prefaced the Boston edition published in 1678, six years after the author's death.

Robert Hutchinson, in the introduction to his edition of *Poems of Anne Bradstreet* (New York: Dover, 1969), gives a concise account of the book's publication. Evidently the author's family, proud of her poetry, felt that it deserved more notice than New England could then give. The Reverend John Woodbridge, Bradstreet's brother-in-law, took with him to England the manuscript of the collection. London at the time had sixty printers; New England, one—and so it must have been difficult, even then, to print poetry in America. "The fact," notes Hutchinson, "that Herrick's *Hesperides* had just appeared in England while the latest venture of Samuel Green, the Cambridge, Massachusetts, printer, was a revision of *The Bay Psalm Book* to rid it of its crudities, gives an indication of the intellectual distance between the two countries."

Walt Whitman, To a Locomotive in Winter, page 474
Emily Dickinson, I like to see it lap the Miles, page 475

Though both of these great nineteenth-century Americans take almost the same subject, in tone and in form the two poems differ as sharply as opera differs from chamber music. (Some students might argue that the mutual subject isn't a moving locomotive, but the poets' praise of it. While seeing a real similarity, they would be missing the distinction between subject and tone.) Whitman addresses his machine in awe and exultation. In lines 14–19 he practically prays to it (almost like Henry Adams on bended knees before the dynamo in *Education*). Dickinson is evidently more playful in her affectionate view of the locomotive as a great beast. It is horselike in that it neighs and has a stable, but it isn't quite a horse: it crawls and hoots. Both poets, incidentally, see not only a locomotive, but a whole train. Dickinson's seeing it "chase itself" suggests cars trying to catch their locomotive as they roll downhill. Dickinson's allusion to Boanerges means no more, we think, than that the locomotive is a servant, and is thunderous.

Whitman's poem is full of diction from music: *recitative, beat, ringing bell, notes, chant, harp, piano, trills.* The locomotive embodies poetry, too, in its *metrical* pant and roar, and in its ability to serve the Muse. The word *recitative* indicates the form the poem will be cast in. In Italian opera, to which Whitman was devoted, Rossini had introduced the use of the full orchestra to accompany the recitative, the passage of half-sung, halfspoken declamation; and it may be that, as Robert D. Faner has argued, such recitative was a basic model for Whitman's poetry. "The recitative, highly rhythmic and emotional, punctuated by instrumental accompaniment with thrilling effect, and in its chanted delivery giving the impression of the rhythms of speech, he found well adapted to the bulk of his work, which he thought of as a sort of bardic chant" *(Walt Whitman & Opera* [Carbondale: Southern Illinois UP, 1951] 234).

Benjamin Alire Sáenz, To the Desert, page 476

Benjamin Alire Sáenz's passionate "To the Desert" is an unrhymed sonnet—fourteen lines of blank verse. (There is also a conscious pattern of assonance at the line ends to suggest rhyme—*night/sky, your/thirst, dios/me*—as well as one slant rhyme, *bend/brand.*) Sáenz's language is both erotic and religious, which is not an unusual situation for Catholic religious poetry, especially in the Spanish tradition. (Sáenz once studied for the priesthood, and the poem's bilingual diction and religious language announces its Latin Catholic heritage.)

"I came to you one rainless August night," the poem begins as it sets up thirst as its central metaphor. In the poem thirst becomes both physical and spiritual, emotional and topographic. Students should be asked to consider how Sáenz's title helps us understand the meaning of the poem. A reader can learn much not only from understanding the speaker of a poem but also from its stated listener. In religious writing, the desert is the place of spiritual self-knowledge, trial, and purification. Sáenz's poem uses that archetype to build a compressed drama of spiritual discovery.

Weldon Kees, FOR MY DAUGHTER, page 477

Weldon Kees, who was born in Beatrice, Nebraska, in 1914, was one of the most talented artists of his generation. In his short life he managed to do distinguished work in poetry, fiction, painting, film, criticism, and music. In 1955, shortly after the breakup of his marriage, Kees disappeared. Most evidence suggests that Kees killed himself by jumping off the Golden Gate Bridge, but some of his friends believed that Kees faked a suicide so that he could go off to Mexico and start a new life. In either event, Kees was never seen again.

"For My Daughter" usually creates a lively classroom discussion, but the conversation often veers in two different directions—one literary, the other ethical. On the literary side, students are often divided on the question as to whether the poet should mislead the reader for thirteen lines and then reveal the truth (that he has no daughter) only in the final line. Some beginning students may feel that the author isn't playing fair with his readers, that he is exploiting their emotions. This discussion can be important for students, since it dramatizes the fact that literature isn't necessarily considerate of our emotions—it has more important goals than leaving us at ease. Kees was a particularly savage poet in respect to pointing out the cruel and unjust parts of life that most people *want* to overlook. The important point is that the speaker comes clean in the last line, and that admission changes the meaning of everything said before. The first thirteen lines, therefore, can be read in two different ways—once coming up to the end (a father's worst fears for his daughter) and again retrospectively from the end (a man's reasons for not wanting children, especially on the brink of a world war).

The other discussion of "For My Daughter" concerns the ethical responsibilities faced by any parent bringing children into the world. (It may be worth noting here that Kees is not striking a hollow pose in this poem. He and his wife decided not to have children.)

One small technical note is worth mentioning: "For My Daughter" is a Shakespearean sonnet.

THE PERSON IN THE POEM

Carter Revard, BIRCH CANOE, page 478

This poem is discussed at some length in the prose paragraph that follows the text. A good question in class is whether a reader would be able to figure out the subject of the poem without knowing the title. The form of the poem is a riddle, a common form for Anglo-Saxon and old Norse verse. These riddles tried to be ingenious, detailed, and difficult. Is Revard's riddle too difficult? Or do students think they could have figured it out? (Remember this is only a hypothetical question; Revard gave us the title.) Another question is what does the poem gain in force or resonance by being spoken in the voice of an inanimate object?

Edwin Arlington Robinson, LUKE HAVERGAL, page 479

Teaching this poem consistently produces some of the most interesting classes that I (DG) have ever conducted. I read the poem aloud in class, then I ask students to answer three questions:

1. Who is the speaker of the poem?

2. What does the speaker ask Luke Havergal to do?

3. Should Luke Havergal follow the speaker's advice?

Students immediately agree that these are sensible questions to ask. In order to answer them, however, they have to learn how to interpret the poem. Have them list on the blackboard everything they know about the speaker (there isn't much to know) in one column. Then have them list essential information they wish they knew but are not told in another column. They will soon discover that the voice speaking claims to be from beyond the grave.

It helps to ask students how many characters are in the poem. There are only three, and each of them—this discovery will show students how much grammar reinforces meaning—is associated with a specific personal pronoun. There is the *I* (the speaker), the *you* (Luke Havergal), and the *she* (Havergal's lost love). Have students collectively put on the blackboard what they can find out about each character.

To figure out what the speaker asks Luke Havergal to do, students must interpret "the western gate." It will help to notice all the imagery of time and seasons in the poem. The *West* in most poetry is often associated with death since the sun sets in the west. (For an illuminating comparison, notice how the aged Ulysses in Tennyson's poem sails west "beyond the sunset, and the baths / of all the western stars until I die.") Let students spend the time necessary to figure "the western gate" out by themselves. At that point, it will be easy for them to discuss whether Havergal should follow this questionable advisor and his deadly suggestion.

Ted Hughes, HAWK ROOSTING, page 480

Hughes's beautifully unnerving "Hawk Roosting" provides an excellent basis for any classroom discussion of poetic voice and persona. The poem is a dramatic monologue spoken by a non-human voice—a powerful antidote to any student who believes all poems are direct autobiographical statements from the author's life. A lesser poet might have settled merely for the basic situation of the poem—

the world seen from the hawk's perspective. Hughes explores the deeper implications of his subject. Using human language, he tries to articulate how alien the hawk's worldview is to our own. The effect is quietly astonishing.

When writers treat animals as their subjects, they often become sentimental. They project human emotions and values—often childish ones—on the animals and overly dramatize these situations, especially the vulnerability of creatures in nature. The resulting stories—from *Bambi* and *The Wind in the Willows* to *Watership Down*—are often compelling stories, but tell us more about the author than the animals because they completely humanize their subjects. Hughes instead emphasizes how differently a hawk might view existence. "Hawk Roosting" reveals a predator's perspective—merciless, efficient, and utterly self-assured. The hawk sits "in the top of the wood" both literally and metaphorically. It rests on the top of the food chain. ("I kill where I please because it is all mine.") Perfectly adapted to its ecological niche, it also sees the world finely suited to its own needs. ("The convenience of the high trees!")

The poem disturbs us not only for its celebration of predation but also because it suggests how many of our own assumptions about the world depend upon being members of our own species, *homo sapiens.*

William Wordsworth, I WANDERED LONELY AS A CLOUD, page 481
Dorothy Wordsworth, JOURNAL ENTRY, page 482

To point out the distance between art and reporting, it may be helpful to read Wordsworth's poem aloud—at least part of it. In their rhythm, lines such as "Fluttering and dancing in the breeze" and "Tossing their heads in sprightly dance" make the motion of the daffodils come alive. By comparison, Dorothy Wordsworth's record of the incident ("the rest tossed and reeled and danced") seems merely excellent prose.

Actually, Wordsworth's sister was a distinguished poet in her own right, as Hyman Eigerman demonstrates in *The Poetry of Dorothy Wordsworth* (New York: Columbia UP, 1940), an anthology of passages from her journals arranged into formally open verse.

James Stephens, A GLASS OF BEER, page 483

The high regard of the Irish for the magical powers of speech has given them a long and glorious tradition of poetic cursing. In the ancient tales of the Ulster saga, we read of kings who wouldn't go to battle without an accompanying druid: a poet-priest charged with pronouncing magnificent metrical curses upon the enemy. Who knows?—in the pubs of Stephens's native Dublin, curses like the one in "A Glass of Beer" may well have seemed ordinary, even mild.

Although the speaker—some frustrated drinker hard up for cash—is in a towering rage at the barmaid who denied him, the tone of the poem is not anger but high amusement. There is irony, too, in the obvious contrast between the speaker's stupendous hyperboles and the puny occasion for them. Save this poem, if you like, for teaching figures of speech.

There is hardly a better modern poem, however, for reminding students that the feelings expressed in poetry aren't always positive. A poem may be written in rage or chagrin, as well as in love or joy. This seems an essential truth, and one that XJK has tried to demonstrate at some length in *Tygers of Wrath: Poems of Hate, Anger, and Invective* (Athens: U of Georgia P, 1981), an annotated anthology showing the tradition of dark emotion in British, Irish, and American poetry from the Middle Ages to the present. Naturally, in this tradition, "A Glass of Beer" holds an honored place.

"A Glass of Beer" is a free translation from the Irish of Daíbhí Ó Bruadair (c. 1625–98). The original with a translation by Thomas Kinsella ("A Shrewish, Barren, Bony, Nosey Servant") is given by Seán Ó Tuama and Kinsella in *An Duanaire: An Irish Anthology* (Philadelphia: U of Pennsylvania P, 1981) 116–17.

William Carlos Williams, THE RED WHEELBARROW, page 484

Evidently many readers have found it easy to admire this poem without feeling a need to know the circumstances in which it was written. For an interesting appreciation, see Louis Untermeyer, *The Pursuit of Poetry* (New York: Simon & Schuster, 1969) 25. Untermeyer views the poem as a kind of haiku that makes us aware of glories in commonplaces. A more sharply critical estimate is that of Roy Harvey Pearce in his fine essay "Williams and the 'New Mode'" in *The Continuity of American Poetry* (Princeton: Princeton UP, 1961) 335–48. Pearce charges the poem with sentimentality: "At its worst this is togetherness in a chickenyard." However, in Pearce's view, the poem also has a better aspect: what "depends" is the poet's vocation as a poet. He needs common objects in order to write poems, and the objects in turn need him to imagine them into poetry.

If the librarian is right about the situation in which the poem was written, "The Red Wheelbarrow" seems a better poem than we had realized: a kind of prayer, a work of compassion. However, that the poem fails to give us an intimation of the reasons for the poet's feelings (and of why we ought to share them) does expose it to Pearce's accusation that it is sentimental. Whatever the instructor's opinion, students may be invited to debate the merits and demerits of the poem.

IRONY

Robert Creeley, OH NO, page 485

"What interests me about 'Oh No' is its tone," Cynthia Edelberg remarks in an interview with the poet. "How would you describe it?" Creeley replies that he sees it as wry irony, the poem being "self-parody," a comment on his feelings at the time. "As Joel Oppenheimer said, that would qualify me to be a Jew. He really liked that poem. It's that kind of humor" (Edelberg's *Robert Creeley's Poetry: A Critical Introduction* [Albuquerque: U of New Mexico P, 1978] 168).

W. H. Auden, THE UNKNOWN CITIZEN, page 486

For making students better aware of irony, Auden's familiar satire remains as dependable as any poem we know. Little seems to have dated in it, other than the praise of the citizen for adding five children to the population. Students are usually good at seeing that, unlike the unknown soldier, the citizen is all too thoroughly identified; and that, nevertheless, his true nature and inmost wants remain unknown. Meaty questions for discussion naturally arise: What are the premises of such a society? It seems dedicated to the proposition that to conform to a norm is the highest virtue—any individual traits, of course, being an annoyance to statisticians. What is a "Modern Man?" One with animal needs, but no aspirations. The epitaph, often overlooked, is worth dwelling on: it tells us at once that the unknown citizen is only a number, and that bureaucrats keep track of him—and, incidentally, like the rest of the poem, the epitaph is in rime.

"The Unknown Citizen" is one of five poems in this chapter in which we hear a voice obviously not the poet's. (The others are the ones by Revard, Robinson, Hughes, and Stephens.)

Sharon Olds, RITES OF PASSAGE, page 487

This poem will not require much explanation. Anyone familiar with six- and seven-year-old boys will understand the situation. The interesting exercise in class is to search out the ironic metaphors and language in the poem ("short men," "small bankers," "celebrating my son's life") and then discussing their effect on our reading of the poem. If some students complain that the poem overstates its case and makes too much of the boys' penchant for mock violence, it will provide a good opportunity to ask the question if a poem (and one might even classify this short descriptive work as "lyric," since it explores a moment's perception) needs to provide a balanced view of life or if it is acceptable to create the sudden, overwhelming, and perhaps unbalanced emotions we feel in a particular moment or situation.

Sarah N. Cleghorn, THE GOLF LINKS, page 488

What a great epigram!—no verbal irony in it, just matter-of-fact notation of a social condition that seems ironic in the extreme. As Robert Frost said, in his introduction to Cleghorn's autobiography, *Threescore* (1936), "There is more high explosive for righteousness in the least little line of Sarah Cleghorn's poem about the children working in the mill . . . than in all the prose of our radical-bound-boys pressed together under a weight of several atmospheres of revolution." (The conservative Frost didn't like Marxists, but he called Cleghorn "a saint and a reformer" anyway.) For a more recent tribute, see Irving Dilliard, "Four Short Lines," *The Nation* 222 (10 Apr. 1976): 444–45.

Stanley Kunitz and Howard Hayward's *Twentieth Century Authors* (New York: Wilson, 1942), in an article on Cleghorn that she apparently helped write, explains the twenty-year hiatus between her early books and her later ones. "This was caused by the fact that her socialism and pacifism made editors and publishers reluctant to use her later writing, and partly by the fact that in middle age she became a teacher." Among her other works is a novel, *The Spinster* (1916), and a last collection, *Poems of Peace and Freedom* (1945).

Thomas Hardy, THE WORKBOX, page 488

Dramatic irony is present in the discrepancy between the carpenter's limited knowledge and the reader's growing conviction that the wife knew John much better than she cares to admit. Her phrase "mere accidental things" contains verbal irony, and in general the whole speech in lines 25–28 is a verbal irony. Cosmic irony may be operating too (and one is sure that it is, knowing Hardy) in the Fate or chance that caused the carpenter to select a piece of poor John's coffin out of all pieces of wood in the world.

To us, the situation in the poem had seemed like that in James Joyce's "The Dead": the wife, by remembering a young man who died of love for her, has a bleak realization that she might have known a joyous life had she married him instead. However, Albert Furtwangler and his students at Mount Allison University found other possible levels of irony, as he kindly wrote to report. For Professor Furtwangler, "The Workbox" is marred by an excess of irony that runs too deep: "it remains fascinating in the long run more as a puzzle than as a clear disclosure of character." Among other readings he considered the two following, which he thinks overingenious and yet consistent with the poem.

The husband, aware of his wife's past, has contrived his present as a cunning torture for her. "He seems to offer it in love, but takes pleasure in drawing out his wife's confused replies . . . thus trapping her in her own hypocrisy."

The husband knows his wife's history; and she knows that he knows it. "But they coexist uneasily with each other by exercising an elaborate fiction of ignorance."

What will you and your students decide?

J. O. Bailey sees in this poem the "ballad-like theme of the lover who died of grief when his beloved married another." Like traditional English and Scottish ballads, the poem has a question-and-answer structure and ends in a surprise. (See *The Poetry of Thomas Hardy* [Chapel Hill: U of North Carolina P, 1970].) Compare "The Workbox" in these respects with "Bonny Barbara Allan" and "Edward."

FOR REVIEW AND FURTHER STUDY

José Emilio Pacheco, HIGH TREASON, page 490

Pacheco is a Mexican poet, but he has chosen to work in the United States and currently teaches at the University of Maryland. He writes in Spanish, but he worked with the noted poet-translator Alastair Reid (himself originally an immigrant from Scotland) on the English versions of his poems. Pacheco's presence in the anthology (along with the inclusion of writers like Octavio Paz, Julia Alvarez, Emanuel di Pasquale, Derek Walcott, and Claude McKay) highlights the importance of immigrants and foreign émigrés in our literary culture.

Pacheco's poem should require little gloss, but the effective and subtle irony of the opening probably deserves a moment's consideration in class to show how irony can be used rhetorically. By saying "I do not love my country" in a poem that celebrates his love for his homeland, Pacheco effectively qualifies the nature of his affection. It is not conventional patriotism but love for its particulars.

It is worth noting that although the poem presumably celebrates Mexico, the images of the poem are deliberately universal. It could be describing Finland or China. The title of this poem is also ironic: Pacheco's treason is a personal love for his country.

William Stafford, AT THE UN-NATIONAL MONUMENT ALONG THE CANADIAN BORDER, page 490

This is a wonderful poem that celebrates an even more wonderful event—two neighboring countries who have lived in peace for nearly two hundred years. (It may be worthwhile in class to ask the obvious *factual* question about what this poem celebrates.)

Stafford's poem uses language memorably in at least two unusual ways. First, the poem characterizes the scene mainly by what did *not* happen there—no battles, no deaths, no monument, no memorable historical events of any kind. Second, Stafford consciously invokes the central non-event by borrowing the diction of patriotic oratory—heroic, soldier, battle, monument, ground, hallowed, people, celebrate. (Was Lincoln's "Gettysburg Address" in the back of Stafford's mind? one wonders.) But Stafford uses these words in exactly the opposite way from an old-fashioned commemorative oration.

Richard Lovelace, TO LUCASTA, page 491

"To Lucasta" may refer to an actual parting. During the Puritan Revolution of 1642–45, Lovelace fought in the service of Charles I. Students will readily see the poet's theme that Honor (duty to God and King) takes priority over duty to Lucasta; the tone of the poem may give them greater difficulty. The closing line makes a serious affirmation: Honor for Lovelace is not an "old Lie," but a creed. Neither grim nor smug, the poem also has wit and loving tenderness. The witty second stanza seems almost comic in its figures of speech: having renounced Lucasta's nunlike chastity and calm, the speaker will now go whet his sword upon the body of someone wilder.

Wilfred Owen, DULCE ET DECORUM EST, page 491

Owen's theme is apparent: <u>death in battle is hideous, no matter what certain ignorant poets say about it.</u> For us, there seems irony in the fact that Owen himself was to be killed in action in France. Although in a wartime letter he called himself "a conscientious objector with a very seared conscience," Owen in this poem does not question that to die for one's country may be necessary. His attitude is overpowering disgust—with the butchery of war, with those who idealize it.

WRITER'S PERSPECTIVE

Wilfred Owen on Writing, WAR POETRY, page 493

Owen's fragmentary notes toward a preface to his still unpublished book are tremendously eloquent. It is interesting to note that Owen's heightened prose often reads like poetry.

A good classroom question is what Owen sees as the purpose of poetry. He does not see the contemporary poet having direct political power, although there was a strong political element in the poems he wrote during the Great War. Instead, Owen sees the poet's role as telling the truth. By speaking the truth about difficult and, in this case, tragic events, the poet *warns*. Owen's sense of truth-telling predicts the current concept of poetry as witnessing.

12 Words

LITERAL MEANING: WHAT A POEM SAYS FIRST

Why a whole section on literal meaning? The need first occurred to XJK in a conversation with Robert Reiter and David Anderson of Boston College. Professor Reiter, who had been using the book in a previous edition, averred that, while it was well to encourage students to read poetry for its suggestions, his students tended to go too far in that direction, and sometimes needed to have their attentions bolted down to the denotations of words on a page. Early in a poetry course, the problem seemed especially large—"I try not to let them look for any symbols until after Thanksgiving!" Mr. Anderson had felt the same difficulty. In teaching Donne's "Batter my heart" sonnet, he had had to argue with students who couldn't see how, in a poem of spiritual aspiration, Donne possibly could be referring to anything so grossly physical as rape. They needed to see the plain, literal basis of Donne's tremendous metaphor, that they might then go on to understand the poet's conception of sanctifying grace.

With these comments in mind, the publishers sent a questionnaire to more than one hundred instructors who had used the book, asking them (among other questions) whether they felt the need for more emphasis on denotation. All who replied said that they would welcome such an emphasis (in addition to the old emphasis on connotation)—all, that is, except for one instructor (God help him) who reported that he couldn't persuade his students ever to rise *above* the level of the literal, if indeed he could get them to rise that far.

Most instructors like to discuss imagery fairly early. They will find nothing to hinder them from taking the chapter on imagery ahead of this one. Another procedure would be to defer "Imagery" until after having discussed both denotation and connotation—taking in sequence the present chapter, "Words," and the following chapter, "Saying and Suggesting."

William Carlos Williams, THIS IS JUST TO SAY, page 500

Williams once recalled that this poem was an actual note he had written to his wife—"and she replied very beautifully. Unfortunately, I've lost it. I think what she wrote was quite as good as this" (conversation with John W. Gerber and Emily M. Wallace in *Interviews with William Carlos Williams,* ed. Linda Welshimer Wagner [New York: New Directions, 1976]).

For parodies of this famous poem, see Kenneth Koch's "Variations on a Theme by William Carlos Williams" in *Contemporary American Poetry,* ed. A. Poulin (Boston: Houghton, 1980) and other anthologies.

Marianne Moore, SILENCE, page 501

This poem appears autobiographical on the surface, but the notes that Marianne Moore scrupulously appended to her poems make it clear that it is a composite, imaginary portrait of a father. (Moore barely knew her father, who had suffered a nervous breakdown shortly after her birth; perhaps, for that reason, imaginary fathers were all the more important to her.) The first five lines were adapted from a "Miss A. M. Homans," according to Moore. "Make my house your inn" is a quote from Edmund Burke, to which Moore added her telling last line. The father in the poem presumably lived in Cambridge, Massachusetts (from references to Longfellow's grave and Harvard), a town in which Moore never resided. We belabor these facts and sources only to demonstrate that poems are often not so autobiographical as they might seem.

A central theme of "Silence" is the eloquence of understatement and restraint. The poet Donald Hall praises this poem in his study *Marianne Moore: The Cage and The Animal* (New York: Pegasus, 1970) saying that by "eschewing the easy words for the ambiguous emotion," Moore displays "a species of honesty and not evidence of lack of depth." Precision is another key term. Notice how important the speaker considers distinctions between related words and situations *(silence/restraint, inn/residence)*.

Robert Graves, DOWN, WANTON, DOWN!, page 502

This poem can be an astonisher, especially if students haven't read it in advance. One freshman group XJK sprang it on provided a beautiful gamut of reactions: from stunned surprise to hilarity. At first, most didn't know quite what to make of the poem, but they soon saw that its puns and metaphors point to details of male and female anatomy; and, in catching these, they found themselves looking to literal meanings. After further discussion, they decided that the poem, however witty, makes a serious point about the blindness of lust. To get at this point, students may be asked to sum up the contrast Graves is drawing between Love and Beauty and the wanton's approach to them.

The title (and opening line) echo a phrase from Shakespeare in a passage about eels being rolled into a pie *(King Lear,* II, iv, 118–23):

Lear: O me, my heart, my rising heart! But down!

Fool: Cry to it, nuncle, as the cockney did to the eels when she put 'em i' th' paste alive. She knapped 'em o' th' coxcombs with a stick and cried, "Down, wantons down!" 'Twas her brother that, in pure kindness to his horse, buttered his hay.

One instructor at a community college in New Jersey has reported an embarrassing experience. One morning, not having had time to prepare for class, he introduced this poem without having read it first. "What's it about?" he queried, and someone in the class replied, "An erection." "WHAT?" he exploded. "Come on, now, let's look at it *closely* . . . . " But as he stared at the poem before him, a chill stole over him. Luckily, he was saved by the bell.

Barbara Howes, LOOKING UP AT LEAVES, page 502

Barbara Howes, who died in 1996, is too little read at present, but she remains an exquisite lyric poet. One understands why Louise Bogan once judged Howes "the most accomplished woman poet of the younger generation—one who has found her own voice, chosen her own material, and worked out her own form." Howes's *Collected Poems: 1945–1990* was published in 1995, and became a finalist for the National Book Award.

Howes wrote in one of the oddest but most important traditions of American poetry. Howes stands with Marianne Moore, Elizabeth Bishop, and ultimately Emily Dickinson in a lineage of women writers passionately committed to the independence and singularity of the poetic imagination. (To this group one might also add Louise Bogan, Julia Randall, May Swenson, and Josephine Miles). They form an eccentric but eminent sorority. In most ways they are modest, even self-deprecating writers, but, in matters they deem important, they are bold and self-assured. They are also quirky writers—alternately erudite and innocent, intimate and reserved, humorous and wistful. They are all temperamentally private artists, but their introspective genius expresses itself matter-of-factly in everyday, even domestic, images. Perhaps what unifies them most obviously is the affirmative quality of their vision. In an essay on Josephine Miles in *The Hollins Critic* (June, 1980), Julia Randall linked several of these poets by saying, "They seem to seek (Bishop) or find (Miles) what women, and I suppose other human beings, most desire: being at home in the world." It is precisely this ability to accept the world as it is that separates them from other, usually more popular women poets who long for some sort of spiritual or personal transformation. When one contrasts the poetry of Moore to that of her contemporary, Edna St. Vincent Millay, or the work of Bishop to that of Adrienne Rich, the fundamental differences become obvious. Their dissimilarities are not merely matters of style but of assumptions about life and poetry.

"Looking Up at Leaves" illustrates Howes's particular lyric gift. She carefully leads the reader through a complex, extended simile. The leaves seem like water lilies, which, in turn, makes the sky into a blue pond. The tree branches become roots seeking the depth of the sky like soil. And so on. The sheer length of the simile takes the reader by surprise. Then the final line caps the comparison with a marvelously quiet pun on the two related meanings of *reflection*. The quiet and affirmative tone of "Looking Up at Leaves" is characteristic of Howes's work. She is a poet who captures the joy of being alive in the natural world.

John Donne, BATTER MY HEART, THREE-PERSONED GOD, FOR YOU, page 503

On Donne's last line: the literature of mysticism is full of accounts of spiritual experience seen in physical terms; and any students who wish to pursue the matter might be directed, for instance, to the poems of St. John of the Cross (which have been splendidly translated by John Frederick Nims).

John E. Parish has shown that Donne's poem incorporates two metaphors, both worn and familiar: the traditional Christian comparison of the soul to a maiden and Christ to a bridegroom, and the Petrarchan conceit of the reluctant woman as a castle and her lover as an invading army. Donne brilliantly combined the two into a new whole. In lines 1 to 4, the sinner's heart is like a walled town, fallen to Satan, the enemy. Now God the rightful King approaches and knocks for entrance. But merely to knock won't do—the King must break open the gates with a battering ram. The verbs in these lines all suggest the act of storming a citadel, "and even *blowe* may be intended to suggest the use of gunpowder to blow up the fortress" ("No. 14 of Donne's *Holy Sonnets*," *College English* 24 [Jan. 1963]: 299–302).

"The paradox of death and rebirth, the central paradox of Christianity" is (according to A. L. Clements in another comment) the organizing principle of the poem. To illustrate the paradox of destroying in order to revive, Donne employs two sorts of figurative language: one, military and destructive; the other, marital and uniting ("Donne's 'Holy Sonnet XIV,'" *Modern Language Notes* 76 [June 1961]: 484–89).

Both the Clements and the Parish articles are reprinted, together with the four other discussions of the poem, in *John Donne's Poetry*, edited by Clements (New York: Norton, 1966).

It is hard to talk for long about rhythm in poetry without citing the opening lines of "Batter my heart." Both in meter and in meaning, they must be among the most powerful lines in English poetry.

THE VALUE OF A DICTIONARY

Henry Wadsworth Longfellow, AFTERMATH, page 505

Like many seemingly abstract words, *aftermath* was originally a concrete descriptive term that referred to the usually meager second-growth of crop in a field that had already been mowed that season [*after* & *math* (an obsolete word for *mowing*)]. Once you read Longfellow's quietly moving poem, you'll never forget the etymology. "Aftermath" shows how poets usually employ words with careful consideration to their histories.

"Aftermath" provides a literal description of mowing the second growth in a winter field, but his treatment suggests a hidden symbolic meaning. Longfellow is careful not to specify exactly what the subtext is and leaves every reader free to project his or her own private meaning into the poem. The structure of Longfellow's insight, however, is painfully clear: to revisit a scene of the past can be devastating.

Fledged means "having feathers" and refers to young birds who are now old enough to have grown feathers and flown from their nests. *Rowen* is a synonym for *aftermath*, a season's second crop, usually of hay.

J. V. Cunningham, FRIEND, ON THIS SCAFFOLD THOMAS MORE LIES DEAD, page 507

Cunningham's epigram states a metaphor: it likens two famous separations decreed by Henry VIII. Separation of the Body (the Church of England) from the

Head (the Pope) is like the decapitation of More, who had opposed it. A possible original for Cunningham's epigram, a Latin epigram by John Owen (1606), has been discovered by Charles Clay Doyle:

Abscindi passus caput est a corpore Morus;
     Abscindi corpus noluit a capite.

In 1659 Thomas Pecke rendered it into English:

What though Head was from Body severed!
     More would not let Body be cut from Head.

Doyle remarks that in fact More played down the role of the Pope as "head" of the Church, preferring the allegorical view (derived from Paul) of Christ as head upon the Church's body ("The Hair and Beard of Thomas More," *Moreana* 18, 71–72 [Nov. 1981]: 5–14).

Kelly Cherry, ADVICE TO A FRIEND WHO PAINTS, page 507

The seemingly incongruous images of this poem are all common subjects in the paintings of Cezanne. The first question to ask the class is "Who is Cezanne?" Then ask how catching that allusion helps us understand the poem. It will also heighten the immediacy of the poem if one brings a book of his paintings into class. Almost any book on the artist will illustrate most if not all of the images in the poem.

Once the role of allusion is understood in the poem, it is interesting to ask students what the final line implies about the speaker's attitude toward the painter-friend in the title. What message does the poem subtly give the "tearing, tugging" painter-friend?

Carl Sandburg, GRASS, page 507

Carl Sandburg's poem, which was written while World War I was still raging, incorporates five place names into its brief length. All five proper nouns are the names of famously bloody battlegrounds. Austerlitz and Waterloo are scenes of major battles in the Napoleonic Wars. Gettysburg refers, of course, to the decisive Civil War battle in Pennsylvania. Ypres and Verdun were the sites of the battles in World War I that still rank among the deadliest military engagements in human history. Since the allusions are all used in parallel ways, a reader should be able to understand the role of any battle he or she does not know from the context as long as he or she recognizes some of the names.

It might be worth asking the class who is speaking in the poem. The speaker is the grass itself, a symbol of the natural world's enduring ability to reassert its power over human history. This aspect of Nature is often viewed in harsh terms, but Sandburg's poem displays it in a gentle, consolatory way. In historical terms, one might consider Sandburg's poem a vision of peace in the final days of World War I.

WORD CHOICE AND WORD ORDER

An exercise to make a class more aware of *le mot juste* is suggested by W. Jackson Bate and David Perkins in *British & American Poets* (San Diego: Harcourt, 1986). Print out several lines of a poem, with an admirably chosen word or words left out. Let students suggest ways to fill in the blank and debate their choices. Then the instructor whips out a trump card: the way the poet filled in the blank—if you're lucky, to "a collective sigh of appreciation."

Josephine Miles, REASON, page 510

Only the reference to Gary Cooper's horse at all dates this concise story-poem, a thing of lasting freshness. "The real characters in this story are the fragments of slang, not the speakers," Lawrence R. Smith has noticed. "Their absence is emphasized by the absence of personal pronouns at the beginning of each line. In place of the pronouns, we simply have 'Said.' This is a poem of pure language." ("Josephine Miles: Metaphysician of the Irrational," *A Book of Rereadings*, ed. Greg Kuzma [Lincoln: Pebble and Best Cellar, 1979] 29).

Kay Ryan, BLANDEUR, page 512

Kay Ryan's witty poem demonstrates that on certain occasions writers can invent the words they need. (Ryan actually coins two related words in her poem—the noun *blandeur* and the verb *blanden*.) Although the poem is in one sense a joke, it also seemingly reflects a sincere desire for the comfortable average rather than the sublime extremes of human experience. The poem states its preference for the undramatic "mean" and not for grand and terrible excess.

Ryan's poem is written in short free verse lines wonderfully interwoven with many irregular rhymes. Many rhymes occur at the ends of lines—*happen/flatten/blanden/Canyon*, *fissures/your*, or *hearts/parts*—but others appear elsewhere in the line like *rondure/fissures*, *hand/remand*, *calving/halving*. The effect of this intricate and unexpected rhyming is to slow down our reading and hear the many interconnections of sound and sense.

Thomas Hardy, THE RUINED MAID, page 513

In a London street, an innocent girl from Dorset encounters a friend who has run away from life on the farm. Now a well-paid prostitute, 'Melia calls herself *ruined* with cheerful irony. That this maid has been made, it would seem, has been the making of her. Hardy, of course, is probably less stricken with awe before 'Melia's glamorous clothes than is the first speaker. As the *ain't* in the last line indicates, 'Melia's citified polish doesn't go deep.

For a sequel to "The Ruined Maid," see "A Daughter Returns" in Hardy's last collection of poetry, *Winter Words*. With "Dainty-cut raiment" and "earrings of pearl," a runaway daughter returns to her country home, only to be spurned by her father for having lost her innocence.

Richard Eberhart, THE FURY OF AERIAL BOMBARDMENT, page 514

Dr. Johnson said that technical language is inadmissible to poetry, but in the case of Eberhart's poem, it is hard to agree. We do not need to know the referents of "belt feed lever" and "belt holding pawl" in order to catch the poet's meaning. Indeed, he evidently chooses these terms as specimens of a jargon barely comprehensible to the unlucky gunnery students who failed to master it. At a reading of his poems in public, Eberhart once remarked that he had added the last stanza as an afterthought. The tone (it seems to us) remains troubled and sorrowful but shifts from loftiness and grandeur to matter-of-fact. This shift takes place in diction as well: from the generality of "infinite spaces," "multitudinous will," "eternal truth," and "the Beast" in man's soul down to "Names on a list," "lever," and "pawl." The poem is a wonderful instance of a poet's writing himself into a fix—getting snarled in unanswerable questions—and then triumphantly saving the day (and his poem) by suddenly returning with a bump to the ordinary, particular world.

Wendy Cope, LONELY HEARTS, page 514

Wendy Cope's bittersweet villanelle demonstrates that old forms can easily accommodate new content, as long as the poet has enough imagination and skill.

Students never seem to have trouble understanding this poem. It is a fun exercise to have students write an additional personal ad in the same rime scheme, but, if you use this idea, be prepared for some odd results.

You might suggest that students read the biographical note on Cope in the "Lives of the Poets" section. Her late-blooming career and personal problems may add a personal dimension to this poem. If she is making gentle fun of the authors of personal ads, she also understands their emotional needs.

FOR REVIEW AND FURTHER STUDY

E. E. Cummings, ANYONE LIVED IN A PRETTY HOW TOWN, page 515

Trained in the classical languages, Cummings borrows from Latin the freedom to place a word in practically any location within a sentence. The first two lines are easy to unscramble: "How pretty a town anyone lived in, with so many bells floating up [and] down." The scrambling is artful, and pedestrian words call attention to themselves by being seen in an unusual order.

The hero and heroine of the poem are anyone and noone, whose names recall the pronoun-designated principals in Cummings's play "Him"—hero Him and heroine Me. Are they Everyman and Everywoman? Not at all: they're different; they're strong, loving individuals whom the poet contrasts with those drab women and men of line 5, "both little and small," who dully sow isn't (negation) and reap same (conformity). Unlike wise noone and anyone, the everyones of line 17 apparently think they're really somebody.

In tracing the history of anyone and noone from childhood through their mature love to their death and burial, Cummings, we think, gives a brief tour through life in much the way that Thornton Wilder does in *Our Town*. But not all readers will agree. R. C. Walsh thinks that, in the last two stanzas, anyone and noone do not literally die but grow into loveless and lifeless adults, whose only hope of rejuvenation is to have children (*Explicator* 22 [May 1964]: item 72). But it seems unlike Cummings to make turncoats of his individualists. Bounded by the passage of the seasons, the rain, and the heavens, the mortal lives of anyone and noone seem concluded in their burial. But in the next-to-last stanza they go on sleeping in love and faith, dreaming of their resurrection.

Robert Herrick, UPON JULIA'S CLOTHES, page 516

This short classic was included in the book due to popular demand. The poem deserves inclusion for beauty's sake alone, but it is also mighty useful in the classroom to illustrate the power of diction. *Liquefaction* is an unforgettable word in Herrick's poem—a strong metaphor clothed in suave music. Note that the poem contains only two Latinate words (one in each stanza)—*liquefaction* and *vibration*. Both of them are employed and positioned for their special resonance. Students will also learn something about the history of English by looking up *brave* in a dictionary. Here Herrick uses it in a now slightly archaic sense to mean "finely-dressed" or "splendidly turned out," though by Shakespeare's time the adjective was also employed, according to the *OED*, as "a general epithet of admiration." Remember Miranda's famous exclamation in *The Tempest*: "O brave new world / That has such people in't."

EXERCISE: *Different Kinds of English*, page 517

Anonymous, CARNATION MILK, page 517
William Wordsworth, MY HEART LEAPS UP WHEN I BEHOLD, page 517
William Wordsworth, MUTABILITY, page 518

Students won't need much help to see that "Carnation Milk" is unschooled speech; that Wordsworth's diction in "My heart leaps up" is plain and unbookish (except for *natural piety*), while his language in "Mutability" is highly formal—not only in diction, but in word order ("Truth fails not").

On the difficult "Mutability" (in case anyone cares to read it for its sense) "the tower sublime" may refer to the Bastille, suggests Geoffrey Durant in his excellent discussion of the poem in *Wordsworth and the Great System* ([Cambridge: Cambridge UP, 1970] 732–735). For other poems with the theme of mutability, see Shelley's "Ozymandias," Shakespeare's "That time of year . . . ," Auden's "As I Walked Out One Evening," Thomas's "Fern Hill," and (in this same chapter) Cummings's "anyone lived in a pretty how town."

Lewis Carroll, JABBERWOCKY, page 518
WRITER'S PERSPECTIVE
Lewis Carroll on Writing, HUMPTY DUMPTY EXPLICATES "JABBERWOCKY," page 520

"Jabberwocky" has to be heard aloud: you might ask a student to read it, alerting him or her in advance to prepare it, and offering tips on pronunciation. ("The *i* in *slithy* is like the i in *slime;* the *a* in *wabe,* like the *a* in *wave.*")

Although Carroll added *chortled* to the dictionary, not all his odd words are invented. *Gyre* of course means "to spin or twist about"—it is used as a noun in Yeats's "Sailing to Byzantium" and "The Second Coming." *Slithy* (sleazy or slovenly), *rath* (an earthen wall), *whiffling* (blowing or puffing), and *callooh* (an arctic duck that winters in Scotland, so named for its call) are legitimate words, too, but Carroll uses them in different senses. *Frabjous* probably owes something to *frab,* a dialect word meaning "to scold, harass, or nag"—as Myra Cohn Livingston points out in her anthology *O Frabjous Day!* (New York: Atheneum, 1977).

Writing in 1877 to a child who had inquired what the strange words meant, Carroll replied:

> I am afraid I can't explain "vorpal blade" for you—nor yet "tulgey wood"; but I did make an explanation once for "uffish thought"—it seems to suggest a state of mind when the voice is gruffish, the manner roughish, and the temper huffish. Then again, as to "burble" if you take the three verbs "<u>b</u>leat," "mu<u>r</u>mur" and "war<u>ble</u>," and select the bits I have underlined, it certainly <u>makes</u> "burble": though I am afraid I can't distinctly remember having made it that way.

Students can have fun unpacking other portmanteau words: *gimble (gamely, gambol); frumious* (which Carroll said is *fuming* plus *furious); vorpal (voracious, purple), galumphing (galloping in triumph),* and so on. (*Uffish* suggests *oafish* too.) Some of these suggestions come from Martin Gardner, who supplies copious notes on the poem (as well as translations of it into French and German) in *The Annotated Alice* (New York: Bramhall, 1960).

All other critics, however, must yield precedence to the estimable Humpty Dumpty whose definite comments are printed in the "Writer's Perspective" following the poem.

13 *Saying and Suggesting*

John Masefield, CARGOES, page 524

Much of the effect of Masefield's contrast depends on rhythms and word-sounds, not just on connotations. In stanza 2, the poet strews his lines with dactyls, producing ripples in his rhythm: *diamonds, emeralds, amethysts, cinnamon*. In the third stanza, paired monosyllables (*salt-caked, smoke stack, Tyne coal, roadrails, pig-lead, firewood*) make for a hard hitting series of spondees. Internal alliteration helps the contrast, too: all those *m*-sounds in the dactyls; and in the harsher lines "Dirty British coaster with a salt-caked smoke stack, / Butting," all the sounds of the *r*, the *t*, and the staccato *k*.

"Cargoes" abounds with lively, meaningful music—and yet Masefield is generally dismissed nowadays as a mere balladeer—a jog-trot chronicler of the lives of the poor and unfortunate. In naming him poet laureate, George V (it is said) mistakenly thought him a hero of the working class; and, unluckily for his later fame, Masefield, like Wordsworth, enjoyed a long senility.

William Blake, LONDON, page 525

Blake's "London" broadens the themes explored in his "The Chimney Sweeper." The personal pathos of "The Chimney Sweeper" becomes a general indictment of a society in which such exploitation is possible. In "London," we see Blake as a prophetic poet—not prophesying the future like a tabloid seer, but speaking as a prophet who declares the moral necessity of just change in a time of evil.

In his essay "On Blake and his Critics" (1934), G. K. Chesterton singled out the third stanza of "London" for special praise. He called the images "two lightning-flashes revealing two separate Visions of Judgment." It is important to remember that Blake was a Londoner born and bred who spent most of his life within the city limits. He is not a country poet describing urban squalor; he is a native morally dissecting his own home town. He knows every image from the inside out.

If Blake were to walk the streets of an American city today, would he find any conditions similar to those he finds in "London"? Is this poem merely an occasional poem, with a protest valid only for its time, or does it have enduring applications?

Please note that Heather Glen's analysis of the background of Blake's "London" appears in the Cultural Studies section of "Critical Approaches to Literature."

Wallace Stevens, DISILLUSIONMENT OF TEN O'CLOCK, page 527

Stevens slings colors with the verve of a Matisse. In this early poem, he paints a suggestive contrast between the pale and colorless homeowners, ghostlike and punctually going to bed at ten and, on the other hand, the dreams they wouldn't dream of dreaming; and the bizarre and exotic scene inside the drunken head of our disreputable hero, the old seafarer. Who in the world would wear a beaded sash or *ceinture?* (A Barbary pirate? An Arabian harem dancer?) Ronald Sukenick has made a terse statement of the poem's theme: "the vividness of the imagination in the dullness of a pallid reality" *(Wallace Stevens: Musing the Obscure* [New York: New York UP, 1967]). Another critic, Edward Kessler, has offered a good paraphrase: "Only the drunkard, the irrational man ('Poetry must be irrational' [*Opus Posthumous* 162]), who is in touch with the unconscious—represented here, and often elsewhere, by the sea can awake his own passionate nature until his blood is mirrored in the very weather" (*Images of Wallace Stevens* [New Brunswick: Rutgers UP, 1972]).

While they will need to see the contrast between pallor and color, students might be cautioned against lending every color a particular meaning, as if the poem were an allegory.

Stevens expressed further disappointment with monotonous neighbors in a later poem, "Loneliness in Jersey City," which seems a companion piece to this. In Jersey City, "the steeples are empty and so are the people," who can't tell a dachshund from a deer. Both poems probably owe some of their imagery to Stevens's days as a struggling young lawyer, living in rooming houses in East Orange, New Jersey, and Fordham Heights, in New York City.

Gwendolyn Brooks, THE BEAN EATERS, page 528

This spare, understated poem seems one of the poet's finest portraits of poor blacks in Chicago. While "We Real Cool" depicts the young, "The Bean Eaters" depicts the old, whose lives are mainly devoted to memories—some happy (*tinklings*, like the sound of their beads) and some painful (*twinges*).

Details are clearly suggestive. The old people are barely eking out a living, eating beans to save money, from *chipware* (chipped tableware, or tableware that chips easily?) set on a creaky old table, using cheap cutlery that doesn't shine.

The long last line, with its extended list, sounds like one of those interminable Ogden Nash lines that Lewis Turco has dubbed "Nashers." Why is its effect touching, rather than humorous? Brooks lists the poor couple's cherished, worthless possessions in detail, and each detail matters. Besides, *twinges / fringes*, a fresh rime, achieves a beautiful closure. We end up sharing the poet's respect and affection for this old pair—no mockery.

Two excellent audio tapes of Gwendolyn Brooks reading her poems and discussing her work and life as a writer are available from: New Letters on the Air, University of Missouri-Kansas City, 5100 Rockhill Road, Kansas City, MO 64110-2499, (816) 235-1159.

Timothy Steele, EPITAPH, page 528

"Silence is golden"—but Sir Tact is obviously a coward, afraid to speak his mind. This epigram is included in Steele's first collection of poems, *Uncertainties and Rest* (Baton Rouge: Louisiana State UP, 1979).

Walter de la Mare, THE LISTENERS, page 528

This much-loved old chestnut, once a favorite of anthologists, still seems a wonderful demonstration of the value to poetry of hints. The identity of the listeners is by no means clear: the more literal-minded will probably think of bats, mice, and crickets, while others will think of ghosts. The latter theory gains support from the poem: these listeners are *phantom* (line 13), not of the *world of men* (16), strange and mute (21–22). If the Traveller is "the one man left awake" (32), are the Listeners men who have fallen asleep (in death)?

In line 5, *turret* suggests a fortress or castle; but as line 14 makes clear, the scene is a house. Which to believe? Perhaps the scene is set in a kind of Loire Valley chateau: a mansion with castlelike touches.

Attempts to guess what happened before "The Listeners" opens may well be irrelevant, but if students will try, they may find themselves more deeply involved with the poem. This much seems clear: The Traveller has accepted some challenge to visit the house: he has given his promise to someone (more than one person, and someone other than the Listeners, whom the Traveller charges to convey his message to "them"). Perhaps this act is one of the deeds required to lift a curse from a kingdom, as in a fairy tale; or as in the Arthurian story of Sir Percival (or Parsifal), who must spend a night in the terrifying Chapel Perilous.

Robert Frost, FIRE AND ICE, page 530

In his first line, Frost probably refers to those who accept the Biblical prophecy of a final holocaust; and in his second line, to those who accept scientists' forecasts of the cooling of the earth. We admire that final *suffice*. A magnificent understatement, it further shows the power of a rime to close a poem (as Yeats said) with a click like a closing box.

Alfred, Lord Tennyson, TEARS, IDLE TEARS, page 530

Tennyson's brooding lyric is a classic example of poetic suggestion. The poem opens with a paradox. The speaker unexpectedly finds himself weeping when "looking on the happy autumn-fields." The tears are declared *idle*, which is to say they seemingly lack any real basis. But are they really mysterious in their origin? The "Writing Assignment" at the end of the chapter asks students to explain why the speaker is weeping.

Tennyson loads the poem with suggestive imagery and situations to answer this question. It might help students to begin by noticing *when* the poem takes place. It is autumn—the time of harvest and completion. The speaker seemingly cannot help but reflect in this season on "the days that are no more." *Where* the poem takes place also reinforces the sense that the speaker is painfully cut off from the past. The speaker weeps while "looking on the happy autumn-fields." Seeing them and remembering the past triggers a series of revealing reveries about "the days that are no more."

The first image associated with the past is light on a sail. First, the sail seems "fresh" and dawn-like—bringing "our friends up from the underworld." The last word of that line, *underworld*, explicitly brings death into the poem. Any reassuring image of the dead returning to us, however, is quickly reversed as the ship sinks "with all we love below the verge." The death imagery becomes more explicit in stanza 3 when the dawn song of the birds falls on "dying ears," and the sun rises to "dying eyes." In the final stanza, the intensity of the speaker's mood heightens appreciably. He speaks explicitly of love—lost love—and the pain of remembering the beloved. By the end of the poem the reader recognizes (at least intuitively) that the speaker weeps from the memory of a dead or lost beloved (*both* circumstances are stated) and the pain of being unable to recapture the past.

The late Cleanth Brooks wrote a penetrating analysis of Tennyson's poem, "The Motivation of Tennyson's Weeper," which is found in his influential 1947 critical collection *The Well Wrought Urn* (Harcourt Brace). Brooks's analysis perfectly illustrates the power of close textual reading. Dean of the New Critics, however, Brooks does not discuss the biographical background of Tennyson's lyric. Although not necessary to understand the poem, the facts of its origin are interesting in themselves. Tennyson wrote the poem in the autumn of 1834 after the death of his closest friend, Arthur Hallam. It was composed—an interesting bit of literary trivia—in the ruins of Tintern Abbey, nearly within sight of Hallam's grave and on the same spot that William Wordsworth had conceived his great ode in 1798.

Richard Wilbur, LOVE CALLS US TO THE THINGS OF THIS WORLD, page 531
WRITER'S PERSPECTIVE
Richard Wilbur on Writing, CONCERNING "LOVE CALLS US TO THE THINGS OF THIS WORLD," page 532

Wilbur suavely explains this richly detailed poem in the "Writer's Perspective" that follows "Love Calls Us to the Things of This World" in the book. The poem may seem a bit difficult to students until they catch the extended metaphor in the first twenty lines (laundry on the line as angels). The poem depends on a series of oppositions (laundry and angels, earth and heaven, soul and body, sleep and waking). Even the poetic language mixes the vulgar and the exalted ("the punctual rape of every blessèd day"). Have students find as many oppositions as possible, and you will watch them grasp the larger themes of the poem in the process. (And you won't believe how many elegant oppositions blissfully coexist in this quietly visionary poem.)

An audio tape of Wilbur reading from his *Collected Poems* is available from: New Letters on the Air, University of Missouri-Kansas City, 5100 Rockhill Road, Kansas City, MO 64110-2499, (816) 235-1159.

14   Imagery

Ezra Pound, IN A STATION OF THE METRO, page 535

Pound recalled that at first this poem had come to him "not in speech, but in little splotches of color." His account is reprinted by K. K. Ruthven in *A Guide to Ezra Pound's Personae* (1926) (Berkeley: U of California P, 1969). Students might like to compare this "hokku-like sentence" (as Pound called the poem) with the more suggestive Japanese haiku freely translated later in this chapter.

For a computer-assisted tribute to this famous poem, see the curious work of James Laughlin and Hugh Kenner, reported in "The Mixpoem Program," *Paris Review* 94 (Winter 1984): 193–98. Following Laughlin's suggestion that the five nouns of "In a Station of the Metro" might interestingly be shuffled, Kenner wrote "A Little Program in Basic" that enabled a computer to grind out 120 scrambled versions of the poem, including these:

> The apparitions of these boughs in the face;
> Crowds on a wet, black petal
>
> The crowd of these apparitions in the petal;
> Faces on a wet, black bough.

Kenner then wrote a program in Pascal that would shuffle eight words and produce 40,320 different versions. We don't know what it all demonstrates, except that Pound's original version still seems the best possible.

Kenner's historical account of the London literary scene and its influences on the composition of this poem is found in the "Critical Approaches to Literature" section of this book.

Taniguchi Buson, THE PIERCING CHILL I FEEL, page 535

Harold G. Henderson, who translates this haiku, has written a good terse primer in *An Introduction to Haiku* (Garden City: Anchor, 1958). Most of Henderson's English versions of haiku rime like this one; still, the sense of the originals (as far as an ignorant reader can tell from Henderson's glosses) does not seem greatly distorted.

T. S. Eliot, THE WINTER EVENING SETTLES DOWN, page 537

This is the first of the series of four poems called "Preludes," originally published in the July 1915 issue of Wyndham Lewis's *Blast*. It was written during Eliot's days at Harvard. The "Preludes," writes Grover Smith in *T. S. Eliot's Poetry &*

Plays (Chicago: U of Chicago P, 1965), belong to the era of "Prufrock." Of "The winter evening settles down," Smith says:

> The first "Prelude" begins with winter nightfall in an urban back street; from indoor gloom and the confined odor of cooking it moves outside into the smoky twilight where gusts of wind whip up leaves and soiled papers, and a shower spatters the housetops. Such adjectives as "burnt out," "smoky," "grimy," "withered," "vacant," "broken," and "lonely" carry the tone.

Some students may point out, though, that the lighting of the lamps seems to end the poem on a note of tranquillity.

Theodore Roethke, ROOT CELLAR, page 537

Probably there is little point in spending much time dividing imagery into touches and tastes and smells; perhaps it will be enough to point out that Roethke's knowledgeable poem isn't all picture-imagery. There's that wonderful "congress of stinks," and the "slippery planks" are both tactile and visual. Most of the language in the poem is figurative, most of the vegetation is rendered animal: bulbs like small rodents, shoots like penises, roots like a forgotten can of fishing worms. Roethke doesn't call the roots lovely, but obviously he admires their tough, persistent life.

Elizabeth Bishop, THE FISH, page 538

This poem is made almost entirely of concrete imagery. Except for *wisdom* (line 63) and *victory* (66), there is no very abstract diction in it.

Obviously the speaker admires this stout old fighter. The image "medals with their ribbons" (line 61) suggests that he is an old soldier, and the "five-haired beard of wisdom" (line 63) suggests that he is a venerable patriarch, of whom one might seek advice.

The poor, battered boat has become magnificent for having the fish in it. The feeling in these lines is joy: bilge, rust, and cracked thwarts are suddenly revealed to be beautiful. In a way, the attitude seems close to that in Yeats's "Sailing to Byzantium," in which the triumphant soul is one that claps its hands and louder sings for every tatter in its mortal dress. The note of final triumph is sounded in "rainbow, rainbow, rainbow!" (line 75). The connotations of *rainbow* in this poem are not very different from the connotations often given the word by misty-eyed romantic poets such as Rod McKuen, but we believe Bishop because of her absolutely hard-eyed and specific view of the physical world. (She even sees the fish with X-ray imagination in lines 27–33.)

Anne Stevenson says in *Elizabeth Bishop* (New York: Twayne, 1966):

> It is a testimony to Miss Bishop's strength and sensitivity that the end, the revelation or "moment of truth," is described with the same attention to detail as the rest of the poem. The temptation might have been to float off into an airy apotheosis, but Miss Bishop stays right in the boat with the

engine and the bailer. Because she does so, she is able to use words like "victory" and "rainbow" without fear of triteness.

Because the fish has provided her with an enormous understanding, the speaker's letting it go at the end seems an act of homage and gratitude.

The poet reads this poem on a recording, *The Spoken Arts Treasury of 100 Modern American Poets*, vol. 10, SA 1049.

Charles Simic, FORK, page 540

Simic's surreal, short poem introduces an object familiar to us, a fork, and presents it as strange and threatening. The central image is plainly stated: the fork "resembles a bird's foot." An evil, indeed violent, world begins to take shape as one looks more closely at Simic's word choice. The fork, we are told at the start of the poem, is evidently visiting from hell. An eerie turn comes in the second stanza when the speaker addresses a "you," who may be the reader, another person in the poem, or the speaker himself. In any case, we are pulled into a dark landscape of cannibals, hell, stabbings, and naked bird heads—a scene right out of Hieronymus Bosch. We are perhaps pulled in against our will, through our familiarity with the object. Each of us has held a fork in our fist, so it is impossible to avoid identifying with the images. That is the real achievement of "Fork"—its surefire inclusion of the reader.

You might begin class discussion by having students point out the words that equip the fork with evil characteristics. A possible writing exercise is to have students come up with their own poems in which a familiar object is treated as foreign and unknown.

Emily Dickinson, A ROUTE OF EVANESCENCE, page 540

"A Route of Evanescence" will probably inspire a heated guessing contest. Contestants will need to pay attention to Dickinson's exact words.

Enclosing this poem in a letter to Thomas W. Higginson, Dickinson gave it a title: "A Humming-Bird."

The poet's report of the hummingbird's arrival from Tunis is fanciful. Besides, the creature could hardly fly 4,000 miles nonstop in one morning. New England hummingbirds don't need to cross the Atlantic; to find a warmer climate, they migrate south. If it was a ruby-throated hummingbird that the poet saw, though, it might indeed have come a long distance: from a winter in Mexico or Central America.

The poet's ornithology may be slightly cockeyed, but her imagery is accurate. Hummingbird wings appear to rotate, but they aren't seated in ball joints; in actuality, they merely flap fast.

Jean Toomer, REAPERS, page 541

This ominous poem, with its contrasts between sound and silence, possibly contains a metaphor. The black field hands are being destroyed by something indifferent and relentless, much as the trapped rat is slain under the blade. (Or, as in "Scottsboro," as a cat stalks a "nohole mouse"?)

A grandson of P. B. S. Pinchback, the black who served for a short time during Reconstruction as acting governor of Louisiana, Toomer had only a brief public career as a writer. His one book, *Cane* (1923), which experimentally combined passages of fiction with poetry, helped to spearhead the Harlem Renaissance. "Reapers" is taken from it.

That Toomer was a man divided between his profound understanding of blacks and his own desire to pass for white emerges in a recent biography, *The Lives of Jean Toomer: A Hunger for Wholeness,* by Cynthia Earl Kerman and Richard Eldridge (Baton Rouge: Louisiana State UP, 1987). *The Collected Poems of Jean Toomer* (Chapel Hill: U of North Carolina P, 1988) is a slim volume of 55 poems, the best of them from *Cane.*

Gerard Manley Hopkins, PIED BEAUTY, page 541

Sumptuously rich in music (rime, alliteration, assonance), this brief poem demands to be read aloud.

Some students might agree with Robert Frost's objection that the poem "disappoints . . . by not keeping, short as it is, wholly to pied things" (1934 letter to his daughter Lesley in *Family Letters of Robert and Elinor Frost* [Albany; State U of New York P, 1972] 162). But, as question 4 tries to get at, Hopkins had more in mind than dappled surfaces. Rough paraphrase of the poem: God is to be praised not only for having created variegation, but for creating and sustaining contrasts and opposites. In lines 5–6, tradesmen's tools and gear, like the plow that pierces and cuts the soil, strike through the surfaces of raw materials to reveal inner beauty and order that had lain concealed.

For a convincing argument that Hopkins in "Pied Beauty," like Dickens in *Hard Times,* complains about a drab, mechanical, industrial-age uniformity in Victorian England, see Norman H. MacKenzie, *A Reader's Guide to Gerard Manley Hopkins* (Ithaca: Cornell UP, 1981) 85–86. Few students will crave to fathom the poet's notions of *instress* and *inscape,* but if you do, see John Pick's unsurpassed *Gerard Manley Hopkins, Priest and Poet,* 2nd ed. (London: Oxford UP, 1966) 53–56.

The point of question 5 is that if the images of the poem were subtracted, its statement of theme also would disappear.

Hopkins discovered the form of "Pied Beauty" and called it the *curtal sonnet* (*curtal,* riming with *turtle:* "crop-tailed"). But, remarks MacKenzie, such sonnets are like a small breed of horse: "compressed, not merely cut short." Instead of two quatrains, the form calls for two tercets; then, instead of a sestet, four lines and brief line more. (Other curtal sonnets by Hopkins: "Peace" and, even more closely cropped, "Ashboughs.")

ABOUT HAIKU

We have kept our enlarged haiku section from the previous edition. Our only changes have been to refresh the contemporary section with a couple of new selections. Instructors should note that we have also added a selection of hokku by Yone Noguchi in "Poems for Further Reading." Please take a look at these early twentieth-century poems. Noguchi was the first Asian-American poet, and he was in many ways the person who first helped bring the haiku tradition over into English. He has been neglected by literary historians, so we are proud to bring his pioneering work some additional attention.

A biographical/critical note on Noguchi is found in this manual (in the commentary on "Poems for Further Reading").

The response to the enlarged haiku coverage has been excellent since it allows instructors enough material to make a separate unit on the subject. Lee Gurga, associate editor of *Modern Haiku* and a master of the form in his own right has praised our coverage of Basho, Buson, and Issa, but he wishes that we had also included work by Shiki (1876–1902), the fourth "Master" of the haiku, who was the originator of the modern haiku in Japan. Shiki was responsible for renaming the form from *hokku* (opening verse) to *haiku* (playful verse). We will consider Gurga's astute suggestion for future editions.

Basho's frogjump poem, "In the old stone pool," may well be the most highly prized gem in Japanese literature: in Japanese there exists a three-volume commentary on it.

For an excellent discussion of the problems of teaching haiku, and of trying to write English ones, see Myra Cohn Livingston's *When You Are Alone / It Keeps You Capone: An Approach to Creative Writing with Children* (New York: Atheneum, 1973) 152–62. Livingston finds it useful to tell students a famous anecdote. Kikaku, a pupil of Basho, once presented his master with this specimen:

Red dragonflies—
Tear off their wings
And you have pepper pods.

As a haiku, said Basho, that's no good. Make it instead:

Red pepper pods—
Add wings
And you have dragonflies.

A moment of triumph, such as all teachers of poetry hope for but seldom realize, has been reported in a letter to XJK from Maurice F. Brown of Oakland University, Rochester, Michigan:

Last year, teaching W. C. Williams in an "invitational" course for a week, I began with "Red Wheelbarrow" . . . and a student hand went up (class of 100): "That's not a poem! That's junk. What if I say, 'Here I sit looking at a blackboard while the sun is shining outside.' Is that a poem?" It was one of those great teaching moments . . . and I did a quick count and wrote it on the board:

Here I sit looking
    At a blackboard while the sun
is shining outside.

Not only a poem . . . a perfect haiku.

A thorough guide to this rocky acre of poetry, by William J. Higginson with Penny Harter, is *The Haiku Handbook: How to Write, Share, and Teach Haiku* (New York: McGraw, 1985).

There are several small journals that focus on haiku and tanka. If you or your students want to pursue studying (and perhaps even publishing) haiku, you will want to look at some of these magazines. *Modern Haiku* has been in existence for over twenty years. The mailing address is *Modern Haiku*, P. O. Box 1752, Madison, WI 53701. Meanwhile, the Haiku Society of America publishes *Frogpond* (Haiku Society of America, 333 East 47th Street, New York, NY 10017). If you write these journals asking for information or submitting your own haiku, make sure you enclose a stamped, self-addressed envelope.

Those interested in the "Three Masters" of the Japanese haiku tradition will want to consult Robert Hass's *The Essential Haiku: Versions of Basho, Buson, and Issa* (Hopewell, NJ: Ecco, 1994). Hass provides both generous selections from the poets and informed introductory essays for each writer.

Looking over the eight contemporary haiku, the reader will see that not every poet adheres to the traditional seventeen syllable pattern. The skillful and illuminating combination of two images or ideas, however, remains central to the haiku's identity in English. The poems are too short to require much commentary, but the title of one poem invites a few remarks.

Why is John Ridland's "The Lazy Man's Haiku" the work of a slothful soul? Because, according to the poet (in a letter), "he's too lazy to write the proper number of syllables in any line—or to get rid of that occidental end-rhyme à la Harold Henderson's ever-unconvincing translations in that old Anchor book." Henderson, in *An Introduction to Haiku* (New York: Anchor Books, 1956), forced all the haiku to rime like his version from Buson given at the beginning of this chapter. (Reading it as a poem in English, we find it profoundly convincing, and suspect it took work.)

FOR REVIEW AND FURTHER STUDY

John Keats, BRIGHT STAR! WOULD I WERE STEADFAST AS THOU ART, page 544

Unlike Petrarchan poets, Keats isn't making the star into an abstraction (Love); he takes it for a visible celestial body, even though he sees it in terms of other things. His comparisons are so richly laden with suggestions (star as staring eye, waters as priestlike), that sometimes students don't notice his insistent negations. The hermit's all-night vigil is *not* what Keats desires. He wants the comfort of that ripening pillow, and (perhaps aware of his impending death) envies the cold star only its imperishability—oh, for unendurable ecstasy, indefinitely prolonged!

Many readers find the last five words of the poem bothersome. Students might be asked, Does Keats lose your sympathy by this ending? If so, why? If not, how would you defend it? We can't defend it; it seems bathetic, almost as self-indulgent as Shelley's lines in "Indian Serenade":

> Oh, lift me from the grass!
>   I die! I faint! I fail!
> Let thy love in kisses rain
>   On my lips and eyelids pale.

Thomas Mauch, of Colorado College, intelligently disagrees, and suggests how "or else swoon to death" may be defended. The *or*, he thinks, is what grammarians call an inclusive *or*, not an exclusive.

> I believe that the speaker is saying, not that if he can't be forever in the close company of the beloved he would rather be dead—sort of like what Patrick Henry said about liberty—but rather that, given the closeness to the woman, dying in that condition would be just as good as experiencing it forever, since in either case he would not undergo a separation from her (and still retain his consciousness of it). I think it is the same point he makes in the "Ode to a Nightingale":

> Now more than ever seems it rich to die,
>   To cease upon the midnight with no pain,
>   While thou art pouring forth thy soul abroad
>   In such an ecstasy!

The poem, Mr. Mauch concludes, illustrates the kind of closure that Keats admired when he affirmed that a poem should "die grandly."

EXPERIMENT: *Writing with Images*, page 545

To write a poem full of images, in any form, is probably easier for most students than to write a decent haiku. (On the difficulties of teaching haiku writing, see Myra Cohn Livingston, cited under "About Haiku.") Surprisingly, there is usually at least one student in every class who can't seem to criticize a poem to save his neck, yet who, if invited to be a poet, will bloom or at least bud.

Walt Whitman, THE RUNNER, page 545

Try reading "The Runner" without the adverbs *lightly* and *partially*. Does the poem even exist without those two delicate modifiers?

T. E. Hulme, IMAGE, page 545

Hulme's poems seem always to have been brief. In his own collection *Personae*, Ezra Pound took two pages to include "The Complete Poetical Works of T. E. Hulme" (in which "Image" does not appear). Pound remarked, "In publishing his *Complete Poetical Works* at thirty, Mr. Hulme has set an enviable example to many of his contemporaries who have had less to say."

Chana Bloch, TIRED SEX, page 545

Chana Bloch's brief poem tells its entire story through images (a very discrete thing to do considering the subject). The first image—the damp matchbook—is particularly clever since the poet develops it to represent both male (the match) and female (the matchbook) sexuality. Bloch also carefully avoids depicting the speaker's inner thoughts but focuses instead on the external images (watching "that sparrow the cat / keeps batting around") that suggest a great deal about what is happening both in bed and in the speaker's mind. The final image of joylessly paging through a supposedly great book provides a final touch of wit to this ingenious poem.

Robert Bly, DRIVING TO TOWN LATE TO MAIL A LETTER, page 546

No doubt the situation in this poem is real: Bly, who lives in frequently snowbound Minnesota, emits hundreds of letters. Compare this simple poem to Frost's "Stopping by Woods on a Snowy Evening," which also has a speaker who, instead of going home, prefers to ogle snowscapes.

Note that this poem is examined in the "Writing Critically" section at the end of this chapter in the main book.

Gary Snyder, MID-AUGUST AT SOURDOUGH MOUNTAIN LOOKOUT, page 546

In brief compass, Snyder's poem appeals to the mind's eye (with *smoke haze, pitch glows on fir-cones, rocks, meadows,* and the imagined vista at the end), the sense of moisture *(after five days rain),* of hot *(three days heat)* and of cold *(snow-water from a tin cup).* The *swarms of new flies* are probably both seen and heard.

For more background to this poem and to Snyder's work in general, see Bob Steuding, *Gary Snyder* (Boston: Twayne, 1976). A fictional portrait of Snyder appears in Jack Kerouac's novel *The Dharma Bums* (New York: Viking, 1958).

H. D. [Hilda Doolittle], HEAT, page 546

Heat becomes a tangible substance in this imagist poem, whose power resides mainly in its verbs, all worth scrutiny. Compare this poem and Snyder's: how does each convey a sense of warmth?

H. D.'s work has enjoyed much critical attention. For a concise, insightful comment on the lyrics and their originality, see Emily Stripes Watts, *The Poetry of American Women from 1632 to 1945* (U of Texas P, 1977) 153–58. Susan Stanford Friedman's *Psyche Reborn: The Emergence of H. D.* (Indiana UP, 1981) is valuable.

Agenda, that excellent, very serious British magazine of poetry, devoted a 200-page special issue to H. D. (vol. 25, nos. 3–4, Autumn/Winter 1987–88). With contributions by the poet herself, Susan Stanford Friedman, Eileen Gregory, Denise Levertov, Alicia Ostriker ("The Open Poetics of H. D.") and others, it is available from 5 Cranbourne Court, Albert Bridge Road, London SW11 4PE.

Billy Collins, EMBRACE, page 547

Billy Collins is a poet with an extraordinary gift for ingenious imagery. "Embrace" is no exception. Here Collins creates an image and then invites the reader to examine it from two sides. The extended image, which begins so playfully and even romantically, soon proves not only devastatingly lonely, but foreboding. This poem contains a lesson every cinematographer knows—the same physical image can elicit a radically different effect depending on the angle from which it is depicted.

A CD of Billy Collins reading his poems, *The Best Cigarette*, has been released by Eric Antonow's small good productions (800-829-7552).

Stevie Smith, NOT WAVING BUT DROWNING, page 547

Stevie Smith reportedly got the initial inspiration for this poem from a newspaper item that described a man who drowned in full view of his friends; they mistook his signals for help as playful waving. Smith pursued the fatal irony of this freak accident and found a chilling universal message in it. Students have no trouble understanding how a person's desperate signals for help can be misunderstood or ignored by others.

If you share the story of the poem's genesis with students, you might also point out how the poem's title reads like a tabloid headline.

It never hurts to belabor the obvious with students. You might suggest they read the short biographical note on Smith and discover that the poet is a woman. Any student particularly interested in Smith should be directed to the superb 1978 film *Stevie* starring Glenda Jackson, which contains an especially powerful rendition of this poem.

WRITER'S PERSPECTIVE

Ezra Pound on Writing, THE IMAGE, page 548

Pound's brief paragraphs on the image may be the most influential critical passage of modern poetry. This passage of his 1913 essay "A Few Don'ts by an Imagiste" (later retitled and incorporated into "A Retrospect") provided a list of issues and opinions that have helped shape the poetic practice of the last nine decades.

Pound's criticism itself unfolds most effectively in short imagistic bursts. Ask students to share the sentence or pair of sentences that most interest them. Are there any ideas with which they fervently agree or disagree?

One word in Pound's passage may need a bit of explanation. As its capitalization indicates, *Mosaic* refers to Moses (and his Ten Commandments).

15 *Figures of Speech*

Alfred, Lord Tennyson, THE EAGLE, page 557

For a hostile criticism of this poem, see Robert Graves, "Technique in Poetry," *On Poetry: Collected Talks and Essays* (New York: Doubleday, 1969) 402–405. Graves finds Tennyson's fragment unable to meet the minimal requirement that a poem should make good prose sense. He complains that if the eagle stands on its hands then its wings must be feet, and he ends up by rewriting the poem the way he thinks it ought to be. Though his remarks are fascinating, Graves reads the poem too literally.

A recent critic has suggested that this poem is a product of Tennyson's hopeless nearsightedness. Celebrating the eagle's 20–20 zoom-lens vision and ability to see a fish from high up, Tennyson yearns for a goal he could not attain: "optical inclusiveness." (See Gerhard Joseph, "Tennyson's Optics: The Eagle's Gaze," *PMLA* 92 [May 1977]: 420–27.)

William Shakespeare, SHALL I COMPARE THEE TO A SUMMER'S DAY? page 557
Howard Moss, SHALL I COMPARE THEE TO A SUMMMER'S DAY? page 558

Shakespeare's original—rich in metaphor, personification, and hyperbole—means more, of course, than Moss's tongue-in-cheek desecration. The only figure of speech in Moss's rewrite is the simile in line 1, and even that is denigrated ("Who says?"). Moss manages to condense 115 great words to 78, a sonnet to a mere thirteen lines. It took a poet skilled in handling rimes to find such dull ones.

Shakespeare's nautical metaphor in line 8 may need explaining: a beautiful young person is a ship in full sail; accident or age can untrim the vessel. Compare this metaphor to "bare ruined choirs where late the sweet birds sang" ("That time of year").

METAPHOR AND SIMILE

Emily Dickinson, MY LIFE HAD STOOD – A LOADED GUN, page 560

This astonishing metaphysical poem (another hymnlike work in common meter) can be an excellent provoker of class debate. Before trying to fathom it, students might well examine its diction. *Sovreign Woods* ("sovereign" would be the more usual spelling) suggest an estate owned by a king. How do the Mountains *reply?* By echoing the gun's report. Apparently the *smile* is the flash from the gun's muzzle; and the *Vesuvian face,* a glimpse of the flaming crater of the volcano. The Eider-Duck, a sea duck, has particularly soft and silky down which is used in pillows and quilts. The gun's *Yellow Eye* seems, again, its flash: and the emphatic *Thumb* is presumably the impact of the bullet that flattens its victim. (Some will say the thumb is a trigger finger, but you don't pull a trigger with your thumb.)

Argument over the meaning of the poem will probably divide the class into two camps. One will see the poem, like "Because I could not stop for Death," as an account of resurrection, with the Owner being God or Christ, who carries away the speaker, life and all, to the Happy Hunting Grounds of Paradise. Personally, we incline toward the other camp. In that view the Owner seems a mere mortal, perhaps a lover. The last stanza reveals that he can die. So taken, the last two lines make more sense. Not having the power to die, the speaker feels something lacking in her. She doesn't wish to outlive her huntsman and be a lonely killer.

Philip Larkin admits the possibility of both views: "This is a romantic love in a nutshell, but who is its object? A religious poet—and Emily was this sometimes— might even have meant God" (*Required Writing* [New York: Farrar, 1984] 193).

A third camp has appeared, proclaiming a feminist interpretation. The poem, as summed up by Adalaide Morris, "tells about a life packed with a potential that the self was not empowered to activate." From this point of view, the poem is overtly political, exhilarating to teach because it recognizes long suppressed animosities ("Dick, Jane, and American Literature Fighting with Canons," *College English* 47 [1985]: 477).

But the poem remains tantalizingly ambiguous. You won't know until you go into class what a discussion may reveal.

Alfred, Lord Tennyson, FLOWER IN THE CRANNIED WALL, page 561

Why does Tennyson say "what God and man is" instead of "what God and man *are*"? Apparently, this isn't faulty grammar, but higher pantheism. God and man are one.

William Blake, TO SEE A WORLD IN A GRAIN OF SAND, page 561

This famous short poem begins Blake's "Auguries of Innocence." Written around 1803 in a notebook and then carefully transcribed by Blake into another notebook made from discarded sheets from his engraving business, this poem was not published until 1863—35 years after the poet's death.

Sylvia Plath, METAPHORS, page 562

Students usually are prompt to see that the central fact of the poem is the speaker's pregnancy. The speaker feels herself to be a walking riddle, posing a question that awaits solution: What person is she carrying? The "nine syllables" are like the nine months of gestation. All the metaphors refer to herself or to her pregnancy, except those in lines 4–5, which refer to the unborn baby: growing round and full like an apple or plum, seeming precious as ivory (and with ivory skin?), fine-timbered in sinew and bone like a well-built house.

The tone of the poem is clear, if complicated. Humor and self-mockery are evident in the images of elephant and strolling melon. In the last line, there is a note of wonder at the inexorability of gestation and birth: "The train there's no getting off."

A lively class might be asked to point out any possible connection between what the poem is saying about the arbitrary, fixed cycle of pregnancy and its form—the nine nine-syllable lines.

As Plath records in her Boston journal for 20 March 1959, the pregnancy she had hoped for ended in a miscarriage. Grieving and depressed, she went ahead and finished this poem, then explicitly called "Metaphors for a Pregnant Woman" (*Journals*, New York: Ballantine, 1983) 298–99.

N. Scott Momaday, SIMILE, page 562

Momaday is best known as a novelist and prose writer; his *House Made of Dawn* won the 1969 Pulitzer Prize in fiction. But Momaday is also an accomplished poet whose work often combines a compressed formal style with the natural imagery of his native Southwest. The Oklahoma-born author of Kiowa ancestry also often incorporates tribal legends into his verse.

"Simile," true to its title, gives us a single, extended simile, but it withholds the emotional motivation for the choice of this particular image. The reader is forced to interpret the behavior of the metaphorical deer in order to answer the *what* of the opening line. Those familiar with T. S. Eliot's concept of "an objective correlative" ("a set of objects; a situation, a chain of events which shall be the formula" that unleashes a particular emotion in a reader) will recognize Momaday's "Simile" as a classic example of that technique. Momaday lets his image work on the reader's unconscious rather than specify its emotional meaning.

EXERCISE: *What Is Similar?*

We'd suggest that this exercise be run through rapidly. We wouldn't give students much time to ponder, but would briskly call on people, and if anyone hesitated for long, would skip to someone else. Give them time to cogitate about these items, and they are likely to dredge up all sorts of brilliant, reached-for similarities in each pair of things—possibly logical, but having nothing to do with the lines. Immediate flashes of understanding are the goal of this exercise, not ponderous explication. Do this one for fun, and so it might be; do it slowly and seriously, and it could be deadly.

OTHER FIGURES

On the subject of puns, students familiar with *Hamlet* and other classics of the Bard may be asked to recall other puns of Shakespeare (besides the celebrated lines about golden lads and girls). If such a discussion prospers, Dr. Johnson's well-known observation in his preface to Shakespeare's works may provide an assertion to argue with:

> A quibble is to Shakespeare what luminous vapors are to the traveler: he follows it at all adventures; it is sure to lead him out of his way, and sure to engulf him in the mire. . . . A quibble is the golden apple for which he will always turn aside from his career or stoop from his elevation. A quibble, poor and barren as it is, gave him such delight that he was content to purchase it by the sacrifice of reason, propriety, and truth. A quibble was to him the fatal Cleopatra for which he lost the world, and was content to lose it.

James Stephens, THE WIND, page 564

As a birthday present to Stephens, James Joyce once translated this poem into five other languages (French, German, Italian, Latin, and Norwegian). These versions are reprinted in *Letters of James Joyce*, ed. Stuart Gilbert (New York: Viking, 1957) 318–19.

Chidiock Tichborne, ELEGY, WRITTEN WITH HIS OWN HAND, page 566

"One must admit the possibility that these verses were written by some other poet, rather than by the protagonist himself," note J. William Hebel and Hoyt H. Hudson in *Poetry of the English Renaissance* (New York: Appleton, 1929). Set to music by a later composer, the "Elegy" was sung as a madrigal.

Margaret Atwood, YOU FIT INTO ME, page 567

The first two lines state a simile. In the second couplet, *hook* and *eye* turn out (to our surprise) to be puns.

John Ashbery, THE CATHEDRAL IS, page 567

Ashbery's unexpected pun on *slated* inspired student Steven B. Stanley of Metropolitan State University to coin "a more contemporary example of a pun" in a one-line poem of his own, "The Spelling Bee Champion":

Studied a spell.

His instructor, Cathy Lewis, took a vote in class: Was Stanley better than Ashbery? Not surprisingly, Stanley triumphed. He adds: "I also came up with: 'The library is booked for demolition.' However, that sounded a little too like Ashbery." Perhaps your students might like to try writing one-liners in this vein, and so realize (as Ashbery does) that it is possible to have fun with poetry.

FOR REVIEW AND FURTHER STUDY

Robert Frost, THE SILKEN TENT, page 568

Although the word *as* in the opening line might lead us to expect a simile, "The Silken Tent" is clearly an immense metaphor, comparing woman and tent in a multitude of ways. What are the ropes or cords? Not merely commitments (or promises to keep) to friends and family, but generous sympathies, "ties of love and thought," on the part of a woman who cares about everything in the world.

While paying loving tribute to a remarkable woman, the poem is also a shameless bit of showing off by a poet cocksure of his technical mastery. Managing syntax with such grace that the poem hardly seems contrived, Frost has sustained a single sentence into an entire sonnet. "The whole poem is a performance," says Richard Poirier, "a display for the beloved while also being an exemplification of what it is like for a poem, as well as a tent or a person, to exist within the constrictions of space ('a field') and time ('at midday') wherein the greatest possible freedom is consistent with the intricacies of form and inseparable from them" (*Robert Frost: The Work of Knowing* [New York: Oxford UP, 1977] xiv–xv). Poirier points out, too, that the diction of the poem seems Biblical, perhaps echoing "The Song of Songs" (in which the bride is comely "as the tents of Kedar") and Psalm 92 (in which the godly "grow like a cedar in Lebanon"). Not only does the "central cedar pole" signify the woman's spiritual rectitude, it points toward heaven.

In teaching this poem, one can quote Frost's remark to Louis Untermeyer, "I prefer the synecdoche in poetry, that figure of speech in which we use a part for a whole." In 1931 Frost recalled that he had called himself a Synecdochist back when other poets were calling themselves Imagists: "Always, always a larger significance. A little thing touches a larger thing" (qtd. in Elizabeth Shepley Sergeant, *Robert Frost: The Trial by Existence* [New York: Holt, 1960] 325).

Denise Levertov, LEAVING FOREVER, page 568

The man seems glad to go: "stones rolling away" suggests the shedding of some great weight, or possibly even a resurrection (an echo of the rolling away of the stone from the Easter tomb?). But in the woman's view the mountain seems like someone rejected and forlorn. The woman's view, expressed in a metaphor and given force by coming last, seems stronger than the man's simile.

Another question: is the poet right to repeat *away, way, away, away*? The sound reverberates with a terrible flat monotony, it is true—but apparently that is the effect necessary.

Jane Kenyon, THE SUITOR, page 569

This economical poem moves from simile to simile: (1) "like the chest of someone sleeping" (steadily rising and falling); (2) "like a school of fish" (flashing their pale bellies), and (3) "like a timid suitor" (hesitant, drawing back, reluctant to arrive).

Until her untimely death from leukemia in 1995, Kenyon lived in Danbury, New Hampshire, with her husband, the poet Donald Hall. *Otherwise: New and Selected Poems* (Graywolf Press) was published posthumously in 1996.

Robert Frost, THE SECRET SITS, page 569

Besides its personification of the sitting Secret, Frost's poem contains an implied metaphor. To dance round in a ring is to make futile efforts to penetrate a secret— merely going around in circles.

H. D., THE POOL, page 569

The figure of speech in H. D.'s "The Pool" is personification. The speaker addresses the pool as if it were a self-conscious and intelligent entity, then questions it about its identity.

A. R. Ammons, COWARD, page 570

Ammons's figure of speech is, of course, a pun, but it is also a pun that underlines the original metaphor of *run* in the expression "runs in my family."

Robert Burns, OH, MY LOVE IS LIKE A RED, RED ROSE, page 570

Figures of speech abound in this famous lyric, similes (lines 1–2, 3–4), a metaphor (*sands o' life*, 12), overstatement (8 and 9, 10), and possibly another overstatement in the last line.

See other professions of love couched in hyperbole, among them Marvell's "To His Coy Mistress" and Auden's "As I Walked Out One Evening." Are the speakers in these poems mere throwers of blarney, whom no woman ought to trust?

For a discussion of this poem that finds more in it than figures of speech, see Richard Wilbur, "Explaining the Obvious," in *Responses* (New York: Harcourt, 1976). Burns's poem, says Wilbur, "forsakes the lady to glory in Love itself, and does not really return. We are dealing, in other words, with romantic love, in which the beloved is a means to high emotion, and physical separation can serve as a stimulant to ideal passion." The emotion of the poem is "self-enchanted," the presence or absence of the lady isn't important, and the very idea of parting is mainly an opportunity for the poet to turn his feelings loose. Absurd as this posture may be, however, we ought to forgive a great songwriter almost anything.

WRITER'S PERSPECTIVE

Robert Frost on Writing, THE IMPORTANCE OF POETIC METAPHOR, page 571

Frost made so many insightful and memorable observations about poetry that it is difficult to select just one passage. Rather than reprint one of his most famous comments, we have selected this fascinating but little known passage from an address he gave at Amherst College in 1930.

In this brief excerpt Frost speculates on the general value of a literary education. He observes how studying poetry trains us to understand metaphors and other figures of speech. Metaphors pervade all types of discourse, Frost remarks, and are used in all walks of life. An education in poetry helps us judge metaphors critically—to see how far they apply to a situation truthfully and where they "break down."

16 *Song*

SINGING AND SAYING

"Song" is an unusual chapter. It approaches poetry in ways different from most other textbooks. We urge new instructors to try this chapter. Most students who write comments about this book say this chapter is the most appealing. "It shows that poetry isn't all found in books," is a typical comment; and many students are glad to see song lyrics they recognize. Most important, the chapter talks to them about poetry by using songs—a context they know a great deal about. It also encourages them to hear poems in a way that they might never have done before if their entire experience was seeing poems on the printed page.

Even if there is not time for a whole unit on song, the instructor who wishes to build upon this interest can use at least some of this chapter to introduce the more demanding matters of sound, rhythm, and form (treated in the chapters that follow). Some instructors take the tack that lyric poetry begins with song, and so begin their courses with this chapter, supplemented by folk ballads elsewhere in the text.

Besides Ben Jonson's classic nondrinking song, many other famous poems will go to melodies. The tradition of poems set to music by fine composers is old and honorable. For lists of such poems with musical settings (and recordings), see *College English* for February 1985 and December 1985.

Ben Jonson, TO CELIA, page 575

Students may not know that in line 2 *I will pledge* means "I will drink a toast." Also, *I would not change for thine* (line 8) in modern English becomes "I would not take it in exchange for yours."

To demonstrate that "To Celia" is a living song, why not ask the class to sing it? Unfortunately, you can no longer assume that the tune is one that everyone knows, so you may need to start them off.

Anonymous, THE CRUEL MOTHER, page 576

Some versions of this ballad start the narrative at an earlier point in time, with a woman discovering that she is pregnant by the wrong man when she is about to marry another. See Alan Lomax's Notes to *The Child Ballads*, vol. 1, Caedmon, TC 1145, an old l.p. record, which contains an Irish version.

If the instructor cares to discuss the bottomless but student-spellbinding topic of archetypes, this ballad will serve to illustrate an archetype also visible in the stepmother figure of many fairy stories.

Run D.M.C., from PETER PIPER, page 578

One reason we chose this excerpt from many other rap lyrics was its density of allusion. "Peter Piper" contains as many literary references as Milton's "Lycidas," but most students don't find them intimidating because they come from popular culture and children's literature. It might be helpful to work through the allusions and discuss how they shape the lyrics' effect on the listener; then use this as a model of how allusions to myth and literature work in traditional poetry. (It's nice to see King Midas in a Run D.M.C. lyric.) Rap is a form of oral poetry, and it's interesting to note how these lyrics incorporate many pieces of the central English-language classic of oral poetry—*Mother Goose.*

A metrical note: notice how once the rap settles into its regular rhythm (line 12) it bounces along in a four-stress line, the standard measure of English-language oral poetry from the Anglo-Saxons till today.

William Shakespeare, TAKE, O, TAKE THOSE LIPS AWAY, page 579

In this short madrigal, Shakespeare wrote in the most popular song form of his era. How many popular song lyrics look this good after three hundred years? Shakespeare had the brevity of the madrigal form working to his advantage; singers busy with elaborate counterpoint didn't need extended lyrics found in simpler strophic forms like the ballad. Although this song was presumably sung by a single voice (the boy who enters with Mariana in the fourth act of *Measure for Measure*), it employs the madrigal form usually associated with three or more voices. Madrigals could take flexible forms ranging from four to thirteen lines, but they always end in a couplet.

The fourth line may confuse some students, "Lights that do mislead the morn" means that the lover's eyes are so radiant that they mislead the morning into believing the sun has risen.

Edwin Arlington Robinson, RICHARD CORY, page 580
Paul Simon, RICHARD CORY, page 581

This pair sometimes provokes lively class discussion, especially if someone in the class maintains that Simon converts Robinson into fresh, modern terms. Further discussion may be necessary to show that Robinson's poem has a starkly different theme.

Robinson's truth, of course, is that we envy others their wealth and prestige and polished manners, but if we could see into their hearts we might not envy them at all. Simon's glib song does not begin to deal with this. The singer wishes that he too could have orgies on a yacht, but even after he learns that Cory died a suicide, his refrain goes right on, "I wish that I could be Richard Cory." (Live rich, die young, and make a handsome corpse!)

Some questions to prompt discussion might include:

1. In making his song, Simon admittedly took liberties with Robinson's poem. Which of these changes seem necessary to make the story singable? What suggestions in the original has Simon picked up and amplified?

2. How has Simon altered the character of Richard Cory? Is his Cory a "gentleman" in Robinson's sense of the word? What is the tone of Simon's line, "He had the common touch"? Compare this with Robinson: "he was always human when he talked." Does Robinson's Cory have anything more than "Power, grace and style"?

3. In the song, what further meaning does the refrain take on with its third hearing, in the end, after the news of Cory's suicide?

4. What truth about life does Robinson's poem help us see? Is it merely "Money can't make you happy" or "If you're poor you're really better off than rich people"? Does Simon's narrator affirm this truth, deny it, or ignore it?

Frank J. D'Angelo has noticed that the name Richard Cory is rich in connotations. It suggests Richard Coeur de Lion, and other words in Robinson's poem also point to royalty: *crown, imperially, arrayed, glittered, richer than a king.*

BALLADS

Anonymous, BONNY BARBARA ALLAN, page 582

Despite the numerous versions of this, the most widespread of all traditional ballads in English, most keep the main elements of the story with remarkable consistency. American versions tend to be longer, with much attention to the lovers' eventual side-by-side burial, and sometimes have Barbara's mother die of remorse, too! Commentators since the coming of Freud have sometimes seen Barbara as sexually frigid, and Robert Graves once suggested that Barbara, a witch, is killing Sir John by sorcery. An Irish version makes Barbara laugh hideously on beholding her lover's corpse.

To show how traditional ballads change and vary in being sung, a useful recording is *The Child Ballads*, vol. 1, Caedmon, TC 1145, containing performances collected in the field by Alan Lomax and Peter Kennedy. Six nonprofessional singers are heard in sharply different versions of "Barbara Allan," in dialects of England, Scotland, Ireland, and Wales.

Dudley Randall, BALLAD OF BIRMINGHAM, page 585

Randall's poem is an authentic broadside ballad: it not only deals with a news event, it was once printed and distributed on a single page. "I had noticed how people would carry tattered clippings of their favorite poems in their billfolds," the poet has explained, "and I thought it would be a good idea to publish them in an attractive form as broadsides" (Interview in *Black World*, Dec. 1971). "Ballad of Birmingham" so became the first publication of Randall's Broadside Press, of Detroit, which has since expanded to publish books and issue recordings by many leading black poets, including Gwendolyn Brooks, Don L. Lee, and Nikki Giovanni.

The poem seems remarkably fresh and moving, though it shows the traits of many English and Scottish popular ballads (such as the questions and answers, as in "Edward," and the conventional-sounding epithets in stanza 5). Randall presents without comment the horror of the bombing—in the mother's response and in the terrible evidence—but we are clearly left to draw the lesson that if the daughter had been allowed to join the open protest, she would have been spared.

Four black girls were killed in 1963, when a dynamite blast exploded in Birmingham's Sixteenth Street Baptist Church. In September, 1977, a Birmingham grand jury finally indicted a former Ku Klux Klansman, aged 73, on four counts of first degree murder.

BLUES

Bessie Smith and Clarence Williams, JAILHOUSE BLUES, page 587

No one knows exactly who wrote this blues song. Authorship is assigned to Smith and Williams because they recorded it in 1923, but their version owes much to a traditional folk blues that survives in several versions. The concept of authorship in a conventional sense has little meaning in an oral tradition like early blues. Singers took songs they heard and transformed them into material for their own performance. One interesting feature of "Jailhouse Blues" is that the singer actually addresses the *blues* itself and converses with it.

W. H. Auden, FUNERAL BLUES, page 587

Auden's poem not only uses many blues elements (especially hyperbolic figures of speech to depict sadness); these lines were also originally written for music. The first two stanzas (followed by different third and fourth stanzas) appeared in *The Ascent of F6*, a play that Auden wrote with Christopher Isherwood in 1936. Set to music by the young Benjamin Britten, the words lamented the death of the play's visionary hero. A few years later Auden and Britten rewrote both the words and music as a cabaret song. (The poem was later set to music again by the American composer Ned Rorem.)

In the process of revision, the song changed from a dirge for a lost political savior to a personal lament for a dead lover. A careful reader will note how the imagery becomes less public and civic in the final two stanzas.

Auden keeps the exaggerated imagery of traditional blues and the flamboyant emotionalism. He also rhymes in couplets, as blues songs conventionally do, but he drops the standard repetition of the first line. "Funeral Blues," therefore employs the mood and style of traditional blues but varies the metrical form.

"Funeral Blues" has long been one of Auden's more popular "songs" (a category the author used in his *Collected Poems*), but thanks to its inclusion in the film *Four Weddings and a Funeral*, it has become one of the most widely known modern love poems.

FOR REVIEW AND FURTHER STUDY

John Lennon and Paul McCartney, ELEANOR RIGBY, page 588

"Eleanor Rigby," we think, is a poem. Although swayed by the superstition that priests are necessarily lonely because celibate, Lennon's portrait of Father

McKenzie and of Eleanor have details that reflect life. Both music and words contain an obvious beat, and if students pick out those syllables in long lines 4 and 7, 14 and 17, and 24 and 27, they will be getting into the subject of meter. (Each of the lines contains a stressed syllable followed by four anapests.)

Bob Dylan, THE TIMES THEY ARE A-CHANGIN', page 589

Bob Dylan's folk song became one of the definitive political anthems of the 1960s, but decades later it holds up extraordinarily well, even on the page. Seen from such a distance, "The Times They Are a-Changin'" is remarkable for its lack of specific topical issues. None of the key political issues of the era is mentioned by name—not even Civil Rights or pacifism. There are a few topical allusions embedded in the text. The lines, "Don't stand in the doorway / Don't block up that hall," for example, refer to the late George Wallace's defiant action to stop school integration in Alabama. But no listener needs to catch that now oblique allusion to get the broader sense of the lines since Dylan has so thoroughly universalized his images. In fact, except for the first line of stanza three with its references to senators and congressmen, there are not even any specifically American references in the song, which otherwise could apply equally to England, Italy, India, or China.

The song's imagery seems more informed by the Bible than the newspaper. The rising waters, the raging battle, the falling old order have an openly prophetic ring to them. (The lines "And the first one now / will later be last" directly allude to the Gospels—Matthew 19:30, Mark 10:31, Luke 13:30.) The poet/songwriter announces himself as the prophet of a new generation that intends to refashion society in direct confrontation with their elders, but no program of reform is offered by the speaker. The nature of this new order is left almost entirely up to our imagination. Perhaps one reason this song proved so powerful and popular was that each listener could project whatever vision of a new society he or she preferred.

WRITER'S PERSPECTIVE

Paul McCartney on Writing, CREATING "ELEANOR RIGBY," page 591

McCartney's comments to the interviewer reveal a great deal about the creative process—how one idea grows unexpectedly out of another. It is interesting to imagine that this song was nearly titled "Daisy Hawkins."

17 Sound

SOUND AS MEANING

Alexander Pope, TRUE EASE IN WRITING COMES FROM ART, NOT CHANCE, page 594

Nowadays, looking at the pages of an eighteenth-century book of poetry, we might think the liberal capitalization and use of italics merely decorative. But perhaps Pope wished to leave his readers little choice in how to sound his lines. Most of his typographical indications seem to us to make sense—like a modern stage or television script with things underlined or capitalized, lest the actors ignore a nuance.

Line 12 is deliberately long: an alexandrine or twelve-syllable line that must be spoken quickly in order to get it said within the time interval established by the other shorter, pentameter lines.

William Butler Yeats, WHO GOES WITH FERGUS?, page 596

Originally a song in Yeats's play *The Countess Cathleen,* this famous lyric over-flows with euphony. Take just the opening question (lines 1–3): the assonance of the various o-sounds; the initial alliteration of *w, d,* and *sh;* the internal alliteration of the *r* in *Fergus, pierce,* and *shore*—musical devices that seem especially meaningful for an invitation to a dance. The harsh phrase *brazen cars* seems introduced to jar the brooding lovers out of their reveries. Unless you come right out and ask what brazen cars are, a few students probably will not realize that they are brass chariots. In ancient Ulster, such chariots were sometimes used for hunting deer—though how you would drive one of them through the deep woods beats us.

If you discuss meter, what better illustration of the power of spondees than "And the WHITE BREAST of the DIM SEA?"

The last line of the poem, while pleasingly mysterious, is also exact. The personification "dishevelled wandering stars" makes us think of beautiful, insane, or distracted women with their hair down: Ophelia in Olivier's film *Hamlet.* That they are wandering recalls the derivation of the word *planet:* Greek for "wanderer." In what literal sense might stars look disheveled? Perhaps in that their light, coming through the atmosphere (and being seen through ocean spray) appears to spread out like wild long hair. For comparable figures of speech, see Blake's "Tyger," in which the personified stars weep and throw spears.

EXERCISE: *Listening to Meaning,* page 596
John Updike, RECITAL, page 597
Frances Cornford, THE WATCH, page 597
William Wordsworth, A SLUMBER DID MY SPIRIT SEAL, page 597

"Recital" shows off Updike as one of America's virtuosos of light verse. The whole poem seems written in imitation of the trochaic "oom-pah" of a tuba, and every line ends in a thumping celebration of the near rime between Mr. Bobo's surname and his chosen instrument. Onomatopoeia is heard even more obviously in Cornford's watch-ticks.

In Wordsworth's Lucy poem, sound effects are particularly noticeable in the first line (the soporific *s*'s) and in the last two lines (the droning *r*'s and *n*'s). If students go beyond the sound effects and read the poem more closely, they might find problems in the first stanza. Is the poet's slumber a literal sleep or a figurative one? That is: is Wordsworth recalling some pleasant dream of Lucy (whether the living Lucy he used to know, or the dead Lucy in Eternity), or is he saying that when she was alive he was like a dreamer in his view of her? If so, he was deluded in thinking that she would always remain a child; he had none of the usual human fears of death or of growing old. However we read the poem, there is evidently an ironic contrast between the poet's seeing Lucy (in stanza 1) as invulnerable to earthly years, and his later view that she is affected, being helplessly rolled around the sun once a year with the other inanimate objects. And simple though it looks, the poem contains a paradox. The speaker's earlier dream or vision of Lucy has proved to be no illusion but an accurate foreshadowing. Now she is a "thing," like rocks and stones and trees; and she cannot feel and cannot suffer any more from time's ravages.

ALLITERATION AND ASSONANCE

A. E. Housman, EIGHT O'CLOCK, page 599

The final *struck* is a serious pun, to which patterns of alliteration begun in the opening line *(st . . . st, r),* and continued through the poem, have led up. The ticking effect of the clock is, of course, most evident in *the clock collected.*

Robert Herrick, UPON JULIA'S VOICE, page 599

Julia, apparently, is singing, for the lutes provide accompaniment. At the beginning and end, this brief poem is particularly rich in music: the sibilance of *so smooth, so sweet, so silv'ry;* and the alliteration (both initial and internal) of the *m-* and *l-* sounds in the last line.

The second line seems a colossal hyperbole, meaning, "Julia, your singing is sweet enough to make the damned in Hell forget to wail." In Herrick's poems, such flattery is never out of place. This is the quality of Herrick's work—a lovely deliberate absurdity—XJK has tried to echo (feebly) in a two-line parody:

When Vestalina's thin white hand cuts cheese,
The very mice go down upon their knees.

This short poem can be compared to Herrick's tribute, "Upon Julia's Clothes."

Alfred, Lord Tennyson, THE SPLENDOR FALLS ON CASTLE WALLS, page 600

If read aloud rapidly, this famous lyric from Tennyson's *The Princess* will become gibberish; and the phrase *Blow, bugle, blow,* a tongue twister. But if it is read with any attention to its meaning, its long vowels and frequent pauses will compel the reader to slow down. Students may want to regard the poem as mellifluous nonsense, but may be assured that the poem means something. In fact, it is based on a personal experience of the poet's. Visiting the lakes of Killarney in 1848, Tennyson heard the bugle of a boatman sound across the still water, and counted eight distinct echoes. "The splendor falls" is the poet's attempt to convey his experience in accurate words.

RIME

William Cole, ON MY BOAT ON LAKE CAYUGA, page 601

This is one of a series of comic quatrains, "River Rhymes," first printed in *Light Year '85* (Case Western Reserve U: Bits Press, 1984).

Hilaire Belloc, THE HIPPOPOTAMUS, page 603

This short amusing poem requires no commentary. Instructors and students alike, however, might enjoy exploring more of Belloc's light verse found in anthologies such as Kingsley Amis's *The New Oxford Book of English Light Verse* (New York, Oxford UP, 1978).

Gerard Manley Hopkins, GOD'S GRANDEUR, page 604

Students who think Hopkins goes too far in his insistence on rimes and other similar sounds will have good company, including Robert Bridges, William Butler Yeats, and Yvor Winters. Still, it is hard not to admire the euphony of the famous closing lines—that ingenious alternation of *br* and *w,* with a pause for breath at that magical *ah!*—and the cacophony of lines 6–8, with their jangling internal rimes and the alliteration that adds more weight to *smeared, smudge,* and *smell.* For Hopkins, of course, sound is one with meaning; and the cacophonous lines just mentioned are also, as John Pick has pointed out, "a summary of the particular sins of the nineteenth century." For a brilliant demonstration that sound effects in Hopkins's poetry have theological meaning, see J. Hillis Miller, *The Disappearance of God* (Cambridge: Harvard UP, 1963) 276–317. Miller finds the poet's theory revealed in his sermons and journals: "Any two things however unlike are in something like"; therefore, "all beauty may by a metaphor be called rhyme."

In the text, it seemed best not to bury the poem under glosses, but to let the instructor decide how thoroughly to explicate it. Here are a few more glosses in case they seem necessary:

Line 7, *man's smudge:* the blight of smoke and ugliness cast over the countryside by factories and mines. As a student for the priesthood in North Wales and as a parish priest in London and Liverpool, Hopkins had known the blight intimately. Another suggestion in the phrase: nature is fallen and needs to be redeemed, like man, who wears the smudge of original sin. Line 12, *morning . . . springs:* The risen Christ is like the sun at dawn. Eastward is the direction of Jerusalem, also of Rome. (Hopkins cherished the hope that the Church of England and the Pope would one day be reconciled.) Lines 13–14, *bent / World:* Perhaps because of its curvature the earth looks bent at the horizon; or perhaps the phrase is a transferred epithet, attributing to the earth the dove's bent-over solicitude. (And as the world seems to break off at the horizon, line 13 breaks at the word bent.) Line 14, *broods:* like a dove, traditional representation of the Holy Ghost.

For still more suggestions, see Pick, *Gerard Manley Hopkins, Priest and Poet,* 2nd ed. (Oxford: Oxford UP, 1966) 62–4; Paul L. Mariani, *Commentary on the Complete Poems of Gerard Manley Hopkins* (Ithaca: Cornell UP, 1970); and (not least) the poet's "Pied Beauty."

A sonnet by Wordsworth also begins "The world is," and Hopkins no doubt knew of it. In their parallel (though different) complaints against trade and commerce, the two deserve to be compared. Both poets find humanity artificially removed from nature: this seems the point of Hopkins's observation in lines 7–8 that once soil was covered (with grass and trees) and feet were bare; now soil is bare and feet are covered. Clearly we have lost the barefoot bliss of Eden, but in answer to Wordsworth, one almost expects Hopkins to cry, "Great God! I'd rather be a Christian." (Wordsworth by *world* means "worldliness.")

Fred Chappell, NARCISSUS AND ECHO, page 604

Fred Chappell is best known as a novelist and short story writer, but his poetry is exceptionally fine. He has often experimented with old verse forms (like Anglo-Saxon stress meter). In "Narcissus and Echo," he revived a virtually defunct form called "Echo Verse," which had not received much attention since the Renaissance. (Note that "Echo Verse" is described in the footnote to the poem.) To complete his *tour de force,* he uses the form to dramatize the plight of the nymph Echo.

Chappell takes the Echo Verse form one difficult step farther than most earlier poets. He makes his echoes form a vertical poem down the right hand side of the page. (Students will usually miss that aspect of the poem unless you point it out to them.) Likewise, Narcissus's speech can be read in isolation, so there are essentially three different poems in this text: Narcissus's self-absorbed solo, Echo's plaintive response, and the pair's lopsided dialogue.

Robert Frost, DESERT PLACES, page 605

Some possible answers to the questions following the poem:

1. *What are these desert places that the speaker finds in himself? (More than one theory is possible. What is yours?)* Terrible pockets of loneliness.

2. *Notice how many times, within the short space of lines 8–10, Frost says* lonely *(or* loneliness*). What other words in the poem contain similar sounds that reinforce these words?* The word *snow,* occurring three times. Other *o*-sounds occur in *oh, going, showing, no, so,* and *home.* The *l* of *lonely* is echoed by alliteration in *looked, last,* and *lairs.*

3. *In the closing stanza, the feminine rimes* spaces, race is, *and* places *might well occur in light or comic verse. Does "Desert Places" leave you laughing? If not, what does it make you feel?* It makes us feel a psychic chill! Yet the feminine rime lightens the grim effect of what is said and gives it a kind of ironic smirk.

For an intriguing if far-out appreciation of this poem that makes much of the sibilent SS-sounds, see Marie Boroff, "Sound Symbolism as Drama in the Poetry of Robert Frost," *PMLA* 107 (1992): 131–144.

READING AND HEARING POEMS ALOUD

Here is a comment by William Stafford on why certain poets read their poems with apparent carelessness. Poets spend their energies in writing poems and are not effective public speakers. Unlike the Russian poet Andrei Voznesensky, a great performer, Stafford remarks,

> Most of the poets I know would feel a little guilty about doing an effective job of reading their poems. They throw them away. And I speak as one who does that. It feels fakey enough to be up there reading something as though you were reading it for the first time. And to say it well is just too fakey. So you throw it away (Interview in *The Literary Monitor* 3.3–4 [1980]).

This comment raises provocative questions for discussion. What is the nature of a poetry reading? Should it be regarded as a performance, or as a friendly get-together?

For a symposium on poetry readings, with comments by Allen Ginsberg, James Dickey, Denise Levertov, and twenty-nine other poets, see *Poets on Stage* (New York: Some/Release, 1978).

A rich and convenient source of recorded poetry, no doubt the best in the country, is the Poet's Audio Center, a nonprofit service to the literary community and academe operated by the Watershed Foundation. The center can supply on cassette more than 500 readings by great and minor poets living and dead, both commercial and noncommercial productions. They issue a catalogue of over 250 recordings. Among the cassette offerings are their own Watershed Tapes, an extremely well produced and interesting series of readings by contemporaries. Address: Poet's Audio Center, P.O. Box 50145, Washington, D.C. 20091.

A catalogue of over 500 radio broadcasts on cassette, including a rich variety of programs featuring contemporary poets such as John Ashbery, Gwendolyn Brooks, John Ciardi, Rita Dove, Allen Ginsberg, Anthony Hecht, Jonathan Holden, Colette Inez, Philip Levine, and many others reading and talking about their work, is available from New Letters on the Air, University of Missouri Kansas City, 5100 Rockhill Road, Kansas City, MO 64110, phone (816) 235–1159.

EXERCISE: *Reading for Sound and Meaning,* page 607
Michael Stillman, IN MEMORIAM JOHN COLTRANE, page 607
William Shakespeare, FULL FATHOM FIVE THY FATHER LIES, page 607
Chryss Yost, LAI WITH SOUNDS OF SKIN, page 608
T. S. Eliot, VIRGINIA, page 608

In Michael Stillman's tribute to the great jazz saxophonist, *coal train* is not only a rich pun on Coltrane's name, it also becomes the poem's central image. The poet has supplied this comment:

> One thing about that poem which has always pleased me beyond its elegiac strain—is the way the technique of the lines and phrases corresponds to a musical effect in Coltrane's playing. He was known for his ability to begin with a certain configuration of notes, then play pattern after pattern of variations. The repetition of "Listen to the coal . . . listen to the . . . listen to . . . listen" was one way to capture a feature of his playing. The image of the coal train disappearing into the night comes, particularly, from a place on the James River, west of Richmond, where I happened to be when I heard of Coltrane's death. Like all jazz musicians, I felt the loss very deeply.

Shakespeare's song contains an obvious illustration of onomatopoeia (the bell's sound), obvious alliteration in the *f*-full first line, and (less obviously) internal alliteration (note the *r* and *n* sounds), and assonance galore. Like a drowned man's bones, ordinary language becomes something "rich and strange" in this song.

The central metaphor of Chryss Yost's poem is weaving, and the author has woven an extraordinarily beguiling fabric of sound. Although the poem is only sixteen short lines long, students will be hard-pressed to find devices of sound Yost does not use. Rhyme, assonance, alliteration, enjambment, stress pattern, syllable count, and repetition are all present. Although the metrical scheme is syllabic, Yost also repeats patterns of stressed and unstressed syllables. Note, for example, how the stress pattern of the first line echoes in the opening line of the second stanza.

The *lai* (or more precisely *lai nouveau*) is a French form of sixteen lines divided into two eight-line stanzas. Each line has a set syllable count of either two or five syllables per line. Students can discover the pattern by analyzing Yost's poem. The form is rarely used in English—probably because of the difficulty of rhyming sixteen lines with only three sounds. (The *a* rhyme must be used twelve times!) Amazingly, Yost not only handles the form in the most natural way but creates a gentle yet deeply expressive lyric poem in which the language of weaving becomes a metaphor for the motions of making love.

Chryss Yost has provided the following commentary on her poem:

The lai, while short, is a deceptively difficult beast to master for at least three reasons. First, unlike most metrical forms in English which count the stressed syllables, the lai measures the syllables in each line. Second, the syllable count is extremely short, just five or two syllables per line. Finally, each stanza uses just two rhymes (*aabaabaa*). In combination with the short lines, this means that the poem must depend on relatively few sounds. A poem with short words and lots of repetition risks falling into obvious, overused rhyme (like *love* and *dove*). I wanted the poem to celebrate the interlocking, tightly-woven form, and I couldn't resist the pun on lai. I went hunting for beautiful and unusual words and discovered *weft*—the threads woven to make fabric. *Weft* has a soft, lingering sound and the meaning seemed to fit the form. *Weft* led to *heft*, *warp*, and *skein*. The technical language of weaving gave me the tools I needed to create an untraditionally sensual poem from a rather restrictive traditional form.

Eliot's "Virginia" is an experiment in quantitative verse, according to George Williamson (*A Reader's Guide to T. S. Eliot* [New York: Noonday, 1957]). You might read aloud "Virginia" and Campion's quantitative "Rose-cheeked Laura" and ask the class to detect any similarity. Ted Hughes has written of "Virginia" with admiration. How is it, he wonders, that Eliot can create so vivid a landscape without specific images? "What the poem does describe is a feeling of slowness, with a prevailing stillness, of suspended time, of heat and dryness, and fatigue, with an undertone of oppressive danger, like a hot afternoon that will turn to thunder and lightning" (*Poetry Is* [New York: Doubleday, 1967]).

WRITER'S PERSPECTIVE

T. S. Eliot on Writing, THE MUSIC OF POETRY, page 609

Eliot's remarks on poetic music are full of significant distinctions—most notably his observation that poetic music does not exist apart from poetic meaning. He also bases poetry firmly in speech ("one person talking to another") and assumes that all poetic music will emerge in some way from the sound and rhythms of conversation.

18   *Rhythm*

STRESSES AND PAUSES

In the first section of this chapter, rhythm is discussed with as few technicalities as possible. For the instructor wishing to go on to the technicalities, the second part of the chapter, "Meter," will give the principles of scansion and the names of the metrical feet.

Except for one teacher at the University of Michigan, James Downer, who would illustrate the rhythms of Old English poetry by banging on his desk for a drum, we have never known anyone able to spend whole classes on meter without etherizing patients. Meter, it would seem, is best dealt with in discussing particular poems.

EXERCISE: *Get with the Beat*, pages 615–616

Browning's four-beat anapestic lines vigorously capture the speed of the scene they describe.

Keeler's loose ballad meter seems suitably rollicking for his down-home subject and tone.

Finch's rhythm is itself an homage to her subject. She has borrowed the hymn stanza that Dickinson used so frequently. Likewise, Finch has deliberately imitated the clear syntax and sonorous cadences of the church hymns to present her images. Although Finch prints her poem in couplets, the rime scheme and syntax fall into Dickinsonian quatrains.

Eisler's lines describing a newspaper photo of Marilyn Monroe have three strong stresses per line, but Eisler creates a different rhythm in each line by varying the number of unstressed syllables. The effect is a jazz-like syncopation. (The first line also has strong secondary stresses on the compound words, *newsprint moonprint*, that makes this especially evocative line read slowly.)

Shakespeare's songs were sung in the theater. Among other things, they provided a break from the iambic pentameter of most characters' speech. This song from *The Tempest* has a loosely iambic rhythm, but the line lengths differ. They follow a lost melody rather than a strict metrical scheme. The rollicking, unpredictable rhythm seems very appropriate to the mood and setting of the song.

Gwendolyn Brooks, WE REAL COOL, page 616

The poet might have ended every line with a rime, as poets who rime usually do:

> We real cool.
> We left school.

The effect, then, would have been like a series of hammer blows, because of so many short end-stopped lines and so many rimes in such quick succession. But evidently Brooks is after a different rhythm. What is it? How to read the poem aloud? Let members of the class take turns trying and compare their various oral interpretations. If you stress each final *We*, then every syllable in the poem takes a stress; and if, besides, you make even a split-second pause at every line break, then you give those final *We*'s still more emphasis. What if you don't stress the *We*'s, but read them lightly? Then the result is a skipping rhythm, rather like that of some cool cat slapping his thighs.

After the class has mulled this problem, read them Brooks's own note on the poem (from her autobiography *Report from Part One* [Detroit: Broadside, 1972] 185), which is reprinted in the "Writer's Perspective" section at the end of this chapter.

As a student remarked about the tone and theme of this poem, "She doesn't think they're real cool, she thinks they're real fool—to die so young like that."

Brooks recorded her own reading of the poem for *The Spoken Arts Treasury of 100 Modern American Poets*, vol. 13, SA 1052.

Alfred Lord Tennyson, BREAK, BREAK, BREAK, page 617

Tennyson's plangent poem displays an interesting rhythmic design. It is written in accentual meter in which the author counts the number of strong stresses per line (rather than in the more conventional accentual-syllabic measure in which one counts both syllables and stresses). The normative line of Tennyson's poem has three strong stresses (though later in the poem, it occasionally broadens to four stresses). By varying the syllable count, Tennyson is able to create all sorts of interesting effects. (It may be worth pointing out to students that Tennyson employs exactly the same technique as Rap in this regard.)

The opening stanza should be scanned as follows:

>   /   /   /
> Break, break, break,

>   U U   /   U   / U /
> On thy cold gray stones, O Sea!

>   U U /   U U   /   U   / U
> And I would that my tongue could utter

>   U   /   U U / U /
> The thoughts that arise in me.

Note how Tennyson's accentual meter can stretch the line from 3 to 9 syllables.

Ben Jonson, SLOW, SLOW, FRESH FOUNT, KEEP TIME WITH MY SALT TEARS, page 617

O sounds slow the opening line, whose every word is a monosyllable. Further slowing the line, eight of the ten monosyllables take heavy beats. "Drop, drop,

drop, drop" obviously racks up still more stresses, as do the spondees that begin lines 4, 5, and 6. The entire effect is that we are practically obliged to read or sing the poem slowly and deliberately—as befits a lamentation.

EXERCISE: *Two Kinds of Rhythm,* page 618
Sir Thomas Wyatt, WITH SERVING STILL, page 618
Dorothy Parker, RÉSUMÉ, page 619

These two poems differ in rhythm: Wyatt compels a heavy pause only at the end of every quatrain, while Parker end-stops every line. Students may be shown that pauses and meanings go together. Both poems are cast in two sentences, but Wyatt develops one uninterrupted statement throughout the entire poem (in sonnet fashion: first the summary of the speaker's problem in the opening three stanzas, then the conclusion beginning with "Wherefore all ye"). "Résumé," as its punctuation indicates, makes a new self-contained statement in every line.

A question on meaning: Must light verse necessarily be trivial in its theme? State Parker's theme in "Résumé." Surely, it isn't trivial. At least in theme, the poem seems comparable to Hamlet's soliloquy, "To be or not to be. . . . "

After *Not So Deep as a Well,* her collected poems of 1936, Parker brought out no more poetry collections. "My verses," she insisted to an interviewer. "I cannot say poems. Like everybody was then, I was following in the exquisite footsteps of Miss Millay, unhappily in my own horrible sneakers" (*Writers at Work: The Paris Review Interviews,* 1st ser. [New York: Viking, 1959]). Parker's wit, acerbic and sometimes macabre, is as clear from "Résumé" as it is from her celebrated remark on being informed that Calvin Coolidge had just died: "How do they know?"

METER

XJK used to think of a meter as a platonic ideal norm from which actual lines diverge, but J. V. Cunningham's essay "How Shall the Poem be Written?" changed his mind. Metrical patterns (in the abstract) do not exist; there are only lines that poets have written, in which meters may be recognized. "Meter," declares Cunningham, "is perceived in the actual stress-contour, or the line is perceived as unmetrical, or the perceiver doesn't perceive meter at all" (*The Collected Essays of J. V. Cunningham* [Chicago: Swallow, 1976] 262).

Max Beerbohm, ON THE IMPRINT OF THE FIRST ENGLISH EDITION OF THE WORKS OF MAX BEERBOHM, page 619

John Updike has paid tribute to this brilliant bit of fluff:

The effortless a-b-a-b rhyming, the balance of "plain" and "nicely," the need for nicely in pronouncing "iambically" to scan—this is quintessential light verse, a twitting of the starkest prose into perfect form, a marriage of earth with light, and quite magical. Indeed, were I high priest of literature, I would have this quatrain made into an amulet and wear it about my neck, for luck.

("Rhyming Max," a review of Beerbohm's collected verse reprinted in *Assorted Prose* [New York: Knopf, 1965].)

EXERCISE: *Recognizing Rhythms*, page 624
Edna St. Vincent Millay, COUNTING-OUT RHYME, page 624
A. E. Housman, WHEN I WAS ONE-AND-TWENTY, page 625
William Carlos Williams, THE DESCENT OF WINTER (SECTION 10/30), page 625
Walt Whitman, BEAT! BEAT! DRUMS! page 626

Probably it is more important that students be able to recognize a metrical poem than that they name its meter. The Millay and Housman poems are thoroughly metrical; the Williams and Whitman are not, but include metrical lines when the poets are describing or imitating the sound of something with a regular rhythm: the clank of freight car wheels, the whistle's *wha, wha*, the beating of drums. In Whitman's poem, besides the refrain (lines 1, 8, and 15) there are primarily iambic lines that end each stanza.

David Mason, SONG OF THE POWERS, page 627

Another powerful poem written in accentual meters. There are two strong stresses in each line. Since nursery rhymes are usually written in accentual meters, and Mason's poem uses the children's game of Scissors, Paper, Stone as its unifying metaphor, the meter is especially appropriate to the subject. But Mason also uses the rough-edged quality of accentual meter to convey the raw, uncompromising nature of his protagonists. Each character (Stone, Paper, Scissors) speaks in turn, each announcing its power, pride, and position. As the poem progresses, these symbolic speakers reveal how unrestrained ambition and desire destroy human relations and community.

WRITER'S PERSPECTIVE

Gwendolyn Brooks on Writing, HEARING "WE REAL COOL," page 628

Brooks's remarks on her poem suggest how she consciously uses rhythm as an instrument of meaning. By placing *we* at the end of each of the first seven lines— in contrast to a more conventional placement at the beginning of each line—she forces the reader to stop and think more probingly about what the lines mean. In the interview, she also stresses that her lineation was not trying to copy a collo-quial rhythm but to express her attitude toward the protagonists in her poem—a significant and provocative distinction.

Kilroy, as students may need to know, was a fictitious—even mythical—char-acter commemorated in graffiti chalked or penciled by U.S. soldiers wherever they traveled in World War II. KILROY WAS HERE was even scrawled in the sands of Anzio, a small testimonial that the graffitist is a person.

19 *Closed Form*

Beginning students of poetry often have had a hard time appreciating either a sonnet or a poem in open verse because they have yet to distinguish one variety of poetry from the other. On first meeting an unfamiliar poem, the experienced reader probably recognizes it as metrical or nonmetrical from its opening lines—perhaps even can tell at first glance from its looks on the page (compact sonnet or spaced-out open verse). Such a reader then settles down to read with appropriate expectations, aware of the rules of the poem, looking forward to seeing how well the poet can play by them. But the inexperienced reader reads mainly for plain prose sense, unaware of the rhythms of a Whitmanic long line or the rewards of a sonnet artfully fulfilling its fourteenth line. Asked to write about poetry, the novice reader may even blame the sonnet for being "too rigid," or blame William Carlos Williams for "lacking music" (that is, lacking a rime scheme), or for "running wild." Such readers may have a right to their preferences, but they say nothing about a poem, nor about the poet's accomplishments.

That is why this chapter and the following one seem essential. To put across to students the differences between the two formal varieties, it isn't necessary to deal with every last fixed form, either. One can do much by comparing two poems (closed and open) on the theme of sorrow—Edna St. Millay's fine sonnet "What lips my lips have kissed" and Stephen Crane's astonishing "The Heart." Before taking up closed form, you might care to teach some song lyrics or a couple of traditional folk ballads. That way the student isn't likely to regard fixed forms as arbitrary constructions invented by English teachers. A stanza, you can point out, is the form that words naturally take when sung to a tune. That is how stanzas began. Sing a second round of a song, and you find yourself repeating the pattern of it.

FORMAL PATTERNS

John Keats, THIS LIVING HAND, NOW WARM AND CAPABLE, page 633

After Keats's death, these grim lines were discovered in the margin of one of his manuscripts. Robert Gittings has pointed out that the burden of the poem is much like that of two letters Keats wrote late in life to Fanny Brawne, charging her conscience with his approaching death and blaming her for enjoying good health. "This," says Gittings, "marks the lowest depths of his disease-ridden repudiation of both love and poetry" (*John Keats* [Boston: Atlantic-Little, 1968] 403). To discuss: can a repudiation of poetry nevertheless be a good poem?

Robert Graves, COUNTING THE BEATS, page 635

At mid-century, Robert Graves was generally considered one of the major English poets of the Modern era. Then shortly before his death he fell out of critical favor. His work almost vanished from the anthologies. Now his reputation is slowly but surely on the rise. Poet, novelist, critic, autobiographer, Graves stands as a diverse and original (if also often eccentric) literary talent—the one surviving British poet of the First World War to achieve a major literary career.

"Counting the Beats" has received almost no critical attention, but it has been a favorite among poets since its first appearance. The poem has an almost hypnotic rhythm. The stanza pattern of the poem is original. The meter is accentual. Each four-line stanza begins with a short two-beat line. The next line has three beats. The long third line of each stanza has five stresses. The stanza then ends with another short two-beat line.

The rime scheme is equally noteworthy and original. Each stanza ends with an *I*-sound, but the first three lines of each stanza repeat a single word as an end-rime. This gives each stanza the effect of the two speakers repeating, refining, and qualifying their ideas as they converse.

Readers interested in learning more about Graves might want to consult the scholarly journal *Focus on Robert Graves and His Contemporaries*, edited by Richard Schumaker and published by the Department of English at the University of Maryland.

John Donne, SONG ("GO AND CATCH A FALLING STAR"), page 636

Maybe it is worth pointing out that, in bringing together short stanzas to make one longer one, Donne hasn't simply joined quatrain, couplet, and tercet like a man making up a freight train by coupling boxcars. In sense and syntax, each long stanza is all one; its units would be incomplete if they were separated.

THE SONNET

William Shakespeare, LET ME NOT TO THE MARRIAGE OF TRUE MINDS, page 638

Shakespeare's enormously popular Sonnet 116 is a meditation on ideal love and romantic fidelity. As one would expect of any famous work by Shakespeare, the meaning of every line in the poem has been debated. Most modern critical discussions have centered on whether the speaker really believes that perfect human constancy is possible or whether the poem is subtly skeptical about its own romantic idealism.

A crucial notion to point out in a classroom discussion is that Shakespeare's poem discusses a spiritual union ("the marriage of true minds," not of bodies). He acknowledges that physical youth and beauty are victim to the ravages of Time. Spiritual love even endures bodily death, the poem asserts, and lasts until Doomsday.

Edna St. Vincent Millay, WHAT LIPS MY LIPS HAVE KISSED, page 638

Millay's originality has been insufficiently appreciated by critics. Too often she has been portrayed as a sentimental traditionalist removed from the mainstream of Modernist innovation. Millay's diction was very traditional, and her devotion to metrical forms like the sonnet seemed conservative when compared to the experimentalism of Pound and Williams. And yet Millay's tone and subject matter was revolutionary in its time, and her strong feminist voice remains powerful. The sexual candor and moral freedom of this 1923 sonnet hardly seems reactionary or conservative.

The female speaker of the sonnet recalls her many previous lovers but—significantly—only in a general sense. They are too numerous for her to individualize. She displays no traditional guilt for her amours. Her only specific remorse concerns her own aging. (By implication, she longs to be young and in love again.)

The sestet of Millay's sonnet explicitly recalls Shakespeare's sonnet "That time of year thou mayst in me behold"—another poem in which an aging lover regrets the passing of youth and approach of old age. Millay boldly appropriates Shakespeare's metaphor of the winter tree and develops it for her own ends. In her excellent essay, "Love's 'Little Day': Time and the Sexual Body in Millay's Sonnets" (printed in *Millay at 100: A Critical Appraisal*, edited by Diane P. Freedman, Carbondale: Southern Illinois UP, 1995), Stacy Carson Hubarb comments:

> The aging speaker as songless tree is an abject figure, one that we might be tempted to read as a prototype of abandoned womanhood, pathetic and powerless, if it were not for the powerful alliance that such abjectness establishes between Millay's speaker and Shakespeare's. The speaker of Shakespeare's sonnet makes a spectacle of his abjection by way of persuasion; so, too, does Millay's, but with the further motive of authorizing herself through poetic echo. To read such self-abjection without a view to literary history would be to mistake it for mere self-pity, a sentimental attachment to the figure of woman as victim, rather than the bold poetic affiliation that Millay surely intends it to be.

Robert Frost, ACQUAINTED WITH THE NIGHT, page 639

This poem first appeared in *West-Running Brook* (1928), Frost's fifth volume, which some critics felt marked a turning in his work toward dark, personal themes. One might argue if Frost's turn to dark themes began here, but it is true that many of his grimmer early poems were cast in a seemingly impersonal narrative form.

"Acquainted with the Night" shows many of the features we associate with Frost's darkly introspective side. Not only is the speaker solitary and alienated from the human community surrounding him; he fatalistically accepts this isolation. The poem begins and ends with the same line, which emphasizes the inescapable quality of the speaker's destiny, though by now *night* has acquired a metaphorical as well as literal meaning.

Although the poem is written in a direct first-person voice, it confides very little to the reader. We know the speaker's desperate isolation but, as William Pritchard observes in his superb study *Frost: A Literary Life Reconsidered* (New York: Oxford UP, 1984), the poem provides "no clues or provocation to significant action." We know what is happening in the poem but not why. Noting that the poem was written in *terza rima*, Randall Jarrell commented that it possessed "Dante's own form and with some of Dante's own qualities." One might elaborate Jarrell's passing remark by saying that one reading of the poem would describe it as the speech of a lost soul wandering in his own private hell.

For the record, it is worth noting that the moody Frost was a compulsive walker whose late night rambles were legendary, though he liked them best with friends.

Kim Addonizio, FIRST POEM FOR YOU, page 640

Anyone who thinks the sonnet form forces a writer into old-fashioned themes should look at this sexy and surprising poem. Addonizio creates a totally contemporary situation and language, and yet she also touches subtly on ancient, indeed primal poetic themes—the impermanence of flesh, the unpredictability of sexual passion, and the mysterious relationship between body and soul.

An interesting question to ask in class: what do the images the speaker's lover has tattooed onto his (or possibly her) body suggest about the person's character? The tattoos depict lightning and blue swirls of water out of which a serpent faces a dragon. These are the only specific images we have of the otherwise unseen lover.

R. S. Gwynn, SCENES FROM THE PLAYROOM, page 640

This ironic, outrageous poem might be valuable to turn to on a day when a class needs waking up.

How much do we know about these people? That this family is wealthy is suggested by the fact that it's the cook's night off. That these brats are treated indulgently is hinted by the children's having apparently killed a series of unlucky goldfish before this latest one. If Mother were alert enough to notice the monstrous acts of her Gestapo brood, much more than onions would make her cry.

Like the reader, the poet deplores both these children and their parents. His attitude is made plain by his drawing the children as Nazis, their parents as blind or foolish.

Of the formalist poets now coming to prominence, Gwynn may be the keenest satirist. This sonnet is from his collection *The Drive-In* (Columbia: U of Missouri P, 1986). He has also written an extended satire on current poets and poetry in the great tradition of Pope's *Dunciad: The Narcissiad* (New Braunfels, TX: Cedar Rock P, 1981). He frequently reviews poetry for *Texas Review, Sewanee Review,* and other literary journals, and is currently a professor of English at Lamar University in Beaumont, Texas.

The Epigram

Alexander Pope, Epigram Engraved on the Collar of a Dog, page 641

Students may be asked: What's the point? Pope makes a devastating comment on society. With few exceptions (such as His Royal Highness), every man is a dog: owned by somebody, accepting handouts, licking his master's hand, learning to heel.

Sir John Harrington, E. E. Cummings, Langston Hughes, J. V. Cunningham, Stevie Smith, Anonymous, Hilaire Belloc, Wendy Cope, A Selection of Epigrams, pages 641–643

Highly various, these nine examples illustrate the persistence of the epigram. Whether the form of an epigram is closed or open, its essence consists of brevity and a final dash of wit.

Besides writing "Of Treason," called the best epigram in English, Harrington has another claim to immortality: he invented the water closet.

Cunningham, the American master of the verse epigram in our time, has had few recent rivals. Instructors who wish further examples of this fixed form will find many to quote in his *Collected Poems and Epigrams* (Chicago: Swallow, 1971).

If the haiku-like brevity of epigrams tempts you to ask your class to write a few, resist the temptation. Even from a bright class the results are likely to depress you. A successful epigrammatist needs, besides the ability to condense, the ability to deliver that final rapier thrust of nastiness. A talented creative writing class, after tackling poems in a few of the less demanding forms (ballads, villanelles, sestinas) might try epigrams, either rimed or rimeless.

If you do ultimately decide to challenge your class with writing an epigram, you might suggest they try the Wendy Cope approach and either update or revise an existing epigram. You'll be surprised how personal some of these revisions can become.

Other Forms

Robert Pinsky, ABC, page 643

The title of Robert Pinsky's short poem suggest its form—an abecediary, a poem which uses the order of the alphabet as its structural principle. Exactly twenty-six words long (not counting the equal sign in the last line) the poem offers one word for each letter of the alphabet in strict order from A to Z. Pinsky turns what might merely be a word game into a concise and evocative meditation on death. The meditation acquires a strange force because it seems to push against the arbitrary limitations of the form. Each new word feels hard-won, a fragment of meaning achieved against the odds. Without the poem's demanding form, Pinsky could easily achieve a more fluent statement of his theme, but that difficult articulation and urgent economy would vanish.

Dylan Thomas, DO NOT GO GENTLE INTO THAT GOOD NIGHT, page 644

No mere trivial exercise (as a villanelle tends to be), Thomas's poem voices his distress at the decline and approaching death of his father. At the time, the elder Thomas was a semi-invalid, going blind, suffering from the effects of tongue cancer. As a teacher of English at Swansea Grammar School, the poet's father had ruled his class with authority; but those who knew him only in his last years knew a different, humbled man. (See Constantine FitzGibbon, *The Life of Dylan Thomas* [Boston: Atlantic-Little, 1965] 294–95.)

Like many other Thomas poems, this one contains serious puns: *good night, grave.* "Another assumption in this poem," says Amy Mulvahill (in a student paper written at Tufts), "may be Thomas's own self-destructive drive that led him to drink himself to death. It's possible that he preferred to taunt death with his boisterous life—to go down unrepentant and brawling."

Repetitious as a villanelle is, the form suits this poem, making its refrains sound like prayers said over and over. If you have any student poets, they might be challenged to write villanelles of their own. The hard part is to make the repeated lines occur naturally, to make them happen in places where there *is* something to be said. But the repetitious form is helpful. Write the two refrain lines and already your labors are eight nineteenths over.

For another instance of Thomas's fondness for demanding, arbitrary forms, see the poem "Prologue," at the beginning of Daniel Jones's edition of *The Poems of Dylan Thomas* (New York: New Directions, 1971). A poem of 102 lines, its first and last lines rime with each other, as do lines 2 and 101, 3 and 100, 4 and 99, and so on, until two riming lines collide in the poem's exact center. Except for that inmost pair of lines, no reader is likely to notice the elaborate rime scheme—rimes so far apart they can't be heard; but apparently it supplied the poet with obstacles to overcome and with a gamelike pleasure.

Robert Bridges, TRIOLET, page 644

The triolet is a form usually associated with light verse, but Bridges's poem demonstrates that it can be used to convey heavier emotional loads, if used with sufficient skill. Bridges's triolet could be used as an example of a short lyric—compressed, evocative, musical, and personal. He also manages to make the opening lines acquire considerable additional force by the end of the poem. We now know both that the couple fell into their passion unawares (they "did not guess") and that love was not only difficult but irretrievably disastrous. Is there a more moving triolet in English?

Elizabeth Bishop, SESTINA, page 645

We would answer the questions following the poem like this.

1. That some terrible loss—a death in the family?—causes the grandmother to weep seems a guess that fits the poem. The old woman tries to hide her grief from the child (lines 6, 10, 31–32); she thinks it was somehow foretold (9).

2. We have no authority to read this poem as autobiography, but the figure of the grandmother—the most important person in Bishop's early life—and the stormy setting (such as we might find in a village on the Nova Scotia coast) invite us to do so. The source of grief may have been the death of the poet's father (hence, an irony that the child draws a man with tear-shaped buttons) or it may have been the illness of her mother, hospitalized several times for a mental disorder. When Bishop was eight months old her father died, and according to Robert Giroux, "The first real home Elizabeth knew was in the coastal town of Great Village, Nova Scotia, where her widowed mother returned in order to be with her parents" (introduction to Bishop's *Collected Prose* [New York: Farrar, 1984]). When the poet was five, her mother had a final breakdown, leaving the girl in the care of her grandmother. Apparently Bishop looked back to her days in Nova Scotia with affectionate yearning. When she was six, her father's wealthy parents moved her to Worcester, Massachusetts, for a less happy stay.

3. Small round pieces of paper. Almanacs (such as *The Old Farmer's*) come with punched holes to make them easy to string and hang on a hook or a nail.

4. The playful ingenuity of the sestina, like that of the villanelle, tempts a poet to wax clever; yet Bishop is writing a deeply felt, moving poem in it. The tone is lightly serious, compassionate—yet with touches of gentle humor: the Little Marvel Stove, the child's drawings. Irony, too, informs the poem: a contrast between the grandmother's sorrow and the child's innocent ignorance.

5. Nims's comment seems an apt description of "Sestina." In the six repeated words, we are given the setting *(house)* the characters *(grandmother, child)*, and key symbols *(Stove, almanac, tears)*. "Sestina" weaves all six into a subtle relationship. This poem is full of things that suggest magic: the prophetic almanac, the teacup (with which fortune-tellers divine), the "marvellous stove." It also is full of secret-keepers: the grandmother, the almanac with its powers of prophecy, the concluding reference to the "inscrutable house." The repetitions are worth tracing: *tears*, in particular, accumulates an effect. In stanza 2 the tears arrive like an equinoctial storm; in 3, the kettle also weeps; in 4, tea is tears; in 5, the man in the child's drawing wears tears; in 6, the almanac weeps paper tears; and finally, in the envoy, tears are flowers. "Time to plant tears" may be literal quotation from the almanac, *tears* being (if memory serves) the name of a small white flower favored by rock gardeners.

Bishop's *Complete Poems* contains another intriguing sestina: "A Miracle for Breakfast." At the time it was written Bishop remarked (in a 1937 letter to Marianne Moore):

It seems to me that there are two ways possible for a sestina—one is to use unusual words as terminations, in which case they would have to be used differently as often as possible—as you say, 'change, of scale.' That would make a very highly seasoned kind of poem. And the other way is to use as colorless words as possible—like Sidney, so that it becomes less of a trick and more of a natural theme and variations. I guess I have tried to do both at once. (Quoted by Nims in his essay, cited in question 5.)

In the later "Sestina," the terminal words seem deliberately usual ones.

For poet Eavan Boland's insightful comparison between "Sestina" and Bishop's poem "One Art," please see the notes on the latter poem in this manual.

WRITER'S PERSPECTIVE

Robert Graves on Writing, POETIC INSPIRATION AND POETIC FORM, page 647

Graves makes the important observation that form emerges naturally from poetic inspiration; form is not something external imposed on it. For Graves, a poet only discovers the form the finished poem wants to take after he or she has written part of it in the trance of inspiration.

20 Open Form

Denise Levertov, SIX VARIATIONS (PART III), page 650

This poem is discussed fairly extensively in the text. Some instructors may worry that the poem is a little too unusual to start the chapter, but its refusal to rest in normal poetic conventions makes it a strong discussion piece. A provocative question to ask a beginning class is "Why would we consider this text poetry? What features does it have that we would consider poetic?"

E. E. Cummings, BUFFALO BILL 'S, page 654

Cleanth Brooks and Robert Penn Warren have taken this poem to be an admiring tribute to William Cody (*Understanding Poetry*, 3rd ed. [New York: Holt, 1960]). But Louis J. Budd, in an interesting dissent, thinks Cummings is satirizing the theatricality of the old sideshow straight shooter and finds Mister Death "a cosmic corporal gathering up defunct tin-gods and stuffed effigies" (*The Explicator* 11 [June 1953]: item 55).

W. S. Merwin, FOR THE ANNIVERSARY OF MY DEATH, page 654

W. S. Merwin's poem is written in unpunctuated free verse. The lines tend to end on natural speech pauses, but without conventional punctuation, the reader cannot know if a phrase or sentence ends until he or she says the line aloud (or reads it carefully) and proceeds to the next line. The effect is one of discovering the full meaning of the lines only as they unfold. The phase "Tireless traveler," for example, is initially ambiguous in syntactical terms. Does it refer to the speaker or the silence of death? Only by going on to the next line ("Like the beam of a lightless star") does the reader understand that the phrase stands in apposition to *silence*. Merwin's lack of punctuation, therefore, both slows down one's reading of the poem and endows its language with an appropriate sense of mystery.

The central idea of the poem is itself a mystery—the exact date of the speaker's death. This question is, of course, a universal one since it is a mystery that every human faces. Merwin uses the occasion of his quandary to meditate on his mortality and praise the beauty of the world in religious terms, though his spiritual impulse reflects the mystery of existence. The speaker bows "not knowing to what." Ultimately, Merwin's "For the Anniversary of My Death" is a contemporary version of the Roman poet Horace's *carpe diem* ode (found in the chapter on Translation) in which the speaker acknowledges the impossibility of knowing the exact time of one's inevitable death and so resolves to seize the day by living fully.

Stephen Crane, THE HEART, page 655
Walt Whitman, CAVALRY CROSSING A FORD, page 655

Two nineteenth-century American poems, the pair seem comparable mainly in brevity and use of narration. The assonance and internal alliteration in Whitman's phrase *silvery river* are echoed in the poem's very opening line: the assonance of the *i*-sound in *line, wind, islands*; the internal alliteration of the *r* in *array, where, green*. But any line of this short poem will repay such inspection. Crane's "The Heart" is obviously less heavy on verbal music, although *Held his heart in his hands* is heavily alliterative; and the second stanza favors the letter *b*. There is rime, too: *it/bitter, bitter/heart*.

Whitman seems to lambaste his poem with sound-effects in his enthusiasm for his grand military spectacle. Crane cares for music, too, and yet his is a subtler, harsher one. Although longer in words, Whitman's "Cavalry" contains fewer pauses than "The Heart" (fifteen compared to Crane's seventeen, if every comma and line-end counts as a pause). The result is, in Crane's poem, a much more hesitant, start-and-stop movement—appropriate, perhaps, to a study of self-immolation. Whitman apparently wants an expansive, continuous progress in his syntax, as in his cavalry.

Wallace Stevens, THIRTEEN WAYS OF LOOKING AT A BLACKBIRD, page 656

Suggestive as blackbirds may be, the theme of the poem is, "Pay attention to physical reality." Stevens chides the thin ascetic men of Haddam who would ignore good blackbirds and actual women for golden phantasms. He also chides that asinine aristocrat who rides about Connecticut (of all places) in a glass coach as if thinking himself Prince Charming. The poem ends in a section whose tone is matter-of-fact flatness, rather as though Stevens were saying, "Well, here's the way the world is; if you don't like it, go read newspapers." Taken as a series of notes for an argument for literalism, this much-discussed poem seems to have unity and to lead to a definite conclusion. For another (and more complicated) view of it, see Helen Hennessy Vendler, *On Extended Wings* (Cambridge: Harvard UP, 1969).

Way-of-looking number 5 recalls Keats's "Grecian Urn": "Heard melodies are sweet. . . ."

Way number 10 eludes final paraphrase. Are the "bawds of euphony" supposed to be, perhaps, crass ex-poets who have sold out their Muses, who utter music to please the box office instead of truth? But blackbirds flying in a green light are so strikingly beautiful that even those dull bawds would be moved to exclaim at the sight of them.

Carolyn Forché, THE COLONEL, page 658

It is possible to argue either way on whether "The Colonel" is a prose poem or a short prose piece, but the stronger case is that it is a poem in prose. Why? First, "The Colonel" displays the compression we usually associate with poetry (prose fiction would unfold more leisurely). Second, by the end of the piece, it becomes apparent that the organization is as much lyric as narrative (the image of the ears pressed to the ground harks back to the *heard* in the opening line and to the auditory images throughout). Third, the density of literary effect (imagery, description, metaphor) has the feel of poetic language. The absence of poetic rhythms and lineation isn't enough to offset these qualities.

The rhetoric of Forché's piece deserves some attention. The effect of the poem depends heavily on the opening sentence ("What you have heard is true.") If we do not—at least initially—accept Forché's piece as reportage, then the poem loses a great deal of its impact. Forché understands this assumption clearly: notice how she dates the incident at the end to increase its verisimilitude. Some critics have questioned whether the episode truly happened as Forché presents it. That is a legitimate historical query, but, in poetic terms, it hardly matters; she has convincingly created the appearance of reality. The exaggerations seem no less credible than the bizarre incidents that fill the newspapers because Forché has captured the tone of factuality.

VISUAL POETRY

For more examples of graphic poetry, see the anthologies edited by Klonsky and Kostelanetz (cited in footnotes to this chapter). Other useful anthologies include Emmett Williams's *Anthology of Concrete Poetry* (New York: Something Else, 1967), Eugene Wildman's *Chicago Review Anthology of Concretism* (Chicago: Chicago Review, 1967), Mary Ellen Solt's *Concrete Poetry: A World View* (Bloomington: Indiana UP, 1969), and Emmett Williams's selection of "Language Happenings" in *Open Poetry: Four Anthologies of Expanded Poems*, ed. Ronald Gross and George Quasha (New York: Simon Schuster, 1973).

George Herbert, EASTER WINGS, *page 659*
John Hollander, SWAN AND SHADOW, *page 660*

The tradition of the shaped poem, or *Carmen figuratum*, seems to have begun in Renaissance Italy, and the form flourished throughout Western Europe in the seventeenth century. English practitioners of the form, besides Herbert, included Robert Herrick (in "The Pillar of Fame") and George Puttenham.

Of "Easter Wings," Joan Bennett has remarked, "The shape of the wings on the page may have nothing but ingenuity to recommend it, but the diminuendo and crescendo that bring it about are expressive both of the rise and fall of the lark's song and flight (Herbert's image) and also the fall of man and his resurrection in Christ (the subject that the image represents)" (qtd. by F. E. Hutchinson in his edition of Herbert's *Works* [Oxford: Oxford UP, 1941]). Visual shape and verbal meaning coincide strikingly when the second stanza dwindles to *Most thin.*

Like Herbert, Hollander clearly assumes that a word-shape has to have a meaningful relation to what is said in it. His reflected swan is one of twenty-five shaped poems collected in *Types of Shape* (New York: Atheneum, 1969). Other graphic poems in the book include a car key, a goblet, a beach umbrella, an Eskimo Pie, and the outline of New York State. Paul Fussell, Jr., discussing "Easter Wings" and Hollander's shaped poems, expresses reservations about this kind of poetry. Most shaped poems, he finds, are directed more to eyes than ears—"or better, we feel that the two dimensions are not married: one is simply in command of the other." But the greatest limitation in the genre is that there are few objects that shaped poems can effectively represent: "their shapes can reflect the silhouettes of wings, bottles, hourglasses, and altars, but where do we go from there?" (*Poetic Meter and Poetic Form* [New York: Random House, 1965] 185–87). Students might be told of Fussell's view and asked to comment. A further disadvantage of most shaped poetry is that it cannot be heard aloud without loss.

Dorthi Charles, CONCRETE CAT, page 662

This trifle first appeared in the second edition of *An Introduction to Poetry* and has been retained out of loyalty to the past. While hunting for an illustration of the sillier kind of concrete poem that simply and unfeelingly arranges words like so many Lincoln Logs, XJK found the very thing in one of William Cole's anthologies of humorous poetry: "Concrete Poem" by the British wit Anthony Mundy. Mundy's work repeats *miniskirt* several times in the form of a miniskirt, and tacks on a couple of *leglegleglegs*. No doubt he was parodying concrete poetry, too. But the cheapskate in XJK rebelled at the thought of paying for permission to reprint such a simple doodad, so decided to cut and paste together a home-made specimen. While constructing the cat, he started having some fun with it, making the tongue a *U*, and so on. As far as we know, however, the pun in the cat's middle stripe (tripes) is the only place where language aspires toward poetry and becomes figurative.

SEEING THE LOGIC OF OPEN FORM VERSE

E. E. Cummings, IN JUST–, page 662

Cummings's poem is one of his "Chansons Innocentes," little songs for children. In it, however, we meet a poet who is familiar with the classics and who naturally associates spring with goat-footed Pan. In Greek mythology, the god's pipes heralded the return of Persephone, and caused birds and beasts to start up at his call. In Cummings's view, he seems a kind of Pied Piper who brings children running.

Line-breaks and capital letters in the poem seem designed to emphasize particulars. *Just-spring,* capitalized, is the name of a holiday: the moment when spring begins. Dividing its name with a line break gives it more importance, perhaps; and *mud - / luscious* similarly takes emphasis. Why are the children's names telescoped (*eddieandbill, bettyandisbel*)? So that these names will be spoken rapidly, pell-mell, the way their owners run and the way children speak about their friends. And when the lame balloonman completes his transformation into Pan, the word *goat-footed* is framed with white space on a line by itself. Except by putting it in capitals, the poet could hardly have thrown more weight on it.

Linda Pastan, JUMP CABLING, page 663

Pastan, in telling us of two cars, divides each line and builds separate columns of words. The last line, all one, fits the proposed action (that the two merge) to the words. Jump cabling we take to be a metaphor for coitus. (For a similar comparison, see E. E. Cummings's well-known "she being Brand / -new," in his *Complete Poems*.) The playful "Jump Cabling" is starkly different in tone from Pastan's "Ethics"; it was first published in an anthology of light verse, Robert Wallace's *Light Year '85* (Cleveland: Bits, 1984).

Lucille Clifton, HOMAGE TO MY HIPS, page 663

Lucille Clifton's poetry exults in everyday images—often viewed from an unusual angle that reveals some transcendent aspect. Her work is also terse and compressed as in this short but definitely not petite poem. Clifton's exuberant poem is, first of all, a dramatic monologue. The speaker celebrates her own hips ("*these* hips" is a repeated phrase). Written in free verse, the poem divides its lines into natural speech units, often short declarative sentences. Another interesting feature of the poem is Clifton's personification of the hips: "They go where they want to go / they do what they want to do." The poem is so conversational that students may easily miss Clifton's sly figures of speech.

An audio tape of Lucille Clifton talking about her poetry is available from: New Letters on the Air, University of Missouri-Kansas City, 5100 Rockhill Road, Kansas City, MO 64110-2499, (816) 235-1159.

Carole Satyamurti, I SHALL PAINT MY NAILS RED, page 664

Satyamurti's poem demonstrates that there are other means than meter for organizing poetic language. In this case, syntax gives the poem a linguistic structure as formal as a sonnet. One might also say the poem has another structure—that of a list, a common genre but not one we usually associate with poetry (though we can upgrade it into the venerable literary device of the *catalogue*, like Homer's catalogue of Greek ships in *The Iliad*). Notice that Satyamurti's lines are grammatically incomplete, unless we read them in conjunction with the title.

All this formal discussion shouldn't blind us, however, to Satyamurti's provocative content. "I Shall Paint My Nails Red" does something that poetry should: it makes us think deeply about part of our everyday world. It asks questions about something we might otherwise take for granted.

WRITER'S PERSPECTIVE

Walt Whitman on Writing, THE POETRY OF THE FUTURE, page 665

Although Whitman created one of the main traditions of American free verse, he has surprisingly little to say about the verse technique he fostered. In this interesting passage from the 1876 preface to the reissue of *Leaves of Grass*, Whitman focuses on two different sorts of innovation—free expression of emotion and direct presentation of character. He sees these features of attitude, tone, and subject leading American poetry into the future.

21 Symbol

T. S. Eliot, THE BOSTON EVENING TRANSCRIPT, page 668

To help a class see the humor of Eliot's poem, try reading it aloud and pronouncing the name of the newspaper slowly and deliberately, in the dullest tones you can muster. This small gem can serve effectively to introduce an early, longer Eliot poem of spiritual desolation, "The Love Song of J. Alfred Prufrock."

Emily Dickinson, THE LIGHTNING IS A YELLOW FORK, page 669

Perhaps the poet would have added more punctuation to this poem had she worked longer on it; a rough penciled draft is its only surviving manuscript. Students may ask, Isn't the fork a symbol? No, it is the other half of a metaphor: what the lightning is like. The lightning (like most literary symbols) is a physical thing or event, reportedly seen. The Apparatus of the Dark (neither fork nor lightning) is whatever dimly glimpsed furniture this cosmic house may hold. The fork seems too simple an instrument to deserve the name of Apparatus. The lightning is doing the revealing, not itself being revealed.

Thomas Hardy, NEUTRAL TONES, page 671

Students usually like to sort out the poem's white, gray washed-out, and ashy things. Can anyone think of a more awful description of a smile than that in lines 9–10? The God in line 2 seems angry and awe-inspiring. He has chided or reproved the sun, and caused it to turn pale in fear (like a schoolboy before a stern headmaster).

Line 8 is a stickler. In Hardy's first draft it read, "On which was more wrecked by our love." Both versions of the line seem awkward, and the present version is obscure, but probably the sense of this and the previous line goes: we exchanged a few words about the question, Which one of us had lost (suffered) the more by our love affair? (That is, after *which* we should mentally insert "of the two of us.")

For speculation about the facts behind "Neutral Tones," see Robert Gittings's fine biography *Young Thomas Hardy* (Boston: Little Brown, 1975) 86–93. Much has been guessed about the possible love affair between young Hardy and his cousin Tryphena Sparks; but if the woman in "Neutral Tones" was indeed real, no one has identified her for sure.

Similar in imagery to "Neutral Tones" is this horrific line from Hardy's novel *The Woodlanders*, chapter 4, when a poverty-stricken woman, Marty South, sees her last hopes expire: "The bleared white visage of a sunless winter day emerged like a deadborn child" (cited by F. B. Pinion in *A Commentary on the Poems of Thomas Hardy* [New York: Barnes, 1977]).

Matthew, THE PARABLE OF THE GOOD SEED, page 672

"The Parable of the Good Seed" is one of three parables that Jesus tells to the crowd describing the "kingdom of heaven" in the thirteenth chapter of Matthew. After Jesus and the disciples leave the crowd and go into a house, the disciples ask him to explain this particular parable. Jesus obliges them with an explication. (We paraphrase the reply in the book following the text of the parable.) Here is his answer from Matthew:

> He answered and said unto them, "He that soweth the good seed is the Son of Man; the field is the world; the good seeds are the children of the kingdom; but the tares are the children of the wicked one; the enemy that sowed them is the devil; the harvest is the end of the world; and the reapers are the angels. As therefore the tares are gathered and burned in the fire; so shall it be in the end of this world. The Son of Man shall send forth his angels, and they shall gather out of his kingdom all things that offend, and them which do iniquity; and shall cast them into a furnace of fire; there shall be wailing and gnashing of teeth. Then shall the righteous shine forth as the sun in the kingdom of their Father. Who hath ears to hear, let him hear." (Matthew 13:37–43)

The special importance of this parable is that Jesus clearly states his own interpretation of the tale. He intends it, therefore, as an allegory with one consistent equivalent meaning assigned to each narrative element. Not all Gospel parables can be so easily allegorized. Some, like the "Parable of the Prodigal Son," are so subtly complex to allow multiple interpretations. Jesus himself told the disciples that his parables allowed two interpretations—one purely narrative reading open to the general public and another, deeper allegorical interpretation available to those who have been initiated in "the mysteries of the kingdom of heaven." (Matthew 13:10–23)

George Herbert, REDEMPTION, page 673

The old burdensome lease that the speaker longs to cancel is original sin, which Christ, by his sacrifice (lines 12–14) allows humankind to throw off. Who is the speaker? Humanity—or perhaps (like Bunyan's Pilgrim) an individual soul in search of salvation.

Robert Frost, THE ROAD NOT TAKEN, page 674

Stanley Burnshaw writes, in *Robert Frost Himself* (New York: Braziller, 1986), that Frost often said "The Road Not Taken" was about himself combined with Edward Thomas, a Welsh poet and good friend. Knowing this, Burnshaw confessed, didn't contribute much to his understanding of the poem. Still, the story is tantalizing. In *Robert Frost: The Years of Triumph* (New York: Holt, 1970) biographer Lawrance Thompson tells about the "excruciations through which this dour Welshman [Thomas] went each time he was required to make a choice." This amused Frost, who once said to Thomas, "No matter which road you take, you'll always sigh, and wish you'd taken another." "The Road Not Taken" (originally called "Two

Roads") was apparently written to poke quiet fun at this failing. When Frost sent the poem in a letter to Thomas, the Welshman apparently missed the joke. He assumed, as have many readers since, that the speaker in the poem was Frost himself. Disappointed, Frost (according to Thompson) "could never bear to tell the truth about the failure of this lyric to perform as he intended it."

Despite the ambiguity that surrounds the poet's intent, the poem succeeds. The two roads are aptly symbolic of the choices we have to make almost every day of our lives. Still, perhaps the poem's essential playfulness is evident in the dramatic "sigh" with which the speaker expects some day to talk about his choice, and in the portentousness of the last line, which seems a bit exaggerated considering that the two roads were "really about the same."

A hard-working introduction to symbolism in poetry is that of Paul Hawkes, of East Stroudsburg University. In a published article, he describes his classroom version of the TV game show "Family Feud," in which teams of students try to guess which meanings of certain symbols have occurred to most of the class. His aim is to show that a symbol, which may have widely familiar and traditional associations, can mean more or less the same to everyone; its meanings aren't the property of one reader alone. Then, to put this insight to use, he takes up "The Road Not Taken."

"I use this poem," he explains, "because it is simple and straightforward, offering little resistance to any student I may ask to summarize the paraphrasable content of the poem." He asks, "What statements in the poem, what choices of diction, suggest that the two roads are to be understood as something more than literal paths in the woods?" And students tend to reply, "A person wouldn't 'sigh' about a choice made years ago unless it was important," or, "The speaker wouldn't regret it 'ages hence' if it were only a path," or, "Why else would he say the decision 'has made all the difference' unless that decision were life-changing?" (We're paraphrasing and condensing Mr. Hawkes's examples.)

Someone will usually guess that the choice of roads suggests Frost's personal choice of careers: Should he or should he not become a poet? Mr. Hawkes then encourages the class to speculate on other possible life choices: marriage, children, a job, relocation. Perhaps this poem is about decision-making; perhaps the nature of the roads need not be specified. As in *Pilgrim's Progress,* a road or a journey on it is a traditional and conventional symbol for life; a fork or crossroads, a decision or turning-point. "The poem," he concludes, "suggests regret not for the way life has turned out but for the severe limitations life imposes on our desire to explore its possibilities." (See "Fire, Flag, Feud, and Frost: Teaching the Interpretation of Symbols," *Exercise Exchange* [Spring 1991] 6–11.)

Christina Rossetti, UPHILL, page 674

This allegorical poem develops a conventional simile: life is like a journey (shades of *Pilgrim's Progress!*). The road is the path of life; the day, a lifespan; the inn at the end of the road, the grave; other wayfarers, the dead; the door, the mouth of the grave (or perhaps the gate of Heaven); the beds, cold clay (or perhaps Heavenly rest). The title suggests another familiar notion: that life is a struggle all the way.

One possible way to paraphrase line 14: "You'll find the end result of your lifelong strivings: namely, death, and the comfort of extinction." A more happily Christian paraphrase is possible, for Rossetti professed herself a believer: "Your labor shall bring you to your goal, the sight of the Lord." Without admitting the possibility of such a faith, the poem will seem grimmer and more cynical than it is.

Do these two characters seem individuals? Not in the least. This is a straight question-and-answer poem, a dialogue between two stick figures.

"Oh No" seems another poem about where you arrive when you die. Creeley, we suspect, kids a conventional notion of Heaven: he makes it a smug, artificial place where the saved sit around smirking at one another.

FOR REVIEW AND FURTHER STUDY

Robinson Jeffers, THE BEAKS OF EAGLES, page 675
Sara Teasdale, THE FLIGHT, page 676

Both of these poems use the eagle as their central symbol (both, in fact, present a mated pair of eagles). Each author, however, uses the symbol in a characteristic way. "The Beaks of Eagles" is a classic Jeffers poem. The speaker adopts an omniscient point of view and describes a local natural environment in precise detail. The narrative is in the present tense, but the speaker adds specific details from the past (e.g. "she was here when the fires of eighty-five raged on these ridges"—an incident that occurred before Jeffers's own birth), and he also speculates on the future. Jeffers's eagle eventually becomes a symbol for the savage beauty and durability of nature in contrast to the frenetic activity and instability of humanity. But Jeffers's eagle, depicted with deep respect and naturalist insight, also never ceases to be a believably real bird.

In contrast, Teasdale's eagles never seem entirely real birds of prey. Her eagles are symbolic from the opening lines. Teasdale's eagles symbolize the adventurous love and passionate union of two people. Their spirits are so closely united that the speaker wishes that when one of them dies, the other will follow— a highly romantic aspiration in contrast to Jeffers's deliberately detached view. (Note how Jeffers destroys any romantic illusion about his mated eagles by stating that the she-eagle's original mate was shot years earlier and that she has now mated with one of her sons. This underscores a crucial difference between the natural eagle and civilized humans.) Teasdale's 1926 poem has a strong musical verve, but it seems decidedly more conventional than Jeffers's expansive free verse poem of the following decade.

William Carlos Williams, POEM, page 677
Ted Kooser, CARRIE, page 677
Lorine Niedecker, POPCORN-CAN COVER, page 678
Wallace Stevens, ANECDOTE OF THE JAR, page 678

"Poem" should be taken literally. "Carrie" presents dust in its traditional role as a symbol for human mortality (although Kooser uses the symbol in a charmingly original way). "Popcorn-can cover" uses literal language in a manner reminiscent of Williams, but the title image of the popcorn-can cover screwed to the wall can be taken as a symbol of the house dweller's poverty and pragmatism. Niedecker does not force the symbolism of the image, but it is there for our notice. "Anecdote of the Jar" contains central symbols.

Students familiar with Stevens sometimes reason, "The jar is a thing of the imagination, that's why it's superior to the wilderness—it makes order out of formless nature, the way Stevens thinks art is supposed to do." But Stevens is constantly warning us of the dangers of mind divorced from the physical world, and we think he means this gray, bare, dominion-taking jar to be ominous. Who could think a wilderness *slovenly* before it came along? Some critics take the phrase *of a port in air* to mean a portal, "an evanescent entry . . . to order in a scene of disorder" (Ronald Sukenick, *Wallace Stevens: Musing the Obscure* [New York: New York UP, 1967]). We read it differently: *portly*, imposing, pompous. Although it is true that Stevens frequently raises the same philosophic or aesthetic questions, from poem to poem he keeps supplying very different answers. See the brilliant essay on Stevens by J. Hillis Miller in *Poets of Reality* (Cambridge: Harvard UP, 1965).

Jerald Bullis has written an intriguing poem in response to "Anecdote of the Jar." Thanks to Peter A. Fritzell of Lawrence University for discovering it.

BUCK IT

Take a shot-up bucket in a swale of woods—
For years "things" have been adjusting to it:
The deer have had to warp their whylom way
Through the fern to honor the order in their blood
That says not to kick it; the visiting woodcock

Probably take it for some kind of newfangled stump,
And doubtless welcome any addition that offers
Additional cover—especially if its imposition
Provides a shelving stay for worm-rich mulch;
A rivulet of breeze low-eddying the swale
Breaks around it much the way a stress's
Flow gets an increment of curvature
From encounter with an old Singer
Sewing machine; the ferns thereabout have turned
A bit more plagiotropic; if it's upright
And the lid's off it's an urn for leaves, bark-bits,
Bird droppings; but in the scope of the whole
Forty-acre woodpatch is it likely
To take dominion everywhere? no more
Than a barbed-wire tangle of words or a good jar.

WRITER'S PERSPECTIVE

W. B. Yeats on Writing, POETIC SYMBOLS, page 679

Symbols were central to Yeats's poetics. They were not arbitrary creations of the writer but primal forms of human communications—arising like Carl Jung's universal archetypes from the unconscious. For Yeats, the symbol is, therefore, in some sense independent of the poet and carries "numberless meanings" beyond the often narrow intentions of the author.

22 *Myth and Narrative*

This chapter has been greatly revised in recent editions to make it more accessible to students. Although the chapter still begins with a discussion of what constitutes myth, there is now an attempt to relate the idea of myth to students' experience with popular culture, especially movies and television. This shift may initially annoy some instructors, but we hope that, if they stick with the chapter, they will discover that we have tried to show how similar myths permeate popular and literary culture. We want to make the material of this chapter less threatening to beginning students while still useful to instructors excited by the prospect of teaching Lawrence, Yeats, and Wordsworth.

Besides the poems in this chapter, other poems in the text will readily lend themselves to the study of myth and its pervasiveness in literature.

Personal myths may be found in the poems of Blake; in Hardy's "Convergence of the Twain"; and in certain poems of Yeats outside this chapter, such as "Leda and the Swan" and "Sailing to Byzantium."

Poems containing central references to familiar classical myths are Cummings's "in Just–," with its reincarnation of the Great God Pan; and Allen Ginsberg's "A Supermarket in California." Christian mythos is of course inseparable from the devotional poems of Donne and Herbert; from Hopkins's poems and Yeats's "The Magi"; from Milton's sonnet on his blindness and from many more.

In this chapter, Thomas Hardy (in "The Oxen") and William Wordsworth (in "The World Is Too Much with Us") sadly contemplate myths in decline.

Robert Frost, NOTHING GOLD CAN STAY, page 684

Many of your students may already be familiar with this popular poem. The relevant detail of the poem in this context is how much narrower its meaning would be if the reference to Eden were dropped. This single mythic allusion expands the resonance of the poem from the transience of spring's beauty to the transience of all perfection.

In his excellent study, *Robert Frost: A Literary Life Reconsidered* (reissued with a new preface in 1993 by the University Press of New England), William Pritchard savors the poem's remarkable compression in the following way:

> The poem is striking for the way it combines the easy delicacy of "Her early leaf's a flower" with monumentalities about Eden and the transient fading of all such golden things, all stated in a manner that feels inevitable. It is as if in writing "Nothing Gold Can Stay," Frost had in mind his later definition of poetry as a momentary stay against confusion. The poem's last word proclaims the momentariness of the "gold" that things like flowers and Eden, dawn and poems share. So the shortness of the poem is also expressive of its sense (Quoted by permission of the author).

Thomas Hardy, THE OXEN, page 684

The legend that farm animals kneel on Christmas Eve is widespread in Western Europe. Hardy takes it to suggest the entire Christian mythos, which "in these years" (since Darwin) few embrace as did the "flock" of children and old people remembered in the opening stanza. The *gloom* in line 15 may resemble the gloom of the unbeliever, and its doleful sound is enforced by its riming with *coomb*—like *barton*, a word from older rural speech.

The tone of "The Oxen" is not hostility toward faith, but wistfulness. Not exactly the village atheist Chesterton said he was, Hardy in late life kept going to church and hoping for a reconciliation between the Church of England and science-minded rationalists.

William Wordsworth, THE WORLD IS TOO MUCH WITH US, page 685

As its sense and its iambic meter indicate, the opening line calls for a full stress on the *with*.

Wordsworth isn't arguing, of course, for a return to pagan nature worship. Rather like Gerard Manley Hopkins's blasting tirade in "God's Grandeur," he is dismayed that Christians, given to business and banking, have lost sight of sea and vernal woods. They should pay less heed to the world, more to the earth. What "powers" have they laid waste? The ability to open themselves to nature's benevolent inspirations. Modestly, the poet includes himself in the *us* who deserve reproof. The impatient outburst ("Great God!") is startlingly unbookish and locates the break in sense between octave and sestet in an unconventional place.

Compare Wordsworth's "Composed upon Westminster Bridge" for a somewhat similar theme.

H. D., HELEN, page 686

H.D.'s celebrated Imagist poem describes Helen of Troy and her fatal beauty in provocatively ambiguous terms. In the full edition of *Literature*, there is a superb student essay on "Helen" by Heather Burke of Wesleyan University. Here is an excerpt.

> In her poem "Helen," H.D. examines the close connection between the emotions of love and hatred as embodied in the figure of Helen of Troy. Helen was the cause of the long and bloody Trojan War, and her homecoming is tainted by the memory of the suffering this war caused. As in many Imagist poems, the title is essential to the poem's meaning; it gives the reader both a specific mythic context and a particular subject. Without the title, it would be virtually impossible to understand the poem fully since Helen's name appears nowhere else in the text. The reader familiar with Greek myth knows that Helen was the wife of Menelaus who ran away with Paris. Their adultery provoked the Trojan War, which lasted for ten years and resulted in the destruction of Troy.

What is unusual about the poem is H.D.'s perspective on Helen of Troy. The poem refuses to romanticize Helen's story, but its stark new version is easy for a reader to accept. After suffering so much for the sake of one adulterous woman, how could the Greeks not resent her? Rather than idealizing the situation, H.D. describes the enmity which defiles Helen's homecoming and explores the irony of the hatred which "All Greece" feels for her.

The central irony of "Helen" is found in the contrast between tone and content. Even as the speaker addresses hate, lines such as "God's daughter, born of love, / the beauty of cool feet / and slenderest knees," reveal an underlying conflict of emotions.

ARCHETYPE

Louise Bogan, MEDUSA, page 687

Bogan's chilling poem is a perfect example of how modern poets have used classical myths to new ends. Bogan presents Medusa quite faithfully to the Greek legend, but she employs the myth for distinctively modern psychological purposes—to portray a state of spiritual and emotional paralysis. The speaker is literally petrified in an eternal moment. Nothing will ever change. One curious feature of "Medusa" is that the speaker shows no surprise, no bitterness, no anger at the paralyzing Gorgon—only total resignation.

Bogan's biographer, Elizabeth Frank, believes the poem portrays the poet's mother as the paralyzing female monster. While there is no specific textual evidence for this interpretation, it is not inconsistent with the facts of Bogan's troubled past. This psychoanalytical/biographical interpretation, however, is not especially useful in reading "Medusa" as poetry. In fact, to reduce the poem to any single allegorical interpretation limits the powerful symbolic resonance of the central situation. The speaker's paralysis can be read with equal validity as emotional, spiritual, imaginative, or artistic. The poem invites us to interpret the speaker's dilemma beyond its literal narrative meaning, but the text does not demand any single construction.

PERSONAL MYTH

William Butler Yeats, THE SECOND COMING, page 688

The brief discussion in the book leaves several points untouched. Students may be asked to explain Yeats's opening image of the falcon and the falconer; to discuss the meaning of the *Blood-dimmed tide* and the *ceremony of innocence;* to explain how the rocking cradle at Bethlehem can be said to "vex" twenty centuries to nightmare; and to recall what they know about the sphinx.

In *A Vision*, Yeats sets forth his notion of the two eras of history (old and new) as two intertwined conelike gyres, revolving inside each other in opposing directions. He puts it succinctly in a note for a limited edition of his poem *Michael Robartes and the Dancer* (1921):

> The end of an age, which always receives the revelation of the character of the next age, is represented by the coming of one gyre to its place of greatest expansion and of the other to that of its greatest contraction. At the present moment the life gyre is sweeping outward, unlike that before the birth of Christ which was narrowing, and has almost reached its greatest expansion. The revelation which approaches will however take its character from the contrary movement of the interior gyre.

Students can be asked to apply this explanation to "The Second Coming." (In fact, this might be a writing assignment.)

For other evidence of Yeats's personal mythology, direct students to "Leda and the Swan" and "Sailing to Byzantium." For alternative versions of "The Second Coming," see Yeats's worksheets for the poem as transcribed by John Stallworthy in *Between the Lines: Yeats's Poetry in the Making* (Oxford: Oxford UP, 1963).

Diane Thiel, MEMENTO MORI IN MIDDLE SCHOOL, page 690

Diane Thiel has provided this note about her poem:

> For years, I wanted to write about this memory of an odd middle school project I presented on Dante's *Inferno*. The piece existed only as notes for some years. About twenty years after the childhood incident described in the piece, the poem finally came together and found its form as *terza rima* (the form Dante invented in the Middle Ages). I chose a rather loose interpretation of *terza rima* for the poem (varying the end-rhymes between exact rhymes, slant rhymes, and assonance) because the variation seemed to best suit the conversational diction and tone of the poem.
>
> I think of *"Memento Mori* in Middle School" as an echo-location, a multi-layered term I invented in the book, *Echolocations* (2001), which contains the poem, to refer to conversations with the past. In the case of this poem, the conversation is with both this work of art from a distant medieval past and the more immediate echoes of a childhood interpretation of the piece. The union of the *Inferno* with that trial-filled middle school age becomes a reflection of threshold crossings that burn themselves into our memories.

An Exercise for Students:

In my writing guide, *Writing Your Rhythm,* I include an exercise which asks students to respond to a poem (preferably choosing from a more distant century) using the form of the chosen piece. This approach helped *"Memento Mori* in Middle School" find its form.

MYTH AND POPULAR CULTURE

Anne Sexton, CINDERELLA, page 692
WRITER'S PERSPECTIVE
Anne Sexton on Writing, TRANSFORMING FAIRY TALES, page 696

"Cinderella" was part of Sexton's fifth collection, *Transformations* (Boston: Houghton, 1971). This volume consisted of seventeen long poems that retold fairy tales in idiosyncratic versions. Although earlier poets like Auden and Jarrell had published revisionist fairy tale poems, Sexton's book proved extremely influential by claiming the fairy tale as the special territory of feminist poets. Some critics (as well as Sexton's editor, Paul Brooks) felt these poems represented a falling off from her more compressed earlier poetry, and there is some truth in that criticism. But the poems have remarkable narrative energy and originality.

"Cinderella" begins like a lyric poem with a series of four rags to riches stories that seem gleaned from the tabloids. But just when it might seem that Sexton would wrap up her short poem, she leaps into an extended narrative. Her version of Cinderella is very close to the Perrault original, although she spices it up with contemporary images and large doses of irony, but, as the story comes to its conclusion, Sexton emphasizes the violent aspects of the original so that it overwhelms the romance. Then in the last stanza, Sexton resumes the original structure of the poem with a bitterly ironic version of "happily ever after."

To use an overworked word, Sexton "deconstructs" the happy ending of a fairy tale; marriage, in her view, is no solution to Cinderella's problems, just the beginning of new ones.

The two letters included in the "Writer's Perspective"—one to her publisher, the other to a fellow writer—describe Sexton's intentions in turning popular fairy tales to her own ends. She wants to make the stories "as wholly personal as my most intimate poems." This attitude may surprise students who don't yet understand how an artist's treatment can transform borrowed material (like myth or legend) into something unique and idiosyncratic.

23 *Poetry and Personal Identity*

"Poetry and Personal Identity" provides students with an introduction to the ways in which a poet's race, gender, cultural background, age, and other factors influence his or her writing. The chapter explores the different ways that poets have defined their personal, social, sexual, and ethnic identities. It also examines the problematic relationship between the author and the poem.

The first section focuses on autobiography and explores the idea of "confessional" poetry. Having drilled students earlier in this book that poems cannot be read as direct autobiography, we are now relaxing a bit and letting them think about the tricky relationship between life and art. This issue usually generates lively classroom discussion. The challenge will be to keep the discussions on track by focusing on the specific text under examination.

With Julia Alvarez's poem, we broaden the discussion by showing how autobiography includes issues of culture, age, and gender as well as purely individual experience. We then look at different approaches toward ethnic writing by contrasting two compelling poems on minority identity—one by Claude McKay, the other by Rhina Espaillat. With Samuel Menashe and Francisco X. Alarcón we see poems about Jewish and Mexican-American identity.

Anne Stevenson's short poem, "Sous Entendu," focuses on gender in terms that students should understand from their everyday life, while Adrienne Rich's poem explores it in more general, archetypal terms. Yusef Komunyakaa's powerful Vietnam poem raises questions of identity that transcend racial categories; he is a black veteran, but he seems to speak for all Vietnam vets without losing his personal identity (reflected in the Vietnam Memorial's black stone). With Donald Justice's striking "Men at Forty," we begin looking at issues of age. Andrew Hudgins's poem explores both religion and the gap between generations. Shirley Geok-lin Lim's poem dramatizes the situation of the immigrant (in this case Chinese) caught between cultures but still rooted in the past.

Sylvia Plath, LADY LAZARUS, page 700

This poem was written over seven days in late October, 1962 (about two weeks after the composition of "Daddy" in the "Poems for Further Reading" chapter). On February 11, 1963, Plath committed suicide by putting her head in a gas oven.

In her 1989 biography of Plath, *Bitter Fame*, Anne Stevenson described "Lady Lazarus" as a "merciless" self-projection of the author who cast herself as "the central figure of her mythic world." Stevenson continues about several of the poems written that final October:

> The poems are extraordinary *performances*—not only in their consummate poetic skill, but in that their central figure is giving a performance as though before a single quelled spectator or in a fairground . . .

Stevenson concludes:

> These poems, penetrating the furthest reaches of disdain and rage, are bereft of all normal "human" feeling. Hurt has hardened to hate, and death is omnipresent.

Surely the dark anger and aching death-wish is tangible in "Lady Lazarus." This poem is spoken by a voice beyond hope. If Plath is a performer, she performs only a script of her own merciless invention.

One stylistic note: "Lady Lazarus" (like "Daddy") is full of German tags. You might ask students why she uses German so much in these late poems. The Nazi connection will be easy for them to see, but it may be worthwhile to mention that Plath's father, Doctor Otto Plath (Ph.D. in entomology), was a German immigrant who spoke with a heavy accent. In other words, there is something to interest both formalist and biographical critics in this chilling, late poem.

Julia Alvarez, THE WOMEN ON MY MOTHER'S SIDE WERE KNOWN, page 703

This poem is discussed at some length in the text. Interested students (and instructors) are encouraged to look up this poem in its original context, a sequence of thirty-three sonnets written about Alvarez turning thirty-three, in her first book of poems, *The Homecoming* (New York: Grove, 1984). Alvarez is currently a professor of literature at Middlebury College. In 1992 she published a novel, *How the Garcia Girls Lost Their Accents* (Chapel Hill: Algonquin Books).

CULTURE, RACE, AND ETHNICITY

Claude McKay, AMERICA, page 704

McKay was one of the first of many black American writers who immigrated from the West Indies. (Students might write an interesting comparison between McKay's sonnet and the later Caribbean poet Derek Walcott's "The Virgins" found in the "Poems for Further Reading" chapter.) McKay was born in Jamaica in 1891 but emigrated to the U.S. in 1912. Although shaped by black experience, "America" reaches for—and indeed achieves—universality of expression; it articulates the frustrated dreams and overpowering desires of any young immigrant. The speaker in this poem defines himself not by his ethnic identity but by his existential identity—as an outsider—in a heartless, if vital society.

Rhina Espaillat, BILINGUAL / BILINGÜE, page 705

Rhina Espaillat has provided this background to her poem "Bilingual / Bilingüe":

> Recent interest in the phenomenon known as "Spanglish" has led me to reexamine my own experience as a writer who works chiefly in her second lan-

guage, and especially to recall my father's inflexible rule against the mixing of languages. In fact, no English was allowed in that midtown Manhattan apartment that became home after my arrival in New York in 1939. My father read the daily paper in English, taught himself to follow disturbing events in Europe through the medium of English-language radio, and even taught me to read the daily comic strips, in an effort to speed my learning of the language he knew I would need. But that necessary language was banished from family conversation: it was the medium of the outer world, beyond the door; inside, among ourselves, only Spanish was permitted, and it had to be pure, grammatical, unadulterated Spanish.

At the age of seven, however, nothing seems more important than communicating with classmates and neighborhood children. For my mother, too, the new language was a way out of isolation, a means to deal with the larger world and with those American women for whom she sewed. But my father, a political exile waiting for changes in our native country, had different priorities: he lived in the hope of return, and believed that the new home, the new speech, were temporary. His theory was simple: if it could be said at all, it could be said best in the language of those authors whose words were the core of his education. But his insistence on pure Spanish made it difficult, sometimes impossible, to bring home and share the jokes of friends, puns, pop lyrics, and other staples of seven-year-old conversation. Table talk sometimes ended with tears or sullen silence.

And yet, despite the friction it caused from time to time, my native language was also a source of comfort—the reading that I loved, intimacy within the family, and a peculiar auditory delight best described as echoes in the mind. I learned early to relish words as counters in a game that could turn suddenly serious without losing the quality of play, and to value their sound as a meaning behind their meaning.

Samuel Menashe, THE SHRINE WHOSE SHAPE I AM, *page 707*

Menashe's poem defines Jewishness in a mystical biological way. "Breathed in flesh by shameless love," he was born from his parents' bodies, and his body contains the history of his people. "There is no Jerusalem but this" means, among other things, that his Jewishness is not found in a geographical place but in himself: his body is the lost temple ("the shrine") of his people, his bones the hills of Zion. This poem may seem difficult to students at first, but once they understand the central metaphor, they usually find it fascinating. A good place to start discussing the poem is its title, which contains the central idea.

Menashe's short, compressed poetry has been repeatedly praised by leading critics such as Stephen Spender, Donald Davie, Kathleen Raine, and Hugh Kenner, but it remains little known. Menashe lives in New York City barely above poverty level in a cold-water flat.

Francisco X. Alarcón, THE X IN MY NAME, *page 707*

Alarcón's poem is about the relation between one's name and one's identity. On a literal level, the X in Alarcón's name stands presumably as an abbreviation for

Xavier, (a name that almost always identifies one as being of Catholic background and most commonly Hispanic descent, though many an Irishman bears it, too). But Alarcón sees the name as a symbol for the X an illiterate peasant must sign on the legal documents that control his or her life. Ultimately, Alarcón also implicitly uses the X (in a way perhaps influenced by Malcolm X) as an algebraic symbol for the elements of his identity lost or repressed in America.

Francisco X. Alarcón teaches at the University of California at Davis. He publishes poetry in both Spanish and English.

Wendy Rose, FOR THE WHITE POETS WHO WOULD BE INDIAN, page 708

Rose's forceful poem raises a central issue in a discussion of race and ethnicity in literature because it is addressed by a Native American speaker to "white poets" who try to identify with Indian experience and world view. Rose's speaker considers this attempt at imaginative identification "a temporary tourism / of our souls." The white poet only wants to visit the Indian's world view as a sort of "instant" substitute for roots. The poem's tone is so angry and dismissive that some readers might claim that it only provides a partial view of the white poets, but it is precisely that same passionate animus that enlivens the poem. A lyric poem is under no obligation to present every side of an issue; instead it must memorably and credibly present the compelling impulse of a particular moment in a particular sensibility. Rose's poem accomplishes this feat quite powerfully. She makes the crucial observation that a temporary, romanticized perusal of Native American culture is insufficient to understand and hopelessly inadequate to portray the complex reality of Indian experience.

Yusef Komunyakaa, FACING IT, page 709

This powerful poem requires little commentary. One feature of the poem requires special mention, since students may overlook it—the *entire* poem describes what the speaker sees on the polished black granite of the Vietnam Veteran's Memorial. What he witnesses there is the combination of the memorial itself and what the mirror-like stone reflects. *Reflection* (line 6) is, therefore, the key word in the poem, which the author uses in both senses, for, as the speaker studies the name on the stone, he reflects back on his wartime experience and flashes back to the death of a fellow soldier. The way the stone both mirrors and transforms the reality around it is the external symbol for the speaker's internal experience.

GENDER

Anne Stevenson, SOUS-ENTENDU, page 710

Students will have no trouble understanding the situation of this poem, but you may need to push them to explore the role of language between the two people. Not only does everything the people say (and don't say) have two meanings—

one literal, the other sexual—but the words they speak metaphorically become part of the clothes they undress.

Emily Grosholz, LISTENING, page 711

The speaker of Emily Grosholz's poem is an expectant mother. The listener is the unborn child in her womb. The speaker develops the idea of how words connect mother and child in a series of metaphors and allusions. She will weave her new son "a birthplace" out of words. Likewise, language will "re-create the gardens of the world," including perhaps the original Garden of Eden, a landscape of pure grace and innocence. Language is also called a "cradle" for the child. All of these images are positive and sustaining. The unborn son "still on his stalk" is implicitly compared to a flower—a part of creation that lacks language. (The stalk is also perhaps a more specific metaphor for the umbilical cord that connects mother and son.) The mother will give him the gift of language "to draw him out" into his full being.

Students might enjoy comparing Grosholz's images and metaphors with those in Sylvia Plath's "Metaphors," which addresses a similar subject.

EXERCISE: *Donald Justice*, MEN AT FORTY, page 712
Adrienne Rich, WOMEN, page 712

As anyone who tries to translate the images and metaphors of either poem into the voice of the opposite gender discovers, these poems are both embedded in the sexual identity of the speaker. But the experiences they describe still speak to the opposite sex. The poems' structures do survive the translation, which demonstrates that good art can be both specific and universal.

For an example of how a skilled poet has translated one set of these images across genders, here is a poem by Andrea Hollander Budy from her award-winning book, *House Without a Dreamer* (Brownsville: Story Line, 1993):

WOMEN AT FIFTY
after Donald Justice

All of their doors
Have closed and their daughters'
Rooms betray a familiar faint perfume
That says *I'll not be back.*

They pause sometimes
At the top of the stairs
To stroke the bannister,
Its perfect knots.

They invite other women now
Only to clean. And like queens in fairy tales
They turn their heads from mirrors
That hold secrets they've kept

Even from themselves,
As they look into their husbands' faces
When their husbands say
They only look.

Women at fifty
Corner a cricket with a broom
And do not kill it, but shoo it out of the house
Into the abundant silence.

(Poem reprinted by permission of the author and Story Line Press.)

FOR REVIEW AND FURTHER STUDY

Shirley Geok-lin Lim, TO LI PO, page 713

Lim's poem explores a common predicament of ethnic Americans: they have lost the language of their ancestors but still feel a deep identification with their family's native land. The last word in the poem—*kin*—is critical to understanding its message.

Lim was born and educated in Malacca, Malaysia, before coming to do a Ph.D. in English at Brandeis. For years she taught at Westchester Community College in New York. She is currently a professor at the University of California at Santa Barbara.

Andrew Hudgins, ELEGY FOR MY FATHER, WHO IS NOT DEAD, page 713

Hudgins's poem explores religious identity—and, by extension, a generation gap. He and his father see death differently. The father has a devout Christian's faith in an afterlife; the speaker, by contrast, is not sure. The son is not against his father's religion; he simply doesn't share its consolations.

Judith Ortiz Cofer, QUINCEAÑERA, page 714

Cofer creates a wonderfully detailed speaker for this coming-of-age poem—a young woman on the brink of adulthood only half cognizant of the mysteries of her new identities. Still partly a child, the speaker embraces her new self with a mixture of awe, fear, and pride. Her childhood is symbolized by the dolls put in the chest "like dead / children." The fifteen-year-old now stands in a middle ground between childhood and marriage. Her new status is represented most clearly by the menstrual blood that privately confirms her new status as an adult woman at least partially independent from her mother (who will no longer wash her clothes and sheets). Although on one level the poem presents a universal female situation, the title, images, and mythology are distinctly Latin Catholic. Cofer's poem demonstrates that a poem does not necessarily lose universality by being embodied in a specific cultural framework. As William Stafford observed, "All events and experiences are local, somewhere."

WRITER'S PERSPECTIVE

Julia Alvarez on Writing, DISCOVERING MY VOICE IN ENGLISH, page 715

Published as an afterword to the revised edition of *Homecoming*, her first book of poems, Alvarez's comments reveal the perspective of over a decade's reflection on her authorial identity. In retrospect, she sees how her younger self was torn between conflicting identities—between languages and cultures. Anyone who reads Alvarez's entire sonnet sequence "33" in *Homecoming* (from which "The women on my mother's side were known" is drawn) will see how greatly these conflicts animated and enriched her poetry.

24 Recognizing Excellence

Ezra Pound long argued for the value of bad poetry in pedagogy. In his *ABC of Reading,* Pound declared that literary education needs to concentrate on revealing what is sham, so that the student may be led to discover what is valid. It is a healthy gesture to let the student see that we don't believe everything contained in a textbook to be admirable. Begin with a poem or two so outrageously awful that the least sophisticated student hardly can take it seriously—some sentimental claptrap such as Cook's "The Old Arm-Chair." From these, you can proceed to subtler examples. It is a mistake to be too snide or too self-righteous toward bad poems, and it is well to quickly turn to some excellent poetry if the classroom starts smelling like a mortuary. There is a certain sadness inherent in much bad poetry; one can readily choke on it. As Allen Tate has said, the best attack upon the bad is the loving understanding of the good. The aim in teaching bad poetry has to be the admiration of good poetry, not the diffusion of mockery.

One further suggestion on bad poetry: a program of really execrable verse orated with straight faces by a few students and members of the faculty can be, with any luck, a fine occasion. For bad poems to work on besides those offered in this chapter, see the dustier stacks in a library of the following anthologies: *Heart Throbs* and *More Heart Throbs,* ed. Joe Mitchell Chapple (New York: Grosset, 1905 and 1911 respectively; many later editions); *The Stuffed Owl: An Anthology of Bad Verse,* ed. D. B. Wyndham Lewis and Charles Lee (London: Dent, 1930; reprinted in the United States by Capricorn paperbacks); *Nematodes in My Garden of Verse,* ed. Richard Walser (Winston-Salem: Blair, 1959); *Worst English Poets,* ed. Christopher Adams (London: Wingate, 1958); *Pegasus Descending: A Book of the Best Bad Verse,* ed. James Camp, X. J. Kennedy, and Keith Waldrop (New York: Macmillan, 1971); and *The Joy of Bad Verse,* ed. Nicholas T. Parsons (London: Collins, 1988).

Anonymous, O MOON, WHEN I GAZE ON THY BEAUTIFUL FACE, page 720

Glorious behind seems inexact, and so does *boundaries* for "boundlessness."

Grace Treasone, LIFE, page 720

Treasone's poem develops a central metaphor, but its language is wildly imprecise. Is the tooth "that cuts into your heart" one's own or somebody else's? (It is probable that the poet means not tooth but "toothache.") Anatomically, the image seems on a par with the "heart's leg" of the tradesman poet quoted by Coleridge. Through the murk of her expression, however, the poet makes clear her theme: the familiar and sentimental notion that life is really all right if you see it through (or have a competent dentist).

Treasone's item first adorned a Dover, New Jersey, newspaper column of local poets called "This Way to Parnassus."

Emily Dickinson, A DYING TIGER – MOANED FOR DRINK, page 721

This is not, by any stretch of critical imagination, a good poem. Besides the poet's innocent lack of perception that *His Mighty Balls* can suggest not eyeballs but testicles, the concluding statement (that the fact that the tiger was dead is to blame) seems an un-Dickinsonian failure of invention. Perhaps the poet intended a religious allegory (Christ the Tiger). Her capitalization of *He* in the last line doesn't seem sufficient proof of such intent, for her habits of capitalization cannot be trusted for consistency.

The failures of splendid poets are fascinating. As in this case, they often seem to result from some tremendous leap that sails over and beyond its object, causing the poet to crash to earth on the other side.

EXERCISE: *Six Terrible Moments in Poetry*, pages 721–722

J. Gordon Coogler, a printer by trade, was said to have displayed a sign in the window of his print-shop in Columbia, S.C.: "POEMS WRITTEN WHILE YOU WAIT."

Mattie J. Peterson has attracted fierce partisans, some of whom see her battling Julia A. Moore for the crown of Queen of American Bad Verse. Richard Walser has brought out of a modern facsimile of her *Little Pansy, A Novel, and Miscellaneous Poetry* (originally 1890; Charlotte: McNally & Loftin, 1967).

Rod McKuen, THOUGHTS ON CAPITAL PUNISHMENT, page 723
William Stafford, TRAVELING THROUGH THE DARK, page 724

McKuen is still popular with some students, and any dogmatic attempt to blast him may be held against you. There may be value in such a confrontation, of course; or you can leave evaluation of these two works up to the class. Just work through McKuen's effusion and Stafford's fine poem, detail by detail, in a noncommittal way, and chances are good that Stafford will win the contest.

It may not be apparent that Stafford's poem is ordered by a rime scheme from beginning to end: *abcb* stanzas and a final couplet. Stafford avoids obvious rimes in favor of the off-rimes *road / dead* and *engine / listen* and the cutoff rimes *killing / belly, waiting / hesitated*, and *swerving / river*—this last a device found in some folk ballads. McKuen's poem announces an obvious rime scheme but fails to complete it. Unlike Stafford, he throws rime out the window in the end, with the effect that his poem stops with a painful inconclusiveness.

Stafford contributes a long comment on his poem to *Reading Modern Poetry: A Critical Introduction*, Paul Engle and Warren Carrier, eds. (Glenview: Scott, 1968).

RECOGNIZING EXCELLENCE

Wllliam Butler Yeats, SAILING TO BYZANTIUM, page 725

Has XJK implied that this poem is a masterpiece so far beyond reproach that no one in his right mind can find fault with it? That is, of course, not the truth. If the instructor wishes to provoke students to argument, he might read them the withering attack on Yeats's poem by Yvor Winters (*Forms of Discovery* [Chicago: Swallow, 1967] 215–16).

This attack really needs to be read in its entirety. Winters is wrong, we believe, but no one can begin to answer his hard-headed objections to the poem without being challenged and illuminated.

Other discussions of the poem, different from XJK's and also short, include Richard Ellmann's *Yeats: The Man and the Masks* (New York: Macmillan, 1949) and John Unterecker's in *A Reader's Guide to William Butler Yeats* (New York: Noonday, 1959). Those who wish to go deeper still and to read a searching examination (informed by study of Yeats's manuscripts) can be directed to Curtis Bradford, "Yeats's Byzantium Poems," *PMLA* 75 (Mar. 1960): 100–25. For those interested in alternatives, John Stallworthy reprints nearly all the legible manuscript versions in *Between the Lines: Yeats's Poetry in the Making* (Oxford: Clarendon, 1963) 87–112.

A deconstructionist reading of "Sailing to Byzantium," subjecting the poem to relentless questioning, showing where it fails to make sense and how it doesn't work, is offered by Lawrence I. Lipking in "The Practice of Theory" (in *Profession 83: Selected Articles from the Bulletins of the Association of Departments of English and the Association of Departments of Foreign Languages*, MLA, 1983). But in his role as a poststructuralist, Lipking confesses himself "a sheep commissioned to say something sympathetic about wolves." He finds deconstructionist tactics offending his students, especially bright idealistic ones who expect their teachers to show them why certain works are great, and who wish poems to "make sense" and to relate to their own lives.

Jean Bauso has used a writing assignment to introduce this challenging poem. "I want you to pretend that you're an old person—someone in his or her eighties," she tells a class. "You've got arthritis, so buttoning or zipping your clothes is slow. Now you will write for ten minutes nonstop in the voice of this old person that you've made yourself into. You want to follow your person's stream of consciousness as he or she sits there thinking about the human condition, about the fact that we human beings have to die." After the students freewrite for ten minutes, they read a few of the results, and she picks up on any comments about wishing for immortality. Then she asks for responses to the name "Byzantium," perhaps holds up some pictures of the Santa Sophia mosaics. She then reads "Sailing to Byzantium" aloud, gives out reading sheets with points for reading it alone, and dismisses the class. For Bauso's detailed account of this lesson plan and her reading sheets, see "The Use of Free-Writing and Guided Writing to Make Students Amenable to Poems," *Exercise Exchange* (Spring 1988).

EXERCISE: *Two Poems to Compare*, page 728

Arthur Guiterman, ON THE VANITY OF EARTHLY GREATNESS, page 728
Percy Bysshe Shelley, OZYMANDIAS, page 728

The title of Guiterman's bagatelle playfully echoes that of a longer, more ambitious poem: Samuel Johnson's "The Vanity of Human Wishes." If Guiterman's achievement seems smaller than Shelley's "Ozymandias," still, it is flawless. "Ozymandias," although one of the monuments of English poetry, has a few cracks in it. Many readers find line 8 incomplete in sense: the heart that fed what, or fed on what? From its rime scheme, we might think the poem a would-be Italian sonnet that refused to work out.

Nevertheless, Shelley's vision stretches farther than Guiterman's. Ozymandias and his works are placed at an incredibly distant remove from us. The structure of the poem helps establish this remoteness: Ozymandias's words were dictated to the sculptor, then carved in stone, then read by a traveler, then told to the first-person speaker, then relayed to us. Ironies abound, more subtle than Guiterman's. A single work of art has outlasted Ozymandias's whole empire. Does that mean that works of art endure (as in "Not marble nor the gilded monuments")? No, this work of art itself has seen better days, and soon (we infer) the sands will finish covering it. Obviously, the king's proud boast has been deflated, and yet, in another sense, Ozymandias is right. The Mighty (or any traveler) may well despair for themselves and their own works, as they gaze on the wreckage of his one surviving project and realize that, cruel as Ozymandias may have been, time is even more remorseless.

What are the facts behind Shelley's poem? According to the Greek historian Diodorus Siculus, Ozymandias was apparently a grand, poeticized name claimed for himself by the Egyptian pharaoh Rameses II. Diodorus Siculus saw the king's ninety-foot-tall statue of himself, carved by the sculptor Memnon, in the first century B.C. when it was still standing at the Ramesseum in Thebes, a mortuary temple. Shelley and his friend Horatio Smith had read a description of the shattered statue in Richard Pococke's *Description of the East* (1742). Smith and Shelley wrote sonnets expressing their imagined views of the wreckage, both of which Leigh Hunt printed in his periodical the *Examiner* in 1818. This is Smith's effort, and students might care to compare it with Shelley's in quality:

> On a Stupendous Leg of Granite, Discovered
> Standing by Itself in the Deserts of Egypt
> In Egypt's sandy silence, all alone,
>> Stands a gigantic leg, which far off throws
>> The only shadow that the desert knows.
> 'I am great Ozymandias,' saith the stone,
>> 'The king of kings: this mighty city shows
>> The wonders of my hand.' The city's gone!—

Nought but the leg remaining to disclose
The site of that forgotten Babylon.

We wonder, and some hunter may express
Wonder like ours, when through the wilderness,
    Where London stood, holding the wolf in chase,
He meets some fragment huge, and stops to guess
    What powerful but unrecorded race
    Once dwelt in that annihilated place.

For more background to the poem, see H. M. Richmond, "Ozymandias and the Travelers," *Keats-Shelley Journal* 11 (1962): 65–71.

William Shakespeare, MY MISTRESS' EYES ARE NOTHING LIKE THE SUN, page 729

Have students state positively each simile that Shakespeare states negatively, and they will make a fair catalog of trite Petrarchan imagery. Poking fun at such excessive flattery is a source of humor even today, as in an old wheeze: "Your teeth are like the stars—they come out at night."

Robert Hayden, THE WHIPPING, page 730

Hayden's poem chillingly depicts the cycles of family and social violence. The old woman beats the boy to avenge the "lifelong hidings / she has had to bear." The narrator stands outside the action of the poem, but the boy's tears trigger his own memories of being beaten by—in a frightening synecdoche—"the face that I / no longer knew or loved." Notice that Hayden deliberately leaves the relationship between "the boy" and "the old woman" unstated. Is she mother, grandmother, aunt, babysitter, foster mother? It doesn't matter in the poem. She is large and powerful while the boy is small and helpless. One might assign this poem together with Hayden's "Those Winter Sundays," for contrasting views of domestic life.

Elizabeth Bishop, ONE ART, page 731

Like Thomas's "Do not go gentle," this villanelle manages to say something that matters while observing the rules of a tricky French courtly form. (For remarks on the villanelle and on writing it, see the entry on Thomas in this manual). A similar feat is performed in Bishop's ingenious recollection of childhood, "Sestina."

Question: What varieties of loss does the poet mention? (She goes from trivial loss—lost door keys—to lost time, to losing beloved places and homes, to loss of love.)

In recalling that she has lost a continent, the poet may be speaking personally: she lived in Brazil for many years, and wrote this poem after returning to America. Early in life, Bishop knew severe losses. Her father died when she was eight months old; when she was five, her mother was confined to an institution.

Perceptively, the Irish poet and critic Eavan Boland has likened "One Art" to Bishop's "Sestina," remarking that "it is obvious that [the poet] entrusted some of her deepest implications of loss to two of the most intricate game forms in poetry." However, she finds differences between the two works: " 'Sestina' is packed with desolate halftones, dropped hints, and the incantatory shadows of nursery rhymes. It manages to convey, at one and the same time, that there is sorrow, yes, and loss, yes, but that they are imperfectly understood. Therefore the poem operates at two different levels. Within it a terrible sorrow is happening. But the teakettle keeps boiling, the cup is full of tea, the stove is warm. Only we, outside the poem, get the full meaning of it all. 'One Art' is quite different. . . . The tone, which is both casual and direct, is deliberately worked against the form, as it is not in 'Sestina.' Once again, Bishop shows that she is best able to display feeling when she can constrain it most." (We quote from her fine essay on Bishop's work, "Time, Memory, and Obsession," *PN Review* [Nov.–Dec. 1991] 18–24.)

EXERCISE: *Re-evaluating Popular Classics,* page 732

Emma Lazarus, THE NEW COLOSSUS, page 733

Most Americans know at least a line or two of this famous sonnet carved on the pedestal of the Statue of Liberty, but surprisingly few can name the author of the poem. The poem and its author have vanished from most anthologies and textbooks. Yet Lazarus's sonnet seems that rare thing—a truly successful public poem. The images are clear and powerful, the language memorable, and the sonnet avoids the chief danger of public poetry—prolixity. The contrast between the original colossus of the ancient world, which represented might, and the new colossus, which represents freedom, is both an original and effective means of dramatizing the difference between the Old World of European despotism and the New World of American democracy, a popular theme of nineteenth-century patriotic poetry, but one rarely so well expressed.

Edgar Allan Poe, ANNABEL LEE, page 733

Students usually adore this poem. Most modern critics hate it. There is some truth in both camps.

Let's catalogue the faults of the poem first. The poem is sentimental: it asks the reader to be sad while reveling in the beauty of the sadness. The poem is also heavy-handed. When Poe gets a nice line or image going, he can't resist repeating it—more often for the sake of sound than sense. (These repetitions make most of the stanza patterns go awry.) The language is abstract and literary (*angels, kingdom, highborn kinsmen, sepulcher, maiden,* etc.). It may be unfair to say that these are not authentic *American* images, but, more to the point, the words seem borrowed from a book rather than observed from life.

And yet, with all its faults neatly noted, the poem remains weirdly beautiful. The very irregularity of the stanzas keeps the form of the poem subtly surprising, despite the bouncy anapestic meter. The abstract quality of the language used in this hypnotic meter—all drenched in emotion—eventually gives the poem a dreamlike reality. That placeless "kingdom by the sea" now begins to resemble the world of memory, and the poem lures us back into our own emotion-drenched childlike memories. ("*I* was a child and *she* was a child," as more than one psychological critic has noted, places the poem in a presexual stage; Annabel Lee is a bride only in the future tense.) The childlike innocence of the language and emotions somehow carry the poem into a sphere where adult critical concerns seem less relevant. "Annabel Lee" somehow marries the style and meter of light verse to the themes of elegiac, if not quite tragic, poetry. Whatever its faults, American poetry would be poorer without it.

When told we were including this poem in a new edition, one instructor (a highly regarded critic adept in literary theory) said "Be gentle. I love that poem. Critics keep showing me why it's awful, but I love it anyway." We hope she feels we've been gentle enough.

WRITER'S PERSPECTIVE

Edgar Allan Poe on Writing, A LONG POEM DOES NOT EXIST, page 735

Do you agree or disagree? If Poe is right, should we discard *The Odyssey, The Divine Comedy,* and "Lycidas"? If he is wrong, then how do you account for the fact that certain long poems contain patches of deadly dullness?

25 *What Is Poetry?*

This chapter is not designed to answer the question of its title in any definitive sense. Instead, we have attempted to create an occasion for reflection and discussion after all the material covered earlier in the book. We have compiled a small anthology of quotations by writers on the nature of poetry. You may want to supplement our list with some you have discovered.

Ha Jin, MISSED TIME, page 740

We end the pedagogic portion of the poetry book with Ha Jin's simple, direct, and moving "Missed Time," a poem the average reader can appreciate on first hearing. Poems need not be complex or challenging to matter. What they need be is expressive, true, and beautiful—though no lover of literature will confuse the beautiful with the merely pretty or decorous.

26 Two Critical Casebooks: Emily Dickinson and Langston Hughes

This greatly expanded chapter offers a representative cross-section of two major American poets—Emily Dickinson and Langston Hughes—one author drawn from the nineteenth century, the other from the twentieth. The selections found in this chapter can be supplemented by additional poems from these two writers elsewhere in the text. There are now 19 Dickinson poems and 15 Hughes poems in the volume as well as substantial prose passages from each author. We have also incorporated visual information into the book with author and documentary photographs relevant to the poems and historical periods. Finally, there is a critical casebook on each poet's work that provides a variety of analytical approaches for the student.

This chapter gives instructors the additional flexibility of using the material for in-depth classroom examinations of the individual poets. The casebooks also provide students with some background—including author biographies and criticism—to prepare essays and term papers, though many instructors may wish students to supplement their reading and research in the library or on our textbook Website.

EMILY DICKINSON

This selection of Dickinson's poems covers her entire career. We have presented many of her most famous poems since students should know these deservedly classic selections, but we have also included a few lesser-known ones to add variety and, we hope, surprise.

Emily Dickinson, SUCCESS IS COUNTED SWEETEST, page 742

When the first collection of Dickinson's *Poems* (1890) was published—four years after her death—by Mabel Loomis Todd and T. W. Higginson, they placed this poem on the first page. The editors implicitly saw that it represents an important theme in the poet's work. They may also have used the poem to symbolize Dickinson's lifelong obscurity. Ironically, this was one of the seven poems Dickinson actually published in her lifetime. It appeared anonymously in 1878 (two decades after its inception) in Helen Hunt Jackson's anthology, *A Masque of Poets*.

The poem articulates one of Dickinson's central themes—how suffering heightens perception and understanding. The nature of success, the poem argues, is best "comprehended" by someone who has tried to secure it but failed. The central image of the poem is the defeated, dying soldier who hears the distant sounds of a victory he will never share. (Some critics—even the learned Judith Farr—comment that the military image is borrowed from the Civil War, which inspired so many poems from Dickinson, but the dating of the poem's first appearance in two manuscripts from 1859 make such a connection impossible.)

In a lecture on Dickinson delivered in 1959 at the bicentennial celebration of the town of Amherst, Richard Wilbur made a cogent case that the poem goes beyond the conventional ideas of compensation ("the idea that every evil confers some balancing good, that through bitterness we learn to appreciate the sweet"). Wilbur speculated that Dickinson's poem:

> is arguing for the *superiority* of defeat to victory, of frustration to satisfaction, and of anguished comprehension to mere possession. What do victors have but victory, a victory which they cannot fully savor or clearly define? They have paid for their triumph by a sacrifice of awareness; a material gain has cost them a spiritual loss ("Sumptuous Destitution" reprinted in *Responses: Prose Pieces 1953–1976*, [New York: Harcourt, 1976]).

Emily Dickinson, WATER, IS TAUGHT BY THIRST, page 742

This short, early poem is unusually compressed even for Dickinson. In only six lines it offers a series of six parallel images and paradoxical observations. Dickinson's poem implies that one learns the nature or the importance of something by experiencing its lack. "Water, is taught by thirst" just as "Land – by the Oceans passed." Each self-contained line presents a different parallel example of instruction by deprivation.

Each line also offers a different contrasting dynamic—positive versus negative experience. The six opening words and initial images of the lines—Water, Land, Transport, Peace, Love, Birds—all have generally positive associations, but each are followed by less comforting and often hostile images—thirst, oceans, throe, battles, Memorial Mold, and snow.

Two glosses might be necessary for the class. By "Memorial Mold" Dickinson means a pictorial representation like a miniature portrait or photograph that lovers might exchange or a family might keep of a dead or absent loved one. "Transport – by throe – " means that ecstasy (or rapture) is achieved by anguish (or a fit of pain). Ultimately, the poem justifies suffering and deprivation as the necessary means by which one understands and appreciates the blessings of life.

Emily Dickinson, I TASTE A LIQUOR NEVER BREWED, page 743

This joyful lyric is a most unusual nature poem—a hymn to the world's beauty in a form reminiscent of a drinking song. The first stanza celebrates a liquor that doesn't exist in the literal sense—it is never brewed but definitely intoxicating. An "Inebriate of Air" (what a gorgeous phrase!) and "Debauchee of Dew," the speaker draws her ecstasy from the everyday world around her rather than from the distant and seemingly romantic "Vats upon the Rhine." As in a good drinking song, the speaker brags about her great capacity to drink in the third and fourth stanzas. She cannot stop imbibing this "liquor never brewed."

In his superb essay on Dickinson, "Sorting Out," J. V. Cunningham quarrels with the traditional efforts to read the poet's work biographically. So much Dickinson criticism and textual scholarship, he observes, tries to create "a reconstructed history of the poet's emotional life." Such an approach obscures the actual surface meaning of the poem—"History would destroy the text to attain the fact." Cunningham then remarks:

> And so it is amusing that one of the best known poems of these [supposedly autobiographical works], "I taste a liquor never brewed" (214), has been until quite recently read as a self-portrait of Legendary Emily, that "Debauchee of Dew," that "little Tippler / Leaning against the – Sun." But it seems more likely that the speaker is not Emily at all, but a hummingbird; that the poem is, as many similar nature poems are, a riddle; and we have long missed the answer, not knowing "Guess Who?" was being asked (*The Collected Essays of J. V. Cunningham* [Chicago: Swallow, 1976]).

Some questions the class might ask include whether the poem is indeed a riddle and whether Cunningham's interpretation is entirely inconsistent with traditional readings. Could the speaker not be both a hummingbird and the poet herself—or, more precisely, be the hummingbird as an allegory for the poet?

Emily Dickinson, WILD NIGHTS — WILD NIGHTS!, page 743

It is worth noting that this famous love poem contains almost nothing explicitly about romantic love. And yet the text radiates erotic passions—mostly through suggestive word choice and imagery.

The first stanza begins with a fantasy of the "wild nights" the speaker would enjoy if she were with her beloved. (We know she speaks to her beloved because of the "Heart" metaphor in the second stanza.) The sexual element of the fantasy is also suggested by the associations of *luxury*, which originally meant *lust* or *lasciviousness*. (Remember the ghost of Hamlet's father admonishing his son: "Let not the royal bed of Denmark be / A couch for luxury and damnèd incest.") Although the word had also acquired its modern meaning by Dickinson's time, the echo of the original sense still remained. Finally, the nocturnal setting of the poem also suggests the obvious setting for the consummation of sexual love.

The second stanza introduces a metaphorical situation that continues through the rest of the poem—a boat in port. The speaker, however, realizes that this metaphor is still fantasy. She both imagines herself a boat in harbor (lines 6–9) and also sees herself in her real situation (lines 11–12) as merely longing to "moor" herself to her beloved.

One more interesting word in this poem is *Eden*. The image of "Rowing in Eden" suggests that fulfillment of the speaker's romantic longings are paradisiacal. The metaphor of Eden further suggests that the speaker's longings—however erotic—are also innocent of sin. Eden, the lost paradise, permitted a sexual freedom unknown to the post-lapsarian world. (Dickinson knew her Milton.) The speaker, therefore, longs for erotic fulfillment in a way that harmonizes body and soul in an idealistic, literally Edenic fashion.

Emily Dickinson, I FELT A FUNERAL, IN MY BRAIN, page 743

There are at least two ways of approaching this stark and powerful poem. We can read it either as a poem about death—the speaker's mental vision of her own extinction—or as a poem that uses death as the central metaphor in an allegory of an unstated psychological anguish.

The poem has an explicit narrative structure. It describes a funeral service and burial. The speaker describes the event simultaneously from two different but related perspectives (a characteristic Dickinsonian device). She places the funeral inside her brain, but she also experiences the ceremony as if she were inside the coffin at the service. Trapped in the coffin, she cannot see the events, only hear them. To borrow a phrase from Judith Farr (whose 1992 study, *The Passions of Emily Dickinson*, places the poet in the context of mid-nineteenth-century American sensibility), the poem is "staged to describe the sensations of lost perception."

Emily Dickinson, I'M NOBODY! WHO ARE YOU?, page 744

Small and simple, this poem is nonetheless memorable. It also illustrates some classic Dickinsonian verbal devices—especially her gift of using everyday words (like *nobody* and *somebody*) in unusual but revelatory ways. Students might enjoy comparing this poem to E. E. Cummings's "anyone lived in a pretty how town," which uses the same verbal device in a more elaborately sustained manner.

Emily Dickinson, THE SOUL SELECTS HER OWN SOCIETY, page 744

"The Soul selects her own Society" is about both solitude and companionship. It is ultimately a love poem, though it does not initially seem so. The first two stanzas are written in the third-person. The speaker views the "Soul" from a distance, though it will eventually seem it is her own soul she describes. The "Soul" chooses her "Society," which proves in the final stanza (now spoken in the first-person) to be a single other person. This "divine Majority" of two suffices for the speaker who then cares little for the rest of the world. She becomes "Like Stone." Even an Emperor kneeling at her doorstep leaves her unmoved.

Emily Dickinson, AFTER GREAT PAIN, A FORMAL FEELING COMES, page 744

The meaning of the poem depends heavily on the first three words, "After great pain." All of the subsequent description and rationale originate as consequences of this suffering. If "outlived," the poem suggests, great pain transforms one.

Like many other Dickinson poems, "After great pain" contains images and suggestions of death—tombs, the "hour of Lead," the "Freezing persons" losing consciousness in the snow. In this poem, however, the implied protagonist has survived the possible brush with death. (It is, in fact, possible to interpret the poem as describing a sort of spiritual resurrection—in contrast to the metaphorical reading of "I felt a Funeral, in my Brain" as describing a spiritual or emotional death and disintegration.)

The style and form of the poem are worth noting. Although it feels intimately personal, the poem is spoken in the third person. The speaker seemingly distances herself from the intensity of emotion she has painfully lived through. The middle stanza is arranged as irregular (5 lines versus the two 4 line stanzas that surround it). Heard aloud, however, the two irregular lines (7 and 8) combine into a metrically standard tetrameter line. Dickinson probably arranged the written text in an irregular fashion to slow the reader down and to emphasize the ideas presented in the lines.

Emily Dickinson, THIS IS MY LETTER TO THE WORLD, page 745

This memorable short poem begins with a characteristic Dickinsonian twist, "This is my letter to the World / That never wrote to Me." As Richard B. Sewall remarks in his detailed volume, *The Life of Emily Dickinson* (Cambridge: Harvard UP, 1980), this poem "too often regarded as a tearful complaint about being neglected is actually a statement . . . of the difficulty of conveying what she calls the 'Message' of Nature." The "Her" in line 5 is clearly nature, but to whom do the "Hands" belong in line 6? It is possible to interpret these hands as belonging to posterity—probably the "countrymen" of line 7 whose tender judgment she implores.

If this poem is not specifically a complaint against being neglected, it is nonetheless a call to posterity. Whatever else it might mean, the poem is also an address to her posthumous audience. She may humbly position herself merely as Nature's messenger, but she nonetheless claims authorship as the transcriber of that message. She also implicitly confided an uncertainty of her own achievement and hopes that her audience will be tender in its judgment.

Emily Dickinson, I HEARD A FLY BUZZ — WHEN I DIED, page 745

Plump with suggestions, this celebrated fly well demonstrates a symbol's indefiniteness. The fly appears in the room—on time, like the Angel of Death—and yet it is decidedly ordinary. A final visitor from the natural world, it brings to mind an assortment of suggestions, some offensive (filth, stenches, rotting meat, offal, and so forth). But a natural fly is a minor annoyance; and so is death, if one is certain of Eternity. Unsure and hesitant in its flight, the fly buzzes as though faltering. It is another failing thing, like the light that comes through the windows and through the eyes (which are, as a trite phrase calls them, "the windows of the soul").

Most students will easily identify "Eyes around" as those of surrounding friends or relatives, and "that last Onset" as death throes. Is "the King" Death or Jesus? It seems more likely that the friends and relatives will behold death. What is the speaker's assignable portion? Physical things: keepsakes bequeathed to friends and relatives; body, to the earth.

Discussion will probably focus on the final line. It may help students to remember that the speaker is, at the present moment of the poem, in Eternity. The scene she describes is therefore a vision within a vision. Perhaps all the last line means is (as John Ciardi has argued), "And then there was no more of me, and nothing to see with." But the last line suddenly thrusts the speaker to Heaven. For one terrible moment she finds herself, with immortal eyes, looking back through her mortal eyes at a blackness where there used to be light.

Emily Dickinson, BECAUSE I COULD NOT STOP FOR DEATH, page 746

QUESTIONS FOR DISCUSSION:

1. *What qualities does Dickinson attribute to death? Why is Immortality going along on this carriage ride?* For the poet, death and immortality go together. Besides, Dickinson is amplifying her metaphor of Death as a gentleman taking a woman for a drive: Immortality, as would have been proper in Amherst, is their chaperone.

2. *Is the poem, as the poet wrote it, in some ways superior to the version first printed? Is* strove *perhaps a richer word than* played? *What is interesting in the phrase* Gazing Grain? *How can grain "gaze"?* It has kernels like eyes at the tips of its stalks. As the speaker dies, the natural world—like the fly in "I heard a Fly buzz"—is watching. *What is memorable in the rhythm and meaning of the line "The Dews drew quivering and chill"?* At *quivering,* the rhythm quivers loose from its iambic tetrameter. The image of cold dampness foreshadows the next stanza, with its images of the grave.

3. *What is the Carriage? What is the House?*

4. *Where is the speaker at the present moment of the poem? Why is time said to pass more quickly where she is now?* Eternity is timeless.

5. *What is the tone of the poem?* Complicated!—seriousness enlivened with delicate macabre humor? Surely she kids her own worldly busyness in the opening line.

William Galperin reads the poem as a feminist affirmation. Not death, he finds, but immortality is Dickinson's subject. In the end the poet asserts a triumph possible only because she has renounced the proposal of Death, that threatening gentleman caller who might have married her ("Emily Dickinson's Marriage Hearse," *Denver Quarterly* Winter 1984: 62–73).

Emily Dickinson, SOME KEEP THE SABBATH GOING TO CHURCH, page 746

This celebration of natural religion was one of the seven poems Dickinson actually published during her lifetime. It appeared in the March 12, 1864, issue of *The Round Table,* a New York weekly published by a relation. (It appeared there under the title "My Sabbath," which may have been Dickinson's own suggestion.)

In the original Massachusetts colony, Sunday church attendance was legally mandatory. By Dickinson's time it was merely a social obligation—but a serious one. Although Dickinson was deeply (if also unconventionally) religious, she stopped attending church by her thirtieth birthday. This poem was published a few years thereafter. The poem makes a clear and cogent case for worshipping God not by attending a church service but by being attentive to God's creation. The poem has a simple rhetorical structure: the speaker contrasts her own practices (what the *I* does) with the customs of *some*. A useful question for class discussion is to ask how each of Dickinson's natural images suitably matches (or exceeds) the ecclesiastic person or object it replaces—chorister, dome, surplice, bell, sexton, and clergyman.

Emily Dickinson, THE BUSTLE IN A HOUSE, page 747

This evocative short poem perfectly illustrates one of Dickinson's greatest imaginative methods—the interpenetration of the domestic and the religious realms. The first stanza describes in clinical terms the busy activity in a house after the death of a loved one. The activity is "solemnest," but the living continue their work. The second stanza, however, reveals a radical shift—first into a symbolic mode and then into a religious one. The domestic activities of the first stanza are now allegorized into emotional symbols—the Heart and Love. The last two lines affirm trust in Eternity (not always the case in Dickinson's work) and close the poem with an epigrammatic click.

Emily Dickinson, TELL ALL THE TRUTH BUT TELL IT SLANT, page 747

Critics have traditionally seen this poem as Dickinson's clearest explanation of her poetic method, and it does remind us of her indirect procedures. Note that the *Truth* is associated with images of light. The poet's job is to make the light illuminating rather than blinding, to ease the viewer into seeing truth gradually. (Even the word *Delight*, which Dickinson wonderfully qualifies with *infirm* to describe the human capacity for truth, contains a possible play on the word *light*.) Likewise, the inability to grasp the truth—to see the light, in the metaphoric world of this poem—is characterized as blindness.

EMILY DICKINSON ON EMILY DICKINSON

Emily Dickinson, RECOGNIZING POETRY, page 747

It may be worth pointing out to students that this famous passage from Dickinson does not exist in any of her writing. It comes from a letter that T. W. Higginson, a critic and novelist who befriended Dickinson after she wrote him, mailed to his wife during a visit to Amherst. Higginson took notes on his conversation with the poet to share with his wife; these brief notes provide a vivid description of both her genius and her eccentricity. (We have reprinted the statement in its full original context in the "Critics on Emily Dickinson" section which follows.)

QUESTIONS FOR DISCUSSION

1. Is Dickinson right about recognizing poetry? Is there any other way to recognize it than by experiencing physical sensation?

2. What poem in the anthology affects you in the way that Dickinson describes? Can you relate the sensations you experience to any particular words or images in the poem?

Emily Dickinson, SELF-DESCRIPTION, page 748

Few letters in literature have generated more commentary—and wild speculation—than Dickinson's April 25, 1862, response to Thomas Wentworth Higginson. Virtually every sentence has been offered several interpretations. The letter is often excerpted, but we have included the whole text to give an accurate impression of Dickinson's unique epistolary style.

Here Dickinson lists her poetic influences—Keats and the two Brownings. For prose she lists Ruskin and Browne, two notably gorgeous and ornate stylists as well as Revelations, a revealing choice among books of the Bible. It is worth noting that all of these choices remain respectable a century and a half later. Dickinson recognized truly good writing in both verse and prose. And amusingly she admits she has never read Whitman because she has been "told that he was disgraceful."

CRITICS ON EMILY DICKINSON, pages 749–757

We have offered five diverse and interesting critical views of Emily Dickinson. The first is **Thomas Wentworth Higginson**'s extensive account of meeting her in 1870. He not only provides a number of superb observations, but he also quotes her remarks extensively. Students will note that Dickinson's famous statement on recognizing poetry ("I feel physically as if the top of my head were taken off") came not from the poet's own letters but from Higginson's account. "I never was with any one who drained my nerve power so much," Higginson remarks at the end of his letter.

Thomas H. Johnson provides an account of discovering Dickinson's manuscripts—one of which we have reproduced. This background will help students understand the unusual nature of the texts of her poems—not an unimportant aspect of interpreting her work. **Richard Wilbur** offers a compelling psychological and biographical portrait of the poet. **Cynthia Griffin Wolff** discusses Dickinson's obsessive central theme, death, and provides a reading of "Because I could not stop for Death," while **Judith Farr** gives a reading of "My Life had stood – a Loaded Gun" that addresses issues of power, gender, and love.

LANGSTON HUGHES

Our selection of Hughes's poetry tries to represent the considerable range of his work—in mood, form, and genre. His special gift of combining traditional and innovational impulses is especially apparent. The juxtaposition with Dickinson's work in this chapter also opens up some interesting comparisons in style and approach that might be used for student essays.

Langston Hughes, THE NEGRO SPEAKS OF RIVERS, page 759

This remarkable poem was written by Hughes while still in his teens. The influence of Walt Whitman and Carl Sandburg, two early models, is evident, but the poem already demonstrates Hughes's characteristic voice. A good discussion question to ask is why Hughes chooses each of the four specific rivers to tell his story of the Negro race. The Euphrates is traditionally the original center of human civilization. By invoking it, Hughes places the Negro at the dawn of humanity. The Congo is the center of black African culture. The Nile represents the source of the most celebrated African culture, and Hughes claims the Negro a role in building this great civilization. Finally, the Mississippi becomes a symbol of the Negro in America, though Hughes selects a joyous moment to represent the race's turbulent place in our history.

Langston Hughes, MOTHER TO SON, page 759

This stark, naturalistic poem contains (and half conceals) a transcendent central symbol—a stairway. While the mother has not spent her life climbing a "crystal stair," she has nonetheless felt confident she was ascending a stairwell. This more mundane stairway is badly maintained, poorly-lit, and slightly dangerous, but the mother has had the drive and courage to climb it. And she insists that her son show the determination to do so, too.

The spare, conversational free verse of "Mother to Son" provides an interesting contrast to the extravagantly syncopated jazz rhythm of "The Weary Blues" or the rich formal measures of "Song for a Dark Girl." Hughes's poems show a wonderful prosodic range.

Langston Hughes, DREAM VARIATIONS, page 760

This poem, according to Hughes's biographer, Arnold Rampersad, was written in response to the poet's 1923 trip to Africa. Presenting a vision of racial harmony, the poem contrasts the "white day" and the gentle dark night in a dream of joyous and unproblematic co-existence. The poem's now famous last line served as the title of John Howard Griffin's *Black Like Me* (1961), an exposé of American racial prejudice and discrimination.

Langston Hughes, LENOX AVENUE: MIDNIGHT, page 760

Harlem's Lenox Avenue is now called Malcolm X Boulevard. Stretching for two miles from West 110th Street to the Esplanade Garden Apartments, Lenox Avenue represented the fashionable and exuberant side of Harlem during the 1920s. (A photograph of Lenox Avenue in 1925 appears in the book at the end of the selection of Hughes's poetry.) Lenox Avenue also appears in the next Hughes poem, "The Weary Blues," which served as the title poem for Hughes's first collection of poems in 1926, and also included "Lenox Avenue: Midnight."

This jazz-like lyric doesn't so much describe Harlem's Lenox Avenue as convey the spirit it fosters. The rhythm of life, the speaker insists, is "a jazz rhythm." What does this claim mean? The middle stanza suggests that a jazz rhythm creates joy out of sorrow—"the broken heart of love" and "the weary, weary, heart of pain."

Langston Hughes, THE WEARY BLUES, page 760

"The Weary Blues" is a poem of rhythmic bravado. Hughes starts with a basic four-beat line ("Droning a drowsy syncopated tune"). He then flamboyantly varies it with jazz-like syncopations as well as contrasts it with interpolated short lines. As in "Song for a Dark Girl," he also incorporates allusive quotations from a traditional song—in this case the blues song of the poem's title. ("The Weary Blues" was published, after all, in the twenties—the same decade as T. S. Eliot's allusive *The Waste Land* and Ezra Pound's *A Draft of XVI Cantos.* Hughes was a populist Modernist but a Modernist nonetheless.)

There are two key characters in "The Weary Blues"—the speaker and the piano-playing blues singer. The poem is a recollection by the speaker of the performance he recently heard in Harlem. (Lenox Avenue was one of the main streets for Harlem nightlife in the twenties. It has now been renamed Malcolm X Boulevard, so Hughes's once famous setting has already become an historical footnote.) The speaker is of unstated race, but the blues singer is repeatedly identified as a Negro. The singer and his song ultimately become a symbol for the sorrows of the modern African American. ("Sweet Blues! / Coming from a black man's soul. / O Blues!") The expression of the blues seems not only cathartic to the singer but almost annihilating. After singing all night, he goes home to sleep "like a rock or a man that's dead."

Hughes's biographer, Arnold Rampersad, has called "The Weary Blues" a work "virtually unprecedented in American poetry in its blending of black and white rhythms and forms." In his autobiographical book, *The Big Sea* (1940), Hughes commented "It was a poem about a working man who sang the blues all night and then went to bed and slept like a rock. That was all." Most readers will find much more in the poem than that summary suggests.

Langston Hughes, I, TOO, page 761

This poem represents Hughes's admirable ability to critique American race-relations and yet maintain a hopeful tone. The speaker's identity is crucial to the symbolic structure of the poem. He is a brother, a spurned darker brother but nonetheless a member of the family who knows he has an unquestioned right to live in the home. The symbolic segregation of being forced to eat in the kitchen obviously reflects the social realities of Southern segregation in that era. The speaker, however, knows his day will come soon—"tomorrow" in line 8—when he will claim his rightful place at the table, confident of his strength and beauty. But, as the last stanza reminds us, it isn't only the threat of the speaker's strength that will intimidate the others but the justice of his cause. They will "be ashamed" of their previous oppression.

The title and opening line is probably an allusion to Walt Whitman's famous passage in part 52 of "Song of Myself":

> I too am not a bit tamed . . . I too am untranslatable,
> I sound my barbaric yawp over the roofs of the world.

Langston Hughes, SONG FOR A DARK GIRL, page 762

One of the most impressive things about reading through Hughes's massive *Collected Poems* is the stylistic diversity of his work. Written in regular rhymed quatrains, "Song for a Dark Girl" shows the tight formal but evocatively modernist side of Hughes's style. The poem uses an ironic, allusive refrain borrowed from Daniel Decatur Emmet's famous minstrel song, "Dixie's Land," which during the Civil War became a marching song for Confederate troops and eventually a nostalgic rallying song for the lost Southern cause. Hughes quotes the song lyric, which is spoken in the faux-black voice of the minstrel, to underscore that the real black experience in "de land ob cotton" is not so joyful. The Christ-like imagery associated with the lynched young man is important to note.

Langston Hughes, BALLAD OF THE LANDLORD, page 762

This ingenious ballad begins to tell its story in the traditional way but then presents an innovative turn midway. The ballad starts in the voice of a black tenant who complains about his negligent landlord. As the poem progresses, the reader realizes that the speaker is arguing with his landlord who is actually present. The argument heats up until the speaker threatens to hit the landlord (in line 20). Suddenly and unexpectedly, the voice of the poem shifts to outside observers, who condemn and overtly misrepresent the tenant. (Note how Hughes also abruptly shifts his meter and lineation once the voices change.) The poem ends with three isolated but sequential newspaper headlines in all capital letters. Hughes's mixture of auditory prosody and visual prosody in this poem is extremely interesting and demonstrates his use of Modernist techniques in seemingly populist works.

Langston Hughes, ISLAND, page 763

This short lyric also has a simple song-like structure. Although printed in couplets, the rime scheme suggests the quatrains of a ballad or popular song. The first six lines state the narrative situation of the poem. The narrator is trying to reach a "fair" island but fears he will drown before achieving his goal. He asks the "wave of sorrow" to spare him. The last two lines deliver a small surprise. The speaker asks the "wave of sorrow" to take him to the island. Suffering is not merely something to survive, the poem suggests, it is also the means by which one can achieve difficult goals. (Students might profitably contrast Hughes's view of sorrow in this poem with Dickinson's similar, though more tragic, view in "Success is counted sweetest" earlier in this chapter.)

Langston Hughes, SUBWAY RUSH HOUR, page 764

In this compressed but vivid depiction of rush hour in the subway, the poet seems to send an optimistic message: that were blacks and whites ever to mingle closely with one another on equal terms, there would be "no room for fear." Notable in the poem is Hughes's imagery. Within his sixteen-word limit he evokes three of the five senses: smell, touch, and sight.

Langston Hughes, HARLEM [DREAM DEFERRED], page 764

Simile by simile, Hughes shows different attitudes, including violent protest, that blacks might possibly take toward the long deferral of their dream of equality. Students might be asked what meaning they find in each comparison. Also worth noting are the strong, largely unpleasant verbs used to characterize the types of decay caused by deferring the dream—*dry up, fester, run, stink, crust and sugar over,* and *sags.* No wonder an explosion is likely to follow.

Hughes's poem supplied the title for Lorraine Hansberry's long-running Broadway play, *A Raisin in the Sun* (1958), in which the Youngers, a family descended from five generations of slaves, come to a Chicago ghetto in hopes of fulfilling their dream.

Donald Ritzhein has written a moving account of what the poem has meant to him, starting when his mother cut it out of a newspaper and pasted it to his bedroom door. "By the time I got to high school . . . I still didn't know a lot about the misery of deferred dreams . . . I knew a little more about them when I heard Martin Luther King, Jr. talk about dreams in Washington. I finally felt a little of what it's like to defer dreams when John F. Kennedy was killed" ("Langston Hughes: A Look Backwards and Forwards," *Steppingstones*, Harlem, Winter 1984: 55–56). Have you any student who would care to write about what the poem has meant to her or him?

Langston Hughes, THEME FOR ENGLISH B, page 764

This poem demonstrates how a great writer in his maturity can turn a routine homework assignment into a memorable piece of literature. If youth is wasted on the young, so perhaps are writing assignments.

Hughes is so convincing a storyteller that you will probably have to remind students—repeatedly—that this poem is not autobiographical. Hughes was not born in Winston-Salem, but in Joplin, Missouri. He did not go to school in Durham, but in Lawrence, Kansas and Cleveland, Ohio. He did attend Columbia (where, by implication, the poem takes place), but left after a year to travel. (He later completed his college education at Lincoln University in Pennsylvania.) He was nearly fifty when he wrote this poem, not twenty-two as the narrator is.

Langston Hughes, HOMECOMING, page 765

The last lines make the speaker's feeling unmistakable: he no longer has a lover, all he has now is vacant space. The title is ironic: *homecoming* usually suggests a warm welcome, not a cold and empty bed. The poem is remarkable for what it leaves unsaid, for the economy with which Hughes portrays utter loneliness.

Langston Hughes, END, page 766

This unusually stark poem presents a chilling vision of death. Hughes's images of death go one step beyond the conventional depictions. Time has not merely stopped; there is no time. Shadows have not fallen; there are no shadows. There is not only no light but also no dark. There is not even a door to exit. There is, by implication, nothing at all. This free verse, imagistic, and consciously impersonal poem demonstrates a different side of Hughes's talent—a darker and colder side—but its immediacy and accessibility remain characteristic.

LANGSTON HUGHES ON LANGSTON HUGHES

Langston Hughes, THE NEGRO ARTIST AND THE RACIAL MOUNTAIN, page 766

Hughes's essay "The Negro Artist and the Racial Mountain" was the key manifesto of the younger African-American artists associated with the Harlem Renaissance. This crucial article originally appeared in the *Nation* as a response to George Schuyler's dismissive article, "The Negro-Art Hokum." Hughes's proud assertion of black identity and unabashed celebration of jazz and the blues struck a responsive chord among many members of the new generation of African-American artists and intellectuals. The new artists saw their role, in the words of Arnold Rampersad, "to assert racial pride and racial truth in the face of either black or white censure or criticism."

Langston Hughes, THE HARLEM RENAISSANCE, page 767

In his autobiography, *The Big Sea* (1940), Hughes gave a vivid account of the Harlem Renaissance. This passage describes both the cultural excitement and the racial tension of Harlem's nightlife after white people began patronizing the local clubs. This profitable influx of white customers led to bizarre situations such as the famous Cotton Club and other nightspots banning African Americans—except as performers and staff—"barring their own race," as Hughes indignantly puts it. But Hughes also celebrates the talent and vitality of the club scene in a way that conveys the African-American side of the Jazz Age.

CRITICS ON LANGSTON HUGHES, pages 769–777

The critical selections on Langston Hughes offer a range of approaches. **Arnold Rampersad**, Hughes's most distinguished biographer, discusses the innovative aspects of the early poetry which blended both black and white literary traditions. **Rita Dove** and **Marilyn Nelson** examine Hughes's role as spokesman for African Americans. **Darryl Pinckney** analyzes in both historical and reader-response terms how Hughes connected with his early African-American readers. **Peter Townsend** analyzes how Hughes used jazz influences and speculates on the social impact of his jazz poetry during his long career. Finally, **Onwuchekwa Jemie** provides a highly sensitive reading of Hughes's most famous poem, "Dream Deferred" (also published under the title "Harlem").

27   *Poems for Further Reading*

Anonymous, EDWARD, page 779

"Edward," with its surprise ending in the last line, is so neatly built that it is sometimes accused of not being a popular ballad at all, but the creation of a sophisticated poet, perhaps working from a popular story. Students might be asked to read the information about ballads in the chapter, "Song," either before or after reading this ballad.

QUESTIONS FOR DISCUSSION:

1. In "Edward," why is the first line so effective as an opening? What expectations does it set up in the hearer's mind? How does the last line also display the skill of a master storyteller?

2. Reading a ballad such as "Edward" on the printed page, we notice that its refrains take up much room. Do you find this repetitiousness a hindrance to your enjoying the poem? Is there anything to be said in favor of the repetitiousness?

3. What is the value to the poem of the question-and-answer method of story-telling? ("Edward" proceeds like a courtroom cross-examination in which the mother, by pointed questioning, breaks down her son's story. Dramatically, the method is powerful, and it holds off until the very end the grimmest revelation.)

4. What else could the author of "Edward" conceivably have told us about this unhappy family? Do you find it troublesome that Edward and his mother behave as they do without our quite knowing why? Might the story have suffered if told by a storyteller who more deeply explored the characters' motivations?

Anonymous, WESTERN WIND, page 780

Originally a song for tenor voices, "Western Wind" probably was the work of some courtier in the reign of Henry VIII. Untouched by modernization, it reads (in its one surviving manuscript):

Westron wynde when wyll thow blow
the smalle rayne douune can rayne
Chryst yf my love wer in my armys
and I yn my bed agayne

This famous poem, according to contemporary poet Deborah Digges, "demands that we create a context for this speaker who is far from home, waiting, it would appear, for the weather to break so that he can return. Is he at sea? Is he lost on the landscape? Is he dying? The poem refuses to answer, lives only by its breath, its longing" ("Lyrics and Ballads of the 15th Century," *Poetry Pilot* [monthly newsletter of the Academy of American Poets] Jan. 1989).

QUESTIONS FOR DISCUSSION:

1. In reading the poem, how does it help to know that the moist, warm west wind of England brings rain and is a sign of spring?

2. What do the first pair of lines and the last pair have to do with each other?

3. Do you agree with a critic who suggested that the speaker is invoking Christ, asking for help in obtaining sex? "By a blasphemous implication Christ is in effect assigned the role of a fertility spirit" (F. W. Bateson, *English Poetry: A Critical Introduction* [London: Longman, 1966]).

4. Consider another critic's view: the unhappy speaker is stressing his (or her) longing to go to bed with his (or her) loved one, and so the word *Christ* is an exclamation. (We prefer this view; see Arthur O. Lewis, Jr., writing in *Explicator* 15 [Feb. 1957]: item 28.)

Anonymous, LAST WORDS OF THE PROPHET (NAVAJO MOUNTAIN CHANT), page 780

This valediction is part of the Mountain Chant of the Navajo translated by Washington Matthews, one of the pioneering linguistic anthropologists. His work helped broaden appreciation for the genius of Native American poetry. The Mountain Chants were performed by the Navajo under the direction of a shaman and contain many archaic words whose meanings were lost even to the priesthood.

Matthew Arnold, DOVER BEACH, page 781

Arnold and his family did such an efficient job of expunging the facts of his early romances that the genesis of "Dover Beach" is hard to know. Arnold may (or may not) have been in love with a French girl whom he called Marguerite, whose egotistic gaiety made her difficult. See Lionel Trilling's discussion of the poem and of Arnold's Marguerite poems in his biography *Matthew Arnold* (New York: Columbia UP, 1949). Marguerite, Trilling suspects, viewed the world as much more various, beautiful, and new than young Arnold did.

A sympathetic reading of "Dover Beach" might include some attention to the music of its assonance and alliteration, especially the *s*-sounds in the description of the tide (lines 12–14). Line 21 introduces the central metaphor, the

Sea of Faith. Students will probably be helped by a few minutes of discussion of the historical background of the poem. Why, when the poem appeared in 1867, was religious faith under attack? Darwin, Herbert Spencer, and Victorian industrialism may be worth mention. Ignorant armies (line 37) are still with us. Arnold probably had in mind those involved in the Crimean War of 1853–56, perhaps also those in the American Civil War. For sources of the poem, see C. B. Tinker and H. F. Lowry, *The Poetry of Matthew Arnold* (New York: Oxford UP, 1940) 173–78.

A dour view of the poem is taken by Donald Hall in "Ah, Love, Let Us Be True" (*American Scholar*, Summer 1959). Hall finds "love invoked as a compensation for the losses that history has forced us to sustain," and adds, "I hope there are better reasons for fidelity than disillusion. . . . Like so many Victorian poems, its negation is beautiful and its affirmation repulsive." This comment can be used to provoke discussion. A useful counterfoil to "Dover Beach" is Anthony Hecht's satiric poem "The Dover Bitch," in his collection *The Hard Hours* (New York: Atheneum, 1960) and in many anthologies. For other critical comment, see William E. Cadbury, "Coming to Terms with 'Dover Beach,'" *Criticism* 8 (Spring 1966): 126–38; James Dickey, *Babel to Byzantium* (New York: Farrar, 1968) 235–38 (a good concise general essay); and A. Dwight Culler, *Imaginative Reason: The Poetry of Matthew Arnold* (New Haven: Yale UP, 1966).

Compare Hardy's attitude in "The Oxen" with Arnold's wistful view of the Sea of Faith.

John Ashbery, AT NORTH FARM, page 782

It is never easy to decide what an Ashbery poem "means." This one is rich with suggestions about which students may be invited to speculate. Who is this threatening catlike "someone" for whom we set out milk at night and about whom we think "sometimes, / Sometimes and always, with mixed feelings"? Is it the Grim Reaper? And yet Death always knows where to find the person he's looking for. And what are we to make of lines 7–11? How can the granaries be "bursting with meal, / The sacks of meal piled to the rafters" if "Hardly anything grows here"? The poet hints at a terrible sterility underlying the visible abundance at North Farm. Perhaps the farm can be regarded as, among other things, a paradigm of the world, rich in material things but spiritually empty. But that is to reduce the poem to flat words. Because such paraphrases tend to slip from Ashbery's poems like seals from icebergs, this poet's work is a favorite of critics. It challenges them to make subtler and stickier paraphrases.

Margaret Atwood, SIREN SONG, page 783

Atwood's "Siren Song" is a wonderfully tricky poem that seduces the reader as cleverly as it does its doomed listener. The reader doesn't realize that he or she has been taken in, until it is too late.

The poem is in three parts. The first section (lines 1–9) recounts the sirens and their deadly songs. Many readers will recognize the legendary monsters (half bird, half woman) from Book XII of the *Odyssey*. "Siren" has become synonymous for any dangerously alluring woman. The second section (lines 10–24) switches gears suddenly, as one of the sirens confesses to us her unhappy plight. She offers to tell us the secret of her irresistible song, but she mainly talks about herself and cries for our help. Then, without knowing it until too late, we are in the final section (the last three lines) in which we realize that we have been lured into the siren's emotional grasp.

Feminist poets have often retold famous myths and legends with a twist. Atwood's "Siren Song" is surely a model of this genre.

W. H. Auden, As I Walked Out One Evening, page 784

This literary ballad, with its stark contrast between the innocent song of the lover and the more knowing song of the clocks, affords opportunities to pay close attention to the poet's choice of words. Auden selects words rich in connotations: the *brimming* of the river (which suggests also the lover's feelings), the *crooked* neighbor (with its hint of dishonesty and corruption as well as the denotation of being warped or bent by Time, like the "diver's brilliant bow"). Figures of speech abound: the opening metaphor of the crowds like wheat (ripe and ready to be scythed by Time the Reaper), the lover's extended use of hyperbole in lines 9–20, the personifications of Time and Justice, the serious pun on *appalling* in line 34 (both awe-inspiring and like a pall or shroud, as in Blake's "London"), the final reconciliation in metaphor between the original "brimming river" and the flow of passing Time. Auden's theme appears to be that as young lovers grow old, their innocent vision is smudged and begrimed by contact with realities—and yet "Life remains a blessing" after all.

The lover's huge promises in stanzas 3 and 4 ("I'll love you Till China and Africa meet . . .") have reminded Richard Wilbur of the hyperbolic boasts of the speaker in Burns's "Oh, my love is like a red, red rose." Burns speaks for the romantic lover, wrapped in his own emotions, but Auden's view of romantic love is skeptical. "The poem then proceeds to rebut [the lover's] lines, saying that the human heart is too selfish and perverse to make such promises" (*Responses* [New York: Harcourt, 1976] 144).

This poem may appear to have too little action in it to resemble folk ballads in more than a few touches. Auden himself, according to Monroe K. Spears, did not call this a ballad but referred to it as "a pastiche of folk-song."

"As I Walked Out One Evening" is one of the "Five Lyrics" included in *W. H. Auden Reading* (Caedmon recording TC 1019). For comparison with the poet's own modest delivery, *Dylan Thomas Reading*, vol. 4 (Caedmon, TC 1061) offers a more dramatic rendition.

W. H. Auden, Musée des Beaux Arts, page 786

In Breughel's *Landscape with the Fall of Icarus* (reproduced with this poem), students may need to have their attention directed to the legs disappearing in a splash, one quarter inch below the bow of the ship. One story (probably apocryphal) is that Breughel's patron had ordered a painting on a subject from mythology, but the artist had only this landscape painting completed. To fill the order quickly, Breughel touched in the little splash, gave the picture a mythological name, and sent it on its way. Question: How does that story (if true) make Breughel seem a shallower man than Auden thinks he is?

Besides the *Landscape*, Auden apparently has in mind two other paintings of Pieter Breughel the Elder: *The Census*, also called *The Numbering at Bethlehem* (Auden's lines 5–8), and *The Massacre of the Innocents* (lines 9–13). If the instructor has access to reproductions, these works might be worth bringing in; however, the *Landscape* seems central to the poem. This painting seems indebted to Ovid's *Metamorphoses*, but in Ovid the plowman, shepherd, and fisherman looked on the fall of Icarus with amazement. The title of Auden's poem, incidentally, is close to the name of the Brussels museum housing the *Landscape*: the Musées Royaux des Beaux Arts.

Edward Mendelson has remarked on the poem in *Early Auden* (New York: Viking, 1981):

> The poetic imagination that seeks out grandeur and sublimity could scarcely be bothered with those insignificant figures lost in the background or in the crowd. But Auden sees in them an example of Christianity's great and enduring transformation of classical rhetoric: its inversion of the principle that the most important subjects require the highest style. If the sufferings of a carpenter turned preacher mattered more to the world than the doom of princes, then the high style, for all its splendor, was a limited instrument. . . . These casually irregular lines make none of the demands for action and attention that marked Auden's earlier harangues on the urgency of the times, yet beneath the apparent surface disorder a deeper pattern of connectedness gradually makes itself felt. The unassertive rhymes, easily overlooked on a first reading, hold the poem together.

Yet another device of language helps bring unity to Auden's meditation, in P. K. Saha's view. Four clauses begin with *how* and one phrase begins with *anyhow* (line 11). These *hows* vary in meaning; still, the repeated *how* is the crucial word in the linguistic pattern of the poem ("Style, Stylistic Transformations, and Incorporators," *Style* 12 [1978]: 18–22).

William Blake, THE TYGER, page 787

"The Tyger" from *Songs of Experience*, is a companion piece to "The Lamb" in *Songs of Innocence*. But while "The Lamb" poses a relatively easy question ("Little lamb, who made thee?") and soon answers it, "The Tyger" poses questions that remain unanswerable. Alert students may complain that some of Blake's questions have no verbs—what dread hand and what dread feet did *what*? While the incompleteness has been explained by some critics as reflecting the agitated tone of the poem, it may have been due to the poet's agitated habits of composition. Drafts of the poem in Blake's notebook show that, after writing the first three stanzas, he began the fourth stanza with the line "Could fetch it from the furnace deep," which would have completed the question in line 12. But then he deleted it, and wrote in stanza four almost as it stands now. (See Martin K. Nurmi, "Blake's Revision of 'The Tyger,'" *PMLA* 71 [1956]: 669–85.) Other useful discussions include that of E. D. Hirsch, Jr., *Innocence and Experience* (New Haven: Yale UP, 1964), who thinks the stars are the rebel angels who threw down their spears when they surrendered; and John E. Grant, "The Art and Argument of 'The Tyger'" in *Texas Studies in Literature and Language 2* (1960): 38–60.

Gwendolyn Brooks, THE MOTHER, page 788

This powerful, direct poem is controversial with many readers, but it so memorably addresses an important contemporary issue that it is worth risking an overheated classroom discussion. Students will easily become polarized according to their moral positions on abortion, so it will help if you focus the discussion on the poem itself rather than broader social, legal, and theological issues. What does this troubling poem say?

First of all, point out that the poem is not spoken by Brooks about herself, but it employs two voices—first a narrator who speaks to another character ("The Mother" of the title), and then the Mother's voice itself. Recognizing this literary distancing device will in itself depoliticize the discussion and allow you to focus on the poem's complex and at times almost contradictory argument. Second, point out the crucial division in the poem. In the first stanza the mother is the *you*. Another voice describes her situation. (This voice can either be seen as an outsider or part of the mother's divided self.) In the second stanza, however, the mother suddenly becomes the *I* and describes her own thoughts, fears, and memories. The *you* now becomes the unborn children. This switch is quiet but startling.

The form of "The Mother" is interesting and unusual—rhymed free verse. Brooks usually rhymes her free verse lines in couplets but in a few places she varies the pattern. A good question to ask students is what effect does the form have on the poem's tone?

Elizabeth Barrett Browning, HOW DO I LOVE THEE? LET ME COUNT THE WAYS, page 789

Dropping this famous sonnet from a previous edition broke more than one teacher's heart. The many requests for this poem, "My Last Duchess," "Mending Wall," "Death be not proud," and Poe's work reminds us how much students enjoy reading famous poems—work that an educational theorist like E. D. Hirsch would claim have "cultural utility." They are poems that are still frequently quoted in newspapers, conversation, and electronic media. Anthologists eager for novelty too often forget that these famous poems remain novel to every new generation.

This is the penultimate sonnet of forty-four constituting Elizabeth Barrett Browning's *Sonnets from the Portuguese*, a book that Ezra Pound once called "The second: that is, a sonnet sequence surpassed in English by one other alone. I would argue for that." The sonnets document the poet's growing love for Robert Browning, whom she married, in defiance of her father's wishes, in her fortieth year. "My little Portuguese" was a pet name Robert often used for Elizabeth: hence the title of her book.

Teachers not opposed to biographical interpretations might direct their students to the notes on both Brownings in the "Lives of the Poets" chapter.

Robert Browning, SOLILOQUY OF THE SPANISH CLOISTER, page 790

The "Soliloquy" is a poem especially valuable to combat the notion that poetry can deal only in love and gladness. Here, the subject is a hatred so intense that the speaker seems practically demented. In the last stanza, he almost would sell his soul to the Devil in order to blight a flowering shrub. A little background information on abbeys, their organization, and the strictness of their rules may help some class members. From internal evidence, it is hard to say whether this is a sixteenth-century cloister or a nineteenth-century one; Barbary corsairs (line 31) plied their trade from about 1550 until 1816. The business about drinking in three sips (lines 37–39) may need explaining: evidently it refers to a symbolic observance, like crossing knife and fork.

It might be stressed that the person in this poem is not the poet: the tone isn't one of bitterness, but of merriment. Comedy is evident not only from the speaker's blindness to his own faults, but from the rollicking rhythm and multisyllable comic rimes *(abhorrence/Lawrence; horsehairs/corsairs; Galatians/damnations; rose-acacia/Plena gratia).*

Questions: With what sins does the speaker charge Brother Lawrence? (Pride, line 23—monogrammed tableware belonging to a monk!; lust, 25–32; and gluttony, 40.) What sins do we detect in the speaker himself? (Envy, clearly, and pride—see his holier-than-thou attitude in stanza 5. How persuasive are his claims to piety when we learn he secretly owns a pornographic novel?) "Soliloquy" abounds in ironies, and class members can spend a lively few minutes in pointing them out.

Samuel Taylor Coleridge, KUBLA KHAN, page 792

The circumstances of this poem's composition are almost as famous as the poem itself, and, for the convenience of instructors who wish to read to their students Coleridge's prefatory note, here it is:

> In the summer of the year 1797, the author, then in ill health, had retired to a lonely farmhouse between Porlock and Linton, on the Exmoor confines of Somerset and Devonshire. In consequence of a slight indisposition, an anodyne had been prescribed, from the effects of which he fell asleep in his chair at the moment that he was reading the following sentence, or words of the same substance, in *Purchas's Pilgrimage:* "Here the Khan Kubla commanded a palace to be built, and a stately garden thereunto. And thus ten miles of fertile ground were inclosed with a wall." The author continued for about three hours in a profound sleep, at least of the external sense, during which time he had the most vivid confidence that he could not have composed less than from two to three hundred lines; if that indeed can be called composition in which all the images rose up before him as *things*, with a parallel production of the correspondent expressions, without any sensation or consciousness of effort. On awaking he appeared to himself to have a distinct recollection of the whole, and taking his pen, ink, and paper, instantly and eagerly wrote down the lines that are here preserved. At this moment he was unfortunately called out by a person on busi-

ness from Porlock, and detained by him above an hour, and on his return to his room, found, to his no small surprise and mortification, that though he still retained some vague and dim recollection of the general purport of his vision, yet, with the exception of some eight or ten scattered lines and images, all the rest had passed away like the images on the surface of a stream into which a stone has been cast, but, alas! without the after restoration of the latter!

It is clearly a vulgar error to think the poem a mere pipe dream, which anyone could have written with the aid of opium. The profound symbolism of "Kubla Khan" has continued to intrigue critics, most of whom find that the pleasure-dome suggests poetry, the sacred river, the flow of inspiration, or instinctual life. About the *ancestral voices* and the *caves of ice* there seems less agreement, and students might be invited to venture their guesses. For a valuable modern reading of the poem, see Humphry House, "Kubla Khan, Christable and Dejection" in *Coleridge* (London: Hart-Davis, 1953), also reprinted in *Romanticism and Consciousness*, ed. Harold Bloom (New York: Norton, 1970).

Some instructors may wish to bring in "The Rime of the Ancient Mariner" as well—in which case it may be a temptation to go on to Jung's theory of archetypes and to other dreamlike poems such as Yeats's "The Second Coming." A fine topic for a term paper might be, after reading John Livingston Lowes's classic source study *The Road to Xanadu* (Boston: Houghton, 1927), to argue whether it is worth trying to find out everything that may have been going on in the back of a poet's mind, and to what extent such investigations can end in certainty.

E. E. *Cummings*, SOMEWHERE I HAVE NEVER TRAVELLED, GLADLY BEYOND, page 793

Why is this exquisite love poem so rarely anthologized? Cummings surely ranks as one of the great love poets in American literature, and this evocative lyric is one of his finest efforts. Many readers prize it greatly. We recently received a wedding announcement that reprinted the poem, and Woody Allen included the entire poem at a pivotal moment in *Hannah and Her Sisters*. The striking last line is one of the most famous in modern American poetry, and serves as epigraph to Tennessee Williams's *The Glass Menagerie*.

The central image of the poem is a rose which the speaker equates with himself. (If one adopted a biographical strategy by which to interpret the text, it is worthwhile to note that Cummings wrote the poem for Anne Barton, an artist's model, whom he married in 1929 and divorced in 1932 after she left him for a wealthy New York surgeon. The interesting aspect of a biographical view is that Cummings's speaker uses the flower image, traditionally a female image, for himself and it becomes a symbol of sexual and emotional awakening in the presence of his beloved.)

The poem moves via paradox and synesthesia. Eyes are "silent." The speaker cannot touch things because "they are too near." Fragility is portrayed as "intense." The effect is to endow the situation with strangeness and mystery. Words are used oddly, the lover's looks *unclose* the speaker. Punctuation is employed for expressive purposes, and normal word order is changed to heighten its musical and semantic effect as in the lovely lines "you open always petal by petal myself as Spring opens

/ (touching skilfully,mysteriously)her first rose." All of these effects are used subtly and unexpectedly. Cummings carefully avoids repeating any verbal trick too often in this poem. Even the form of the poem is alluringly elusive. Many lines slip into iambic pentameter, but the poem never falls into a predictable rhythmic pattern. There are also rhymes hidden throughout the poem, but only in the last stanza do they appear conventionally at the ends of the lines. The sheer density of beautifully employed poetic effects and the constant shifting from one effect to another create an intoxicating almost hypnotic spell on the listener.

John Donne, DEATH BE NOT PROUD, page 794

During the Renaissance, when life was short, a man of the cloth like Donne would have surprised no one by being on familiar terms with death. Still, "Death be not proud," one of Donne's "Holy Sonnets," is an almost startling put-down of "poor death." Staunchly Christian in its sure expectation of the resurrection, Donne's poem personifies death as an adversary swollen with false pride and unworthy of being called "mighty and dreadful." (For another bold personification, see "Batter my heart, three-personed God," also one of the "Holy Sonnets," in which Donne sees God as ravisher.)

In "Death be not proud" the poet accuses death of being little more than a slave bossed around by "fate, chance, kings and desperate men"—a craven thing that keeps bad company, such as "poison, war, and sickness." Finally Donne taunts death with a paradox: "death, thou shalt die."

Of interest, though perhaps of less than immediate usefulness in the classroom, are the articles on Donne's religious poetry by Helen Gardner, Louis L. Martz, and Stanley Archer in *John Donne's Poetry: Authoritative Texts, Criticism*, ed. A. L. Clements (New York: Norton, 1966). All three explore the extent to which Jesuit methods of meditation might have influenced the "Holy Sonnets."

It might be instructive for students to compare two personifications of death: Donne's and Emily Dickinson's in "Because I could not stop for Death," where death appears in the guise of a courtly gentleman who stops by to take the poet for a pleasant ride.

John Donne, THE FLEA, page 795

This outrageous poem is a good class-rouser on a dull day, but we don't urge you to use it unless the class seems friendly. (Some women students tend to be offended by Donne's levity; men tend to be put off by his ingenuity.)

A little familiarity with a seventeenth-century medical notion may help make Donne's metaphor clear. Conception, it was thought, took place when the blood of men and women mingled during intercourse. That is why Donne declares in line 11 that "we almost, yea more than married are." Bitten by the flea containing his blood, the woman may already be pregnant.

Instructors fond of Donne's knotty poems will be grateful for Theodore Redpath's valuable crib-book *The Songs and Sonnets of John Donne* (London: Methuen, 1956; also New York: University Paperbacks, 1967). Redpath works through the poems line by line, explicating difficulties. He explains line 18: The woman would commit "three sins in killing three" in that she'd commit murder in killing him, suicide in killing herself, and sacrilege in killing the flea. Why sacrilege? Because she would be attacking a "marriage temple."

Patricia Meyer Spacks has treated the poem to scrutiny in *College English* 29 (1968): 593–94.

Rita Dove, DAYSTAR, page 795

What suggestions can be found in the title of Dove's poem? The word is a trove of connotations. You may wish to make sure at the start that your students are familiar with the dictionary meaning of *daystar*: the morning star or, poetically, the sun. From the poem's last line, we infer that it was the sun the poet had in mind. Why *daystar* instead of sun? Does the word suggest to the poet, as to us, joy and happiness? Also, a star is a "self-luminous, self-containing mass of gas in which the energy generated by nuclear reactions in the interior is balanced by the outflow of energy to the surface and the inward-directed gravitational forces are balanced by the outward-directed gas and radiation pressures." Perhaps the poet is suggesting that a similar state of balance is what the wife and mother in the poem seeks—and finds—when she sits behind the garage, "building a palace," while her children are taking their naps. The chance to daydream in solitude sustains her not only through her toils but "that night when Thomas rolled over and / lurched into her."

Thomas and Beulah, in which "Daystar" appears, won the 1987 Pulitzer Prize for poetry. The book contains a series of poems about the lives and concerns of an ordinary black couple.

In 1993, Rita Dove became the U.S. Poet Laureate, the first African American to hold this prestigious position.

T. S. Eliot, THE LOVE SONG OF J. ALFRED PRUFROCK, page 796

Teaching any basic course in literature, an instructor would have to be desperate for time not to devote to "Prufrock" at least a class or two. Eliot's early masterpiece can open such diverse matters as theme, tone, irony, persona, imagery, figures of speech, allusion, symbolism, and the difference between saying and suggesting. Most students will enjoy it and remember it.

QUESTIONS FOR DISCUSSION:

1. *Why the epigraph from Dante? What expectations does it arouse?* Perhaps that this "song" will be the private confession of someone who thinks himself trapped and unredeemable, and thinks it of his hearer, too.

2. *What facts about J. Alfred can we be sure of? His age, his manner of dress, his social circles? What does his name suggest? Can you detect any puns in it?* A prude in a frock—a formal coat.

3. *What do you make of the simile in lines 2–3? What does it tell us about this particular evening? Etherized* suggests fog, also submission, waiting for something

grim to happen. *What does it tell you about Prufrock's way of seeing things?* "A little sick," some students may say, and with reason.

4. *What gnaws at Prufrock?* Not just his sense of growing old, not just his inability to act. He suffers from Prufrock's Complaint: dissociation of sensibility. In line 105, unable to join thought and feeling, he sees his own nerves existing at one remove from him, as if thrown on a screen by a projector.

5. *Who are "you and I" in the opening line? Who are "we" at the end?* Some possibilities: Prufrock and the woman he is attending. Prufrock and the reader. Prufrock and Prufrock—he's talking to himself, "you" being the repressive self, "I" being the timid or repressed self. Prufrock and the other eggheads of the Western world—in this view, the poem is Eliot's satire on the intelligentsia.

6. *What symbols do you find and what do they suggest? Notice those that relate to the sea, even* oyster-shells *(line 7).* XJK points out blatantly that water has connotations of sexual fulfillment, and quotes "Western Wind." Eliot hints that unlike Prufrock, the vulgar types who inhabit cheap hotels and fish shops have a love life.

7. *Try to explain the last three lines.*

8. *Now summarize the story of the poem. What parts does it fall into?* Part one: Prufrock prepares to try to ask the overwhelming question. Then in lines 84–86 we learn that he has failed to ask it. In 87–110 he tries to justify himself for chickening out. From 111 to the end, he sums up his static present and hollow future.

That Eliot may have taken the bones of his plot from Henry James's story "Crapy Cornelia" (1909) is Grover Smith's convincing theory. "This is the story of White-Mason, a middle-aged bachelor of nostalgic temperament, who visits a young Mrs. Worthington to propose marriage but reconsiders owing to the difference in their worlds." (*T. S. Eliot's Poetry and Plays* [Chicago: U of Chicago P, 1960] 15).

"The meter of 'Prufrock' is peculiar," observes John Heath-Stubbs. "It is not simply free verse, as in [Eliot's] earlier Laforgueian pieces, but in its lines of irregular length, many but not all of which rhyme, suggests a free version of the Dantesque Canzone." This suggestion, and the poem's epigraph from the *Inferno*, point to Eliot's growing preoccupation with Dante ("Structure and Source in Eliot's Major Poetry," *Agenda* [Spring–Summer 1985]: 24).

T. S. Eliot Reading His Poetry (Caedmon recording TC 1045) includes the poet's rendition of "Prufrock."

Cleanth Brooks has written an essay full of wisdom and practical advice, "Teaching 'The Love Song of J. Alfred Prufrock,'" which you can find in *Eliot's Poetry and Plays*, one of the MLA's valuable "Approaches to Teaching" series (1988).

Louise Erdrich, INDIAN BOARDING SCHOOL: THE RUNAWAYS, page 801

For discussion: Have you ever been somewhere you wanted to run away home from? If so, how does your memory of that experience compare with that of the speaker in this poem?

This poem is long on wounds: the railroad tracks are scars (6), the runaways' old welts are like roads (15), the names they wrote in wet cement and the leaves they pressed into the sidewalk before it dried recall "delicate old injuries" (22–24). All these things carry powerful connotations of being wounded, mistreated, beaten down—like the runaways themselves.

Jacklight (New York: Holt, 1984), the collection in which this poem appears, contains several other realistic poems of Indian life. Since the success of *Love Medicine* (1984), *The Beet Queen* (1986), and *Tracks* (1988), Louise Erdrich is best known as a novelist, but we think her poetry warrants attention too.

Erdrich, born in Little Falls, Minnesota, grew up in Wahpeton, North Dakota, and now lives in New Hampshire.

Robert Frost, BIRCHES, page 801

"Birches," according to Lawrance Thompson, was written during a spell of homesickness in 1913–14, when Frost and his family were living in Beaconsfield, Buckinghamshire, England (*Robert Frost: The Years of Triumph* [New York: Holt, 1970] 37, 541).

Students may be led to see the poem as much more than a nostalgic picture of boyhood play. From line 43 on, the poem develops a flamboyant metaphor. Richard Poirier has given us a good summary of the poem's theme; "While there are times when the speaker [of "Birches"] would 'like to get away from earth awhile,' his aspiration for escape to something 'larger' is safely controlled by the recognition that birch trees will only bear so much climbing before returning you, under the pressure of human weight, back home" (*Robert Frost: The Work of Knowing* [Oxford: Oxford UP, 1977] 172).

One line in "Birches" meant most to Frost, the line about feeling lost in the woods, facing too many decisions about which way to go. He pointed it out to audiences on several occasions: "It's when I'm weary of considerations" (line 43). Reading the poem at Bread Loaf in July 1954, he remarked of the line, "That's when you get older. It didn't mean so much to me when I wrote it as it does now" (*Robert Frost: A Living Voice,* ed. Reginald Cook [Boston: U of Mass P, 1974] 51). Radcliffe Squires has written interestingly of the birch tree as a path toward heaven fraught with risk, suspense, even a kind of terror. The climbing boy performs his act of birch-bending gracefully, but in doing so goes almost too far, like one filling a cup "even above the brim" (*The Major Themes of Robert Frost* [Ann Arbor: U of Michigan P, 1963] 55–56).

Sidelights on the poem: Frost wrote to his friend, Charles Madison, in 1950, "'Birches' is two fragments soldered together so long ago I have forgotten where the joint is." Can anybody find it? . . . A particular word he congratulated himself on finding was *crazes* in line 9: "cracks and crazes their enamel" (Cook, 230).

Frost's concern for scientific accuracy is well known. He sought evidence to confirm his claim that birches bend to left and right. "With disarming slyness, he said: 'I never go down the shoreline [from Boston] to New York without watching the birches to see if they live up to what I say about them in the poem.' His birches, he insisted, were *not* the white mountain or paper birch of northern New England *(Betula papyrifera)*; they were the gray birch *(Betula populifolia)*" (Cook, 232).

Robert Frost, MENDING WALL, page 803

This familiar poem is often misread, or loaded with needless symbolism. Some possible notions you might meet:

1. That the poem is an allegory: the wall stands for some political barrier such as segregation, immigration quotas, or the Iron Curtain. But can the text of the poem lend such a notion any support? Frost, according to Louis Untermeyer, frowned on all attempts to add to the wall's meaning: "He denies that the poem says anything more than it seems to say" (Note in *Robert Frost's Poems* [New York: Washington Square P, 1964]).

2. Frost's theme is that fences should be destroyed. Up with communal land, away with private property! But as Radcliffe Squires points out, none of Frost's other poetry supports such a left-wing view. Neither does "Mending Wall" support it, "for the poet-narrator himself cooperates with the wall-builder, replacing the stones in the spring even as he protests in spirit" (*The Major Themes of Robert Frost* [Ann Arbor: U of Michigan P, 1963]).

3. The maxim "Good fences make good neighbors" is just a smug platitude for which the speaker has only contempt. This view would make him out to be a cynic. Yet, by cooperating in the wall-mending, the speaker lends the maxim some truth. Although limited in imagination, the neighbor isn't an idiot. (Frost is portraying, by the way, an actual farmer he liked: the cheerful Napoleon Guay, owner of the farm next door to the Frosts' farm in Derry, New Hampshire. See *New Hampshire's Child: The Derry Journals of Leslie Frost* [Albany: State U of New York P, 1969].)

At the center of the poem is a contrast between two ways to regard mending a wall. The speaker's view is announced in the first line; the neighbor's is repeated in the last. "The opposing statements," says Untermeyer, "are uttered by two different types of people—and both are right." Students may be asked to define the very different temperaments of speaker and neighbor. A hard-working farmer to whom spring means walls to mend, the neighbor lacks fancy and frivolity. Spring is all around him, yet he *moves in darkness*, as though blind. Lines 30–40 compare him to a man of the Stone Age. A conservative from habit, he mends walls mainly because his father did. The speaker, full of mischief and imagination, is presumably a poet who wants to do no more hard labor than he can help. The speaker enjoys having some fun with the neighbor, telling him that apple trees won't invade pines. Mending walls is a kind of spring ritual, and the speaker likes to pretend there is magic in it: using a spell to make stones balance, blaming the wear-and-tear of winter upon elves—or more exactly, upon some Something not to be offended.

Robert Frost, STOPPING BY WOODS ON A SNOWY EVENING, page 804

Students will think they know this poem from their elementary school textbooks, in which it is usually illustrated as though it were about a little horse, but they may need to have its darker suggestions underlined for them. Although one can present a powerful case for seeing Frost as a spokesman for the death wish, quoting other Frost poems such as "Come In," "To Earthward," and "Into My Own," we think it best to concentrate on this familiar poem and to draw the class to state what it implies. The last stanza holds the gist of it. What would he do if he *didn't* keep his promises? There is sense, however, in an objection a student once made: maybe he'd just stay admiring the snow for another fifteen minutes and be late for milking. "People are always trying to find a death wish in that poem," Frost told an audience at the Bread Loaf Writers' Conference in 1960. "But there's a life wish there—he goes on, doesn't he?"

Ask students if they see anything unusual about the rime scheme of the poem (rimes linking the stanzas as in *terza rima* or as in Shelley's "Ode to the West Wind"), and then ask what problem this rime scheme created for the poet as the poem neared its end. How else would Frost have ended it if he hadn't hit upon that magnificent repetition? In 1950 Frost wrote to a friend, "I might confess the trade secret that I wrote the third line of the last stanza of 'Stopping by Woods' in such a way as to call for another stanza when I didn't want another stanza and didn't have another stanza in me, but with great presence of mind and a sense of what a good boy I was I instantly struck the line out and made my exit with a repeat end" (qtd. in Lawrance Thompson, *Robert Frost: The Years of Triumph* [New York: Holt, 1970] 597–98). On another occasion Frost declared that to have a line in the last stanza that didn't rime with anything would have seemed a flaw. "I considered for a moment winding up with a three line stanza. The repetend was the only logical way to end such a poem" (letter of 1923 to Sylvester Baxter, given by R. C. Townsend, *New England Quarterly* 36 [June 1963]: 243).

That this famous poem may be sung to the old show tune "Hernando's Hideaway" (from *The Pajama Game*) was discovered by college students working as waiters at the Bread Loaf Writers' Conference in 1960.

Paper topic: Read Lionel Trilling's speech at Frost's eighty-fifth birthday dinner, in which Trilling maintained, "I think of Robert Frost as a terrifying poet" ("A Speech on Robert Frost: A Cultural Episode," *Partisan Review* 26 [Summer 1959]: 445–52; also reprinted in *Robert Frost: A Collection of Critical Essays*, ed. James M. Cox [Englewood Cliffs: Prentice, 1962]). Referring to "Stopping by Woods" and other Frost poems, state to what extent you agree with Trilling's view or disagree with it.

Frost reads the poem on *An Album of Modern Poetry* (Library of Congress, PL 20) and on *Robert Frost Reading His Own Poems*, record no. 1 (EL LCB 1941, obtainable from the National Council of Teachers of English, 1211 Kenyon Road, Urbana, IL 61801). Both recordings also include "Fire and Ice."

Allen Ginsberg, A SUPERMARKET IN CALIFORNIA, page 805

A comparison of this poem with Walt Whitman's "I Saw in Louisiana a Live-Oak Growing" and "To a Locomotive in Winter" demonstrates the extent to which Ginsberg, in his tribute to Whitman, uses very Whitmanlike "enumerations." Ginsberg's long sentences, use of free verse, parentheses, and fulsome phrases ("childless, lonely old grubber," "lonely old courage-teacher," etc.) are further indications that he is paying tribute to Whitman in part by echoing his style.

There is in "A Supermarket in California" as well a quality of surrealism that is Ginsberg's own. The existence of a "Neon fruit supermarket," the juxtaposition of past and present, the inclusion of Spanish poet García Lorca (like Ginsberg and Whitman, a homosexual) "down by the watermelons," and the references to Charon and to the River Lethe all hover at the edges of dream.

Questions for discussion: What does Ginsberg mean when he speaks of "the lost America of love"? What does the poem say about loneliness? about death? (Whitman's death, in the poem, is as lonely a journey as Ginsberg imagines his life to have been.)

Dana Gioia, CALIFORNIA HILLS IN AUGUST, page 806

When this poem was first added to this anthology in 1986, Dana Gioia provided the following note (little suspecting he would one day become a co-conspirator in editing future editions of the book):

> "California Hills in August" was conceived as a defense of the special beauty of the dry landscape of California and the American Southwest. While the poem admits that an outsider might initially find this environment harsh and even hostile in the summer months, it asks that the landscape be seen on its own terms and not judged as some deficient form of conventionally verdant summer scenery.
>
> Strangely, I did not write this poem until I had been living in the Northeast for several years. It was only then that I realized how foreign the sparse August hills of California seemed to most Americans who came from areas which are lushly green and overgrown during the summer. Likewise, living back East, I finally understood how much the symbolic framework of traditional English poetry depended on the particular kind of climate shared by England and Eastern America. Until then the seasonal patterns of this poetry with its snowy winters and green summers had always seemed remote and artificial to a Westerner like me, raised in a climate which endowed a radically different sense of Nature's cycles. I wondered why Western writers had not played with that paradox more forcefully in their poetry.
>
> These thoughts must have been in the back of my mind when suddenly I returned home for a family emergency. Two sleepless days later, after it had been resolved, I took a noontime walk through some nearby hills. In the strangely heightened consciousness of physical exhaustion and dislocating travel, I found myself overwhelmed by the delicate, sun-

bleached beauty of the place. This was a landscape which I had left long enough ago both to hunger for as a native and to recoil from as an outsider. Sorting out these contradictions as I walked home, I heard myself say the first few lines of the poem. Writing out the opening stanzas later that day, I realized how image by image this poem had been forming for a long time in my unconscious.

The poem divides into two uneven parts. The first four stanzas view the landscape through the eyes of an imaginary Easterner who sees only the emptiness, deprivation, and savagery of the place. But then in the final stanza the speaker suddenly upsets everything said up to this point by suggesting how a native might see the same place from a different perspective. Isn't one of the purposes of poetry to make us see the unexpected beauty of some person, place or thing we previously took for granted or dismissed? That transformation was what I hoped to accomplish in "California Hills in August."

Thom Gunn, THE MAN WITH NIGHT SWEATS, page 807

Thom Gunn's particular genius has been to embody the human and artistic contradictions of his age. Reading his extravagantly diverse *Collected Poems* (1994), one finds poems on LSD and San Francisco street hustlers next to lyrics on Catholic saints and Caravaggio—all of them recognizably drawn from the same imagination. Gunn is the crown prince of incongruity, a Romantic entranced by classical control, an experimentalist who never renounced rhyme and meter, an anti-authoritarian ruled by mandarin standards.

When Gunn first came to California from England in 1954, he was only twenty-five but had already published a celebrated book of poems. Having won a writing fellowship to Stanford, the young gay poet with "a promiscuous love of experience" studied with the famously rigorous Yvor Winters. Gunn's already incisive style sharpened under Winters's formalist tutelage, but his tone and subject kept their rebellious edge. His second book may have begun with rhymed iambic stanzas, but they described a motorcycle gang on the move.

Gunn's greatest moment as a poet came at his most difficult time—the AIDS epidemic. In a single month he lost four close friends. Out of this personal and public crisis grew *The Man with Night Sweats* (1992), which will probably stand as the finest poetic testament of those plague years. While most AIDS poetry relied on naked grief and raw emotion, Gunn's lucid but lyric meditations were simultaneously realistic and transcendent. He did not merely give voice to the lost—he gave them poetry, as in the title piece, which begins: "I wake up cold, I who / Prospered through dreams of heat / Wake to their residue, / Sweat, and a clinging sheet."

The speaker in Gunn's poem faces the impending certainty of his own death. The language is precisely phrased and classically balanced in the tradition of English death poems like Chidiock Tichborne's "Elegy" or John Keats's "When I have fears that I may cease to be." Both of those earlier poems would provide illuminating contrasts for class discussion or possible student essays. What words would suffice to face one's own death?

Thomas Hardy, THE CONVERGENCE OF THE TWAIN, page 807

The discovery in September 1985 of the well-preserved wreck of the *Titanic* in the North Atlantic, and the subsequent squabble over possession of it, has given this old favorite poem a certain immediacy. Most students will be familiar with the history of this great disaster from news reports or from the many popular films and books. Still, a few facts may need to be recalled. The fateful day was April 15, 1912. The pride of the British White Star lines, the *Titanic* was the world's largest ship in its day, celebrated for luxurious trappings (including Turkish baths and a fully equipped gym). Many of the unlucky passengers were wealthy and famous. One reason the *Titanic* sank with such cost of life was that the builders, smugly assuming the ship to be unsinkable, had provided lifeboats for fewer than half the 2,200 passengers. (Only 705 survived.) Hardy wrote the poem for the souvenir program of a benefit show for the *Titanic* Disaster Fund (to aid survivors and the bereaved) given at Covent Garden, May 14, 1912.

Hardy has been seen as an enemy of science and industrialism, those spoilers of rural England, but Donald Davie argues that "The Convergence of the Twain" shows no such animosity. The poem censures vanity and luxury, "but not the technology which built the great ship and navigated her" (*Thomas Hardy and British Poetry* [Oxford: Oxford UP, 1972]). Although Hardy personally knew two victims of the disaster, the "Convergence," as J. O. Bailey points out, is not a personal lament; indeed, the drowned are hardly mentioned. The poem is a philosophic argument, with the Immanent Will punishing man for pride: "It acts like the Greek concept of Fate that rebukes *hubris*" (*The Poetry of Thomas Hardy* [Chapel Hill: U of North Carolina P, 1970]). Fate, however, seems personified in the poem as the Spinner of the Years, a mere agent of the Will.

Students can concentrate profitably on the poet's choice of words: those that suggest the exotic unnaturalness of the *Titanic's* furnishings *(salamandrine, opulent, jewels . . . to ravish the sensuous mind, gilded).* Diction will also point to the metaphor of the marriage between ship and iceberg: the *intimate welding* and the *consummation.* The late Allen Tate was fond of reading this poem aloud to his friends, with mingled affection and contempt, and remarking (according to Robert Kent) that it held "too many dead words, dead then as now, and all the more obtuse for having been long dead in Shelley. 'Stilly,' for example." From Hardy's original printed version of the poem, as given in *The Variorum Edition of the Complete Poems of Thomas Hardy,* ed. James Gibson (New York: Macmillan, 1979), it appears that he originally cast line 6: "The cold, calm currents strike their rhythmic tidal lyres." Isn't *thrid* an improvement, even though it is stiltedly archaic?

Robert Hayden, THOSE WINTER SUNDAYS, page 809

QUESTIONS FOR DISCUSSION:

1. Is the speaker a boy or a man? How do you know?

2. Summarize the poem's theme—its main idea.

3. What do you understand from "the chronic angers of that house"?

4. How does this poet's choice of words differ from that of most writers of prose? Suggestion: Read the opening five lines aloud.

This brief poem, simple in the word's best sense, has a depth that rewards close reading. That the speaker is a boy is a safe inference: most grown-ups do not lie abed while their fathers polish their shoes. Besides, evidently years have intervened between the speaker today and his previous self—the observing child. Now the speaker understands his father better, looks back on himself, and asks, "What did I know?"

The poem states its theme in its wonderful last line (worth quoting to anyone who distrusts abstract words in poetry). Students can miss Hayden's point unless they understand its vocabulary. *Austere* can mean stern, forbidding, somber, but it can also mean (as it does here) ascetic, disciplined, self-denying. To rise in the freezing house takes steely self-discipline. That the father's life is built on austerity we get from his labor-worn hands. What is an *office*? A duty, task, or ceremony that someone assumes (or has conferred on him): the tasks of shining shoes, of stirring banked fires in a furnace (or a coal-burning stove?). James Wright, a keen admirer of Hayden's poem, has spoken of it in an interview:

> The word *offices* is the great word here. *Office*, they say in French. It is a religious service after dark. Its formality, its combination of distance and immediacy, is appropriate. In my experience uneducated people and people who are driven by brute circumstance to work terribly hard for a living, the living of their families, are very big on formality. (*The Pure Clear Word: Essays on the Poetry of James Wright*, ed. Dave Smith [Urbana: U of Illinois P, 1982] 10)

Perhaps the "chronic angers" belong to the father: the boy gets up slowly and fearfully as though in dread of a tongue-lashing. Yet this reading does not seem quite in keeping with the character of the father as he emerges: stoic, patient, long-suffering, loving. Hayden does not invest these angers in the father exclusively. Perhaps any tenant of this bitterly cold house has reason to dread getting up in it.

When read aloud, the opening stanza reveals strong patterns of sound: the internal alliteration of the *k*-sound in *blueblack, cracked, ached, weekday, banked, thanked* (and, in the next stanza, in *wake, breaking, chronic*)—staccato bursts of hard consonants. Rather than using exact rime at the ends of lines, Hayden strengthens lines by using it internally: *banked/thanked* (line 5), *wake/breaking* (6); perhaps off-rime, too: *labor/weather* (4), *rise/dress* (8). Alliteration and assonance occur in *clothes . . . cold* (2), *weekday weather* (4). If you assign this poem early in your investigation of poetry, probably it matters more that students hear and respond to the rich interplay of repeated sounds than that they be able to give these devices labels.

"Those Winter Sundays" is the most often reprinted poem of Robert Hayden. A black poet who grew up in Detroit and who for many years was an English professor at the University of Michigan, he has written other poems apparently drawn from childhood and memory, among these "Obituary," another moving tribute to his father. Hayden's posthumous *Collected Poems* (New York: Norton/Liveright, 1985) belongs, we think, in every library.

Seamus Heaney, DIGGING, page 810

When Irish poet Seamus Heaney went to Lewiston, Maine, in 1986 to receive an honorary degree at Bates College, he read "Digging" aloud to the assembled graduates, parents, and friends. It seemed an appropriate choice. Some of the Maine students in his audience must have found expressed in Heaney's poem their own ambition for hardworking forebears whose course through life they had decided not to follow. Is the speaker in the poem uneasy about choosing instead to be a poet? It is clear that he admires the skill and strength his father and grandfather displayed in their work. But the poem ends on a positive note. The poet accepts himself for what he is.

In "Feeling into Words," an essay in his *Preoccupations* (New York: Farrar, 1980), Heaney likens the poetry to digging up archaeological finds. Apparently it is a matter of digging a spade into one's past and unearthing something forgotten. "Digging," written in 1964, was his earliest poem in which it seemed that his feelings had found words. "The pen/spade analogy," he adds, "was the simple heart of the matter and *that* was simply a matter of almost proverbial common sense." As a schoolboy, he was often told to keep studying "because 'learning's easily carried' and 'the pen is lighter than the spade.'"

George Herbert, LOVE, page 811

Herbert's poem is often read as an account of a person's reception into the Church; the eaten *meat*, as the Eucharist. Herbert's extended conceits or metaphors are also evident in "Redemption."

For discussion: compare "Love" with another seventeenth-century devotional poem, Donne's "Batter my heart." What is the tone of each poem? Herbert may seem less intense, almost reticent by comparison. Douglas Bush comments, "Herbert does not attempt the high pitch of Donne's 'Divine Poems.' His great effects are all the greater for rising out of a homely, colloquial quietness of tone; and peace brings quiet endings—'So I did sit and eat'" (*English Literature in the Earlier Seventeenth Century* [New York: Oxford UP, 1945] 139).

Herbert, by the way, is an Anglican saint—the only one who does not also appear in the Roman Catholic calendar.

Robert Herrick, TO THE VIRGINS, TO MAKE MUCH OF TIME, page 812

Roses would have suited Herrick's iambic meter—why is *rose-buds* richer? Rosebuds are flowers not yet mature, and therefore suggest virgins, not matrons. There may be a sexual hint besides: rosebuds more resemble private parts than roses. But in this poem, time flies, the rosebuds of line 1 bloom in line 3. Rose-buds is also rhythmically stronger than roses, as Austin Warren has pointed out: it has a secondary stress as well as a primary. Warren has recalled that when he first read the poem in college in 1917, he misread *rose-buds* as *roses*, kept misreading it ever after, and only a half-century later realized his mistake and found a new poem in front of him. "In untutored youth, the sentiment and the rhythm suffice: the exactness of the language goes unnoticed. And in later life a remembered favorite escapes exact attention because we think we know it so well" ("Herrick Revisited," *Michigan Quarterly Review* 15 [Summer 1976]: 245–67).

Question for discussion: What do you think of Herrick's advice? Are there any perils in it?

Gerard Manley Hopkins, SPRING AND FALL, page 813

Hopkins's tightly wrought syntax may need a little unraveling. Students may be asked to reword lines 3–4 in a more usual sequence ("Can you, with your fresh thoughts, care for leaves like the things of man?") and then to put the statement into more usual words. (An attempt: "Do you, young and innocent as you are, feel as sorry for falling leaves as for dying people?") Lines 12–13 may need a similar going-over and rough paraphrase. ("Neither any human mouth nor any human mind has previously formed the truth that the heart and spirit have intuited.") "Sorrow's springs are the same"—that is, all human sorrows have the same cause: the fact that all things pass away. A world of constant change is "the blight man was born for": an earth subject to death, having fallen from its original state of a changeless Eden. The difficulties of a Hopkins poem result from a swiftly thoughtful mind trying to jam all possible meaning into a brief space (and into words that are musical).

Wanwood is evidently a term the poet coined for pale autumn woods. W. H. Gardner, editor of Hopkins's poems, finds in it also the suggestion of "wormwood"—bitter gall, also wood that is worm-eaten. The term *leafmeal* reminds him of "piecemeal," and he paraphrases line 8: "One by one the leaves fall, and then rot into mealy fragments."

Gerard Manley Hopkins, THE WINDHOVER, page 814

"The best thing I ever wrote," said Hopkins. If your students have enjoyed "Pied Beauty" or "God's Grandeur" without too much difficulty, then why not try "The Windhover," despite its famous ambiguities? Some students may go afield in reading the opening line, and may take *I caught* to mean that the poet trapped the bird; but they can be told that Hopkins, a great condenser, probably means "I caught a glimpse of."

Dispute over the poem often revolves around whether or not the windhover is Christ and around the meaning of *Buckle!* Most commentators seem to agree that the bird is indeed Christ, or else that Christ is like the bird. (Yvor Winters, who thought the poem "minor and imperfect," once complained, "To describe a bird, however beautifully, and to imply that Christ is like him but greater, is to do very little toward indicating the greatness of Christ.") Some read *Buckle!* as a plea to the bird to descend to earth; others, as a plea to all the qualities and things mentioned in line 9 (*Brute beauty, valor, act*) to buckle themselves together into one.

Still others find the statement ending in *Buckle!* no plea at all, but just an emphatic observation of what the poet beholds. If Christ is the windhover (other arguments run), in what sense can he be said to buckle? Two of the answers: (1) in buckling on human nature and becoming man, as a knight buckles on armor; (2) in having his body broken on the cross. Students can be asked to seek all the words in the poem with connotations of royalty or chivalry—suggestive, perhaps, of Christ as King and Christ as noble knight or chevalier. Why the *sheer plod?* Hopkins reflects (it would seem) that if men will only buckle down to their lowly duties they will become more Christ-like, and their spiritual plowshares will shine instead of collecting rust. Hopkins preached a sermon that expressed a similar idea: "Through poverty, through labor, through crucifixion His majesty of nature more shines." The *embers*, we think, are a metaphor: moist clods thrown by the plow going down the sillion. Hopkins likes to compare things to hearth fire: for instance, the "fresh-firecoal chestnut-falls" in "Pied Beauty."

For detailed criticism, one might start with Norman H. MacKenzie, *A Reader's Guide to Gerard Manley Hopkins* (Ithaca: Cornell UP, 1981). MacKenzie provides facts from ornithology and his own kestrel-watching: no other birds are so expert in hovering, body horizontal, tail and head pointing down as they study the ground for prey. To hang stationary in the air over one spot, they must fly into the wind "with rapidly quivering (*wimpling,* line 4) wings, missing a few beats as gusts die, accelerating as they freshen"—responding to variations in the wind with nearly computer speed. Once in about every eight hovers, the kestrel will dive, not inertly but with wings held tense and high—it doesn't "buckle" in the sense of *collapse.* If it finds no victim, the bird swings and banks and takes an upward "stride," to hover once more. Hopkins's "how he rung upon the rein" doesn't mean that the kestrel climbs in a spiral. No gyring Yeats-bird, he.

An interesting view of the religious imagery informing this poem can be found in James Finn Cotter's study, *Inscape: The Christology and Poetry of Gerard Manley Hopkins* (Pittsburgh: U of Pittsburgh P, 1972). Cotter, who is formidably learned in theology, examines traditional Christian writings to discover how they shaped Hopkins's sense of imagery. Cotter maintains that "Hopkins fashioned a myth of his own making," but that his private vision drew from a wide variety of philosophical and theological sources. In his long, careful reading of "The Windhover" Cotter observes:

> Circular motion and form dominate "The Windhover": the kestrel moves in slow, wide, sharp, and gliding circles which the rhythm and language perfectly mimic. Christ is present here as throughout the other sonnets, in the sun illuminating the scene; he is the dawn drawing the bird to a brilliant expression of itself and hence of its Lord.

Despite his fondness for Old and Middle English, Hopkins luckily refrained from calling the windhover by its obsolete name: *fuckwind* or *windfucker.* (No, that *f* is not a long *s.*) Thomas Nashe in *Lenten Stuffe* (1599) speaks of the "Kistrilles or windfuckers that filling themselves with winde, fly against the winde evermore." See *windfucker* in the *Oxford English Dictionary.* (For this dumbfounding discovery, thanks to David Lynch, who copyedited *Literature,* 4th ed.)

A. E. *Housman*, LOVELIEST OF TREES, THE CHERRY NOW, page 815

What is Housman's theme? Good old *carpe diem*. If you ask students to paraphrase this poem (it's not hard), a paraphrase might add, to catch the deeper
implication, "Life is brief—time flies—I'd better enjoy beauty now."

Not part of the rough poem Housman began with, the second stanza was
added last. Lines 9–10 originally read: "And since to look at things you love /
Fifty times is not enough." What can be said for Housman's additions and
changes? (These and other manuscript variations are given by Tom Burns Haber
in *The Making of "A Shropshire Lad"* [Seattle: U of Washington P, 1966].)

A. E. *Housman*, TO AN ATHLETE DYING YOUNG, page 815

"To an Athlete Dying Young" is another *carpe diem* poem—but with a mostly ret-
rospective perspective. Rather than advising one to take advantage of life's
opportunities before it is too late, the elegiac poem celebrates the passing of a
young man who dies at the height of his physical glory. The deceased was a town
hero, a champion runner. Housman's timeless imagery of footracing and laurels
provides the poem with a classical, almost Roman, feel.

Help the students point out and explain the significance of repeating images
and phrases, especially the various thresholds and the "shoulder-high" carrying
of the athlete—first in his victor's chair, and later his coffin. You might also discuss the poem's most famous lines, "And early though the laurel grows / It with-
ers quicker than the rose." What do *laurel* and *rose* represent here? Ask the students to state the theme of "To an Athlete Dying Young," and have them recall living proof of Housman's observation that sometimes the name dies before the man
(forgotten pop stars, retired athletes).

Randall *Jarrell*, THE DEATH OF THE BALL TURRET GUNNER, page 816

The speaker seems an unknown citizen like Auden's. Jarrell's laconic war poem
is complex in its metaphors. The womb is sleep; the outside world, waking; and
the speaker has passed from one womb to another—from his mother into the
belly of a bomber. His existence inside the ball turret was only a dream, and in
truth he has had no mature life between his childhood and his death. Waking
from the dream, he wakes only to nightmare. In another irony, the matter-of-fact
battle report language of the last line contrasts horribly with what is said in it.
How can the dead gunner address us? Clearly the poet had written his epitaph
for him—and has done so as Jarrell said he wrote "The Woman at the Washington Zoo," "acting as next friend."

Robinson *Jeffers*, TO THE STONE-CUTTERS, page 817

If students will compare this poem with Shakespeare's sonnet "Not marble nor the
gilded monuments," they'll be struck by a sharp difference of view. Shakespeare, evidently, is the optimist. For him, a poem can confer immortality and inspire love until

doomsday. For Jeffers, poems will merely bring a little respite to "pained thoughts"—much as a spoonful of honey helps a hangover, according to one popular belief.

For a short assignment: Write a paraphrase of each of these two poems. Bring your work to class, ready to read it aloud. We'll discuss the poems, taking off from your work on them.

For another pessimistic view of monuments, direct students to Shelley's "Ozymandias." You might ask them to compare its theme with those of Shakespeare and Jeffers.

A sidelight on this poem: Any doubt he may have had that stone monuments last long didn't prevent Jeffers from building, with his own hands, a stone tower next to his home at the ocean's edge in Carmel, California.

Ben Jonson, ON MY FIRST SON, page 817

This heartbreaking poem from Jonson's *Epigrammes*, requested by several instructors, repays close reading. What is "the state [man] should envy?" Death. Why the dead child should be envied is made clear in the lines that immediately follow (7–8). The final couplet is difficult in its syntax, and contains a pun on *like* in a sense now obsolete. The speaker vows, or prays (*vow*, along with *votive*, comes from the Greek *euchesthai:* "to pray"), that anyone whom he loves may not live too long. The seriousness of Jonson's wit is shown in this colossal pun: *like* meaning "thrive, do well, get on" as well as "to be fond." See *like* in the *OED* for other illustrations:

> Shallow to Falstaff: "By my troth, you like well and bear your years very well." (*Henry IV*, P.2, 3.2.92)
>
> "Trees generally do like best that stand to the Northeast wind." (Holland's Pliny, 1600)

"Poems Arranged by Subject and Theme" in this manual lists the book's other poems about fathers and children. In this section, see especially the father-and-son poems by Stephen Shu-ning Liu and James Wright ("Autumn Begins in Martins Ferry, Ohio").

Donald Justice, ON THE DEATH OF FRIENDS IN CHILDHOOD, page 818

There is more emotional distance, less grief in this poem than in Ben Jonson's. Neither does the speaker in "On the Death of Friends in Childhood" seem to be mourning one specific loss. The "Friends" he mentions suggest friends in general, perhaps other people's as well as his own. Yet, though time has softened the impact of long-ago losses, the narrator urges that we remember dead childhood friends and what was shared with them.

John Keats, ODE ON A GRECIAN URN, page 818

Why is the symbol of the urn so endlessly suggestive? It may help students to recall that Grecian urns are vessels for the ashes of the dead, and that their carved or painted figures *(Of deities or mortal, or of both)* depict a joyous afterlife in the Elysian fields. The urn being circular, its design appears to continue endlessly. What greater image for eternity, or for the seamlessness of perfected art?

Most good discussions of the "Urn" confront a few of the poem's celebrated difficulties. Some questions to help speed the confrontation:

1. *Assuming that the urn is said to be* sylvan *because it displays woodland scenes, in what sense is it a* historian? *What history or histories does it contain, or represent?*

2. *How can unheard melodies be sweeter than heard ones?*

3. *Why are youth, lover and loved one, trees, and musicians so lucky to exist upon the urn? (Lines 15–27.)*

4. *What disadvantages do living lovers labor under? (Lines 28–30.)*

5. *In stanza four, the procession of thought turns in a new direction. What additional insight occurs to the poet?* That the urn, whose world had seemed perfect, is in some ways limited and desolate. The altar cannot be reached nor sacrifice fulfilled, nor can the unseen little town ever be returned to.

6. *Paraphrase the statement that the urn "dost tease us out of thought / As doth Eternity."* The urn lures us out of our habit of useless cogitation. Eternity also stops us from thinking because, for us mere mortals, it too is incomprehensible.

7. *How is the urn a "Cold Pastoral"?* Literally, it's lifeless clay; figuratively, it stands aloof from human change and suffering. Compare Stevens's "Jar."

8. *How then can a Cold Pastoral be called "a friend to man"?* It provides a resting place for human ashes; it inspires and delights; and, as the last lines attest, it teaches us.

John Keats, ON FIRST LOOKING INTO CHAPMAN'S HOMER, page 819

QUESTIONS FOR DISCUSSION:

1. What are the *realms of gold?* Can the phrase have anything to do with the fact that early Spanish explorers were looking for El Dorado, a legendary city of treasure in South America?

2. Does Keats's boner about Cortez mar the poem?

3. Did you ever read anything that made you feel like a stout Cortez? If so, what?

John Keats, WHEN I HAVE FEARS THAT I MAY CEASE TO BE, page 820

Students will see right away that the poem expresses fear of death, but don't let them stop there: there's more to it. Why does the poet fear death? Because it will end his writing and his loving. The poem states what both loving and writing poetry have in common: both are magical and miraculous acts when they are spontaneous. Besides favoring "unreflecting love" for its "fairy power," Keats would write "with the magic hand of chance." And—if you care to open up a profundity—what might the poet mean by those "huge cloudy symbols of a high romance"? Literal cloud shapes that look like Tristram and Isolde's beaker of love-potion, or what?

Note that this poem addresses not Keats's beloved Fanny Brawne, but "the memory of the mysterious lady seen in adolescence one brief moment at Vauxhall long ago in the summer of 1814," according to Robert Gittings in *John Keats* (Boston: Atlantic, 1968) 188. The poem is about a "creature of an hour." (Fanny, of course, occupied not one hour but many.)

Gittings has found in the poem echoes of two sonnets of Shakespeare, both about devouring time: #60 ("Like as the waves make towards the pebbled shore, / So do our minutes hasten to their end") and #64 ("When I have seen by Time's fell hand defaced"). In the copy of the *Sonnets* that Keats co-owned with his friend Reynolds, these two were the most heavily marked.

This poem has had a hefty impact on later poets, notably John Berryman, who took from it the title for an autobiographical collection of his own poems on ambition and desire: *Love and Fame* (1972).

Philip Larkin, POETRY OF DEPARTURES, page 821

The speaker wonders why he doesn't break with his dull, tame life, just walk out, chuck everything, launch into the Romantic unknown like a highwayman. What an appealing notion! Question: Have you ever yearned to do that very thing? (Who hasn't?)

Well, why doesn't he take off? Because he sees all too clearly and painfully that such a grandiose gesture would be ridiculous. Commenting on lines 25–27, in which the speaker imagines himself swaggering nut-strewn roads and crouching in the fo'c'sle, David Timms finds him "unconvinced by such daydreams, though sympathetic to the dreamers, for he is one himself." And so he dismisses his Romantic urge as too studied and belabored, ultimately false. Still, just because he sees through those dreams, he won't let himself feel superior. The dreams may be artificial, but so is his own tame life, his room, his specially chosen junk. As he is well aware, at the end, his greatest danger is to be trapped in owning things and neatly arranging them: books, china, all fixed on shelves in an order "reprehensibly perfect." (We have somewhat expanded on Timms's paraphrase, from *Philip Larkin* [Edinburgh: Oliver & Boyd, 1973] 87.)

William H. Pritchard has remarked that Larkin himself expunged Romantic possibilities from his life, the better to entertain them in his writing ("Larkin's Presence," in *Philip Larkin: The Man and His Work*, ed. Dale Salwak [Iowa City: U of Iowa P, 1989] 74–75).

Irving Layton, THE BULL CALF, page 822

Sentimental poets frequently shed tears over concrete objects, while (in their imagery and diction) failing to open their eyes to the physical world. Such is not the case of Layton's "The Bull Calf," in which the poet tells us that he weeps only after having portrayed the dead calf in exact detail ("one foreleg over the other").

Layton's poem develops a series of contrasts. In the first section, the calf's look of nobility ("the promise of sovereignty," "Richard II") is set against his immaturity. The "fierce sunlight," in an implied metaphor, is compared to the calf's mother: taking in maize, licking her baby. In line 14, the "empty sky," suggestive of the calf's coming death, seems the turning point of the poem. In the remainder, the calf, which had been portrayed at first as full of life and pride, becomes an inanimate object, "a block of wood," a numb mass that emits ugly sounds when handled ("a sepulchral gurgle"). But in the closing lines, introducing still another contrast, Layton seems to show the calf as a living sleeper, or perhaps a statue or finished work of art.

Probably the best-known living poet in Canada, Layton was born in Rumania and came to Montreal early in life. Standing outside both British and French communities, Layton's perspective often has been that of an outsider, a Jew, a satirist, and a revolutionary. *The Selected Poems of Irving Layton*, with an introduction by Hugh Kenner (New York: New Directions, 1977), is an attempt to widen his audience south of the border.

Philip Levine, ANIMALS ARE PASSING FROM OUR LIVES, page 823

Remarkable about this poem is its point of view—a pig's—and its insouciant tone, considering the circumstances. This pig is on its way to market, and to death. An intelligent animal with a startlingly human persona (even jauntily condescending to the boy who, it says, thinks it will act "like a beast" [line 22]), it knows exactly the kind of death that awaits, and takes pride in facing its fate with courage. Its English is colloquial ("squeal / and shit like a new housewife / discovering television," "Not this pig"), its manner breezy.

Levine's title seems ironic. It leads us to expect a self-consciously "significant" poem about endangered species and the urgent need to save them. But in fact, it surprises us by focusing instead on meat animals, killed in great numbers every day without our thinking twice. Like Simic in "Butcher Shop," Levine sets forth the unpalatable details of the slaughter and the discomfort sensitive people feel when they reflect on the bloodshed necessary to provide meat for the table. Levine, describing the dreams in which the snouts of slaughtered pigs "drool on the marble," calls attention as well to the hypocrisy of "the consumers / who won't meet their steady eyes / for fear they could see." Given the title and the opening lines, who could predict where this poem was going?

Stephen Shu-ning Liu, MY FATHER'S MARTIAL ART, page 824

Born in China, Stephen Shu-ning Liu has lived in this country since 1952 and currently teaches at Clark County Community College in Las Vegas. In *Breaking*

Silence, An Anthology of Contemporary Asian American Poets edited by Joseph Bruchac (New York: Greenfield Review, 1983) he remarks:

> My philosophy in writing poetry is that poetic language should be simple, clear and direct. Like fresh air and wholesome bread, poetry is for the crowd; and the poet, since he is just another human being, does not necessarily have a tattoo or a weird hairdo. A poet should work alone and leave group exercise to the football players.

In "My Father's Martial Art," the father has apparently died ("the smog / between us deepens into a funeral pyre"). His son remembers him and his skill with the martial arts, learned during a three-year stay in a monastery. The poignant final stanza makes evident the speaker's love and longing for his absent father. "But don't retreat into night, my father" calls to mind another elegy for a father, Dylan Thomas's famous "Do not go gentle into that good night."

Dream Journeys to China, an English-Chinese bilingual edition of his poems (Beijing: New World Press, 1982) is available from the China Publications Center, P. O. Box 399, Beijing, People's Republic of China.

Robert Lowell, SKUNK HOUR, page 825

Students should have no trouble in coming up with the usual connotations of skunk, but they may need help in seeing that the title is a concise expression of Lowell's theme. This is an evil-smelling hour in the speaker's life; and yet, paradoxically, it is the skunks themselves who affirm that life ought to go on. After the procession of dying and decadent people and objects in the first four stanzas, the mother skunk and her kittens form a triumph: bold, fecund, hungry, impossible to scare. Although they too are outcasts (surrounded by their aroma as the poet is surrounded by his madness and isolation?), they stick up for their right to survival.

The poem is rich in visual imagery. In the mind's eye, there are resemblances between the things contained in stanza 5 (the Ford car and the hill's skull), also the objects set in fixed rows (love-cars, tombstones, beached hulls). Water and the sea (by their decline or absence) are to this poem what they are to Eliot's *Waste Land*. Even the Church is "chalk-dry"; its spire has become a spar like that of a stranded vessel.

This poem is intensively analyzed in *The Contemporary Poet as Artist and Critic: Eight Symposia*, ed. Anthony Ostroff (Boston: Little, 1964). Richard Wilbur, John Frederick Nims, and John Berryman comment on the poem, after which Lowell comments on their comments. Lowell calls the opening of the poem "a dawdling, more or less amiable picture of a declining Maine sea town. . . . Sterility howls through the scenery, but I try to give a tone of tolerance, humor, and randomness to the sad prospect." He sees the skunk hour itself as a sort of dark night of the soul and refers readers to the poem by Saint John of the Cross. Lowell's night, however, is "secular, puritan, and agnostical." Lowell notes that the phrase *red fox stain* was intended only to describe the color of vegetation in the fall on Blue Hill, a mountain in Maine.

Elizabeth Hardwick, Lowell's wife when "Skunk Hour" was written, has affirmed that all the characters in the poem were actual—"were living, more or less as he sees them, in Castine [Maine] that summer. The details, not the feeling, were rather alarmingly precise, I thought. But fortunately it was not read in town for some time" (quoted by Ian Hamilton, *Robert Lowell: A Biography* [New York: Random, 1982] 267).

Sandra M. Gilbert, who sees the poem as "richly magical," reads it for its embodiment of myth. She explores it as a vision of Hell, pointing out that its events happen not on Halloween, but "somewhere in Hallowe'en's ritually black and orange vicinity." (The decorator's shop is "sacramentally orange.") The summer millionaire has departed in fall, like a vegetation deity—Osiris or Attis. Nautilus Island's witchlike hermit heiress is Circe, Hecate, Ishtar, Venus, "the goddess of love turned goddess of death in an All Soul's Night world" ("Mephistopheles in Maine: Rereading Lowell's 'Skunk Hour,'" *A Book of Rereadings*, ed. Greg Kuzma [Lincoln, NE: Pebble and Best Cellar, 1979] 254–64).

Andrew Marvell, TO HIS COY MISTRESS, page 826

QUESTIONS FOR DISCUSSION:

1. *"All this poet does is feed some woman a big line. There's no time for romance, so he says, 'Quick, let's hit the bed before we hit the dirt.'" Discuss this summary. Then try making your own, more accurate one. Suggestion: The poem is divided into three parts, each beginning with an indented line. Take these parts one at a time, putting the speaker's main thoughts into your own words.* There's a grain of truth to this paraphrase, rude though it be. We might question, however, whether Marvell's speaker is trying to hoodwink his loved one. Perhaps he only sums up the terrible truth he knows: that time lays waste to youth, that life passes before we know it. He makes no mention of "romance," by the way—that's the paraphraser's invention. A more nearly accurate paraphrase, taking the three divisions of the poem one by one, might go like this:

    Lines 1–20: If we had all the room in the world and if we were immortal, then our courtship might range across the globe. My love for you could expand till it filled the whole world and I could spend centuries in praising your every feature (saving your heart for last). After all, such treatment is only what you deserve.

    Lines 21–32: But time runs on. Soon we'll be dead and gone, all my passion and all your innocence vanished.

    Lines 33–46: And so, while you're still young and willing, let's seize the day. Let's concentrate our pleasure into the present moment. Although we can't make the sun stand still (like Joshua in the Bible), we'll do the next best thing: we'll joyously make time fly.

    Now, obviously, any such rewording of this matchless poem must seem a piddling thing. But if students will just work through Marvell's argument part by part, they may grasp better the whole of it.

2. *In part one, how much space would be "world enough" for the lovers? Exactly how much time would be enough time?* To point out the approximate location of the Humber and the Ganges on a globe [or a simple circle drawn on a blackboard] can drive home the fact that when the poet says *world enough*, he spells out exactly what he means. A little discussion may be needed to show that in defining "enough" time, Marvell bounds it by events [the conversion of the Jews], numbers the years, and blocks out his piecemeal adoration. Two-hundred years per breast is a delectable statistic! Clearly, the lover doesn't take the notion of such slow and infinitely patient devotion seriously.

3. *What is the main idea of part two? How is this theme similar to that of Housman's "Loveliest of trees"?* Both Marvell and Housman in "Loveliest of trees" are concerned with the passage of time; they differ on what needs to be done about it. Marvell urges action; Housman urges filling one's youth with observed beauty. Of these two expressions of the *carpe diem* theme, Housman's seems the more calm and disinterested.

4. *Paraphrase with special care lines 37–44. Is Marvell urging violence?* In lines 37–44, Marvell's point seems to be that time works a gradual, insidious violence. It is like a devouring beast (*slow-chapped*), holding us in its inexorable jaws. Some students will find the imagery odd, even offensive in a love poem: *birds of prey* (who want to eat, not be eaten), the cannonball of strength and sweetness that batters life's iron gates. Violence is not the speaker's counsel, but urgency. His harsh images lend his argument intensity and force.

5. *Considering the poem as a whole, does the speaker seem playful, or serious?* This fifth question presents an easy dichotomy, but of course Marvell's speaker is both playful and serious. In making clear the tone of the poem, a useful poem for comparison is Marlowe's "Passionate Shepherd." What are the two speakers' attitudes toward love? Marvell's seems more down-to-earth, skeptical, and passion-driven: a lover in a fallen world, not [like Marlowe's shepherd] a lover in a pastoral Eden.

If later on, in teaching figures of speech, you want some great lines for illustrations, turn back to this inexhaustible poem. There's hyperbole in lines 7–20, understatement ("But none, I think, do there embrace"), metaphor, simile, and of course the great personification of chariot-driving time.

Telling a class that Marvell was a Puritan usually shakes up their overly neat assumption. Some may be surprised to learn that one can be a Puritan and not necessarily be puritanical.

Defending the poem against charges that its logic is fallacious, a recent critic, Richard Crider, has shown that "the speaker's appeal is not merely to the lady's passion, . . . but to a more inclusive and compelling value—completion and wholeness." A good student of Aristotle's logic as well as Aristotle's ethics, Marvell's speaker calls on his listener to exercise all her human powers, among them reason. "Although no single net will capture all the resonances of the final couplet, near the heart of the passage is the thought of living life completely, in accordance with natural law" ("Marvell's Valid Logic," *College Literature* [Spring 1985]: 113–211).

John Milton, WHEN I CONSIDER HOW MY LIGHT IS SPENT, page 828

While this famous sonnet is usually taken to refer to the poet's lost eyesight, some critics have argued that it is not about blindness at all. The familiar title "On His Blindness" was not given by Milton, but by a printer a century later.

QUESTIONS FOR DISCUSSION:

1. *If the poem is not about blindness, what might it be about?* Possible suggestions: Milton's declining powers of poetry; Milton's fame as a Puritan apologist.

2. *Is "talent" a pun referring to Milton's talent for writing poetry? What other meanings of the word seem appropriate in this poem?* In the New Testament parable (Matthew 25:14–30), the hidden talent is money that should have been earning interest. That Milton is thinking primarily of work and business can be plausibly argued; other words in the poem convey such connotations—*spent, true account, day-labor,* and perhaps *useless,* which suggests the Medieval Latin word for interest, *usura.*

The theme of frustration in life (and reconciliation to one's lot) is dealt with differently in Shakespeare's "When, in disgrace with Fortune and men's eyes."

Marianne Moore, POETRY, page 828

Marianne Moore was a singular poet both on the page and in real life. Her elaborate verse style, complex syllabic meters, and penchant for collage and quotation mirror in some mysterious way her carefully cultivated eccentricity and wry personal reticence. One peculiar feature of her work is that most of her poems—directly or indirectly—explore aesthetics, especially the nature of literary art. In this respect, "Poetry" occupies an important position in her work. This superbly observed and intellectually provocative poem also illustrates a central irony of her work—the more overtly abstract her poem appears the more covertly personal it proves to be.

"Poetry" appears in several versions in Moore's various collections. Hardly had she first published the poem in 1921 than she began revising it. By the time she published her *Complete Poems* in 1967, Moore had grotesquely cut the poem down to only three lines. For this anthology we have reprinted her original version, which seems to us the finest and fullest one. (Instructors should make sure they compare our version to others they may have in different books.)

"Poetry" is both a defense of poetry as an important human enterprise and—to quote critic Helen Vendler—Moore's "indirect self-reproach for her painstaking absorption in 'all this fiddle.'" While eventually justifying the art of poetry for its heightened attention to genuine phenomena, the poem also admits its own skepticism about the elaborate "fiddle" of poetry and its recognition of the failure of "half poets" and "derivative" writers. Moore's aesthetic ideal is best summarized in her famous (and wondrously oxymoric) image "imaginary gardens with real toads in them." Boldly the poet affirms the utility of poetry. Poetry is "useful" to Moore when it genuinely encompasses both external and internal reality.

The poet Donald Hall, who knew Moore, has commented in similar terms on the poem:

> In her well-known poem, "Poetry," Miss Moore begins, "I too, dislike it." This line has been interpreted as ironic, as an attempt to disarm, or as evidence that she practices her art only half-seriously. Quite obviously, however, her reasoning is serious. She refers to a kind of poetry that is neither honest nor sincere but that has found fashionable approval by virtue of its very obscurity.
> (*Marianne Moore: The Cage and the Animal* [New York: Pegasus: 1970] 40)

The form of "Poetry" is also worth discussing. It might help to ask the class if the poem has a form—to see what features they discover on their own. Moore shaped the version of "Poetry" reprinted here into five complex syllabic stanzas of six lines each. Students can count out the syllables in each line to determine the stanza pattern. The stanzas also rhyme—although the rhymes are more visible to the eye than audible in her run-on enjambed lines. The rhyme scheme is *abbccd*. The poem unfolds in the manner of an impassioned, learned conversation, and it employs prose rhythms in its elaborate syllabic pattern. Spoken aloud, it sounds like free verse; on the page, however, the reader sees how carefully wrought it is as formal verse.

Marilyn Nelson, A STRANGE BEAUTIFUL WOMAN, page 830

This strange and beautiful short poem has the simplicity of a haiku—a single image doubled in a mirror followed by a single question also doubled. The poem's power rests in its suggestiveness, and it works—like the mirror—in two ways at once. The poem is affirmative in the speaker's recognition of her own beauty, but it is also subtly self-critical in noting that the speaker is insufficiently familiar with admitting her own beauty, which initially seems "strange" to her. In the same way, the speaker's surprised question—"Hey, / I said, / what you doing here?"—acquires a more disturbing existential quality when the reflection repeats it. What is the speaker doing, the image seems to ask, in and with her own life?

Yone Noguchi, A SELECTION OF HOKKU, page 830

Yone Noguchi, the first Asian-American poet of significant influence, was born in Tsushima, a small town near Nagaya, Japan. He became interested in English language and literature in public school. He later studied English at Keio University in Tokyo, but after two years he decided to immigrate to America. He arrived in San Francisco in December 1893, where he worked for a Japanese-language paper while studying American poetry. In 1896 he met the popular Western poet

Joaquin Miller who encouraged his literary ambitions. For three years Noguchi lived in a hut on Miller's hillside property above Oakland, and he associated with *Les Jeunes*, a group of young San Francisco writers including Gelitt Burgess. Noguchi soon published two books, *Seen & Unseen* (1897) and *The Voice of the Valley* (1897), which showed the influence of Miller and Walt Whitman. Although written in slightly odd English, these early books were praised for their freshness. His next two collections of poetry, *From the Eastern Sea* (1903) and *The Summer Cloud* (1906), not only display more confidence and originality, they also incorporate more traditional Japanese elements of style and structure. *The Summer Cloud*, which presented sixty-two prose poems, also demonstrated Noguchi's early interest in literary modernism. In 1904 Noguchi returned to Japan—leaving behind his American lover, Leonie Gilmour, and their newborn son, Isamu Noguchi (who would become an internationally celebrated sculptor).

Noguchi corresponded with Ezra Pound and William Butler Yeats about Japanese literary aesthetics. He, therefore, played an important but little-known role in influencing the development of Imagism. He also helped popularize haiku as an English-language form. His volume *Japanese Hokkus* (1920), which was dedicated to Yeats, stills stands as a major early milestone in the American haiku tradition. Noguchi understood his unique role as a conduit between the Japanese and English-language literary tradition. "We must lose our insularity," he wrote hopefully of Japanese literature, but he could certainly have claimed to have helped broaden the perspective of American letters.

Sharon Olds, THE ONE GIRL AT THE BOYS' PARTY, page 831

This poem whimsically describes a talented little girl, "her math scores unfolding in the air around her," during a pool party at which all the other guests are boys. *They* in lines 2 and 15, *their* in lines 18 and 19 seem to refer only to the boys. In lines 5, 7, and 11, the word *they* apparently includes the girl. You might ask students to note the pairs of adjectives that affirm the child's strength and composure: she is "smooth and sleek" (line 3), her body is "hard and / indivisible as a prime number" (lines 5–6), her face is "solemn and / sealed" (lines 16–17). The adjectives make clear the narrator-mother's respect for her brilliant daughter. Notable too is the metaphor of wet ponytail (itself a by-now-dead metaphor!) as pencil (line 12). That and the "narrow silk suit / with hamburgers and french fries printed on it" remind us that she is in some ways a very typical little girl.

It is the mathematical figures of speech that make this poem unique. Why not ask students to point out and discuss them? Are they apt? Do they ever appear forced? Which ones succeed best?

Wilfred Owen, ANTHEM FOR DOOMED YOUTH, page 832

Metaphorically, this sonnet draws a contrast between traditional funeral trappings and the actual conditions under which the dead lie on the field of battle: with cannon fire instead of tolling bells, rifle bursts instead of the patter of prayers, the whine of shells instead of choirs' songs, the last lights in dying eyes instead of candle-shine, pale brows (of mourning girls, at home?) instead of shrouds or palls, the tenderness of onlookers (such as the poet?) instead of flowers—an early draft of the poem reads, "Your flowers, the tenderness of comrades' minds"—and the fall of night instead of the conventional drawing down of blinds in a house where someone has died.

For another Owen war poem, see "Dulce et Decorum Est." For other war poems, see in this manual "Poems Arranged by Subject and Theme."

The poet's revisions for this poem, in four drafts, may be studied in the appendix to C. Day Lewis's edition of Owen's *Collected Poems* (London: Chatto, 1963). In its first draft, the poem was called "Anthem for Dead [not Doomed] Youth," and it went, in our reading of the photographed manuscript:

What minute bells for these who die so fast?
Only the monstrous anger of our guns.
Let the majestic insults of their iron mouths
Be as the priest-words of their burials.
Of choristers and holy music, none;
Not any voice of mourning, save the wail
The long-drawn wail of high, far-sailing shells.
What candles may we hold for these lost souls?
Not in the hands of boys, but in their eyes
Shall many candles shine, and [?] will light them.
Women's wide-spreaded arms shall be their wreaths,
And pallor of girls' cheeks shall be their palls.
Their flowers, the tenderness of all men's minds,
And every dusk, a drawing-down of blinds.

Linda Pastan, ETHICS, page 832

As a student, the narrator, like others in her class, found her teacher's ethical puzzler irrelevant. Now the mature woman pondering the "real Rembrandt" in the museum finds the question still remote from her vital concerns, but for different reasons. The approach of her own old age has shown her that nothing lasts, that with the onflow of years our choices, whatever they may be, fade into insignificance.

One way of entering the poem: students may be asked to sum up its theme. Is it *carpe diem?* Is the poet saying, with Housman in "Loveliest of trees," "Life is fleeting; I'd better enjoy beauty while I can"? No, for the poet seems not to believe in day-seizing. Is it *ars longa, vita brevis est?* No, for both art and life seem pitifully brief and temporary. The point, rather, is that all things pass away despite our efforts to hold on to them. But instead of telling them what the point is, you might ask students to paraphrase the poem's conclusion that "woman / and painting and season are almost one / and all beyond saving by children."

To discuss: In what ways does "Ethics" differ from prose? Pastan's language seems far more musical. She makes beautiful music of alliteration and assonance. Read the poem aloud. And central to "Ethics" is a huge metaphor: old woman, season, earth, painting, and poet become one—all caught in time's resistless fire.

In a previous Instructor's Manual, we wondered: How many times did the speaker have to repeat that ethics course? To our relief, on a recent visit to the

University of Arizona in Tucson, Linda Pastan supplied an answer reported to us by Ila Abernathy of the Poetry Center. Pastan went to the Ethical Culture School in New York City, a private school run by the Ethical Culture Society and serving both elementary and high school students. The school's curriculum hits ethics hard: the poet was required to take once-a-week ethics classes for twelve years.

Linda Pastan chose "Ethics" to represent her in *The Poet's Choice*, an anthology of poets' own favorite poems edited by George E. Murphy, Jr. (Green Harbor, MA: Tendril, 1980).

Octavio Paz, WITH OUR EYES SHUT (CON LOS OJOS CERRADOS), translated by *John Felstiner*, page 833

This short poem by Nobel laureate Octavio Paz is simple enough that anyone with basic Spanish can follow it in the original. (The original text will also give any native Spanish speakers in your class a chance to show off their bilingual abilities.) The poem explores a paradoxical conceit—shutting one's self off from physical light, one can experience an inner light. Becoming a "blind stone" to the outside, "You light up from within." The second stanza allows the metaphor to become erotic, although Paz is deliberately ambiguous about whether the lovers are together or apart. "Night by night" the speaker recreates his love with his eyes shut—perhaps carving her features from memory or perhaps touching her with his hands. The final stanza celebrates how the lovers enlarge their existence from knowing one another "with our eyes shut."

Sylvia Plath, DADDY, page 834

There are worse ways to begin teaching this astonishing poem than to ask students to recall what they know of Dachau, Auschwitz, Belsen (line 33), and other Nazi atrocities. "Every woman adores a Fascist"—what does Plath mean? Is she sympathizing with the machismo ideal of the domineering male, lashing his whip upon subjugated womankind? (No way.) For an exchange of letters about the rightness or wrongness of Plath's identifying with Jewish victims of World War II, see *Commentary* (July and October 1974). Irving Howe accuses Plath of "a failure in judgment" in using genocide as an emblem of her personal traumas.

Incredible as it seems, some students possess an alarming fund of ignorance about Nazis, and some might not even recognize the cloven foot of Satan (line 53); so be prepared, sadly, to supply glosses. They will be familiar with the story of Dracula, however, and probably won't need much help with lines 71–79. Plath may be thinking of *Nosferatu*, F. W. Murnau's silent screen adaptation of Bram Stoker's novel *Dracula*, filmed in Germany in 1922. Hitler's propagandists seized on the Nosferatu theme and claimed that the old democratic order was drinking the country's blood. Plath sees Daddy as doing the same to his daughter.

Edgar Allan Poe, TO HELEN, page 837

The first version of this poem appeared in Poe's third volume, *Poems* (1831), which was published while the author was a cadet at West Point. (At twenty-two he had already published two earlier books!) Poe circulated a subscription among his fellow cadets to underwrite a volume of his verse. Many of them subscribed in the expectation that Poe would publish the satirical squibs he had written about their teachers and officers. Imagine their surprise on opening the volume to discover delicate lyrics like "To Helen" and "Israfel." Poe later revised it slightly in 1841 to polish its most famous lines to read: "To the glory that was Greece / And the grandeur that was Rome." (It is a worthwhile exercise to ask students to differentiate between the implications of *glory* and *grandeur.*)

Poe (whose comments on his own poems are famously unreliable) claimed that "To Helen" was written in youth "to the first, purely ideal love of my soul." That statement seems uncharacteristically accurate. The woman in "To Helen" seems less a flesh and blood beauty than an object of aesthetic contemplation. Notice how, in the final stanza, Helen becomes transformed in the speaker's mind into a statue, as she stands in the window niche.

Poe's idealized notion of love seems more maternal than sexual—not a surprising thing for a sensitive boy who lost his mother before his third birthday. "To Helen" makes a very interesting comparison piece to "Annabel Lee."

Alexander Pope, A LITTLE LEARNING IS A DANG'ROUS THING, page 837

This passage is an excerpt (lines 215–232) from Pope's "An Essay on Criticism," which he published when he was only twenty-three years old. It was this poem, which Joseph Addison immediately proclaimed "a Master-piece in its kind," that made Pope a literary celebrity.

Many teachers object to using excerpts from long works; such selections, they feel, betray the author's original intentions. In general, we agree; we favor including complete poems, so that each part of the work may be seen in relation to the whole. Pope, however, provides a special case. All of his greatest poems are too long to include in total. But it would seem too cruel to deny both teachers and students alike the pleasures of Pope's work, so we have bent the rules several times to introduce this satiric master's work to a new generation. As every teacher knows, one sometimes needs to bend critical rules a bit.

As long as we are bending the rules, we should point out how much this excerpt from a long didactic poem looks like a self-standing lyric in its new form. Examining these eighteen lines in isolation, we see how carefully Pope arranged the images in each line to build toward a cumulative poetic as well as intellectual effect. The final image of the weary traveler looking over the mountaintop at the endless Alps rising ahead is a brilliant stroke that seems closer to a romantic sensibility than a neo-classical one.

Ezra Pound, THE RIVER-MERCHANT'S WIFE: A LETTER, page 838

After the death of Ernest Fenollosa, a scholar devoted to Chinese language and literature, Pound inherited Fenollosa's manuscripts containing rough prose versions of many Chinese poems. From one such draft, Pound finished his own version of "The River Merchant's Wife." Fenollosa's wording of the first line went:

My hair was at first covering my brows (child's method of wearing hair)

Arthur Waley, apparently contemptuous of Pound for ignoring dictionary meanings of some of the words of the poem, made a translation that began:

Soon after I wore my hair covering my forehead . . .

Pound's version begins:

While my hair was still cut straight across my forehead . . .

Pound, says the recent critic Waj-lim Yip, has understood Chinese culture, while Waley has not, even though he understands his dictionary. "The characters for 'hair/first/cover/forehead' conjure up in the mind of a Chinese reader exactly this picture. All little Chinese girls normally have their hair cut straight across the forehead." Yip goes on to show that Pound, ignorant of Chinese as he was, comes close in sense and feeling to the Li Po original. (*Ezra Pound's Cathay* [Princeton: Princeton UP, 1969] 88–92.)

    What is the tone of the poem? What details make it seem moving and true, even for a reader who knows nothing of Chinese culture?

Henry Reed, NAMING OF PARTS, *page 839*

This is one of the most teachable poems ever written. There are two voices: the voice of the riflery instructor, droning on with his spiel, and the voice of the reluctant inductee, distracted by the springtime. Two varieties of diction and imagery clash and contrast: technical terms opposed to imagery of blossoming nature. Note the fine pun in line 24, prepared for by the rapist bees in the previous line. Note also the connotations of the ambiguous phrase *point of balance* (line 27)—a kind of balance lacking from the recruits' lives?

    Students need to be shown the dramatic situation of the poem: the poor inductee, sitting through a lecture he doesn't want to hear. One would think that sort of experience would be familiar to students, but a trouble some instructors have met in teaching this poem is a yearning to make out of it a vast comment about Modern Civilization.

    The poet himself has recorded the poem for *An Album of Modern Poets*, 1 (Library of Congress, PL 20). Dylan Thomas reads "Naming of Parts" even more impressively in his *Reading, Vol. IV: A Visit to America and Poems* (Caedmon, TC 1061).

Adrienne Rich, LIVING IN SIN, *page 840*

The title of Adrienne Rich's powerfully pensive poem may need explaining nowadays to some students, and it is essential that they understand the phrase since it sets up the narrative situation of the poem. As the title indicates, Rich's pair of lovers (who are referred to only as "he" and "she") are living together but not married—a bolder lifestyle in 1955 than today. The woman has expected their life together to be romantic and carefree—"no dust upon the furniture of love"— but the daily reality of housework and habitual intimacy proves dull and disillusioning. This deflation of romantic fantasy suggests the secondary meaning of the title—the Adam and Eve of her hoped-for lover's Eden have fallen from grace into the humdrum world of everyday disappointment.

Rich has neatly divided the two worlds of the protagonists' experience into night and day. The night remains romantic—if also diminished from the woman's original expectations—but the dawn brings only disappointment. The poem never directly states whether the woman's vacillating feelings will bring matters to a crisis, but the relative impact of each emotional state is suggested by the fact that the evening world of love receives three lines of treatment whereas the daylight world of disillusionment gets twenty-three. These proportions give "Living in Sin" the feel of an Anton Chekhov short story in which the final outcome remains unstated but the narrative situation has been so carefully presented as to make the conclusion inevitable.

For this reason, "Living in Sin" would be a good poem to use in a classroom discussion of "Saying and Suggesting." Rich's poem leaves a great many important things unsaid but implicit. The images suggest conclusions the protagonist seems not yet able to articulate—like the "beetle-eyes" staring at her from the shelf. The poem also has an interesting point of view. Although narrated in the third person, the poem adopts the subjective point of view of the woman.

"Living in Sin" is an early Rich poem (published in 1955 in her second collection, *The Diamond Cutters*). It is tempting, therefore, to read the poem as a narrative that prefigures Rich's turn to feminism. "Living in Sin" certainly responds to such interpretation. The woman in the poem has mistakenly sought fulfillment by creating a domestic world designed to please her male lover. (The particulars of the apartment "had risen at his urging.") Now she begins to understand the mistaken idealism and unintentional subjugation of that decision. Some changes—some escape—must happen, even if the particular course of action has not yet been imagined. What must come next, to quote the title of a subsequent Rich volume, is "the will to change."

Edwin Arlington Robinson, MINIVER CHEEVY, page 841

"Miniver Cheevy" is one of Robinson's great character portraits. These miniature character studies (see also "Richard Cory") are a genre that Robinson perfected. Based on the dramatic and narrative poems of poets like George Crabbe and Robert Browning, Robinson compressed the portrait poem into tighter, often lyric structures. His work with its stark realism, bitter antiromanticism, and concise form marks the true beginning of modern (but not Modernist) American poetry.

Mr. Cheevy of the title is a man unable to face reality. He lives in a fantasy world of "the days of old." Cheevy imagines he would have lived a more exciting and fulfilling life in an earlier age, but Robinson makes it clear that Cheevy's fantasies are pure self-deception. Robinson undercuts Cheevy's delusions with irony ("He missed the medieval grace / Of iron clothing").

Writing the introduction to Robinson's posthumous *King Jasper* in 1935, Robert Frost reminisced about reading "Miniver Cheevy" in London in 1913 with Ezra Pound. They laughed over the fourth *thought* in "Miniver thought, and thought, and thought / And thought about it." "Three 'thoughts' would have been 'adequate,' as the critical praise then was," Frost remembered ". . . the fourth made the intolerable touch of poetry, with the fourth, the fun began."

Theodore Roethke, ELEGY FOR JANE, page 842

By piling up figures of speech from the natural world, Roethke in "Elegy for Jane" portrays his student as a child of nature, quick, thin, and birdlike. A *wren*, a *sparrow*, a *skittery pigeon*, Jane has a *pickerel smile* and neck curls *limp and damp as tendrils*. She waits *like a fern, making a spiny shadow*. She has the power to make shade trees and (even more surprising) mold burst into song. For her, leaves change their whispers into kisses.

Then she dies. The poet acknowledges that for him there is no consolation in nature, in the "sides of wet stones" or the moss; his grief is not assuaged. Because he mourns the girl as teacher and friend, no more, he recognizes a faint awkwardness in his grief as he speaks over her grave:

> I, with no rights in this matter,
> Neither father nor lover.

Roethke, writing about this poem in *On the Poet and His Craft* (Seattle: U of Washington P, 1965) 81–83, reminds the reader that it was John Crowe Ransom (to whose "Bells for John Whiteside's Daughter" this poem has often been compared) who first printed "Elegy for Jane." Roethke discusses his use of enumeration, calling it "the favorite device of the more irregular poem." He calls attention to one "of the strategies for the poet writing without the support of a formal pattern," a strategy he uses in "Elegy for Jane": the "lengthening out" of the last three lines in the first stanza, balanced by the progressive shortening of the three lines at the poem's end.

Some readers have interpreted "Elegy for Jane" as the work of a man who never had children of his own; but in fact Roethke as a young man had fathered a daughter for whom he felt great affection. Although "neither father nor lover" of Jane, he at least could well imagine a father's feelings.

William Shakespeare, NOT MARBLE NOR THE GILDED MONUMENTS, page 843

To discuss: Is Shakespeare making a wild boast, or does the claim in lines 1–8 seem at all justified? (Time has proved him right. Here we are, still reading his lines, 500 years after they were written! Of course, the fact that he happened to be Shakespeare helped his prediction come true.)

For teaching this poem in tandem with Robinson Jeffers's "To the Stone-cutters," see the entry on Jeffers in this manual.

William Shakespeare, THAT TIME OF YEAR THOU MAYST IN ME BEHOLD, page 844
William Shakespeare, WHEN, IN DISGRACE WITH FORTUNE AND MEN'S EYES, page 844

Shakespeare's magnificent metaphors probably will take some brief explaining. How is a body like boughs, and how are the bare boughs like a ruined choir loft? Students will get the general import, but can be helped to visualize the images. "Consumed with that which it was nourished by" will surely require some discussion. Youth, that had fed life's fire, now provides only smothering ashes. The poet's attitude toward age and approaching death stands in contrast to the attitudes of poets (or speakers) in other poems of similar theme: admiration for the exultant sparrows in William Carlos Williams's "To Waken an Old Lady"; defiance in Yeats's "Sailing to Byzantium."

Figures of speech are central to "That time of year," but rarely enter into "When, in disgrace" until the end, when the simile of the lark is introduced. The lark's burst of joy suggests that heaven, called *deaf* in line 3, has suddenly become keener of hearing. Critical discussion of both sonnets goes on: *Shakespeare's Sonnets*, edited with analytic commentary by Stephen Booth (New Haven: Yale UP, 1977) is especially valuable.

Charles Simic, BUTCHER SHOP, page 845

"Butcher Shop" is a constellation of metaphors. Associating the everyday instruments of a butcher's trade with things we wouldn't expect—things whose connotations are emotionally powerful—Simic works a kind of nighttime transformation. The light recalls a convict struggling to escape. Knives recall church, cripple, and imbecile. Most pervasive of the metaphors in the poem is the river of blood (lines 8 and 14). In a sense, we are nourished by a river of blood when we dine on the flesh of animals. Perhaps (like convict, cripple, and imbecile) the animals too are sufferers. Perhaps all of these victims in chorus lift the mysterious voice that the poet hears in the closing line.

Louis Simpson, AMERICAN POETRY, page 846

Simpson's brilliant short poem would make an excellent classroom assignment in a discussion that could also include Archibald MacLeish's "*Ars Poetica,*" and Marianne Moore's "Poetry." All three are classic statements of modern poetics. Simpson's is both the most recent work (1963) and the only one specifically focused on what makes American poetry different from other literatures. The short imagistic poem combines odd and usually seemingly unpoetic items (rubber, coal, uranium) with more traditional literary elements (moons, poems). The final stanza develops this principle of contradictory assemblage into the surreal extended simile of the shark-like poem swimming through the desert uttering cries that are almost human. Clearly Simpson's poem is not conceptual and discursive, but suggestive and symbolic. What does the shark symbolize? At the very least, the image suggests the restless, untamed, omnivorous, and even dangerous nature of American poetry. How does this vision of the art compare to Moore's or MacLeish's?

David R. Slavitt, TITANIC, page 846

In "The Convergence of the Twain," Hardy censures the vanity, luxury, and pride that prompted Fate to ram the *Titanic* into an iceberg. Slavitt's poem about the same tragedy takes another tack. He makes dying on the *Titanic* sound almost like fun—all aboard!

If they sold passage tomorrow for that same crossing, who would not buy?

Slavitt's point is that, since we all have to die, it's certainly more glamorous, more desirable to do it "first-class" (note the double meaning of "go" in the last line) than to die less comfortably, in more mundane ways, and soon be forgotten.

Cathy Song, STAMP COLLECTING, page 846

Song's poem depends upon an original and illuminating conceit: the speaker views the countries of the world through the stamps they issue. Understanding that the subject of each stamp reflects in some way the culture and geography that produced it, the speaker speculates on the national vision and self-image behind her stamps. "Stamp Collecting" is a political poem, but it unfolds with such delicate observations and employs such ingenious language that it may be easy for students to miss the political content. Moreover, the poem has no specific ideological ax to grind. "Stamp Collecting" explains the concept of national self-identity rather than any particular political cause.

Wallace Stevens, THE EMPEROR OF ICE-CREAM, page 848

Choosing this poem to represent him in an anthology, Stevens once remarked, "This wears a deliberately commonplace costume, and yet seems to me to contain something of the essential gaudiness of poetry; that is the reason why I like it." (His statement appears in *Fifty Poets: An American Auto-Anthology*, ed. William Rose Benet [New York: Diffield, 1933].)

Some students will at once relish the poet's humor, others may discover it in class discussion. Try to gather the literal facts of the situation before getting into the poem's suggestions. The wake or funeral of a poor old woman is taking place in her home. The funeral flowers come in old newspapers, not in florists' fancy wrappings; the mourners don't dress up, but wear their usual street clothes; the refreshments aren't catered but are whipped up in the kitchen by a neighbor, a cigar-roller. Like ice cream, the refreshments are a dairy product. Nowadays they would probably be a sour cream chip-dip; perhaps in 1923 they were blocks of Philadelphia cream cheese squashed into cups for spreading on soda crackers. To a correspondent, Stevens wrote that *fantails* refers not to fans but to fantail pigeons (*Letters* [New York: Knopf, 1966] 341). Such embroidery seems a lowbrow pursuit: the poor old woman's pathetic aspiration toward beauty. *Deal* furniture is cheap. Everything points to a run-down neighborhood, and to a woman about whose passing nobody very much cares.

Who is the Emperor? The usual guess is Death. Some students will probably see that the Emperor and the muscular cigar-roller (with his creamy curds) suggest each other. (Stevens does not say that they are identical.) Ice cream suggests the chill of the grave— and what besides? Today, some of its connotations will be commonplace: supermarkets, Baskin-Robbins. To the generation of Stevens, ice cream must have meant more: something luxurious and scarce, costly, hard-to-keep, requiring quick consumption. Other present-day connotations may come to mind: sweetness, deliciousness, childhood pleasure. Stevens's personal view of the ice cream in the poem was positive. "The true sense of 'Let be be finale of seem' is let being become the conclusion or denouement of appearing to be: in short, ice cream is an absolute good" (*Letters* 341). An absolute good! The statement is worth quoting to students who have doubts about the poet's attitude toward ice cream—as did an executive of the Amalgamated Ice Cream Association, who once wrote to the poet in perplexity (see *Letters* 501–2). If ice cream recalls sweet death, still (like curds) it also contains hints of mother's milk, life, and vitality.

On a visit to Mount Holyoke, XJK was told that, as part of an annual celebration, it is customary for the trustees and the seniors to serve ice cream (in Dixie cups) to the freshman class at the grave of Mary Lyon, founder of the college. In a flash he remembered Stevens's poem, and embraced Jung's theory of archetypes.

Alfred, Lord Tennyson, ULYSSES, page 849

The following inadequate précis, meant to make lovers of Tennyson's poem irate, might be quoted to students to see whether they agree with it: A hardy old futzer can't stand life in the old folks' home, and calls on his cronies to join him in an escape, even though the whole lot of them are going to break their necks.

For criticism, see Paul F. Baum, *Tennyson Sixty Years After* (Chapel Hill: U of North Carolina P, 1948) 92–94; and John Pettigrew, "Tennyson's 'Ulysses': A Reconciliation of Opposites," *Victorian Poetry* 1 (Jan. 1963): 27–45.

Dylan Thomas, FERN HILL, page 851

Fern Hill is the farm of Thomas's aunt, Ann Jones, with whom he spent boyhood holidays. In line 2 the poet cites a favorite saying of his father's, "Happy as the grass is green." The saying is echoed again in line 38. As students may notice, Thomas likes to play upon familiar phrases and transform them, as in line 7, "once *below* [not *upon*] a time."

It came as a great shock when we first realized that this poem, which XJK had thought a quite spontaneous burst of lyric energy, is shaped into a silhouette, and that the poet contrived its form by counting syllables. Such laborious working methods were customary for Thomas. John Malcolm Brinnin has recalled seeing more than 200 separate and distinct versions of "Fern Hill"—a fact worth conveying to students who think poets simply overflow.

We take the closing line to express Thomas's view of his own poetry, lyrical and rule-bound at the same time: a song uttered in chains. Of course, the last line also means that the boy in the poem was held in chains by Time, the villain, who informs the whole poem (except for stanzas 3 and 4, which see childhood as Eden). Students may be asked to trace all the mentions of Time throughout the poem, then to sum up the poet's theme. William York Tindall, who offers a line-by-line commentary, makes a fine distinction: "Not how it feels to be young, the theme of 'Fern Hill' is how it feels to have been young" (*A Reader's Guide to Dylan Thomas* [New York: Noonday, 1962]). And we'd add, "how it would have felt to grow old, if the boy had realized he wouldn't live forever."

According to Tindall (in a lecture), Thomas used to grow huffy whenever asked if he were an admirer of Gerard Manley Hopkins. Still, to hear aloud both "Fern Hill" and Hopkins's "Pied Beauty" is to notice much similarity of sound and imagery. Hopkins studied Welsh for a time, while Thomas never did learn the language; but both at least knew of ancient Welsh poetry and its ingeniously woven sound patterns.

Thomas's magnificent (or, some would say, magnificently hammy) reading of this poem can be heard on Caedmon recording TC 1002, cassette 51002, compact disk Z1002. The recording, *A Child's Christmas in Wales and Other Poems,* also contains "Do not go gentle into that good night."

John Updike, EX-BASKETBALL PLAYER, page 852

Updike's ex-basketball player suffers the fate that Housman's athlete escapes by dying young. Flick Webb has to live on, unsung, in "fields where glory does not stay." The man whose "hands were like wild birds" now uses those hands to pump gas, check oil, and change flat tires. "Once in a while, / As a gag, he dribbles an inner tube." In his spare time, he sits in Mae's luncheonette and "just nods / Beyond her face toward bright applauding tiers / Of Necco Wafers, Nibs, and Juju Beads." (Are today's students still familiar with those brand names?)

Updike's light tone does not obscure the pathos of Flick's situation. (Students might be asked if they know anyone like Flick Webb.) Though Updike has written notable light verse, he says of this early poem, his second to be accepted by the *New Yorker,* that it "is 'serious' and has enjoyed a healthy anthology life, though its second stanza now reads strangely to students. . . . That is, they have never seen glass-headed pumps, or gas stations with a medley of brands of gasoline, or the word *Esso*" (foreword to a new edition of Updike's first book, *The Carpentered Hen* [New York: Knopf, 1982]).

See how quickly your class can identify the poem's form as blank verse.

Derek Walcott, THE VIRGINS, page 853

Walcott provides an ironic view of the main seaport of the Virgin Islands. The irony begins with the title in which the islands seem waiting to be raped or seduced by outsiders. The sun is like a drug ("sun-stoned"), and the term *free port* is used sarcastically to underscore how little of any worth freedom has brought this city. The dense images and careful rhetoric of this poem create the impression of a dead place where no genuine life is possible.

Edmund Waller, GO, LOVELY ROSE, page 854

In some ways quieter than Marvell's "To His Coy Mistress" or Herrick's "To the Virgins, to Make Much of Time," this poem has the same theme: *carpe diem*. "Go, Lovely Rose" merits admiration for its seemingly effortless grace and for the sudden, gently shocking focus on our mortality in the poem's final stanza.

Students may enjoy reading Ezra Pound's imitative tribute to Waller: the "Envoi" to *Hugh Selwyn Mauberley,* beginning "Go, dumb-born book . . . ," in *Personae,* Pound's collected shorter poems (New York: New Directions, 1949).

Walt Whitman, A NOISELESS PATIENT SPIDER, page 855

"A Noiseless Patient Spider" isn't a poem about human beings reaching out in love to other human beings, but about the soul trying to form contact with higher reality. It may be used effectively in discussing symbolism in poetry, as well as figures of speech. Whitman's poem is open in form, and yet certain lines fall into traditional measures (almost into rime, too), as would be indicated by rearranging them:

> Till the bridge you will need be form'd
> Till the ductile anchor hold,
> Till the gossamer thread you fling
> Catch somewhere, O my soul.

Walt Whitman, I SAW IN LOUISIANA A LIVE-OAK GROWING, page 856

Whitman often regards some other living thing and sees himself reflected in it. In "Live-Oak" (one of the *Calamus* poems), the tree becomes his mirror in line 4; and one might expect the poem, like "A Noiseless Patient Spider," to extend the comparison. But the poem takes a surprising twist: Whitman himself cannot abide the oak's solitude. (This poem has not been shown to refer to any particular friends or events in the poet's life.)

Pablo Neruda's tribute to Whitman may well be applied:

> There are many kinds of greatness, but let me say (though I be a poet of the Spanish tongue) that Walt Whitman has taught me more than Spain's Cervantes: in Walt Whitman's work one never finds the ignorant being humbled, nor is the human condition ever found offended (qtd. by Gay Wilson Allen in *Poetry Pilot* [Nov. 1976]).

Richard Wilbur, THE WRITER, page 856

A searching criticism of Wilbur's work, and this poem, is offered by Andrew Hudgins (*Hudson Review,* Winter 1989). Sometimes Wilbur implies that it is possible to master the world and its complicated problems in much the same way that a poet, in a successful poem, masters the language—but it isn't, of course. Wilbur thus places himself in a dilemma, one he is aware of. Hudgins summarizes "The Writer" and interprets it:

. . . Hearing his daughter as she types a story in her room, he compares the house to a ship and the sound of the typewriter keys to "a chain hauled over a gunwale," while the "stuff" of his daughter's life is "a great cargo and some of it heavy." Then, rather glibly, he wishes her a "lucky passage." As soon as he's completed the metaphor, however, he rejects the "easy figure" because he remembers how difficult the life of a writer can be. The next metaphor he advances is embedded in the anecdote of a "dazed starling" that once became trapped in the same room his daughter is now working in. . . . Though the poem is touching and even powerful, the implied final metaphor, and the ending of the poem, while infinitely better than the rejected first metaphor of the ship, still have a bit of its premeditated neatness about them.

Whether or not the poem is autobiography, Wilbur does have a daughter, Ellen Wilbur, now a widely published fiction writer, author of *Wind & Birds & Human Voices*, a collection of short stories (Stuart Wright, 1984: NAL paperback, 1985).

William Carlos Williams, SPRING AND ALL, page 857

QUESTIONS FOR DISCUSSION:

1. *Why cannot Williams's attitude toward spring be called "poetic" and "conventional"? What is his attitude toward the approaching season? By what means is it indicated? Consider especially lines 14–15 and 24–25, and the suggestion of conta-*gious *in the opening line.* Spring is stealing over the land as a contagious disease infects a victim. But spring is not a disease: it has a "stark dignity."

2. *An opinion: "This poem clearly draws from the poet's experience as a pediatrician who had attended hundreds of newborns, and whose work was often to describe with clinical exactness the symptoms of his patients." Discuss.* Lines 16–18 especially seem to contain a metaphor of newborn infants. The adjectives *mottled, dried, sluggish* could occur in a physician's report. In lines 9–13 also, the description of bushes, trees, and vines seems painstakingly exact in its detail.

Recalling his life as writer and physician in an article for a popular magazine, Williams once told how poems would come to him while driving on his daily rounds. "When the phrasing of a passage suddenly hits me, knowing how quickly such things are lost, I find myself at the side of the road frantically searching in my medical bag for a prescription blank" ("Seventy Years Deep," *Holiday* [Nov. 1954]: 78). "By the road to the contagious hospital" was one such poem, originally recorded on prescription blanks (Roy Miki, "Driving and Writing," *William Carlos Williams: Man and Poet*, ed. Carroll F. Terrell [Orono: National Poetry Foundation, 1983] 113).

Scholars have speculated that the brief lines of many of Williams's poems may have been decreed by the narrow width of a prescription blank, but we don't buy that guess. Had he wanted longer lines Williams would have turned the blanks sideways, or composed in smaller handwriting.

William Carlos Williams, To Waken an Old Lady, page 859

Questions for Discussion:

1. *By which words or phrases does Williams suggest the physical ravages of old age? What very different connotations do the phrases* broken / seedhusks *and* shrill / piping *carry, as well as the suggestions of feeble and broken senility?* Broken husks suggest a feast, piping suggests merriment.

2. *What is the* dark wind? *Can a wind be literally dark?* No, it can't; Williams means dark in the sense of sinister or menacing. This wind is like the passage of time that buffers or punishes.

3. *What is the dictionary definition of* tempered? *What does the word mean in this poem?*

William Wordsworth, Composed Upon Westminster Bridge, page 859

Imaginary conversation:

> *Instructor:* What do you make of the title? Is this a poem composed upon the subject of a bridge, or a poem composed while standing on a bridge's sidewalk?
> *Student:* The latter, obviously.
> *Instructor:* How do you know?
> *Student:* His eye is located up on the bridge. Otherwise he wouldn't see with such a wide-angle lens.
> *Instructor:* You genius! To the head of the class!

Whose is the "mighty heart"? Wordsworth is describing the city as a sleeping beauty about to awaken. Of course, the brightness of the scene is increased by the poet's being out for his stroll before a hundred thousand chimneys have begun to smoke from coal fires preparing kippers for breakfast. Charles Lamb, in a letter to Wordsworth, had chided the poet that the urban emotions must be unknown to him, so perhaps this famous sonnet is an answer to the charge.

Compare "The World Is Too Much with Us" for a different Wordsworth attitude toward commerce; or compare Wordsworth's London of 1807 with Blake's "London" of 1794—practically the same city, but a different perspective. (Wordsworth up on the bridge at dawn, letting distance lend enchantment; Blake down in the city streets by night, with the chimney sweep, the teenage whore, and the maimed veteran.)

James Wright, Autumn Begins in Martins Ferry, Ohio, page 860

Martins Ferry was Wright's home town. The speaker of the poem describes the men of Martins Ferry sitting in the high school stadium, the only place in the vicinity where heroes are likely to appear. Certainly these working-class men have given up dreams of heroism in their own lives. Grey-faced, ruptured, worn out by their jobs in heavy industry, they sit in taverns over their beer "ashamed to go home" to their wives. Unable even to satisfy the romantic or sexual longings of their wives, who are "dying for love," these men turn to their sons for inspiration. In October, as the year begins to die, they watch the heroic spectacle of their sons' football games. While there is something gloriously primal about Wright's scene, there is also something darkly ironic. Will the sons of Martins Ferry achieve true heroism on the gridiron? Or will they just bang up their knees and dislocate their shoulders for a season or two before they go on to equally unheroic adult lives? The poem masterfully has it both ways—both heroic and doomed.

Perhaps the fathers were once football heroes themselves, as George S. Lensing and Ronald Moran point out in *Four Poets and the Emotive Imagination* (Baton Rouge: Louisiana State UP, 1976), a study that discusses nearly the whole of Wright's work. "From this there is the suggestion that the futures of the current community heroes may be as bleak as the present time assuredly is for the fathers."

Did Wright mean to protest the violence of football—at least, football of the Martins Ferry kind? Not according to the poet himself, who once played on an Ohio River Valley semipro team. Although the high school games were "ritualized, formalized violence," they had positive qualities: "the expression of physical grace," "terrific aesthetic appeal." Wright's own high school produced not just lads doomed to frustration (like their fathers), but at least one football hero—Lou Groza, placekicker for the Cleveland Browns. (Wright made his remarks in an interview reprinted in *The Pure Clear Word: Essays on the Poetry of James Wright*, ed. Dave Smith [Urbana: U of Illinois P, 1982] 3–4.)

In the same critical anthology, Robert Hass sees football in the poem as a harvest ritual, which, like all good harvest rituals, celebrates sexual potency and the fruitfulness of the earth (two positive qualities apparently not conspicuous in Martins Ferry). "Even the stanzaic structure of the poem participates in the ritual. The first two stanzas separate the bodies of the men from the bodies of the women, and the third stanza gives us the boys pounding against each other, as if they could, out of their wills, effect a merging" (210).

Jan Hodge, of Morningside College in Sioux City, Iowa, wrote us a long letter full of insights about this poem. (We have incorporated a few of his remarks into our comments above.) He ends his reading of the poem with some especially interesting observations:

> Isn't the third stanza (introduced by that powerful placement of "Therefore" on a line by itself) the logical culmination of the first *two* stanzas—the point being that it is because of *both* the larger community's need for heroes *and* their father's need to find (vicarious) pride in them that the sons give themselves so suicidally (and so beautifully?) to football? The speaker understands the harshness of the lives around him and why therefore football becomes so important. He is also I think compassionate, but refuses to sentimentalize either the game or the failures he sees so accurately. I find Wright's use of the two oxymorons—"suicidally beautiful" and "gallop terribly"— particularly effective to express his ambiguous attitude toward football, the

sons, the fathers, and the workers. If there is violence, there is also a kind of grace in their sacrifice—all the more poignant because (as you and others have pointed out) it is almost certainly futile.

"Does Wright mean to protest the violence of football?" you ask. A majority of my students argue so—but less I think because of the poem than because they think (wrongly) I am opposed to football and assign the poem for that reason. I end up in discussion defending the poem against their second-guessing of it. I had assumed for years that such a protest was not Wright's intent; your notes confirm my view.

Finally, some comments by poet William Virgil Davis of Baylor University, who considers "Autumn Begins in Martins Ferry" to be the key poem in Wright's work. In an article on "James Wright's *Cogito*" in *Notes on Contemporary Literature* (Jan. 1993), Davis describes the structure of the poem:

> The poem follows the pattern of a logical argument, the three stanzas parallel-ing the arrangment of a syllogism. Indeed, the first stanza asserts, "I think it" (1. 2) and the third begins, "Therefore" (1. 9). The two "terms" of the argument are defined at the conclusions of stanzas one and two in the parallel phrases, "Dreaming of heroes" (1. 5) and "Dying for love" (1. 8). These are respectively associated with men (fathers) and women (mothers), and the results of these kinds of "deaths" create situations in which the "sons" of such parents "grow suicidally beautiful / At the beginning of October, / And gallop terribly against each other's bodies" (11. 10–12). This conclusion, following the "There-fore" of line 9, is more than the "*sum*" of Descartes's principle, but, like it, it defines a being born of the realization of a logical argument: what one is is what he believes and feels, based upon his past experiences and his personal history. Still, the "essence," although born of "existence," exceeds it. This is, then, beauty born out of the death of self for the sake of self-realization.

Therefore, what the poem "means" is what the speaker reads or feels at the end of it; and, even if the argument is invalid, it is true.

Mary Sidney Wroth, IN THIS STRANGE LABYRINTH, page 861

Recent feminist scholarship has uncovered many unjustly neglected works by women, but surely Mary Sidney Wroth must rank among the most interesting—and most overdue—additions to the canon. The niece of Sir Philip Sidney and Lady Mary Herbert, the Countess of Pembroke, Mary Sidney grew up in a tal-ented and cultivated family. An arranged marriage to Sir Robert Wroth, however, proved unhappy during his lifetime and financially precarious after his death.

Wroth's sonnets were added to her prose romance, *Urania* (1621), which she boldly published under her own name. Titled *Pamphilia to Amphilanthus*, the poems (which constitute the first sonnet sequence by an Englishwoman) speak in the voices of the prose romance's two main characters, but the poems also reflect her personal experience after her husband's death, especially her romantic liaison with her married cousin, the Earl of Pembroke, by whom she had two children.

"In this strange labyrinth" employs the image of the labyrinth as a symbol for erotic confusion. Each direction the speaker contemplates taking poses some danger or disappointment. This conceit is developed for thirteen lines until a detail from the myth—Ariadne's thread—is introduced in the final line. As Ariadne's thread guided her lover through the dangers of the labyrinth, so will "the thread of love" guide the speaker.

Sir Thomas Wyatt, THEY FLEE FROM ME THAT SOMETIME DID ME SEKË, page 862

Surely Wyatt knew what he was about. Sounding the final *e*'s helps to fulfill the expectations of iambic pentameter in lines 2, 12, 15, 17, 20, and 21, lines that otherwise would seem to fall short. In other lines, however, Wyatt appears to make the rhythm deliberately swift or hesitant in order to fit the sense. Line 7 ("Busily seeking with a continual change") seems busy with extra syllables and has to be read quickly to fit the time allotted it. Such a metrical feast seems worthy of Yeats, as does line 11, in which two spondees ("loose gown," "did fall") cast great stress upon that suddenly falling garment.

What line in English love poetry, by the way, is more engaging than "Dear heart, how like you this?" And when have a lover's extended arms ever been more nicely depicted? (This line may be thrown into the teeth of anyone who thinks that, in descriptive writing, adjectives are bad things.)

William Butler Yeats, CRAZY JANE TALKS WITH THE BISHOP, page 863

Piecing together a history from this Crazy Jane poem and others, John Unterecker has identified the Bishop as a divinity student who had courted Jane in his youth. She rejected him in favor of a wild, disreputable lover: Jack the journeyman. As soon as he got enough authority, the Bishop-to-be had Jack banished, but Jane has remained faithful to her lover (at least, in spirit). (See *A Reader's Guide to William Butler Yeats* [New York: Noonday, 1959].) In this poem, the Bishop's former interest in Jane has dwindled to a concern for her soul only. Or has it? Perhaps the Bishop, no doubt a handsome figure in his surplice, may be demonstrating Yeats's contention that fair needs foul. Jane is living in lonely squalor. The grave, she says, can affirm the truth that her friends are gone, for it holds many of them; and her own empty bed can affirm that Jack is gone, too. Still, she firmly renounces the Bishop and his advice.

Each word of the poem is exact. Love has *pitched* his mansion as one would pitch a tent. The next-to-last line ends in two immense puns: *sole or whole*. The Bishop thinks that soul is all that counts, but Jane knows that both soul and hole are needed. Such puns may be why Yeats declared (in a letter) that he wanted to stop writing the Crazy Jane series: "I want to exorcise that slut, Crazy Jane, whose language has become unendurable."

What does Yeats mean by the paradoxical statement in the last two lines? Perhaps (1) that a woman cannot be fulfilled and remain a virgin—that, since fair and foul are near of kin, one cannot know Love, the platonic ideal, without going through the door of the physical body; and (2) that the universe is by nature a yin/yang combination of fair and foul (or, as Yeats would have it in *A Vision*, a pair of intertwining gyres). Crazy Jane may be crazy, but in Yeats's view she is a soothsayer.

William Butler Yeats, LEDA AND THE SWAN, page 864

The deliberately awful off-rime *up / drop* ends the sonnet with an appropriately jarring plop as the God-swan discards the used Leda and sinks into his postejaculatory stupor.

Other questions that can be raised:

1. What *knowledge* and *power* does Yeats refer to in line 14?

2. Do the words *staggering* (line 2) and *loosening* (line 6) keep to the basic meter of the poem or depart from it? How does rhythm express meaning in these lines? (It staggers on *staggering* and loosens on *loosening*.)

3. Compare this poem to Donne's sonnet "Batter my heart." Is the tone of Yeats's sonnet—the poet's attitude toward this ravishing—similar or dissimilar?

For an early draft of the poem, see Yeats's *Memoirs*, ed. Denis Donoghue (New York: Macmillan, 1973) 272–74.

William Butler Yeats, WHEN YOU ARE OLD, page 864

Yeats wrote this poem to the actress Maud Gonne in October, 1891. It is based very loosely on Ronsard's sonnet, "Quand Vous Serez Bien Vielle," but it is not a translation. Yeats merely took Ronsard's premise (an old woman rereading the verses a poet wrote to her in their youth) and developed it in his own way.

In this gentlest of love poems, the speaker is resigned to not winning the woman he loves. He is merely one of many men who love her. His claim, however, is that his love was not for the surface charms of her grace or beauty; he alone loved her for her searching soul. And he has the satisfaction of being able to preserve the unique quality of his devotion in words. Yeats's lyric, therefore, celebrates the ennobling power of both love and poetry.

To be candidly emotional risks seeming sentimental, but may we end the notes to the "Poems for Further Reading" by hoping that many years from now a few of our students take down this book to reread a few of the poems we taught them and realize that we spoke to "the pilgrim soul" in them?

Envoi

Let us end this section with another poem about teaching poetry—one by Paul Lake, a professor at Arkansas Technical University in Russellville. Lake's "Introduction to Poetry" appears in his collection, *Another Kind of Travel* (Chicago: U of Chicago P, 1988).

Introduction to Poetry

She comes in late, then settles like a sigh
On the first day, returning every week
Promptly at ten, each Monday Wednesday Friday,
To study Shakespeare, Jonson, Donne, and Blake;

Enters the room to an approving murmur,
Straightens her dress, then, brushing back her hair,
Arches her body with the slightest tremor,
And sits, while the room grows breathless, in her chair;

Sits for an hour, while busy sophomores worry
Each turgid line, a Botticellian smile
On her rapt face, who's learned how little study
Love involves; who, walking down the aisle,

Knows in her bones how little poetry
Words breathe, and how—on turning to go home—
All eyes will watch her rise above her "C"
And walk off, like a goddess on the foam.

DRAMA

28   *Reading a Play*

In many parts of the country, students rarely if ever see plays other than school or other amateur productions, and the instructor may encounter some resistance to the whole idea of studying drama. But all students are steeped in film and television drama, and it may be useful to point out that such drama begins with playscripts. One might reason somewhat like this: Movies and television, it's true, give plays hard competition in our society, and a camera does have advantages. In moments, film can present whole panoramas and can show details in close-up that theaters (with their cumbersome sets and machinery) cannot duplicate. Movies used to be called "photoplays," but the name implies an unnecessary limitation, for there is no point in confining the camera to recording the contents of a picture-frame stage. But a play—whether staged in a proscenium theater or in a parking lot—has its own distinct advantages. It is a medium that makes possible things a camera cannot do. Unlike movies and television, a play gives us living actors, and it involves living audiences who supply it with their presences (and who can move one another to laughter or to tears). Compared, say, to the laughter of live spectators at a comedy, the "canned" laughter often dubbed into television programs is a weak attempt to persuade television viewers that they are not alone.

A PLAY IN ITS ELEMENTS

Susan Glaspell
TRIFLES, page 869

The comeback of *Trifles* may be due, we think, not only to Glaspell's pioneering feminist views but also to its being such a gripping, tightly structured play. Whether or not you have much time to spend on the elements of a play, we think you will find *Trifles* worth teaching; students respond to it.

Topic for writing or discussion: What common theme or themes do you find in both *Trifles* and *Antigonê*? (A conflict between the law and a woman's personal duty.)

The Provincetown Players, who performed in a theater on an abandoned wharf, had a fertile summer in 1916. Besides *Trifles*, with Glaspell herself playing Mrs. Hale, their season included the first Eugene O'Neill play to be produced, *Bound East for Cardiff*. Glaspell has said that she derived the plot of *Trifles* from a murder case she had investigated as a reporter in Des Moines.

TRAGEDY AND COMEDY

David Ives
SURE THING, page 887

In 1993 I (DG) attended the original off-Broadway production of David Ives's six one-act comedies, *All in the Timing*. By the end of the evening I knew that one of these little comic gems would have to go into the next edition of *Literature*. When *All in the Timing* opened, Ives was a relative unknown in American theater. Soon he became a minor celebrity. A shy but witty man, Ives wore his newfound fame with comic nonchalance. When *New York* magazine listed him as one of the "100 Smartest New Yorkers," Ives told a reporter from the *Columbia University Record* that he didn't approve. "Lists," he explained, "are anti-democratic, discriminatory, elitist, and sometimes the print is too small." Audiences of all kinds respond to Ives's work. *All in the Timing* has gradually become one of the most widely produced contemporary plays in America.

Sure Thing demonstrates how quickly innovative theatrical technique is incorporated into mainstream drama. Ives bases his play in equal parts on modernist experimental theater and popular comedy—half Luigi Pirandello, one might say, and half Groucho Marx. One might add further that Ives uses the modernist techniques of dramatic distancing, stylization, and fragmentation to tell the most traditional story possible—a young man and woman meeting to fall in love. (Youthful romance has been a central subject of comedy since Menander and Plautus.) The resulting work is both surprising and familiar. The best new art often works exactly as Ives's *Sure Thing* does by creating a meaningful conversation between the ancient and the new.

If the fragmentary technique of *Sure Thing* isn't just a clever theatrical gimmick, what meaningful conversations does it open up? By dramatizing every moment of mutual attraction and rejection, Ives's disjointed narrative structure provides a candid and detailed anatomy of modern romance. It also shows how individuals both speak and listen in social code. *Sure Thing* is as much about language as romance. Ives embodies the mutual exploration of these two characters entirely in language. There is no physical comedy in the play. The only non-verbal element is the bell that punctuates the action to announce that one of the characters has lost interest in the other. (The bell editorializes only once with multiple rings after Betty begins to talk about astrological signs, but this auditory gag is merely an intensification of its normal role.)

Perhaps the most interesting idea found in *Sure Thing* is the notion that human personalities are so changeable that the timing of an experience is critical to its proper reception. (And, of course, in no mode of human communication is timing more important than in comedy.) When Betty says that she can't believe she has waited so long to read Faulkner, she initiates a crucial exchange that comments on both the theme and style of the play:

BILL. You never know. You might not have liked him before.

BETTY. That's true.

BILL. You might not have been ready for him. You have to hit these things at the right moment or it's not good.

BETTY. That's happened to me.

BILL. It's all in the timing.

Bill's final phrase became the title of Ives's award-winning night of comedies as well as the title for his collection of fourteen one-act plays, *All in the Timing* (New York: Vintage, 1995). One suspects it wasn't just the theatrical pun that made the phrase so attractive but also the aesthetic it suggests.

Instructors should remember how easy it is to produce *Sure Thing* in the classroom. All one needs is two actors, two chairs and a bell (or whistle or buzzer). The play takes less than fifteen minutes to perform. Students can also be asked to write and perform additional scenes of their own.

Students interested in writing on Ives should be directed to the other plays in *All in the Timing*. It contains two short plays that provide interesting parallels to *Sure Thing*. This first is *Words, Words, Words*, which presents three monkeys (named Milton, Swift, and Kafka) who have been placed in a laboratory at Columbia University with three typewriters to produce the text of *Hamlet*. The second play is *The Universal Language* in which a young woman takes an introductory lesson in a phony universal language (a parody of Esperanto) that proves to be an educational scam. Both of these plays are not only hilarious, but they offer an insightful critique of language. Ives's preface to *All in the Timing* is in itself a brilliant comic performance.

WRITER'S PERSPECTIVE

Susan Glaspell on Drama
CREATING *TRIFLES*, page 897

Over the past quarter century Susan Glaspell has slowly regained her rightful position as an important innovator in modern American drama. *Trifles* is now securely in the twentieth-century canon, but the rest of Glaspell's work remains too little known; and despite some fine recent work, her critical coverage is still incommensurate with her achievement. (Glaspell wrote thirteen plays, ten novels, and nearly fifty short stories.) There is also not yet a comprehensive, full-length modern biography. Much important scholarship needs to be done.

Given the lack of critical and biographical commentary, it is puzzling that Glaspell's 1927 autobiography, *The Road to the Temple*, is not better known. The excerpt from her autobiography in the "Writer's Perspective" has never appeared in any textbook before (though surely some other enterprising editor will soon lift it—with our compliments).

In this section of *The Road to the Temple*, Glaspell provides a first-hand account of two important events in the history of American drama—the creation of the Provincetown Players and the unusual genesis of her first play, *Trifles*, in 1916. As her autobiography makes abundantly clear, Glaspell and George Cram "Jig" Cook's marriage was deeply fulfilling for both partners. It is a gentle irony that Glaspell's feminist play was written at the prompting of her supportive husband. (He also helped create the Provincetown Players to spur her talent.) American literature has had few nicer moments than this one.

The Road to the Temple (New York: Stokes, 1927) is now long out of print. It took me (DG) several months to search out a copy by canvassing major dealers in modern literature, but most large university libraries will have a copy. Glaspell's style is very casual, but the book is fun to read. In addition to her own life story, she provides interesting accounts of American theatrical and bohemian life in the first three decades of the twentieth century. Cambridge's edition of Susan Glaspell's *Plays* (1987), edited by C. W. E. Bigsby, reprints four one-act plays and has excellent scholarly apparatus and a fine introduction. It is indispensable for students of this pioneering playwright.

Sophocles

OEDIPUS THE KING, page 913

One problem in teaching this masterpiece is that students often want to see Oedipus as a pitiable fool, helplessly crushed by the gods, thus stripping him of heroism and tragic dignity. (A classic bepiddlement of the play once turned up on a freshman paper: "At the end, Oedipus goes off blinded into exile, but that's the way the cookie crumbles.") It can be argued that Oedipus showed himself to be no fool in solving the riddle of the Sphinx or in deciding to leave Corinth; that no god forced him to kill Laïos or to marry Iocastê.

Another problem in teaching this play is that some students want to make Oedipus into an Everyman, an abstract figure representing all humanity. But Oedipus's circumstances are, to say the least, novel and individual. "Oedipus is not 'man,' but Oedipus," as S. M. Adams argues in *Sophocles the Playwright* (Toronto: U of Toronto P, 1957). On the other hand, Freud's reading of the play does suggest that Oedipus is Everyman—or, better, that every man is Oedipus and like Oedipus wishes to kill his father and marry his mother. A passage from Freud's celebrated remarks about the play is included in the casebook.

Despite Freud's views, which usually fascinate students, critical consensus appears to be that Oedipus himself did not have an Oedipus complex. Sophocles does not portray Oedipus and Iocastê as impassioned lovers; their marriage was (as Philip Wheelwright says) "a matter of civic duty: having rid the Thebans of the baleful Sphinx by answering her riddle correctly, he received the throne of Thebes and the widowed queen as his due reward" (*The Burning Fountain* [Bloomington: Indiana University Press, 1954]). Wheelwright also notes, incidentally, that the title *Oedipus Tyrannus* might be translated more accurately as "Oedipus the Usurper"—a usurper being (to the Greeks) anyone who gains a throne by means other than by blood succession. Actually, of course, Oedipus had a hereditary right to the throne. (Another interpretation of the play sees Laïos and Iocastê as having incurred the original guilt: by leaving a royal prince to die in the wilderness, they defied natural order and the will of the gods.)

For the nonspecialist, a convenient gathering of views will be found in *Oedipus Tyrannus*, ed. Luci Berkowitz and Theodore F. Brunner (New York: Norton, 1970). Along with a prose translation of the play by the editors, the book includes the classic comments by Aristotle, Nietzsche, and Freud, and discussions by recent critics and psychologists. Seth Bernardete offers a detailed, passage-by-passage commentary in *Sophocles: A Collection of Critical Essays*, ed. Thomas Woodard (Englewood Cliffs, NJ: Prentice, 1966). Francis Fergusson has pointed out that the play may be read (on one level) as a murder mystery: "Oedipus takes the role of District Attorney; and when he at last convicts himself, we have a twist, a *coup de théâtre,* of unparalleled excitement." But Fergusson distrusts any reading so literal, and questions attempts to make the play entirely coherent and rational. Sophocles "preserves the ultimate mystery by focusing upon [Oedipus] at a level beneath, or prior to any rationalization whatever" (*The Idea of a Theatre* [Princeton: Princeton UP, 1949]). Refreshing, after you read many myth critics, is A. J. A. Waldock's *Sophocles the Dramatist* (Cambridge: Cambridge UP, 1951; reprinted in part by Berkowitz and Brunner). According to Waldock, the play is sheer entertainment, a spectacular piece of shock, containing no message. "There is no meaning in the *Oedipus Tyrannus.* There is merely the terror of coincidence, and then, at the end of it all, our impression of man's power to suffer, and of his greatness because of this power." Pointing out how little we know of Sophocles' religion, Waldock finds the dramatist's beliefs "meagre in number and depressingly commonplace."

Although the religious assumptions of the play may not be surprising to Waldock, students may want to have them stated. A good summing-up is that of E. R. Dodds, who maintains that Sophocles did not always believe that the gods are in any human sense "just"; but that he did always believe that the gods exist and that man should revere them ("On Misunderstanding the Oedipus Rex," *Greece and Rome* [Oxford: Oxford UP, 1966] Vol. 13).

"Possibly the best service the critic can render the *Oedipus Rex,*" says Waldock, "is to leave it alone." If, however, other criticism can help, there are especially valuable discussions in H. D. F. Kitto, *Greek Tragedy,* 3rd ed. (London: Methuen, 1961), and *Poiesis* (Berkeley: U of California P, 1966); Richmond Lattimore, *The Poetry of Greek Tragedy* (Baltimore: Johns Hopkins UP, 1958); and Patrick Mullahy, *Oedipus, Myth and Complex* (New York: Grove, 1948).

In the "Suggestions for Writing" at the end of the chapter there is one especially challenging topic (number 3): to compare translations of the play. For any student willing to pick up the challenge, we think this topic might produce a great term paper. The differences between versions, of course, are considerable. Sheppard's rendition, or Kitto's, is more nearly literal than that of Fitts and Fitzgerald and much more so than that of Berg and Clay. In the latter team's version of 1978, the persons of the tragedy all speak like formally open lyrics in current little magazines. Lots of monosyllables. Frequent pauses. Understatement. Lush imagery. Berg and Clay perform this service brilliantly, and it might be argued: why shouldn't each generation remake the classics in its own tongue?

Still impressive is the film *Oedipus Rex* (1957), directed by Tyrone Guthrie, a record of a performance given in Stratford, Canada. Although the theater of the play is more Stratfordian than Athenian, the actors wear splendid masks. The text is the Yeats version. The film (88 minutes long, 16 mm, in color) may be bought or rented from Contemporary/McGraw-Hill Films, 1221 Avenue of the Americas, New York, NY 10020, or from their regional distributors.

In July 1984, the Greek National Theater presented a much-discussed *Oedipus Rex* at the Kennedy Center in Washington. Bernard Knox offers an admiring account of it in *Grand Street* for Winter 1985. The director, Minos Volankis, staged the play on a "circular, dark brown plate, tilted toward the audience" and etched with a labyrinth pattern. In Volankis's version, Oedipus and Iocastê cannot see the pattern and ignore it as they move about the stage, but the chorus and Teiresias are aware of the labyrinth and respectfully trace its curves in their movements. Oedipus is a clean-shaven youth, the only young person in the play—"caught in a web spun by his elders."

In a useful recent article on teaching *Oedipus,* W. A. Senior of Broward Community College suggests ways to present the play as meaningful to freshmen who wonder how anything so ancient and esoteric as classical drama can help them in their lives today and advance their pursuit of a C.P.A. degree. His approach is to demythify the character of Oedipus, stressing that the protagonist is no god or superman, but a confused, deceived human being at the center of a web of family relationships (to put it mildly) and political responsibilities. Like a business executive or professional today, Oedipus has to interrogate others, determine facts, and overcome his natural reluctance to face painful realities.

To help students come to terms with the central character, Senior has used specific writing assignments. "I have them compose a letter to Oedipus," he reports, "individually or at times in groups, at the height of the action in the third act to advise him on what to do or to explain to him what he has done wrong so far. In a related essay taking a page from *Antigonê* and its theme of public versus private good, which is foreshadowed in *Oedipus Rex,* I ask them to write an editorial on Oedipus as politician; each student must adopt a position and defend it" ("Teaching Oedipus: The Hero and Multiplicity," *Teaching English in the Two-Year College* [Dec. 1992], 274–79).

ROBERT FITZGERALD ON SOPHOCLES

TRANSLATING SOPHOCLES, PAGE 954

Now half a century after they first appeared, Robert Fitzgerald and Dudley Fitts's versions of Sophocles remain the finest translations in English. They not only capture the dignity, power, and beauty of the Greek, Fitts and Fitzgerald also created eminently stageworthy versions of the ancient classics.

In an afterword to his 1941 solo translation of *Oedipus at Colonus,* Fitzgerald offered a commentary on the challenges of translating Sophocles. His remarks examine the issue of finding poetic language that was neither too elevated nor too common.

Instructors may be interested to know that Dudley Fitts was the young Robert Fitzgerald's Latin master at the Choate School. They became lifelong friends and collaborated on three celebrated translations of Greek tragedies. When they corresponded, they usually wrote their letters in Latin. Fitts's mentorship helped guide Fitzgerald to his career as the most distinguished American translator of Greek and Roman classical poetry, including *The Iliad, The Odyssey,* and *The Aeneid.* Fitzgerald later became the Boylston Professor at Harvard. For an account of Fitzgerald's teaching methods, see Dana Gioia's memoir "Learning from Robert Fitzgerald" in the Spring 1998 issue of the *Hudson Review.*

CRITICS ON SOPHOCLES, pages 955–960

This critical casebook on Sophocles tries to provide a representative sampling of the many opinions on the tragedian. We begin with two indispensable critiques of *Oedipus the King*—the celebrated commentaries of Aristotle and Freud. **Aristotle's** discussion of *Oedipus the King* in his *Poetics* is undoubtedly the single most influential statement in Western drama criticism. In his analysis he tries to define the special psychological and artistic effects of tragic theater. In investigating these questions, the philosopher examines the nature of tragic plotting and characterization.

The father of modern psychology, **Sigmund Freud,** was also, by nature if not by occupation, a literary critic. Many of his major psychoanalytic concepts came from his close reading of texts—from Sophocles and the Old Testament to Shakespeare and da Vinci. In this short passage from *The Interpretation of Dreams* (1900) Freud expounds one of his most influential ideas, the Oedipus complex. Trying to account for the powerful effect Sophocles' tragedy has on modern audiences, Freud hypothesizes that both the Oedipus myth and the ancient Greek play must touch something universal within the audience—namely "our first sexual impulse towards our mother and first hatred and our first murderous wish against our father." The importance of introducing students to these two texts can hardly be overestimated. They are necessary components of cultural literacy as well as illuminating contributions to any discussion of Sophocles.

E. R. Dodds, one of the great Greek scholars of modern times, provides a provocative reading about the nature of Oedipus's character. Taking a critical rather than a scholarly perspective (discussing his own reaction, that is, rather than trying to ascertain Sophocles' original intention), Dodds sees Oedipus as a great tragic character not because of his powerful worldly position as king but because of his interior and intellectual qualities. Oedipus seems great, Dodds maintains, as a symbol of restless human intelligence.

By contrast, **A. E. Haigh** discusses a more general topic, the pervasive role of irony in Sophocles' plays. The concept of irony is difficult for many students to grasp, but they need to understand it in order to approach *Oedipus*. Haigh's treatment is so clear and well organized—with its helpful categories of "conscious" and "unconscious" irony—that his explanation will be very useful to assign to students, especially in introductory courses.

William Shakespeare

OTHELLO, THE MOOR OF VENICE, page 965

For commentary on the play, some outstanding sources of insight still include A. C. Bradley's discussion in *Shakespearean Tragedy* (1904; rpt. ed. [New York: St. Martin's, 1965]); and Harley Granville-Barker, "Preface to *Othello*," in *Prefaces to Shakespeare*, II (Princeton UP, 1947), also available separately from the same publisher (1958). See also Leo Kirschbaum, "The Modern *Othello*," *Journal of English Literary History* 2 (1944), 233–96; and Marvin Rosenberg, *The Masks of "Othello"* (Berkeley: U of California P, 1961). A convenient gathering of short studies will be found in *A Casebook on Othello*, ed. Leonard Dean (New York: Crowell, 1961). For a fresh reading of the play, see Michael Black, who in *The Literature of Fidelity* (London: Chatto, 1975) argues that the familiar view of Othello as a noble figure manipulated by the evil Iago is wrong and sentimental. According to Black, we see ourselves and our destructive impulses mirrored in both characters; hence, we are disturbed.

Lynda E. Boose has closely read the confrontation scene between Othello and Brabantio, the father of Desdemona, in front of the Duke (I, iii), and has found in it an ironic parody of the traditional giving away of the bride at a marriage ceremony. Instead of presenting his daughter to Othello as a gift, the thwarted Brabantio practically hurls her across the stage at the Moor. (The scene resembles Lear's casting away of Cordelia in *King Lear*, I, i.) In most of Shakespeare's plays, the father of the bride wants to retain and possess his daughter. Prevented by law and custom from doing so, he does the next best thing: tries to choose her husband, usually insisting on someone she does not desire. But Shakespeare, in both comedy and tragedy, always stages the old man's defeat ("The Father and the Bride in Shakespeare," *PMLA* 97 [May 1982]: 325–47).

Still another opinion that students might care to discuss: "No actress could credibly play the role of Desdemona if the character's name were changed to, say, Sally" (Frank Trippett, "The Game of the Name," *Time*, 14 Aug. 1978).

General question 3: "How essential to the play is the fact that Othello is a black man, a Moor, and not a native of Venice?" That Othello is an outsider, a stranger unfamiliar with the ways of the Venetians, makes it easier for Iago to stir up Othello's own self-doubts; and so the fact seems essential to the plot. (See especially III, iii, 215–23, 244–47, 274–84.) Venice in the Renaissance had no commerce with black Africa but Shakespeare's many references to Othello's blackness (and Roderigo's mention of the Moor's "thick lips," I, i, 68) have suggested to some interpreters that Othello could even be a coastal African from below the Senegal. On the modern stage, Othello has been memorably played by African-American actor Paul Robeson and by Laurence Olivier, who carefully studied

African-American speech and body language for his performance at the Old Vic (and in the movie version). A critic wrote of Olivier's interpretation:

> He came on smelling a rose, laughing softly with a private delight; bare-footed, ankleted, black. . . . He sauntered downstage, with a loose, bare-heeled roll of the buttocks; came to rest feet splayed apart, hips lounging outward. . . . The hands hung big and graceful. The whole voice was charac-terized, the o's and the a's deepened, the consonants thickened with faint, guttural deliberation. "Put up yo' bright swords, or de dew will rus' dem": not quite so crude, but in that direction. It could have been caricature, an embarrassment. Instead, after the second performance, a well-known Negro actor rose in the stalls bravoing. For obviously it was done with love; with the main purpose of substituting for the dead grandeur of the Moorish empire one modern audiences could respond to (Ronald Bryden, *New States-man*, I May 1964).

For a fascinating study of the play by a white teacher of African-American students at Howard University, see Doris Adler, "The Rhetoric of *Black* and *White* in *Othello*," in *Shakespeare Quarterly* 25 (Spring 1974): 248–57. Iago, Roderigo, and Brabantio hold negative and stereotyped views of black Africans which uncomfortably recall modern racial prejudices. In their view, Othello is "lascivious" (I, i, 126), an unnatural mate for a white woman (III, iii, 245–49), a practitioner of black magic (I, ii, 74–75). Under the influence of Iago's wiles, Othello so doubts himself that he almost comes to accept the stereotype forced on him, to reflect that in marrying him Desdemona has strayed from her own nature (III, iii, 243). Such, of course, is not the truth Shakespeare reveals to us, and the tragedy of Othello stems from a man's tragic inability to recognize good or evil by sight alone. "Eyes cannot see that the black Othello is not the devil," Adler observes, "or that the white and honest Iago is."

In answer to general question 4 ("Besides Desdemona and Iago, what other pairs of characters seem to strike balances?"): Alvin Kernan in his introduction to the Signet edition of *Othello* comments,

> The true and loyal soldier Cassio balances the false and traitorous soldier Iago. . . . The essential purity of Desdemona stands in contrast to the more "practical" view of chastity held by Emilia, and her view in turn is illuminated by the workaday view of sensuality held by the courtesan Bianca. . . . Iago's success in fooling Othello is but the culmination of a series of such betrayals that includes the duping of Roderigo, Brabantio, and Cassio.

The last general question ("Does the downfall of Othello proceed from any flaw in his nature, or is his downfall entirely the work of Iago?") is a classic (or cliché) problem, and perhaps there is no better answer than Coleridge's in his *Lectures on Shakspere*:

> Othello does not kill Desdemona in jealousy, but in a conviction forced upon him by the almost superhuman art of Iago—such a conviction as any man

would and must have entertained who had believed in Iago's honesty as Othello did. We, the audience, know that Iago is a villain from the beginning; but in considering the essence of the Shakesperian Othello, we must perseveringly place ourselves in his situation, and under his circumstances. Then we shall immediately feel the fundamental difference between the solemn agony of the noble Moor, and the wretched fishing jealousies of Leontes. . . . Othello had no life but in Desdemona: the belief that she, his angel, had fallen from the heaven of her native innocence, wrought a civil war in his heart. She is his counterpart; and, like him, is almost sanctified in our eyes by her absolute unsuspiciousness, and holy entireness of love. As the curtain drops, which do we pity the most?

On the suggestion for writing: Thomas Rymer's famous objections to the play will not be easy to refute. At least, no less a critic than T. S. Eliot once declared that he had never seen Rymer's points cogently refuted. Perhaps students will enjoy siding with the attack or coming to the play's defense.

Was the Othello-Desdemona match a wedding of April and September? R. S. Gwynn of Lamar University writes: "Has anyone ever mentioned the age difference between Othello and Desdemona? Othello speaks of his arms as 'now some nine moons wasted.' Assuming that this metaphor means that his life is almost 9/12 spent, he would be over 50! Now if a Venetian girl would have normally married in her teens (think of the film version of *Romeo and Juliet*), that would make about 30 years difference between him and his bride." This gulf, Othello's radically different culture, his outraged father-in-law, and Iago's sly insinuations, all throw tall obstacles before the marriage.

"If we are to read the play that Shakespeare wrote," maintains Bruce E. Miller, "we must acknowledge that Othello as well as Iago commits great evil." In *Teaching the Art of Literature* (Urbana, IL: NCTE, 1980), Miller takes *Othello* for his illustration of teaching drama and stresses that Othello went wrong by yielding to his gross impulses. In demonstrating why the play is a classic example of tragedy, Miller takes advantage of students' previously having read Willa Cather's "Paul's Case." The latter story illustrates "the difference between sadness and tragedy. Paul's death is sad because it cuts off a life that has never been fulfilled. But it is not tragic, for Paul lives and dies in this world of human affairs." But Othello's death has the grandeur of tragedy. Realizing at last that Desdemona has been true and that in staying her he has destroyed his own hopes of happiness, the Moor attains a final serenity of spirit, intuiting the true order of things.

BEN JONSON ON SHAKESPEARE

ON HIS FRIEND AND RIVAL WILLIAM SHAKESPEARE, page 1064

Anyone who claims that William Shakespeare did not author the plays that bear his name must reckon with the testimony of the poet and dramatist Ben Jonson who left two accounts of the Bard of Avon—one in verse, the other (reprinted here) in conversation with poet and nobleman, William Drummond of Hawthorden, who entertained Jonson and kept detailed notes. (The selection we reprint is the closest thing Jacobean literature has to a literary interview.) Jonson, who never enjoyed consistent box office success in commercial theater, had a jealous but affectionate relationship with his immensely popular rival. Here in conversation we overhear Jonson grumbling about the man he claimed to love "on this side idolatry." Students interested in pursuing the relationship between the two playwright-poets should also read Jonson's magnificent verse, "To the Memory of My Beloved, The Author, Mr. William Shakespeare, And What He Hath Left Us," which appeared as the dedication to the First Folio of Shakespeare's works in 1623. The poem begins:

> To draw no envy, Shakespeare, on thy name,
>   Am I thus ample to thy book and fame;
> While I confess thy writing to be such
>   As neither man nor muse can praise too much.

(Note, too, that three poems by Jonson appear in the "Poetry" section of *Literature*.)

CRITICS ON SHAKESPEARE, pages 1065–1067

The large selection of Shakespeare criticism we have reprinted in the casebook hardly touches the surface of the vast scholarship available, but it does provide students with a broad cross-section of critical opinion. It is easy for students to become intimidated by the mountains of material in Shakespeare studies. The important thing is to get them *started* somewhere engaging and reliable. We strove to put together an informed but accessible set of selections that both students and instructors could find useful.

Poet **W. H. Auden** was fascinated with Shakespeare. He wrote and lectured fascinatingly on a substantial number of the plays. In Auden's recently published *Lectures on Shakespeare* (2000) alone, he discusses thirty-five of the plays as well as *The Sonnets*.

This discussion of Iago comes from Auden's 1961 essay, "The Joker in the Pack," reprinted in his critical collection, *The Dyer's Hand* (1962). In analyzing *Othello*, Auden notes how differently the villain operates in the play compared to Shakespeare's other tragedies. Iago and not the title character stands at the center of *Othello*, Auden observes, since he motivates the crucial dramatic actions. It is not Fate that dooms Othello; it is another human being. Auden's view of Iago neatly complements Maud Bodkin's identification of Iago as a diabolical figure. The devil, after all, leads persons to voluntary doom by evil advice.

Anyone interested in Auden's relation to Shakespeare should also read his superb introduction to *The Sonnets*, which is reprinted in *Forewords & Afterwords* (New York: Random House, 1973). Auden also wrote a sequel to *The Tempest*—his 1944 dramatic poem, *The Sea and the Mirror*.

Three questions you may ask students about Auden's analysis are:

1. What aspects of *Othello* does Auden consider unique?

2. What character does Auden assert stands at the center of Shakespeare's play? What is unusual about this character?

3. What is peculiar about Othello's fall in relation to the fall of most tragic heroes?

Maud Bodkin's *Archetypal Patterns in Poetry* (1958) remains a useful guide to mythological criticism as a perspective on English poetry. In the volume she analyzes both *Hamlet* and *Othello* (among many other classics). Her examination of Iago as a satanic figure is persuasive and revealing. In the volume she expands on this central insight to explicate Shakespeare's tragedy as a conflict between heroic values (embodied by Othello) and diabolic chaos (expressed by Iago). Her psychoanalytical/mythic reading of Iago places him as both a mythic devil and as the internal mental force that can deny or destroy a person's ideal values.

Virginia Mason Vaughan's "Black and White in *Othello*" offers the insight of both historical criticism and cultural studies. She places Shakespeare's characterization within the social and cultural context of the early Jacobean period, especially the assumptions of the "predominately white audience" that viewed the play. Othello is, in her analysis, the Other, and his darkness is "the visual signifier of his Otherness." Whether that Otherness is portrayed as an "African" or "Moor" does not matter; Othello stands perpetually as alien to the other characters and the audience.

Probably no modern novelist thought more deeply about William Shakespeare than **Anthony Burgess**. His 1964 novel, *Nothing Like the Sun*, is generally considered the most compelling fictional work about the enigmatic Bard of Avon. His late novel, *Enderby's Dark Lady* (1984), also begins and ends with brilliant short stories about Shakespeare. Burgess also wrote a full-length critical study of the dramatist as well as a novel about Christopher Marlowe in which Shakespeare appears. Before he began writing fiction (at the age of 38), Burgess worked for the British government as a cultural officer in Asia. The selection printed in *Literature* comes from a talk the polyglot Burgess gave at an international conference on translation. He addresses several interesting issues about how literary works travel across languages and cultures. He also speculates on why Shakespeare's work has proved nearly universal in its appeal. Finally, he reminds us that literary translation involves far more than finding equivalent words. Two questions you might ask students to start discussion:

1. In Burgess's experience, who seemed to be the only British author with universal appeal in Malaysia? How does Burgess account for this fact?

2. According to Burgess, what does translation involve besides words?

31   *The Modern Theater*

REALISM AND NATURALISM

Henrik Ibsen
A DOLL'S HOUSE, page 1072

At the heart of the play, as its title indicates, is its metaphor of a house of make-believe. In the play's visible symbols, we see Ibsen the poet. In Act I, there is the Christmas tree that Nora orders the maid to place in the middle of the room—a gesture of defiance after Krogstad had threatened her domestic peace and happiness. In the Christmas gifts Nora has bought for the children—sword, toy horse, and trumpet for the boys, a doll and a doll's bed for the girl Emmy—Nora seems to assign boys and girls traditional emblems of masculinity and femininity and (in Rolf Fjelde's phrasing) is "unthinkingly transmitting her doll-identity to her own daughter." When the curtain goes up on Act II, we see the unfortunate Christmas tree again: stripped, burned out, and shoved back into a corner—and its ruin speaks eloquently for Nora's misery. Richly suggestive, too, is Nora's wild tarantella, to merry music played by the diseased and dying Rank. Like a victim of a tarantula bite, Nora feels a kind of poison working in her; and it is ironic that Rank has a literal poison working in him as well. (The play's imagery of poison and disease is traced in an article by John Northam included in Rolf Fjelde's *Ibsen: A Collection of Critical Essays* [Englewood Cliffs, NJ: Prentice, 1965]). Significant, too, is Nora's change of costume: taking off her fancy dress, she divests herself of the frivolous nonsense she has believed in the past and puts on everyday street attire.

Ibsen's play was first performed in Copenhagen on December 21, 1879; no doubt many a male chauvinist found it a disquieting Christmas present. Within a few years, *A Doll's House* had been translated into fourteen languages. James Gibbons Huneker has described its fame: when Nora walked out on Helmer, "that slammed door reverberated across the roofs of the world." With the rise of feminism, *A Doll's House* gradually became Ibsen's most frequently performed play—not only on the stage but also in television and film adaptations. In 1973, for example, two screen versions were issued almost simultaneously: Joseph Losey's overly solemn version starring Jane Fonda, and Hilliard Elkin's superior adaptation featuring Claire Bloom (expertly assisted by Anthony Hopkins, Ralph Richardson, Denholm Elliott, and Edith Evans).

Ibsen, to be sure, was conscious of sexual injustices. In preliminary notes written in 1878, he declared what he wanted his play to express:

A woman cannot be herself in contemporary society; it is an exclusively male society with laws drafted by men, and with counsel and judges who judge feminine conduct from the male point of view. She has committed a crime and she is proud of it because she did it for love of her husband and to save his life. But the husband, with his conventional views of honor, stands on the side of the law and looks at the affair with male eyes.

Clearly, that is what the finished play expresses, but perhaps it expresses much more besides. A temptation in teaching Ibsen is to want to reduce his plays to theses. As Richard Gilman says, the very name of Henrik Ibsen calls to mind "cold light, problems, living rooms, instruction" (*The Making of Modern Drama* [New York: Farrar, 1964]).

But is the play totally concerned with the problems of the "new woman"? Ibsen didn't think so. At a banquet given in his honor by the Norwegian Society for Women's Rights in 1898, he frankly admitted,

I have been more of a poet and less of a social philosopher than people have generally been inclined to believe. I thank you for the toast, but I must decline the honor of consciously having worked for women's rights. I am not even quite sure what women's rights really are. To me it has been a question of human rights.

Elizabeth Hardwick thinks Ibsen made this statement because he had "choler in his bloodstream" and couldn't resist making a put-down before his admirers. She finds Ibsen nevertheless admirable: alone among male writers in having pondered the fact of being born a woman—"To be female: What does it mean?" (*Seduction and Betrayal* [New York: Random, 1974]). Perhaps there is no contradiction in arguing that Ibsen's play is about both women's rights and the rights of all humanity.

Another critic, Norris Houghton, suggests a different reason for the play's timeliness. "Our generation has been much concerned with what it calls the 'identity crisis.' This play anticipates that theme: Ibsen was there ahead of us by ninety years" (*The Exploding Stage* [New York: Weybright, 1971]). Houghton's view may be supported by Nora's declared reasons for leaving Torvald: "If I'm ever to reach any understanding of myself and the things around me, I must learn to stand alone."

The play is structured with classic severity. Its first crisis occurs in Krogstad's initial threat to Nora, but its greatest crisis—the climax—occurs when Helmer stands with the revealing letter open in his hand. We take the major dramatic question to be posed early in Act I, in Nora's admission to Mrs. Linde that she herself financed the trip to Italy. The question is larger than "Will Nora's husband find out her secret?"—for that question is answered at the climax, when Helmer finds out. Taking in more of the play, we might put it, "Will Nora's happy doll house existence be shattered?"—or a still larger question (answered only in the final door slam), "Will Nora's marriage be saved?"

Ibsen's magnificent door slam has influenced many a later dramatist. Have any students seen Stephen Sondheim and Hugh Wheeler's musical *Sweeney Todd, The Demon Barber of Fleet Street* (1979) on stage or on television? At the end, Todd slams a door in the faces of the audience, suggesting that he would gladly cut their throats.

For a dissenting interpretation of Ibsen's play, see Hermann J. Weigand, *The Modern Ibsen* (New York: Dutton, 1960). Weigand thinks Nora at the end unchanged and unregenerate—still a wily coquette who will probably return home the next day to make Torvald toe the line.

A topic for class debate: Is *A Doll's House* a tragedy or a comedy? Much will depend on how students interpret Nora's final exit. Critics disagree: Dorothea Krook thinks the play contains all the requisite tragic ingredients (*Elements of Tragedy* [New Haven: Yale UP, 1969]). Elizabeth Hardwick (cited earlier) calls the play "a comedy, a happy ending—except for the matter of the children."

To prevent North German theater managers from rewriting the play's ending, Ibsen supplied an alternate ending of his own "for use in an emergency." In this alternate version, Nora does not leave the house; instead, Helmer makes her gaze upon their sleeping children. "Oh, this is a sin against myself, but I cannot leave them," says Nora, sinking to the floor in defeat as the curtain falls. Ibsen, however, thought such a change a "barbarous outrage" and urged that it not be used. Students might be told of this alternate ending and be asked to give reasons for its outrageousness.

Citing evidence from the play and from Ibsen's biography, Joan Templeton argues that those critics who fail to see *A Doll's House* as a serious feminist statement have distorted its meaning and unintentionally diminished its worth ("*The Doll House* Backlash: Criticism, Feminism, and Ibsen," PMLA: January 1989).

For a cornucopia of stimulating ideas, see *Approaches to Teaching Ibsen's* A Doll's House, edited by Yvonne Shafer (New York: Modern Language Association, 1985), one of the MLA's likable paperback series "Approaches to Teaching Masterpieces of World Literature." June Schlueter writes on using the play as an introduction to drama, and notes that, unlike *Oedipus,* the play does not create an inexorable progress toward disaster. "At any point, we feel, justifiably, that disaster might be avoided." Irving Deer recommends approaching the play by considering "how it deals with decaying values and conventions." J. L. Styan urges instructors to have a class act out the play's opening moments, before and after discussing them, so that Ibsen's wealth of suggestive detail will emerge, which students might otherwise ignore. Other commentators supply advice for teaching the play in a freshman honors course, in a course on women's literature, and in a community college. Joanne Gray Kashdan, author of this latter essay, reports that one woman student exclaimed on reading the play: "I realized I had been married to Torvald for seven years before I divorced him!"

WRITER'S PERSPECTIVE

George Bernard Shaw on Drama

IBSEN AND THE FAMILIAR SITUATION, page 1129

QUESTIONS

1. How, according to Shaw, does *A Doll's House* reflect Ibsen's originality? In the play's time, what was so new about it?

2. How does Shaw explain the origin of drama?

3. Which playwright does Shaw prefer: Ibsen or Shakespeare? Why?

TRAGICOMEDY AND THE ABSURD

Milcha Sanchez-Scott
THE CUBAN SWIMMER, page 1133

Very little criticism has been written about Milcha Sanchez-Scott, but she is a genuine dramatic talent. *The Cuban Swimmer* is one of the most interesting experimental plays in recent American theater. Sanchez-Scott is also one of the most profusely talented Hispanic playwrights now active. She is not a prolific writer, but her best work is richly conceived and brilliantly executed. Her plays like *Latina* (1980), *The Cuban Swimmer* (1984), and *Roosters* (1987) are important additions to contemporary American drama.

The Cuban Swimmer* is an experimental play in both form and style, but, unlike most experimental drama, it succeeds. This play requires no critical intervention to clarify its aims. Audiences intuitively follow Sanchez-Scott's innovative devices, and the play's cumulative impact is considerable. *The Cuban Swimmer* creates three distinct but inter-dependent worlds—the swimmer in the water, her family in the boat behind her, and the radio newscasters in the helicopter. Obviously, none of these worlds can be presented realistically on-stage. They must be stylized in some way by the director and the designer. This factor highlights the symbolic—almost allegorical—atmosphere of the play, a quality the author both indulges and satirizes.

Perhaps the most interesting aspect of *The Cuban Swimmer* is the bilingual texture of the dialogue. Sanchez-Scott creates two separate linguistic worlds—the mixture of Spanish and English spoken by the Suárez family and the cliché-ridden media English of the newscasters. These two "dialects" also differ in another crucial sense—one is the private language of love, duty, and tradition; the other is the public language of hyperbole and manipulation. Although *The Cuban Swimmer* brilliantly employs the visual potential of theatrical spectacle, the play centers on language. Significantly, one does not need to know Spanish to enjoy the play (although a sizable portion of the text is *en Español*). Sanchez-Scott carefully positions the Spanish so that a monolingual English-speaker can guess most of it from context while still experiencing the cultural richness of the characters' bilingual existence.

There is so much family drama going on in *The Cuban Swimmer* that an attentive reader might meaningfully examine almost every relationship—across generations, across genders, across cultures. At the center of the family drama is Eduardo Suárez, whose driving ambition is for his daughter Margarita to achieve athletic fame and success. As both her coach and father, he projects his own complex set of needs and desires (as father, immigrant, and exile) on Margarita. The play signals some of his desires overtly and others indirectly. His boat, for instance, is named *La Havana*, an ironic moniker for a political exile who runs a salvage yard. His wife is—Sanchez-Scott revels in such symbolic possibilities— the former Miss Cuba. His nineteen-year-old daughter is the "Cinderella entry" in the "Wrigley Invitational Women's Swim to Catalina," and probably the only amateur among the professional swimmers.

The ending of *The Cuban Swimmer* deserves some commentary. The play has flirted with symbolism from the opening (in a dozen details from the generically named *Abuela* to the religious prayers and oaths said by the family), but now it unfolds into a sort of Magic Realism reminiscent of García Márquez. Pushed by her father past endurance, Margarita seems to drown. She certainly disappears. Then she miraculously reappears on the breakers off Santa Catalina to win the race. The radio announcers call her upset victory in language that bespeaks not only media hype but also the Latin Catholic imagery that is woven through the play. Here are the play's final words:

> This is indeed a miracle! It's a resurrection! Margarita Suárez, with a flotilla of boats to meet her, is now walking on the waters, through the breakers . . . onto the beach, with crowds of people cheering her on. What a jubilation! This is a miracle!

Shakespeare's *The Tempest* and Milton's "Lycidas" also seem to be hovering around the play's climax—or, at the very least, the traditional myths of death, sea-change, and resurrection. Sanchez-Scott has so carefully prepared us for the magical final tableau that it seems simultaneously both surprising and inevitable for this daughter of Miss Cuba and the head usher of the Holy Name Society to be reborn miraculously out of the sea to *Santa* Catalina—like Jesus walking on the waves. *The Cuban Swimmer's* comic tone allows us to view this final scene ironically, but the play's tight symbolic structure also suggests we should take it seriously. That so complex and ambitious an ending could work testifies to Sanchez-Scott's imaginative power.

Sandra Santa Cruz directed a production of *The Cuban Swimmer* in 1997 at the University of Colorado, Boulder. (The photo for *The Cuban Swimmer* found in the book was taken from this production.) She wrote an interesting account of her experiences selecting, producing, and directing the play, from which we offer a few excerpts:

> In selecting a play, I began to search for a work that would look at the Hispanic experience, a community we are not normally accustomed to seeing in American theater. I was disappointed to encounter a number of one-act plays written by Hispanic playwrights whose stories seemed to focus negatively on Hispanic life. While I am not particularly interested in a one-sided, idealized portrait of the Hispanic experience, I don't agree with those works which portray Hispanics, or any other community, from a demoralizing, degrading perspective. In my opinion, this negative imagery only serves to

reinforce and perpetuate harmful stereotypes. Rather, I am interested in works that present a range of choices. I found Milcha Sanchez-Scott's *The Cuban Swimmer* to represent a realistic portrait of a family who oscillates between adversity and triumph; frustration and hope.

From the outset, *The Cuban Swimmer* seemed to capture the imagination, interest and excitement of people throughout the Theater department. It presented a unique set of challenges, the most obvious of which is the setting—the ocean! How would that environment be created? Secondly, it portrays the experience of a Cuban family. How would a cast who was largely unfamiliar with this particular culture and language relate to the language and characterization? Although only a seemingly short one-act play, the events of *The Cuban Swimmer* range from stasis to crisis, from calm to fury. The external world imposes itself through the television media and the natural world through calamity. . . .

In my opinion, *The Cuban Swimmer* explores the fundamental question of identity; one's own image of "self," how that "self" is defined and how that self-identity is tested. It's about the loss of dignity and confidence in oneself and how that affects self-image. The play is driven by the emotional, physical, and spiritual survival of a family whose hopes and dreams have been undermined by a callous external world. Despite the dangers and hardships of the open sea, the real battle lies within the family itself; especially when their image of "self" is shattered.

. . . Ultimately, Margarita finds the inner strength to emerge triumphant; transcending limitations imposed by an external world and in full possession of her self—"self-possessed," so to speak.

WRITER'S PERSPECTIVE

Milcha Sanchez-Scott on Drama
WRITING *THE CUBAN SWIMMER*, page 1147

Milcha Sanchez-Scott provides an extremely interesting account of her life and literary development in M. Elizabeth Osborn's valuable anthology, *On New Ground: Contemporary Hispanic-American Plays* (New York: Theater Communications Group, 1987). This book also reprints Sanchez-Scott's *Roosters*. The excerpt reprinted in *Literature* describes the author's discovery of herself as a writer as well as the initial inspiration for *The Cuban Swimmer*.

32 *Evaluating a Play*

This chapter may be particularly useful for students to read before they tackle a play about whose greatness or inferiority you have any urgent convictions. The chapter probably doesn't deserve to be dealt with long in class, but it might lead to a writing assignment: to comment on the merits of any play in the book.

If you assign students to write a play review (see "Writing About a Play" page 1417), you might like to have them read this chapter first. To help them in forming their opinions, they may consult the list of pointers in the "Writing Critically" section on pages 1154–55.

33 Plays for Further Reading

David Henry Hwang
THE SOUND OF A VOICE, page 1158

David Hwang's short play, *The Sound of a Voice,* is simple, direct, and deeply mysterious. The play unfolds like an eerie folktale. A nameless man visits an enigmatic female hermit, who is reputed to be a witch. Although they both recognize that they are potential foes, they fall into a doomed love affair. Eventually, one of them is destroyed. Hwang's treatment combines elements from both the Eastern and Western traditions. *The Sound of a Voice* borrows many features from Nō drama, the courtly theater of Japan. Despite their elaborate and allusive language, Nō plays have simple narrative structures, and they mostly focus on the interaction of two principal characters (one of whom is usually a ghost haunting some mysterious locale). Like Nō drama, *The Sound of a Voice* prominently deploys music to build a brooding atmosphere rife with emotive impact and symbolic significance. *The Sound of a Voice* also resembles the short symbolist plays of William Butler Yeats, J. M. Synge, and August Strindberg. Yeats's plays, which masterfully combine elements of Nō drama with English verse tragedy to create a poetic form for folk material, seem particularly influential on *The Sound of a Voice.*

The main reason to outline the rich literary background of *The Sound of a Voice* is not because the play needs such explication. Hwang's play wears its learning lightly; the influences have all been assimilated into a remarkably straightforward and accessibly contemporary style. The importance of Hwang's diverse sources is to demonstrate the complex heritage of an Asian-American playwright. There is sometimes a temptation to reduce the work of minority writers to mere autobiography, but in this short play, Hwang consciously draws from a Japanese genre that has nothing directly to do with either the Chinese heritage of his family or the historical traditions of the author's native language, English. Hwang himself has complained about how narrowly he has been stereotyped as a writer:

> I first became aware of the simplistic nature of this stereotyping when I did the two Japanese plays *The Sound of a Voice* and *The House of Sleeping Beauties.* I thought this work was a departure because these were the first plays I'd written that didn't deal with being Chinese-American, with race and assimilation; I felt that they were tragic love stories. Yet they were not perceived as being a departure, because they had Asian actors. (*Contemporary Authors,* vol. 132. Susan M. Trosky, ed. Detroit: Gale Research)

While *The Sound of a Voice* draws from Hwang's consciousness as an Asian writer, it is also a work that grows out of the traditions of American experimental theater.

QUESTIONS

1. *How does Hwang's names for his two characters ("Man" and "Woman") affect our reading of the play?* Although the author lets the woman's name (Hanako) slip into the stage directions, he otherwise refers to them only by their generic titles of Man and Woman. The two characters never give one another their true names but only self-evident fictions (Yokiko, Man Who Fears Silence, and Man Who Fears Women). By refusing to name them, Hwang encourages us to see them as archetypal or symbolic characters. The visitor is all men, and Hanako is, implicitly, womankind. Their story, by extension, bears some symbolic significance to all male-female relations. When the Woman suggests "Man Who Fears Women" as a name for her visitor, she underscores the symbolic nature of their relationship. The action generally seems not to be realistic in detail but symbolic in import. Hwang is not trying to recreate the texture of daily reality as a naturalistic dramatist might; instead, he attempts to portray a mythic drama—a folk legend come to life. Although the action of Hwang's play takes place in Japan, one could easily imagine a staged production of it set in rural New England or on the Louisiana bayou. All you would have to change is to substitute a Cajun violin or Vermont fiddle for the *shakuhachi*.

2. *Why does the man visit the woman in her remote house?* We never know *exactly* why he visits, but we gradually learn that he came on a quest or dare to kill her. The woman tells of other men who arrived because "great glory was to be had by killing the witch in the woods." He initially believes (as do the nearby villagers) that she is a witch who enchants and destroys the men who visit her home. He even imagines (scene 7) that her flowers contain the trapped spirits of her previous lovers. As the man falls in love with her, his desire to kill her disappears, but he is nonetheless plagued by guilt at his failure to keep to his quest.

3. *The woman is unsure of the length of time since her last visitor. What effect does that uncertainty have on our sense of the dramatic situation?* This detail contributes to the mythic quality of the action. It seems possible that she is a supernatural being unaffected by human mortality; or, perhaps more to the point, that this particular plot is played again and again between her and generations of young men. Moreover, at the very least, it adds to the sense of mystery that pervades the play.

4. *Does this play have a central conflict?* Like Japanese etiquette, the action of Hwang's play is understated; the real drama is implied mostly in the details. Both the man and the woman understand from the opening scene that they are locked in a potentially mortal combat, but neither of them directly admits their knowledge. Everything concerning the central conflict emerges slowly—and often indirectly—at least insofar as the audience is concerned. But Hwang's deliberately low-key style, however, eventually intensifies the dramatic tension since it creates a heavy sense of mystery we become anxious to resolve. The central dramatic conflict is the symbolic battle that the man and woman play out. The woman seems to

win by removing the man's fears and arousing love in him. Ironically, however, the man, who could not defeat her by force, manages to destroy her by love. His decision to abandon her after their professions of devotion drives her to suicide.

5. *When we read a play, we focus mostly on the text. When we see a play in the theater, however, we experience it visually as well as verbally. What nonverbal elements play important roles in Hwang's play?* The Sound of a Voice illustrates the importance of nonverbal elements in achieving theatrical effects. Two complete scenes (scenes 4 and 6), as well as the conclusion, are played without words. Another episode (scene 8) depends on a visual trick (the man balancing his chin on the point of a sword) to create dramatic tension. Likewise, one of the central contests between the two characters is a physical fight with wooden sticks. The play's finale is a visual tableau. Music also plays an important role in establishing and maintaining the mood of the play. Students will be able to find other nonverbal elements of the play. Hwang reminds us of the importance of spectacle, even in a modest, two-character play. A play works by total representation of a drama, not by the words alone.

There are a great many possible topics for papers based on Hwang's play. Students could trace a single image from the play (flowers would be an obvious candidate) and discuss its significance. Another interesting notion would be to discuss the use of music in the play: what does it contribute to the atmosphere and tone that words could not? Another good subject would be to examine the two scenes in the play (scenes 4 and 6) that are played without words: what effect do they have on the structure and feeling of the drama? Students could also discuss the end of *The Sound of a Voice:* is the woman's death tragic? The theme of suicide would also be an illuminating topic since both characters contemplate the idea, and the woman hangs herself at the end of the play. Finally, students could compare and contrast *The Sound of a Voice* with one of its models—either a Nō drama or one of Yeats's short plays. Nō plays are generally very brief (around ten pages). Arthur Waley's classic, *The Nō Plays of Japan* (New York: Grove, 1957) provides an excellent starting point. Any play by Seami, such as *Tsunemasa* or *Kumasaka* (both in the Waley book), the most celebrated master of the form, would work well. Several of Yeats's short plays provide excellent contrasts to Hwang's piece, most notably, *Deidre, The Only Jealousy of Emer,* and *Purgatory.*

WRITER'S PERSPECTIVE

David Henry Hwang on Drama

MULTICULTURAL THEATER, page 1172

QUESTIONS

1. What events contributed to Hwang's heightened consciousness of his Asian roots?

2. What importance does Hwang feel mythology has in drama?

3. On what does Hwang think the notion of "ethnic theater" depends?

Terrence McNally
ANDRE'S MOTHER, page 1173

One of the major genres of contemporary American theater has been the AIDS play—dramas that explore the painful social, moral, and personal issues that came into public prominence in the epidemic of Acquired Immune Deficiency Syndrome. Terrence McNally has examined these issues with his characteristic mixture of humor and humanity in *Andre's Mother*, a dramatic vignette of extraordinary compression. At the center of this compelling scene is the title character, a role without words. Students find this play provocative. Not only does it address a highly visible public issue, but the play's literary structure focuses the reader's attention on puzzling out what goes on inside Andre's Mother's mind.

QUESTIONS

1. *What relation does Andre's Mother have to the other characters in the play?* Her only connection is through her dead son, but they come from a part of his life she never knew—or at least never acknowledged. She has never met the other three people, although they played important roles in her son's life. She seems to be isolated in her grief and her unspoken disapproval of her son's homosexuality. Arthur, Penny, and Cal are articulate, sophisticated, witty people. Andre's Mother is neither urbane nor worldly (Andre is described by Cal as a "country boy"). There is a social distance between her and them. McNally portrays her intense isolation, confusion, and initial resentment through her silence.

2. *Andre's Mother, the title character of this piece, never says a word in the course of the play. What thoughts and emotions do you think she experiences in the final scene? Give reasons for your opinions.* The dramatic point of this vignette is to make the audience project their feelings onto the silent, suffering mother. McNally does not portray her in an entirely positive light. She refuses to speak, even as Cal desperately begs her for some response. She has also apparently never acknowledged that her son was gay. Her presumed disapproval made it impossible for Andre to speak to her either about his homosexuality or illness, and yet we feel the intensity and isolation of her grief. All we know about her feelings, however, are her external actions, which in the final scene appear understandably ambiguous. She wants to hold on to the balloon. She starts to let it go, then pulls it back to kiss it before finally letting it sail away. Her fixed stare on the balloon, however, suggests she cannot let go of her son or break his "last earthly ties" with her. However harshly we may have judged her earlier in the play, we are probably touched by her evident love and pain in this final moment.

3. *Is the balloon a symbol in* Andre's Mother? *If so, what does it represent?* This becomes the dominant symbol of McNally's vignette. Cal explains what he con-

siders the balloons' significance. "They represent the soul," he explains. "When you let go, it means you're letting his soul ascend to Heaven. That you're willing to let go. Breaking the last earthly ties." It seems uncertain, however, whether Andre's Mother would share Cal's interpretation. When she finally lets go of her balloon, her slow, agonized gestures seem to confirm the permanence of her earthly ties. A more focused interpretation of the balloon is probably in order. The balloons may be intended to represent all the things that Cal claims, but they also come to symbolize the relationship each character has with the deceased. Arthur and Penny let go first; they knew him least well. Each expresses his or her personal perspective on him. Cal's farewell is more deeply complicated, especially since he speaks it to Andre's silent Mother. One might even suggest that the Mother's painful silence suggests all that went unspoken between her and her son. The balloons also become surrogates for Andre, whose presence haunts the play he never enters. Can your students suggest other symbolic associations of the balloons?

A good writing exercise would be to have students create a final speech for Andre's Mother. Ask them to write 500 words for her character to speak alone on the stage about her reactions to Andre's death. An alternate version of the assignment would be to have her speak to Andre's spirit, as if he could hear her.

WRITER'S PERSPECTIVE

Terrence McNally on Drama
HOW TO WRITE A PLAY, page 1176

McNally offers invaluable advice to all aspiring authors: the best way to become a writer is to write. He expresses himself with a light touch, but he puts forward some important ideas. Writing is a process, McNally asserts, that does not fully begin until one writes. Many students labor under the misconception that inspiration happens entirely away from one's desk or keyboard. McNally's sensible comments not only illuminates his own creative process but provide students with a helpful perspective on their own writing.

Arthur Miller
DEATH OF A SALESMAN, page 1177

QUESTIONS

1. Miller's opening stage directions call for actors to observe imaginary walls when the action is in the present, and to step freely through walls when the scene is in the past. Do you find this technique of staging effective? Why or why not?

2. Miller has professed himself fascinated by the "agony of someone who has some driving, implacable wish in him" (*Paris Review* interview). What—as we learn in the opening scene—are Willy Loman's obsessions?

3. What case can be made for seeing Linda as the center of the play: the character around whom all events revolve? Sum up the kind of person she is.

4. Seeing his father's Boston side-girl has a profound effect on Biff. How would you sum it up?

5. Apparently Biff's discovery of Willy's infidelity took place before World War II, about 1939. In this respect, does *Death of a Salesman* seem at all dated? Do you think it possible, in the present day, for a son to be so greatly shocked by his father's sexual foibles that the son's whole career would be ruined?

6. How is it possible to read the play as the story of Biff's eventual triumph? Why does Biff, at the funeral, give his brother a "hopeless" look?

7. How are we supposed to feel about Willy's suicide? In what way is Willy, in killing himself, self-deluded to the end?

8. What meanings do you find in the flute music? In stockings—those that Willy gives to the Boston whore and those he doesn't like to see Linda mending? In Biff's sneakers with "University of Virginia" lettered on them (which he later burns)? In seeds and gardening?

9. Of what importance to the play are Charley and his son Bernard? How is their father-son relationship different from the relationship between Willy and Biff?

10. What do you understand Bernard to mean in telling Willy, "sometimes . . . it's better for a man just to walk away"?

11. Explain Charley's point when he argues, "The only thing you got in this world is what you can sell. And the funny thing is that you're a salesman, and you don't know that." (Miller, in his introduction to the play, makes an applicable comment: "When asked what Willy was selling, what was in his bags, I could only reply, 'Himself.'")

12. What do you make of the character of Ben? Do you see him as a realistic character? As a figment of Willy's imagination?

13. Suppose Miller had told the story of Willy and Biff in chronological order. If the incident in the Boston hotel had come early in the play, instead of late, what would have been lost?

14. Another death of another salesman is mentioned in this play: that of Dave Singleman. How does Willy view Singleman's death? Is Willy's attitude our attitude?

15. In a famous speech in the final Requiem, Charley calls a salesman a man who "don't put a bolt to a nut"; and Charley recalls that Willy "was a happy man with a batch of cement." Sum up the theme or general truth that Charley states. At what other moments in the play does this theme emerge? Why is Willy, near death, so desperately eager to garden?

16. When the play first appeared in 1949, some reviewers thought it a bitter attack upon the capitalist system. Others found in it social criticism by a writer committed to a faith in democracy and free enterprise. What do you think? Does the play make any specific criticism of society?

17. Miller has stated his admiration for Henrik Ibsen: "One is constantly aware, in watching his plays, of process, change, development." How does this comment apply to *A Doll's House*? Who or what changes or develops in the course of *Death of a Salesman*?

Directed by Elia Kazan, with Lee J. Cobb superbly cast as Willy Loman, *Death of a Salesman* was first performed on Broadway on February 10, 1949. Originally, Miller had wanted to call the play *The Inside of a Head*, and he had planned to begin it with "an enormous face the height of the proscenium arch which would appear and then open up." Fortunately, he settled upon less mechanical methods to reveal Willy's psychology. In later describing what he thought he had done, Miller said he tried to dramatize "a disintegrating personality at that terrible moment when the voice of the past is no longer distant but quite as loud as the voice of the present." *Death of a Salesman* has often been called "poetic," despite its mostly drab speech. At first, Miller had planned to make its language more obviously that of poetry and in an early draft of the play wrote much of it in verse. He then turned it into prose on deciding that American actors wouldn't feel at home in verse or wouldn't be able to speak it properly. Miller's account of the genesis of the play is given in his introduction to his *Collected Plays* (New York: Viking, 1959).

In the same introduction, Miller remarks why he thinks the play proved effective in the theater but did not make an effective film. Among other reasons, the movie version transferred Willy literally to scenes that, in the play, he had only imagined, and thus destroyed the play's dramatic tension. It seems more effective—and more disturbing—to show a man losing touch with his surroundings, holding conversations with people who still exist only in his mind. Keeping Willy fixed to the same place throughout the play, while his mind wanders, objectifies Willy's terror. "The screen," says Miller, "is time-bound and earth-bound compared to the stage, if only because its preponderant emphasis is on the visual image. . . . The movie's tendency is always to wipe out what has gone before, and it is thus in constant danger of transforming the dramatic into narrative." Film buffs may care to dispute this observation.

Miller's play is clearly indebted to naturalism. Willy's deepening failure parallels that of his environment: the house increasingly constricted by the city whose growth has killed the elms, prevented anything from thriving, and blotted out human hope—"Gotta break your neck to see a star in this yard." Heredity also works against Willy. As in a Zola novel, one generation repeats patterns of behavior established by its parent. Both Willy and Biff have been less successful than their brothers; presumably both Willy and his "wild-hearted" father were philanderers; both fathers failed their sons and left them insecure. Willy explains, "Dad left when I was such a baby . . . I still feel—kind of temporary about myself."

The play derives also from expressionism. Miller has acknowledged this debt in an interview:

> I know that I was very moved in many ways by German expressionism when I was in school: . . . I learned a great deal from it. I used elements of it that were fused into *Death of a Salesman*. For instance, I purposefully would not give Ben any character, because for Willy he *has* no character—which is, psychologically, expressionist because so many memories come back with a simple tag on them: something represents a threat to you, or a promise. (*Paris Review* 38 [Summer 1966])

Ben is supposed to embody Willy's visions of success, but some students may find him a perplexing character. Some attention to Ben's speeches will show that Ben does not give a realistic account of his career, or an actual portrait of his father, but voices Willy's dream versions. In the last scene before the Requiem, Ben keeps voicing Willy's hopes for Biff and goads Willy on to self-sacrifice. Willy dies full of illusions. Unable to recognize the truth of Biff's self-estimate ("I am not a leader of men"), Willy still believes that Biff will become a business tycoon if only he has $20,000 of insurance money behind him. One truth gets through to Willy: Biff loves him.

Class discussion will probably elicit that Willy Loman is far from being Oedipus. Compared with an ancient Greek king, Willy is unheroic, a low man, as his name suggests. In his mistaken ideals, his language of stale jokes and clichés, his petty infidelity, his deceptions, he suffers from the smallness of his mind and seems only partially to understand his situation. In killing himself for an insurance payoff that Biff doesn't need, is Willy just a pitiable fool? Pitiable, perhaps, but no mere fool: he rises to dignity through self-sacrifice. "It seems to me," notes Miller (in his introduction to his *Collected Plays*), "that there is of necessity a severe limitation of self-awareness in any character, even the most knowing . . . and more, that this very limit serves to complete the tragedy and, indeed, to make it all possible." (Miller's introduction also protests against measuring *Death of a Salesman* by the standards of classical tragedy and finding it a failure.)

In 1983 Miller directed a successful production in Peking, with Chinese actors. In 1984 the Broadway revival with Dustin Hoffman as Willy, later shown on PBS television, brought the play new currency. Hoffman's performance is available on video cassette from Teacher's Video Company at (800) 262-8837. Miller added lines to fit the short-statured Hoffman: buyers laughing at Willy call him "a shrimp." The revival drew a provocative comment from Mimi Kramer in the *New Criterion* for June 1984: she was persuaded that Miller does not sympathize with Willy Loman and never did.

Since 1949 certain liberal attitudes—towards aggression, ambition, and competitiveness—have moved from the periphery of our culture to its center, so that the views of the average middle class Broadway audience are now actually in harmony with what I take to have been Miller's views all along. In 1949 it might have been possible to view Willy as only the victim of a big, bad commercial system. In 1984, it is impossible not to see Miller's own distaste for all Willy's attitudes and petty bourgeois concerns, impossible not to come away from the play feeling that Miller's real judgment of his hero is that he has no soul.

For a remarkable short story inspired by the play, see George Garrett's "The Lion Hunter" in *King of the Mountain* (New York: Scribner's, 1957).

A natural topic for writing and discussion, especially for students who have also read *Othello* and a play by Sophocles: How well does Miller succeed in making the decline and fall of Willy Loman into a tragedy? Is tragedy still possible today? For Miller's arguments in favor of the ordinary citizen as tragic hero, students may read his brief essay "Tragedy and the Common Man" in the "Writer's Perspective" following the play.

For other comments by Miller and a selection of criticism by various hands, see *Death of a Salesman: Text and Criticism*, ed. Gerald Weales (New York: Viking, 1967). Also useful is *Arthur Miller: A Collection of Critical Essays*, ed. Robert W. Corrigan (Englewood Cliffs, NJ: Prentice, 1969). In *Arthur Miller* (London: Macmillan, 1982), Neil Carson seeks to relate *Death of a Salesman* to the playwright's early life.

WRITER'S PERSPECTIVE

Arthur Miller on Drama
TRAGEDY AND THE COMMON MAN, page 1248

QUESTIONS

1. *In arguing that a tragedy can portray an ordinary man, how does Miller find an ally in Sigmund Freud?* See Miller's second paragraph and Freud's comments on Oedipus, page 957.

2. *According to Miller, what evokes in us "the tragic feeling"? Compare his view with Aristotle's view found on page 955.* Unlike the Greek theorist, Miller finds the sense of tragedy arising not from pity and fear, but from contemplating a character who would give his life for personal dignity.

3. *In Miller's view, why is not tragedy an expression of pessimism? What outlook does a tragedy express?*

4. *Consider what Miller says about pathos, and try to apply it to* Death of a Salesman. *Does the play persuade you that Willy Loman would have won his battle? That he isn't witless and insensitive? Or is the play (in Miller's terms) not tragic, but only pathetic?*

Tennessee Williams
THE GLASS MENAGERIE, page 1251

QUESTIONS

1. How do Amanda's dreams for her daughter contrast with the realities of the Wingfields' day-to-day existence?

2. What suggestions do you find in Laura's glass menagerie? In the glass unicorn?

3. In the cast of characters, Jim O'Connor is listed as "a nice, ordinary, young man." Why does his coming to dinner have such earthshaking implications for Amanda? For Laura?

4. Try to describe Jim's feelings toward Laura during their long conversation in Scene VII. After he kisses her, how do his feelings seem to change?

5. Near the end of the play, Amanda tells Tom, "You live in a dream; you manufacture illusions!" What is ironic about her speech? Is there any truth in it?

6. Who is the main character in *The Glass Menagerie?* Tom? Laura? Amanda? (It may be helpful to review the definition of a protagonist.)

7. Has Tom, at the conclusion of the play, successfully made his escape from home? Does he appear to have fulfilled his dreams?

8. How effective is the device of accompanying the action by projecting slides on a screen, bearing titles and images? Do you think most producers of the play are wise to leave it out?

For Williams's instructions for using the slide projector, see "How to Stage *The Glass Menagerie*" in the "Writer's Perspective" following the play. Personally, we think the slide projector a mistake. In trying to justify it, Williams underestimates the quality of his play's spoken lines—but what do your students think?

The gracious world of the old South lives on in Amanda's memories. No doubt its glories shine brighter as the years go by, but all three members of the Wingfield family, in their drab little apartment, live at several removes from the real world. Laura is so shy that she cannot face strangers, yet her mother enrolls her in a business school where she is, of course, doomed to failure. Next, quite ignoring the fact that Laura has no contact with anyone outside her own family, Amanda decides that her daughter ought to marry, and cheerfully sets about finding her a gentleman caller. Some students will want to see Amanda as a silly biddy and nothing more, so that it may help to ask: In what ways is she admirable? (See Williams's initial, partially admiring description of her in the cast of characters.)

A kindly, well-intentioned young man, Jim O'Connor, is a self-styled go-getter, a pop psychologist. Like Biff Loman in *Death of a Salesman*, Jim is a high school hero whose early promise hasn't materialized. He was acquainted with Laura in school but now remembers her only when prompted. Laura's wide-eyed admiration for him flatters Jim's vanity, and in her presence he grows expansive. Gradually, Laura awakens in him feelings of warmth and protectiveness, as well as a sense that her fragility bespeaks something as precious and rare as her glass unicorn. It is with genuine regret that he shatters her tremulous, newly risen hopes with the revelation that he is engaged to be married to Betty, a young woman as unremarkable as himself.

Laura's collection of glass animals objectifies her fragility, her differentness, her removal from active life. Significantly, the unicorn is her favorite. "Unicorns, aren't they extinct in the modern world?" asks Jim; and he adds, a few lines later, "I'm not made out of glass." When Jim dances with Laura and accidentally breaks off the unicorn's horn, the mythical creature becomes more like the common horses that surround him, just as Laura, by the very act of dancing, comes a few steps closer to being like everyone else. Although Jim can accept the broken unicorn from Laura as a souvenir, he cannot make room in his life for her. Her fleeting brush with reality does not in the end alter her uniqueness or release her from her imprisonment.

Amanda's charge that Tom manufactures illusions seems a case of the pot calling the kettle black. As we know from Amanda's flighty talk and far-fetched plans for Laura, the mother herself lives in a dream world, but she is right about Tom. A would-be poet, a romantic whose imagination has been fired by Hollywood adventure movies, Tom pays dues to the Merchant Seamen's union instead of paying the light bill. So desperate is he to make his dreams come true, he finally runs away to distant places, like his father before him. In truth, each character in the play has some illusions—even Jim, who dreams of stepping from his warehouse job into a future as a millionaire television executive. And as Tom's commentaries point out, at the time of the play's action all Americans seem dazzled by illusions, ignoring the gathering threat of World War II. "In Spain, there was Guernica! But here there was only hot swing music and liquor, dance halls, bars, and movies, and sex that hung in the gloom like a chandelier and flooded the world with brief, deceptive rainbows."

For a challenging study of the play, see Roger B. Stein, "*The Glass Menagerie* Revisited: Catastrophe without Violence," *Western Humanities Review* 18 (Spring 1964):141–53. (It is also available in *Tennessee Williams: A Collection of Critical Essays*, ed. Stephen S. Stanton [Englewood Cliffs, NJ: Prentice, 1977].) Stein finds in the play themes of both social and spiritual catastrophe: the failure of both Christianity and the American dream. Although some of the play's abundant Christian symbolism and imagery would seem just decoration, students may enjoy looking for it. Scene V, in which Tom tells his mother that Laura will have a gentleman caller, is titled on the screen "Annunciation." Laura says she has dreaded to confess she has left business school, because her mother, when disappointed, wears a look "like the picture of Jesus' mother." Amanda is also identified with the music of "Ave Maria." When Tom comes home drunk, he tells Laura of seeing the stage magician Malvolio, an Antichrist who can escape from a nailed coffin and can transform water to wine (also to beer and whiskey). Jim O'Connor is another unsatisfactory Savior: he comes to supper on a Friday night and (symbolically?) is given fish, but unlike the Christ whose initials he shares, he can work no deliverance. Laura is described as if she were a saint, or at least a contemplative. When she learns that Jim is engaged to Betty, "the holy candles in the altar of Laura's face have been snuffed out." Compare Williams's instructions to lighting technicians in his production notes:

> Shafts of light are focused on selected areas or actors, sometimes in contradistinction to what is the apparent center. For instance, in the quarrel scene between Tom and Amanda, in which Laura has no active part, the clearest pool of light is on her figure. This is also true of the supper scene. The light upon Laura should be distinct from the others, having a peculiar pristine clarity such as light used in early religious portraits of female saints or madonnas.

Most suggestive of all, Williams keeps associating candles with lightning. Amanda's candelabrum, from the altar of the Church of the Heavenly Rest, had been warped when the church was struck by lightning. And when Tom, in his final speech, calls on Laura to blow her candles out, he declares that "nowadays the world is lit by lightning." The playwright suggests, according to Stein, that a hard, antireligious materialism now prevails. (At least, this line of reasoning may be worth an argument.)

The character of Laura, apparently, contains traits of Williams's sister Rose. Although the painfully shy Laura is not an exact portrait of his sister (Laura "was like Miss Rose only in her inescapable 'difference,'" Williams has written), the name of Rose suggests Laura's nickname, "Blue Roses." A young woman with "lovely, heartbreaking eyes," Rose felt acute anxiety in male company. She was pressed by her mother to make a painful social debut at the Knoxville Country Club. For a time she was courted by a junior executive, an ambitious young man who soon suspended his attentions. After the breakup, Rose suffered from mysterious illnesses, showed symptoms of withdrawal, and eventually was committed to the Missouri State Asylum. Williams tells her story in his *Memoirs* (New York: Doubleday, 1975) 116–28. Like Tom Wingfield, apparently Williams as a young man was a restless dreamer and aspiring writer who left home to wander the country.

In his own memoir, William Jay Smith, who knew Williams in St. Louis as a fellow college student at Washington University, remarks on the background of the play:

> I am frequently amused by those who take Tom's autobiographical projection of his family in *The Glass Menagerie* literally and picture him as having inhabited a run-down, seedy old house, if not a downright hovel. The house

on Arundel Place, with its Oriental rugs, silver, and comfortable, if not luxurious furniture, was located in an affluent neighborhood. . . . Our entire bun-
galow on Telegraph Road would have fitted comfortably into one or two of
its rooms. Mrs. Williams presided over it as if it were an antebellum mansion.
(*Army Brat* [New York: Persea, 1980] 190)

Tennessee Williams reads excerpts from *The Glass Menagerie* on cassette tape,
available from the American Audio Prose Library, Inc., Box 842, Columbia, MO
65205; phone number for orders, (800) 447–2275. An excellent reading of the complete play with Montgomery Clift, Julie Harris, and Jessica Tandy is also available
on audio cassette from Caedmon (A-301). Additionally, Paul Newman's 1987 version of *The Glass Menagerie*, starring Joanne Woodward and John Malkovich, with
Karen Allen and James Naughton, is available on video cassette from Teacher's
Video Company at (800) 262-8837.

WRITER'S PERSPECTIVE

Tennessee Williams on Drama

HOW TO STAGE *THE GLASS MENAGERIE*, page 1300

QUESTIONS

1. How does Williams feel about theatrical "realism"?

2. How does Williams argue for his use of the slide projector? If you were
producing *The Glass Menagerie*, would you follow the playwright's instructions
and use the projector, or leave it out?

3. What other antirealistic devices would Williams employ? Would you
expect them to be effective?

August Wilson

JOE TURNER'S COME AND GONE, page 1302

QUESTIONS

1. What does Bynum's "shining man" represent? What is the significance of
his telling Bynum to rub blood on himself? What action of Loomis's in Act III
does this ritual foreshadow?

2. What is implied when, in Act II, Scene 2, Bynum asks Loomis whether he
has ever been in Johnstown?

3. Who is Joe Turner? What does he represent?

4. At what moment does the crisis occur in *Joe Turner's Come and Gone*?

5. After reading Wilson's play, what would you say is the Secret of Life that Bynum learns from the shining man?

6. What, if anything, does Wilson's play have to say about religion?

7. For discussion: Do you think the play would have been more effective had Herald Loomis and his wife decided to stay together once they had been reunited?

8. Comment on the spelling of Loomis's name. Is he a herald? If so, what message does he impart?

9. What is the theme of *Joe Turner's Come and Gone*? Is it stated in the play, or only implied?

David Savran remarks about Wilson's play:

Joe Turner's Come and Gone, which takes place in 1911, performs a ritual of purification, setting African religious tradition against American Christianity. It documents the liberation of the spiritually bound Herald Loomis, who years before had been pressed into illegal servitude by the bounty hunter named in the play's title. In the course of the play the details of everyday life in a Pittsburgh boarding house give way to the patterns of African religion and ritual. With the help of Bynum, an African healer, a "Binder of What Clings," Loomis effects his own liberation. He recognizes that his enslavement has been self-imposed; this man "who done forgot his song" finds it again. Bynum explains to him: "You bound on to your song. All you got to do is stand up and sing it, Herald Loomis. It's right there kicking at your throat. All you got to do is sing it. Then you be free." (*In Their Own Words: Contemporary American Playwrights* [New York: Theatre Communications Group, 1989] 289)

The lines Savran quotes, appearing in the play's final scene, are perhaps as good a statement of the play's theme as there is.

The troubled Loomis is a herald, it seems—Bynum's "One Who Goes Before and Shows the Way" (see Bynum's long speech in Act I, Scene 1). What Loomis learns, and shows the others, is that African-Americans, if they search, can find within themselves and their African traditions the power to be free. This is apparently the Secret of Life that Bynum has learned from his "shining man." Everyone has to find his own song. Only then can he make his mark on life.

Bynum, the conjure man, is a pivotal character. At the start of the play, he is the only one who has found his song (though Bertha and Jeremy seem closer to having found theirs than do some of the other characters). Loomis, when he first appears, is still under the influence of Joe Turner, the cruel bounty hunter who personifies all the evils of slavery. Thus Loomis frightens the others, seems to them crazy and unpredictable. Though Seth knows where Martha Pentecost is, he refuses to tell Loomis. In fact, Loomis is a man searching for his song.

Bynum also realizes that, after their long period of slavery and separation, black people have to seek and find one another. That's why his magic is aimed at bringing people together. That's also why he likes the People Finder, and why he encourages Jeremy to go "down to Seefus" to play his guitar, even though Bertha warns him the place might get raided. "That's where the music at," Bynum says. "That's where the people at. The people down there making music and enjoying themselves. Some things is worth taking the chance going to jail about." Several of the characters in Wilson's play are in search of the right person to connect with. What makes this play so life-affirming is that some of them, by reaching out, find what they're looking for.

The turning point in the play seems to come at the end of Act I, when Loomis has his vision, making such a commotion that Seth tells him he'll have to leave the boarding house. Only Bynum realizes how crucial that vision is to Loomis's spiritual health. By this time he clearly believes that Loomis is a shining man. That's why he asks, on the following day, whether Loomis has ever been in Johnstown. It was in Johnstown that Bynum had the experience with the shining man that he tells Selig about in Act I, Scene 1.

By singing the Joe Turner song in Act II, Scene 2, Bynum gets Loomis to unburden himself, to reconnect with his own African roots. As if by instinct, Loomis seems to know he can do so by rubbing himself with his own blood, thus acting out the ritual Bynum has described to Selig in Act I, Scene 1. Wilson is clearly aware that blood functions as a Christian symbol of purification. Martha urges Loomis to be washed in the blood of the Lamb. But Loomis rejects the Christianity that sustains his wife. Purification comes for Loomis and Bynum not through Christianity but through the powerful African rituals of their forefathers. "I don't need nobody to bleed for me!" Herald says. "I can bleed for myself." Loomis's song is "the song of self-sufficiency." When he learns to sing it, he becomes a shining man.

Students need to pay attention to Wilson's prologue ("The Play," preceding Act I, Scene 1). The world of *Joe Turner's Come and Gone* is a now-vanished corner of American society—a world of poor drifters, of migrants from the cotton fields to the booming Pittsburgh steel mills of 1911. But although times have changed, the situation of the characters ("foreigners in a strange land" seeking "a new identity") may recall that of any new settlers in a big city, whether Africans, Hispanics, or Asians. For class discussion: How does the play remind us of the lives (and problems) of minority people today, who find themselves transplanted to an American city from a very different culture?

For another topic for discussion, have students read Wilson's comments to his interviewer, Bill Moyers, in "Black Experience in America" in the "Writer's Perspective" following the play. How does the play reflect Wilson's views? Particularly interesting may be Wilson's opinion that African-Americans were ill advised to leave the South.

Here are three suggested writing topics:

1. The importance of magic in *Joe Turner's Come and Gone.*

2. Is Wilson a symbolist? (That he imparts a message and that he portrays real and recognizable people does not prevent his play from being richly suggestive. Joe Turner, Bynum's "shining man," and the blood rituals that are part of the quest for an individual song all hint at larger meanings. Students may find others as well.)

3. For a long paper, one entailing some research in a library: In what ways has life for most African-Americans changed since the 1911 of which Wilson writes? In what ways have problems and conditions of life stayed the same?

Wilson's play was first performed in a staged reading in 1984 at a playwright's conference at the Eugene O'Neill Theater Center. Later, in 1986 and 1987, it had two productions by the Yale Repertory Theater. Shortly thereafter, in 1988, a successful Broadway production received great acclaim: "haunting, profound, indescribably moving" (Frank Rich in *The New York Times*); "Wilson's best play" (William A. Henry III in *Time*).

Students might be asked to comment on this summing up by Henry in *Time* for April 11, 1988, and if necessary argue with it:

> At the end, when Loomis seems pathetically shorn of his consuming purpose . . . the most spiritual boarder perceives in him instead the "shiny man" of a folkloric religious vision. In that moment, spectators too find themselves transported from pity to admiration: Loomis has transformed his pointless suffering into an ennobling search for life's meaning.

Shortly after Wilson received a second Pulitzer Prize for *The Piano Lesson* in April 1990, he made a few revealing comments to an interviewer. Nothing in his work is autobiographical, he declared; nothing he has written has been taken from his own experience. He has successfully avoided studying other playwrights. He claims to have read nothing by Shakespeare except *The Merchant of Venice* (in high school), nothing by Ibsen, Miller, or Tennessee Williams. The only other playwrights whose work he admits to knowing are Amiri Baraka, Ed Bullins, and Athol Fugard. He doesn't go to the theater himself, hasn't been to a movie in ten years. "Part of this creative isolation is self-protective fear," explains the interviewer, Kevin Kelly. "Wilson is afraid of tampering with those chaotically rich and whimsically independent forces in his head, terrified of confusing their voices and stories with the voices and stories of other writers" ("August Wilson's True Stories," *Boston Globe*, April 29, 1990).

WRITER'S PERSPECTIVE

August Wilson on Drama

BLACK EXPERIENCE IN AMERICA, page 1352

QUESTIONS

1. *What does Wilson see as a part of his purpose in writing plays?* "To see some of the choices that we as blacks in America have made."

2. *How does* Joe Turner's Come and Gone *illuminate any such choices?* Wilson has respect and affection for black folk culture, with its elements of myth and magic. Perhaps, he hints, it risks disappearance when transplanted to the urban North.

3. *What light do Wilson's remarks throw on the line in the play, "Everyone has to find his own song"?* These characters, as the playwright sees them, are looking for their African identities. That they are embarked on any such quest won't be obvious to most readers. Students will need to do some thinking and discussing in order to make sense of Wilson's claim. What is an African identity? How does Herald Loomis end up with one at the end? Carefully reread the playwright's explanatory stage directions in the last moments of the play.

WRITING

This chapter is no more than a brief guide and a small work of reference. If you find it useful, you might ask students to read it before they plan their papers. As succinctly as we can, we set forth in the section "Writing About Literature" a few general critical approaches to a story, poem, or play; then we escort the student through the various procedures of finding a topic and organizing, drafting, revising, and finishing a paper.

Such matters need not divert much classroom time from the livelier task of reading literature. Perhaps it would be sufficient, after students have tried "Writing About Literature," to take a few minutes to question them on this material, to make sure at least that they are aware of it. At the same time, you might invite their own questions about essay writing (to which, no doubt, you will have your own answers).

If this chapter fulfills its purpose, it will save you some breath and spare you from reading many innocent almost-plagiarisms, floating unidentified quotations (of the kind that suddenly interrupt the student's prose with Harold Bloom's prose in quotation marks), and displays of ill-fitting critical terminology.

Some instructors assign few papers and exact from their students rather highly polished prose; others prefer to keep students scribbling away constantly, on the assumption that the practice in writing is valuable (whether or not the instructor reads all their output word by word). Instructors who favor the latter approach report that they simply assign selections in the book that have questions after them, and ask students to answer some questions in writing outside of class. These papers are collected and the instructor later skims through them and selects a few of the livelier points to quote and discuss at the next class. (The papers are not returned.)

Once—at the end of a class in which argument had waxed over the question "Is 'Naming the Parts' an antiwar poem or isn't it?"—XJK made the mistake of cutting off the discussion and telling students to go home and write their opinions down on paper. The result was to cool future class discussions: students were afraid that if they talked animatedly, they would be told to write. A different approach is that of an instructor who would halt a class discussion that had grown driveling, or bad-tempered, or without heart, and cry, "For God's sake, let's all stop talking! Now get out your pencils and write me a paragraph. . . . " He claimed that in the next class the discussion improved markedly.

Anonymous

A LITTLE POEM REGARDING COMPUTER SPELL CHECKERS, page 1365

This poem, which was first shown to us by Cara Nusinov, of Miami, Florida, has long circulated on the Internet. We have spent a considerable amount of time trying to track down its author. What we discovered was both interesting and surprising. The poem reprinted in our book seems to be based on a longer piece of light verse by Jerrold H. Zar, who is the Associate Provost for Graduate Studies of Northern Illinois University. His original poem was titled "Candidate for a Pullet Surprise" (note the pun) and was first published in *Journal of Irreproducible Results* (vol. 39 No. 1, Jan./Feb. 1994). The Internet seems to have worked rather like the old oral tradition in compressing and modifying his text into a new collective and anonymous version, but Professor Zar deserves proper credit for being its ultimate progenitor. The anthology went to press before his identity was discovered, but he will be noted in future editions.

35 *Writing About a Story*

If your students complain, "I've never written about *stories* before—what am I supposed to do?" you can have them read this section. We can't imagine spending whole class hours with this material; it is supplied here mainly to provide students with illustrations of acceptable papers written by each of three usual methods, and a few pointers on format and mechanics. If you like, you can assign this section for outside reading when you first make a writing assignment.

XJK comments: The card report (pages 1391–92) may well be God's gift to the instructor overwhelmed with papers to grade. At least, I can't take credit for its creation. This demanding exercise first impressed me as a student in the one course I took at Teachers College, Columbia. The professor, Lennox Grey, assigned us aspiring literature teachers to pick ten great novels we hadn't read and to write card reports on them. Among the novels were *War and Peace* and *Les Misérables*, and although Grey allowed us as many as two cards to encompass them, I must have spoiled a pack of cards for every novel I encompassed. But the task was an agreeable challenge, and I felt it obliged me to look more closely at fiction than I ever had. Later, as a graduate student in Ann Arbor, I found the same device heavily worked by Kenneth Rowe, Arthur Miller's teacher of playwriting, in a popular course in modern drama. Every week, students were expected to read two full-length plays and to turn in two card reports. Nearly a hundred students swelled the course, and Rowe employed two teaching assistants to do the grading. As one of them, I soon realized the beauty of the method. Even a novice like me could do a decent job of grading a hundred card reports each week without being crushed under the toil, either. For an hour a week Rowe met with the other assistant and me and superintended our labors a little, and we thrashed out any problem cases.

If you care to give such an assignment a try, don't feel obliged to write a card report of your own as a Platonic ideal to hold your students' reports up to. When you gather in the sheaves, you can compare a few of them (looking hard at the reports of any students whom you know to be intelligent and conscientious) and probably will quickly see what a better-than-average report on a story might encompass. In grading, it isn't necessary to read every item on every card: you may read the plot summaries with intermittent attention and concentrate on the subtler elements: symbol, theme, evaluation. Because extensive remarks by the instructor don't seem called for (and anyway, wouldn't fit on the card), your comments may be short and pointed. If a student reporting on "The Tell-Tale Heart" has omitted a crucial symbol, you may simply query, "The eye?" or "The heartbeat?" One can probably grade thirty card reports in less than an hour and do an honest job; whereas a set of thirty essays, even brief ones, takes at least four hours.

By asking students to produce so few words, you need not feel that their writing skills are being slighted. To get the report to fit the card, a good student has to do several drafts and revisions, none of which the instructor has to read. A shoddy job by a student who hasn't thoroughly read the story is painfully obvious. Once in a while, after a surfeit of expansive essays, I have asked a class for a card report just to rest my eyes and to remind them of the virtues of concision. Some students inevitably grumble, but most are in for a reward, some will even be delighted that the assignment is so clearly defined and limited!

Warn your students to allow plenty of time to do this job right. Stephen Marcus, of the University of California, Santa Barbara, tells us that some of his students were appalled to find it took them two or three hours to write one card report. That sounds about par for the assignment; if you want to abbreviate it, you can omit some of the required elements.

To read nothing but card reports all term is, however, a mind crusher. Essays, of course, develop different skills of thinking and organization and will probably still seem necessary. In choosing an essay topic, if given a choice, many students have trouble deciding how large a topic to attempt in an assigned word length, and many are tempted to choose a topic larger than they can handle. Some want to make sure they'll have enough ideas to fill the word length. Even if you don't care to assign any of the topics suggested in the text, having students read the lists in the "Suggestions for Writing" section may give them a clearer notion of the right amplitude of topics for papers of various lengths.

If this list, the writing assignments in each "Writing Critically" section, the "Suggestions for Writing" at the end of most chapters, and your own inspiration don't suffice, still more topics for writing may be quarried from the questions after the stories.

36   *Writing About a Poem*

Here are notes on the two poems contained in "Writing About a Poem."

Robert Frost
DESIGN, page 1400

"Design" is fruitful to compare in theme with Walt Whitman's "A Noiseless Patient Spider." One could begin by comparing the early versions of the two poems, Whitman's "The Soul, reaching" and Frost's "In White." What are the themes of these versions? It is more difficult to tell from these vaguer, more general poems. In rewriting, both poets seem not only to have made their details more specific, but also to have defined their central ideas.

If you wish to deal with this section in class, you might have students read "Design," then the two student papers that follow the poem. What did these writers notice about the poem that you didn't notice? What did you notice about it that they left out?

Besides Jarrell's classic explication, many other good discussions of the poem can be consulted. Elizabeth Drew has a succinct explication in *Poetry: A Modern Guide to Its Understanding and Enjoyment* (New York: Norton, 1959), and there is a more detailed reading by Richard Ohmann in *College English* 28 (Feb. 1967): 359–67.

Abbie Huston Evans
WING-SPREAD, page 1408

The student's evaluation seems just to us. While "Wing-Spread" is not so vivid a cameo as "Design," nor so troubling in its theme, and while it contains trite rimes (except for *beryl/peril*), we think it a decent poem and admirably terse.

Insufficiently recognized (like most poets), Evans (1881–1979) had a long, productive life. Her *Collected Poems* was published in 1970 by the University of Pittsburgh Press. There are dozens of poems better than "Wing-Spread" in it.

SUGGESTIONS FOR WRITING

Here are a few more topics for paper assignments to supplement the list at the end of the chapter.

Topics for Brief Papers (250–500 words)

1. A *précis* (French, from Latin: "to cut short") is a short abstract or condensation of a literary work that tries to sum up the work's most essential elements. Although a précis, like a paraphrase, states the poet's thought in the writer's own words, a paraphrase is sometimes as long as the original poem, if not longer. A précis, while it tends to be much briefer than a poem, also takes in essentials: theme, subject, tone, character, events (in a narrative poem), and anything else that strikes the writer as important. A précis might range in length from one ample sentence to a few hundred words (if, say, it were condensing a long play or novel, or a complex longer poem). Here, for instance, is an acceptable précis of Robert Browning's "Soliloquy of the Spanish Cloister":

   > The speaker, a monk in a religious community, voices to himself while gardening the bitter grudge he has against Brother Lawrence, one of his fellow monks. He charges Lawrence with boring him with dull talk at mealtime, sporting monogrammed tableware, ogling women, drinking greedily, ignoring rituals (unlike the speaker, who after a meal lays knife and fork in a cross—which seems overly scrupulous). Having vented his grudge by slyly scissoring Lawrence's favorite flowering shrubs, the speaker is now determined to go further, and plots to work Lawrence's damnation. Perhaps he will lure Lawrence into misinterpreting a text in Scripture, or plant a pornographic volume on him. So far gone is the speaker in his hatred that he is even willing to sell his soul to the devil if the devil will carry off Lawrence's; and so proud is the speaker in his own wiles that he thinks he can cheat the devil in the bargain. Vespers ring, ending the meditation, but his terrible grudge seems sure to go on.

   As the detailed précis makes clear, Browning's poem contains a chronicle of events and a study in character. The précis also indicates the tone of the poem and (another essential) its point of view.

   Students might be supplied with a copy of the above material to guide them and be asked to write précis of four or five poems, chosen from a list the instructor compiles of six or eight poems in the "Poems for Further Reading."

2. Find a poem that you like, one not in this book so it may be unfamiliar to other members of the class. Insert into it a passage of five or six lines that you yourself write in imitation of it. Your object is to lengthen the poem by a bit of forgery that will go undetected. Type out the whole poem afresh, inserted lines and all, and have copies duplicated for the others in the class. Then let them try to tell your forged lines from those of the original. A successful forgery will be hard to detect, since you will have imitated the poet's language, handling of form, and imagery—indeed, the poet's voice.

TOPICS FOR MORE EXTENSIVE PAPERS (600–1,000 WORDS)

1. Relate a personal experience of poetry: a brief history of your attempts to read it or to write it; a memoir of your experience in reading poetry aloud; a report of a poetry reading you attended; an account of how reading a poem brought a realization that affected you personally (no instructor-pleasing pieties!); or an account of an effort to foist a favorite poem upon your friends, or to introduce young children to poetry. Don't make up any fabulous experiences or lay claim to profound emotions you haven't had; the result could be blatantly artificial ("How I Read Housman's 'Loveliest of trees' and Found the Meaning of Life"). But if you honestly can sum up what you learned from your experience, then do so, by all means.

2. After you have read several ballads (both folk ballads and literary ballads), write a ballad of your own, at least twenty lines long. If you need a subject, consider some event recently in the news: an act of bravery, a wedding that took place despite obstacles, a murder or a catastrophe, a report of spooky or mysterious happenings. Then in a prose paragraph, state what you learned from your reading of traditional or literary ballads that proved useful to you as a ballad composer yourself.

TOPICS FOR LONGER PAPERS (1,500 WORDS OR MORE)

1. Leslie Fiedler, the critic and novelist, once wrote an essay in which he pretended to be a critic of the last century ("A Review of *Leaves of Grass* and *Hiawatha* as of 1855," *American Poetry Review* 2 [Mar.–Apr. 1973]). Writing as if he subscribed to the tastes of that age, Fiedler declared Whitman's book shaggy and shocking, and awarded Professor Longfellow all the praise. If you can steep yourself in the literature of a former age (or recent past year) deeply enough to feel confident, such an essay might be fun to write (and to read). Write about some poem once fashionable, now forgotten; or about some poem once spurned, now esteemed. Your instructor might have some suggestions.

2. For a month (or some other assigned period of time), keep a personal journal of your reading of poetry and your thinking about it. To give direction to your journal, you might confine it to the work of, say, half a dozen poets who interest you; or you might concentrate on a theme common to a few poems by various poets.

WRITING A POEM *(Some notes by XJK)*

These notes are provided mainly for the instructor who employs this anthology in a creative writing course. Some may be of interest, however, to anyone who in teaching composition includes a unit on writing poems. Such an instructor will probably have firm persuasions about poetry and about the teaching of poets. Instead of trying to trumpet any persuasions of my own, let me just set down some hunches that, from teaching poetry workshops, I have come to feel are mostly true.

In reading a student's poem, you have to look at it with your mind a blank, reserving judgment for as long as possible. Try to see what the student is doing, being slow to compare a fledgling effort to the classics. There's no use in merely reading the poem and spotting any influences you find in it—"Ha, I see you've been reading Williams!" You can, however, praise any virtues you discover and you can tell the student firmly, kindly, and honestly any adverse reactions you feel. Point to anything in the poem that causes you to respond toward it, or against it. Instead of coldly damning the poem's faults, you can inquire why the writer said something in such-and-such a way, rather than in some other. You can ask to have anything you don't understand explained. If a line or a passage doesn't tell you anything, you can ask the student to suggest a fresh way of wording it. Perhaps the most valuable service you can perform for a student poet is to be hard to please. Suggest that the student not settle for the first words that flash to mind, but reach deeper, go after the word or phrase or line that will be not merely adequate, but memorable.

The greatest method of teaching poetry writing I have ever heard of was that of the late John Holmes. Former students at Tufts remember that Holmes seldom made comments on a poem, but often would just lay a finger next to a suspect passage and fix the student with a look of expectancy until the silence became unendurable, and the student began explaining what the passage meant and how it could be put better. (I have never made the Holmes method succeed for me. I can't keep from talking too much.)

Most workshop courses in poetry fall into a classic ritual. Students make copies of their poems, bring them in, and show them around to the class. This method of procedure is hard to improve upon. Some instructors find that the effort of screening the work themselves first and deciding what to spend time on in class makes for more cogent class sessions, with less time squandered on boring or inferior material. In general, class sessions won't be any more lively and valuable than the poems that are on hand. (An exception was a workshop I once visited years ago at MIT. The poems were literal, boring stuff, but the quality of the students' impromptu critical analyses was sensational.) Often a great class discussion will revolve around a fine poem with deep faults in it.

The severest challenge for the instructor, incidentally, isn't a *bad* poem. A bad poem is easy to deal with; it always gives you plenty of work to do—passages to delete, purple adjectives to question. The challenge comes in dealing with a truly surprising, original, and competent poem. This is risky and sensitive work because genuine poets usually know what they are doing to a greater degree than you or any other outsider does; and you don't want to confuse them with reactions you don't trust. For such rare students, all a poetry workshop probably does is supply an audience, a little encouragement, and sometimes even an insight.

There are natural temptations, of course, to which teachers of poets fall prey. Like coin collectors, they keep wanting to overvalue the talents they have on hand, to convince themselves that a student is a Gem Mint State poet, when a less personal opinion might find the student just an average specimen, although uncirculated. It's better to be too slow than too quick to encourage a student to seek nationwide publication. It is another temptation, if you have a class with a competent poet in it, to devote most of each session to that poet's latest works, causing grumblings of discontent (sometimes) among the other paying customers. I believe that a more competent poet deserves more time, but you have to conduct a class and not a tutorial.

Poetry workshops can become hideously intimate. They are bound to produce confessional or diary poems that, sometimes behind the thinnest of fictive screens, confide in painful detail the writer's sexual, psychic, and religious hangups. I have known poetry workshops where, by semester's end, the participants feel toward one another like the members of a hostile therapy group. That is why I believe in stressing that a poem is not merely the poet's self-revelation. It usually helps to insist at the start of the course that poems aren't necessarily to be taken personally. (See "Poetry and Personal Identity," if you want any ammunition.) Everybody will know, of course, that some poets in the class aren't capable of detached art and that a poem about a seduction may well be blatant autobiography; but believe me, you and your students will be happier if you can blow the trumpet in favor of the Imagination. There is no use in circulating poems in class anonymously, pretending that nobody knows who wrote them. Somebody will know and I think that the sooner the members of the class freely admit their identities, the more easy and relaxed and open the situation will be. To know each one personally, as soon as you can, is essential.

As the workshop goes on, I don't always stick to a faithful conference schedule. Some will need (and wish for) more of your time than others, but I like to schedule at least one conference right away, at the beginning of the course. This is a chance to meet with students in private and get a sense of their needs. I tell them to bring in a few poems they've already written, if they've written any. But I make it clear that class sessions will deal only with brand-new poems. At the end of the course, I program another such conference (instead of a final exam), sit down with each student, and ask, "Well, where are you now?"

Some students will lean on you for guidance ("What shall I write about?"); others will spurn all your brilliant suggestions and want to roar away in their own directions. Fine. I believe in offering the widest possible latitude in making assignments—but in having some assignments. Even the most inner-directed poet can learn something from being expected to move in a new direction. Having a few assignments will discourage the customers who think they can get through any number of creative writing courses by using the same old yellowed sheaf of poems. Encourage revision. Now and then, suggest a revision as an assignment instead of a new poem.

In "Writing a Poem" I offer a radical suggestion: that the students memorize excellent poems. Feeling like a curmudgeon for making this recommendation, I was happy to find some support for it in the view of Robert Bly, who remarked in *Coda* (June/July 1981):

> I won't even read a single manuscript now, when I visit a university workshop, unless the poet in advance agrees to memorize fifty lines of Yeats. At

the first workshop I visited last fall it cut the number of graduate-student writers who wanted to see me from 15 to 2. Next year I'm changing that to fifty lines of *Beowulf.*

Bly may seem unreasonably stern, but he and I agree on the value of memorization. I believe it helps coax the writing of poetry down out of the forebrain, helps it unite with the pulse.

Bly has sane things to say, in this same article, about the folly of thirsting for publication too early. And incidentally, here's one of his unorthodox exercises for a writing workshop (imparted in an interview in the *Boston Globe Magazine* for April 10, 1988):

> One workshop, I brought in an onion for each of the students. I asked everybody to spend 10 to 15 minutes describing the exterior of the onion, using all of their senses. That requires every bit of observation you have, to remain looking at the onion. Then, in the second part of the exercise, I said, "Now I want you to compare the onion to your mother."

That must have rocked 'em! I wonder if it produced any good results.

For a textbook wholly devoted to the writing of poetry, quite the best thing of its kind, see Robert Wallace's *Writing Poems*, Third Edition (New York: Harper-Collins, 1991).

Another book crammed with teaching hints and lively writing exercises for student poets is *The Teachers & Writers Handbook of Poetic Forms*, edited by Ron Padgett (1987), and sold by Teachers & Writers Collaborative, 5 Union Square West, New York, NY 10003. Besides supplying unstuffy definitions and examples of many expected forms, the Handbook deals with blues poems, collaborations, ghazals, insult poems, light verse, pantoums, performance poems, raps, renga, and more.

FURTHER NOTES ON TEACHING POETRY *by XJK*

These notes are offered in response to the wishes of several instructors for additional practical suggestions for teaching poetry. They are, however, mere descriptions of a few strategies that have proved useful in my own teaching. For others, I can neither prescribe nor proscribe.

1. To a greater extent than in teaching prose, the instructor may find it necessary to have poems read aloud. It is best if students do this reading. Since to read a poem aloud effectively requires that the reader understand what is said in it, students will need advance warning so that they can prepare their spoken interpretations. Sometimes I assign particular poems to certain people, or ask each person to take his or her choice. Some advice on how to read poetry aloud is given in the chapter "Sound." I usually suggest only that students beware of waxing overemotional or

rhetorical, and I urge them to read aloud outside of class as often as possible. If the student or the instructor has access to a tape recorder, it may be especially helpful.

2. It is good to recall occasionally that poems may be put back together as well as taken apart. Sometimes I call on a student to read a previously prepared poem, just before opening a discussion of the poem. Then, the discussion over and the poem lying all around in intelligible shreds, I ask the same student to read it over again. It is often startling how the reading improves from the student's realizing more clearly what the poet is saying.

3. I believe in asking students to do a certain amount of memorization. Many groan that such rote learning is mindless and grade-schoolish, but it seems to me one way to defeat the intellectualizations that students (and the rest of us) tend to make of poetry. It is also a way to suggest that we do not read a poem primarily for its ideas: to learn a poem by heart is one way to engrave oneself with the sound and weight of it. I ask for twenty or thirty lines at a time, of the student's choice, then have them write the lines out in class. Some students have reported unexpected illuminations. Some people, of course, can't memorize a poem to save their souls, and I try to encourage but not to pressure them. These written memorizations take very little of the instructor's time to check and need not be returned to the students unless there are flagrant lacunae in them.

4. The instructor has to sense when a discussion has gone on long enough. It is a matter of watching each student's face for the first sign of that fixed set of the mouth. Elizabeth Bishop once wisely declared that, while she was not opposed to all close analysis and criticism, she was against "making poetry monstrous and boring and proceeding to talk the very life out of it." I used to be afraid of classroom silences. Now, I find it helps sometimes to stop a discussion that is getting lost, and say, "Let's all take three minutes and read this poem again and think about it silently." When the discussion resumes, it is usually improved.

Some of the finest, most provocative essays on teaching poetry in college I have seen are these:

Alice Bloom, "On the Experience of Unteaching Poetry," *Hudson Review* (Spring 1979): 7–30. Bloom: "I am interested in the conditions of education that would lead a student to remark, early in a term, as one of mine did, that 'I wish we didn't know these were poems. Then it seems like it would be a lot easier.'"

Clara Clairborne Park, "Rejoicing to Concur with the Common Reader" in her volume *Rejoining the Common Reader: Essays, 1962–1990* (Evanston: Northwestern, 1991). Park is now a professor at Williams College, but for many years she taught in a community college. This essay recounts the joys and disappointments of working with students who were just discovering literature. Park is most concerned by how to relate literature to the lives of her students without condescending to them. She praises a kind of simplicity in approaching literature that "need not mean narrowness." Discussing the teacher's realization that he or she participates "in a process that changes lives," Park writes an essay that proves both moving and enlightening.

ON INTEGRATING POETRY AND COMPOSITION

How do you teach students to read poetry and, at the same time, to write good prose? Instructors who face this task may find some useful advice in the following article, first published in *The English Record*, bulletin of the New York State English Council (Winter 1981). It is reprinted here by the kind permission of the author, Irwin Weiser, director of developmental writing, Purdue University.

THE PROSE PARAPHRASE
INTEGRATING POETRY AND COMPOSITION

Irwin Weiser

Many of us teach composition courses which demand that we not only instruct our students in writing but that we also present literature to them as well. Such courses often frustrate us, since a quarter or a semester seems too brief to allow us to teach fundamentals of composition alone. How are we to integrate the teaching of literature with the teaching of writing? What are we to do with a fat anthology of essays, fiction, poetry, or drama and a rhetoric text and, in some cases, a separate handbook of grammar and usage?

Recently, I tried an approach which seemed to provide more integration of reading and writing than I previously had felt I attained in similar courses. The course was the third quarter of a required freshman composition sequence; the departmental course description specifies the teaching of poetry and drama, but also states "English 103 is, however, primarily a composition, not a literature, course. Major emphasis of the course should be on writing." The approach I will describe concerns the study of poetry.

Because this is a writing course, I explained to my students that we would approach poetry primarily as a study of the way writers can use language, and thus our work on denotation and connotation, tone, irony, image, and symbol should help them learn to make conscious language choices when they write. Chapters in Kennedy/Gioia's *Literature* entitled "Words," "Saying and Suggesting," and "Listening to a Voice" fit nicely with this approach. Further, because this is a writing course, I wanted my students to have frequent opportunities to write without burying myself under an even greater number of formal, longish papers than I already required. An appropriate solution seemed to be to have my students write prose paraphrases of one or two poems from those assigned for each discussion class.

During the first week of the course, we discussed and practiced the paraphrase technique, looking first at Kennedy's explanation of paraphrasing and then at his paraphrase of Housman's "Loveliest of trees, the cherry now." By reading my own paraphrase, not among the ablest in the class, I was able to place myself in the position of coinquirer into these poems, most of which I had not previously taught. This helped establish a classroom atmosphere similar to that of a creative writing workshop, one conducive to the discussion of both the poetry in the text and the writing of the students. In fact, while the primary purpose of assigning the paraphrases was to give my students extra writing practice, an important additional result was that throughout the quarter their paraphrases, not the teacher's opinions and interpretations, formed the basis for class discussion. There was rarely a need for the teacher to *explain* a poem or a passage: someone, and frequently several people, had an interpretation which satisfied most questions and resolved most difficulties.

At the end of this essay are examples of the prose paraphrases students wrote of Emily Dickinson's "I heard a Fly buzz—when I died." Two of the paraphrases, at 90 and 112 words, are approximately as long as Dickinson's 92-word poem; the 160-word third paraphrase is over 75% longer because this student interpreted as she paraphrased, explaining, for example, that the narrator willed her earthly possessions in a futile attempt to hasten death. Such interpretation, while welcome, is not at all necessary, as the two shorter, yet also successful, paraphrases indicate. In fact I had to remind students that paraphrases are not the same as analyses, and that while they might have to interpret a symbol—as these students variously explained what the fly or the King meant—or unweave a metaphor, their major task was to rewrite the poem as clear prose.

The first paraphrase is perhaps the most straightforward of this group. The author's voice is nearly inaudible. He has stripped the poem of its literary qualities—no "Heaves of Storm," only "the air before a stone"; no personification; the author is only present in the choice of the word "sad" to describe the final buzz of the fly. His paraphrase is a prose rendering of the poem with no obvious attempt to interpret it.

Paraphrase II seems to ignore the symbolic importance of the fly, and perhaps in the very casualness of the phrase "and the last thing I was aware of was this fly and its buzz" suggests the same insignificance of death from the perspective of the hereafter that Dickinson does. More interesting is this student's treatment of the willing of the keepsakes: the formal diction of "proper recipients," "standard fashion," and "officially ready to die" suggests death as a ritual. Unexpected interpretations like this appear frequently in the paraphrases, demonstrating the flexibility and richness of language, emphasizing the error in assuming that there is one right way to interpret a poem, and sometimes, when the interpretations are less plausible, leading to discussions of what constitutes valid interpretation and how one finds support for interpretations of what one reads.

The third paraphrase, as I suggested before, offers more interpretation as well as a stronger authorial voice than the previous two. The author adds a simile of her own, "as if the winds had ceased temporarily to catch their breaths," and more obviously than the other students uses the fly as a metaphor for death in her final sentence.

I will not take the space for a thorough analysis of these paraphrases, but I think that they suggest what a teacher might expect from this kind of assignment. Clearly, these three students have read this poem carefully and understand what it says, the first step towards understanding what it means. Small group and classroom discussions would allow us to consider these paraphrases individually and comparatively, to point out their merits and weaknesses, and then to return to the original verse with new perspectives.

Most heartening were the comments of several students during the quarter who told me that they felt more confident about reading poetry than they previously had. Though I doubt that my students are any more ardently devoted to poetry now than they were before the course began, they are not intimidated by verse on the page. They have an approach, a simple heuristic, for dealing with any unfamiliar writing. Ideally, my students will remember and use their ability to paraphrase and their ability to use their paraphrases to understand and evaluate what they read when they come upon a particularly difficult passage in their chemistry or history texts during the next three years or in the quarterly reports or technical manuals or journals they will read when they leave the university and begin their careers.

Appendix: Sample Paraphrases

Paraphrase I

I heard death coming on. The stillness in the room was like the stillness in the air before a storm. The people around me had wiped their eyes dry, and they held their breaths waiting for that moment when death could be witnessed in the room. I wrote a will which gave away my possessions—that being the only part of me I could give away. A fly then flew between the light and me making a sad, uncertain buzz. My eyesight faded and I could not see to see.

Paraphrase II

I heard a fly buzz as I was about to die. The sound of the fly broke the quietness in the room which was like the calm before a storm. The people sitting around waiting for me to die cried until they could not cry anymore. They began to breathe uneasily in anticipation of my death when God would come down to the room to take me away. I had willed all of my valuables to the proper recipients in the standard fashion. I was officially ready to die, going through the final dramatic moments of my life, and the last thing I was aware of was this fly and its buzz.

Paraphrase III

I could feel the approach of death just as I could hear the buzz of an approaching fly. I knew death was buzzing around, but I did not know when and where it would land. The stillness of death was like the calmness that exists between storms, as if the winds had ceased temporarily to catch their breaths.

I was aware of the sorrow in the room. There were those who had cried because death was near, and they waited for death to stalk into the room like a king and claim its subject.

I willed all of my earthly possessions, all that could legally be assigned to a new owner, in an attempt to hasten death. But there was no way to control death;

I was at the mercy of its timing. And then like the fly that finally lands on its choice place, death fell upon me, and shut my eyes, and I could no longer see.

* * *

Mr. Weiser reported in a letter that, once again, he had used the method of poetry paraphrase in his writing course, and remained pleased with it. "My students," he remarked, "no longer treat poems as holy scripts written in some mystical code, but attack them fearlessly." The course had proved fun both for them and for him, and he felt he was paying his dues to both writing and literature.

37 *Writing About a Play*

In an introductory literature course that saves drama for last, there seems never enough time to be fair to the plays available. That is why many instructors tell us that they like to have students read at least two or three plays on their own and write short papers about at least one or two of them.

Among the "Topics for More Extended Papers" (page 1424), number 5 invites the student to imagine the problems of staging a classic play in modern dress and in a contemporary setting. If you prefer, this topic could be more general: Make recommendations for the production of any play. In getting ready to write on this topic, students might first decide whether or not the play is a work of realism. Ask them: Should sets, lighting, and costumes be closely detailed and lifelike, or perhaps be extravagant or expressionistic? Would a picture-frame stage or an arena better suit the play? What advice would you offer the actors for interpreting their roles? What exactly would you emphasize in the play if you were directing it? (For a few insights into methods of staging, they might read Tennessee Williams's "How to Stage *The Glass Menagerie*" on page 1300.)

PURPOSE OF CRITICAL APPROACHES

This chapter is designed to introduce students to the variety of possible approaches they can take in analyzing literature. Theory and criticism have become such important aspects of undergraduate literary study that many instructors need an informed beginner's guide to the subject. Our objective has been to cover the area intelligently without overwhelming or confusing the beginning student.

This section presents overviews of ten critical approaches. While these ten methods do not exhaust the total possibilities of literary criticism, they represent the most influential and widely used contemporary approaches. Each approach is introduced with an overview designed to explain to beginning students the central ideas of the critical method. The general note does not try to explain every aspect of a critical school or summarize its history; instead, it focuses on explaining the fundamental insights that motivate each approach. While many contemporary critics combine methodologies, it seemed wisest to keep the categories as simple and separate as possible, since students may be wrestling with these ideas for the first time.

CRITICAL SELECTIONS

After the introductory note each critical school is illustrated by two critical excerpts. The first excerpt is usually a theoretical statement explaining the general principles of the approach. In each case, we have selected a passage from one of the methodology's leading practitioners that summarizes its central ideas in an accessible way. There is, for example, Cleanth Brooks listing the principles of Formalist Criticism, Elaine Showalter outlining the issues of Feminist Poetics, Northrop Frye explaining the concept of Mythic Archetypes, and Stanley Fish presenting the parameters of the Reader-Response method. These selections reinforce and broaden the ideas found earlier in the introductory notes. They also familiarize the student with a major figure in each school.

This general statement is then followed by a critical excerpt that discusses actual works in the book. These critical analyses have been selected with great care to provide illuminating but accessible examples of each school. These excerpts are not only well argued and informed analyses, but they are also clearly written with a minimum of theoretical jargon. Footnotes have also been added to explain any references that might be unfamiliar to students.

It was not always possible to find critical excerpts that could do the double duty of illustrating a school of thought while analyzing a text at hand. Sometimes we chose the clearest exposition available of an influential critical concept. (We also felt that students would profit by seeing where these influential ideas originated.) Some of these critical texts are challenging because the ideas are subtle and complex, but—once again—we have always tried to find the most accessible excerpt possible.

LITERARY WORKS DISCUSSED

Critical methods are always easier to understand when they discuss a poem, play, or story you know. Consequently, we have tried to find noteworthy excerpts that illustrate a particular critical approach and *that also focus on a literary text found in the book*. This feature allows the instructor the possibility of assigning many of these critical texts as ancillary readings.

The criticism on fiction lends itself well to classroom use. Daniel Watkins's Marxist reading of D. H. Lawrence's "The Rocking-Horse Winner," for example, would surely help students understand the symbolic structure of that arresting story. Edmond Volpe's analysis of "Barn Burning" illuminates the mythic structure under Faulkner's story. Juliann Fleenor's discussion of "The Yellow Wallpaper" will show students how contemporary attitudes toward gender did not apply even in medical sciences in Charlotte Perkins Gilman's time. Many instructors may want a new twist on teaching "The Tell-Tale Heart" (that classic chestnut that students often rate their favorite story). Daniel Hoffman's brilliant psychological reading will help students see below the story's surface into its fascinating subtext. The formalist analysis of "Sonny's Blues" by Michael Clark examines the interplay of symbol and meaning in James Baldwin's story.

In poetry, Brett Millier's biographical comment on Elizabeth Bishop's "One Art" might broaden a discussion of the villanelle into other issues. Hugh Kenner recreates the heady atmosphere of Modernist London in a way that places Ezra Pound's "In a Station of the Metro" in a historical context. Joseph Moldenhauer provides students with an informed but accessible historical account of how Andrew Marvell used elements of the Renaissance tradition in "To His Coy Mistress," while Geoffrey Hartman deconstructs Wordsworth's "A Slumber Did My Spirit Seal."

USING THE CHAPTER

Some instructors may want to use "Critical Approaches to Literature" as a formal part of the course, but more, we suspect, will prefer to use it in a less systematic way as a resource that can be tailored to whatever occasion seems suitable. An excellent way to introduce students to the section is to assign a short paper analyzing a single poem according to the critical approach of their choice. This method allows them to explore the introductory material for each critical school and then learn one approach in depth by trying it on a specific text.

Many poems in the book lend themselves to this assignment. Some likely choices (from the first few POETRY chapters) would include: D. H. Lawrence's "Piano," Robert Browning's "My Last Duchess," Theodore Roethke's "My Papa's Waltz," Anne Bradstreet's "The Author to Her Book," Wilfred Owen's "Dulce et

Decorum Est," Josephine Miles's "Reason," Langston Hughes's "Theme for English B," and Alfred Tennyson's "Tears, Idle Tears." All of these poems invite multiple readings from a variety of perspectives.

Certain stories also naturally suggest multiple readings. Poe's "The Tell-Tale Heart," for instance, easily allows formalist, biographical, psychological, mythological, reader-response and deconstructionist readings. Charlotte Perkins Gilman's "The Yellow Wallpaper" is similarly open to multiple interpretations. Openly autobiographical, it directly addresses issues of gender, sociology, psychology, and myth. Other stories that invite wide approaches include Faulkner's "A Rose for Emily," Tan's "A Pair of Tickets," Joyce's "Araby," Hawthorne's "Young Goodman Brown," Walker's "Everyday Use," O'Connor's "A Good Man Is Hard to Find," and Cather's "Paul's Case." If you want to assign a single work for students to try the critical approach of their choice, you could probably not do better than Kafka's *The Metamorphosis*.

Plays like *Oedipus the King* or *Othello* have already been analyzed from every conceivable critical perspective, but there's no reason why a student shouldn't try his or her own hand at them. *A Doll's House*, *Trifles*, and *Death of a Salesman* are also naturally open to multiple approaches. Finally, Milcha Sanchez-Scott's *The Cuban Swimmer* profitably invites mythic, psychological, sociological, formal and biographical readings.

OTHER RESOURCES

If any of your brighter students should start writing papers following any of these critical approaches, and you should wish to provide them with models longer than the brief illustrative samples we supply, a new series of paperbacks may be helpful to them. It will be still more helpful if they are familiar with a classic such as *Frankenstein*, *The Scarlet Letter*, *Wuthering Heights*, *Heart of Darkness*, *Hamlet*, *Portrait of the Artist as a Young Man*, *Gulliver's Travels*, *The Awakening*, or *The House of Mirth*. Titles dealing with each of these classics and others have appeared, or will appear shortly, in the series "Case Studies in Contemporary Criticism," whose general editor is Ross C. Murfin of the University of Miami (Bedford Books and St. Martin's Press). Each book contains five essays on its novel, illustrating five different approaches: psychoanalytic criticism, reader-response criticism, feminist criticism, deconstruction, and the new historicism. There are also readable essays that explain each critical school, and bibliographies of critical books representing each of them.

Index of Authors with Titles

NOTES

NOTES

NOTES

NOTES